Mobile Computing

Technology, Applications, Issues and Research Directions

SECOND EDITION

Mobile Computing

Technology, Applications, Issues and Research Directions

SECOND EDITION

Brijesh Kumar Gupta

Ph.D. (IIT–R), MISET

Professor & Head
Department of MCA
IIMT College of Engineering
Greater Noida–201 306, India

Formerly:

Asst. Prof. & Coordinator R & D Cell
Department of Computer Applications
G.C.E.T., Greater Noida – 201 306, India

Asst. Prof. & Coordinator Computer Center
Dept. of Computer Science & Engineering
C.O.E.R., Roorkee –247 667, India
&
Civilian Gazetted Officer
Ministry of Defense, Govt. of India, India

KHANNA BOOK PUBLISHING CO. (P) LTD.

Publisher, of Science, Technology and Engineering Books

4C/4344, Ansari Road, Darya Ganj, New Delhi-110002
Phone: 011-23244447-48 **Mobile:** +91-99109 09320
E-mail: contact@khannabooks.com
Website: www.khannabooks.com

Dear Readers,

To prevent the piracy, this book is secured with HIGH SECURITY HOLOGRAM on the front title cover. In case you don't find the hologram on the front cover title, please write us to at contact@khannabooks.com or whatsapp us at +91-99109 09320 and avail special gift voucher for yourself.

Specimen of Hologram on front Cover title:

Moreover, there is a SPECIAL DISCOUNT COUPON for you with EVERY HOLOGRAM.

How to avail this SPECIAL DISCOUNT:

Step 1: Scratch the hologram
Step 2: Under the scratch area, your "coupon code" is available
Step 3: Logon to www.khannabooks.com
Step 4: Use your "coupon code" in the shopping cart and get your copy at a special discount
Step 5: Enjoy your reading!

Thanks,
Khanna Publishing House

MOBILE COMPUTING *by*

Brijesh Gupta

ISBN: 978-93-86173-21-8

First Edition: 2008
Reprint: 2024, 2025, 2026

To view complete list of books, please scan the QR Code: 

Published by:
Khanna Book Publishing Co. (P) Ltd.
CIN: U22110DL1998PTC095547

Visit us at: www.khannabooks.com
Write us at: contact@khannabooks.com

Printed in Bharat.

Dedicated
to
The God's Gifts
Aakarsh & Agrim

About the Author

Dr. Brijesh Kr. Gupta is currently serving as Professor and Head in the Department of MCA at Galgotias College of Engineering & Technology, Greater Noida. He joined teaching profession in 1991 after his Post Graduation. He has 22 years of teaching, research and administrative experience at various levels in Indian Education System. He served in Ministry of Defense, Govt. of India as a Civilian Officer. To carry out his research work in the area of High Speed Communications, he enrolled himself at Indian Institute of Technology – Roorkee, India in Jan., 1999. He has worked on two major research projects sponsored by U.G.C. New Delhi, and A.I.C.T.E., New-Delhi and completed them successfully. He has served in reputed technical institutes of U.P. Technical University(GBTU & MTU), Lucknow since 2003, after completing his Ph.D.

The courses taught by Dr. Gupta for Post Graduate (M.Tech., M.B.A., M.C.A.) are Advanced Computer Networks, Data Network, Data Communication and Computer Networks, Management Information System, and Mobile Computing. Similarly courses taught by him for undergraduate classes are Multimedia Communication, Wireless Communication, Computer Networks, Fundamental of Computer Communication System, Information System etc. He has guided more than 130 projects for Post Graduate and Graduate students in the areas of Computer Networking, Satellite Communication, Robotics, Management Information System, Network Security, VoIP, Wireless Communication, and Software Engineering. He always achieved 98% -100% result (students got distinction marks also) for these theory courses, and awarded by the technical institute.

He has published 41 research papers in International and National Journals and Conference Proceedings and authored a book on Mobile Computing. He is Co- Editor of two Proceedings of the workshop / faculty development program sponsored by Department of Science and Technology (DST), Govt. of India, and AICTE-New Delhi. He has attended total number of 32 International, Continental, and National Conferences, Workshops and Symposium in India and abroad and Chaired Technical Sessions in several International Conferences.

He has guided several M. Phil. and M.Tech. Students for their dissertations. At present several students are under his supervision for their Ph.D. research work. He organized several National Conference, workshop and faculty development programs sponsored by D.S.T. New Delhi, and A.I.C.T.E. New Delhi, and delivered inspirational lectures as a resource person during these programs to improve Teaching- Learning Process and Research Standards. He has keen interest to organize Industry – Institute Collaboration Programs e.g. Software Development Training Program, IT Infrastructure Management, Faculty Enablement Program etc.

Dr. Gupta is providing his services as a Member of Editorial Board to International Journal of Hybrid Computation Intelligence, India. He is life member for Indian Society for Earthquake Technology, INDIA, Education Wing of Rajyoga Education & Research Foundation, Mount Abu, INDIA and Center for Education Growth & Research, New Delhi, INDIA. He is member of Technical Program Committee and Paper Review Committee of several reputed Int'l Conferences since 2006.

Preface to the Second Edition

It is my proud privilege to present the second edition of 'Mobile Computing' to my beloved readers. In the last few years Mobile Computing has achieved high maturity level rapidly because of introduction of Android and new hardware innovations and improvements in chip technology.

Mobile Computing is rapidly becoming a way of life accepted by all parts of the Globe. It is distributed computing that involves elements, whose location changes in the course of computation. Elements may be software components - such as mobile agents, data, hardware - such as palmtops and wireless phones or users. This being a very broad definition, the common underlying issue is location and its management.

The term Mobile Computing is very often used for Wireless Mobile Computing, the use of portable devices capable of wireless networking. Wireless Mobile Computing faces additional constraints induced by the characteristics of wireless communications and the demand for portability. Mobile Wireless Computing enables access to data at any time and from any place towards the vision of ubiquitous or pervasive computing.

This book is organized into 5 Units: Introduction, Mobile Data Management, Location Management, Transaction Management, and Ad hoc Networks.

Though Mobile Computing covers a variety of different hardware and software platforms as well as diverse applications, many common issues arise.Security is one of the concerning and very important issue. In the end of each unit myself tried to highlight this major issue of security in mobile environment.

In this edition a good number of questions and answers related with the subject, alongwith solved paper are added. I hope, the readers will be benefited after going through all these.

I would like to welcome to receive your feedback, suggestions, and any other comment that will enable to improve the next edition of this book in future.

Please send your relevant and healthy suggestions to: profbkgupta @gmail.com

Dr. Brijesh Kr. Gupta

Greater Noida, India
Date: October 13, 2013

Acknowledgements

I would like to extend my heartfelt thanks to Mr. Suneel Galgotia, Chairman, Galgotias Educational Institutions(GEI), and Mr. Dhruv Galgotia, CEO-GEI, who have given an opportunity to me to serve at Galgotias College of Engineering & Technology, Greater Noida. I feel proud to serve in such Institute, which is celebrating over a decade of leadership in technical education and provides a strong values based education system, an excellent academic platform.

I am grateful to Dr. R. Sundaresan, Director, Galgotias College of Engineering & Technology for his inspirations, motivation and valuable thoughts.

Myself highly thankful to my research guides Dr. S.C.Sharma, Associate Prof., and Dr. Mohan Lal, Associate Prof., IIT - Roorkee for their encouragement and wholehearted co-operation in understanding the relevant technology.

My thanks to Dr. Gagan Varshney, Prof. and Dean, IMS Engineering College, Ghaziabad for his moral support alongwith best wishes.

My deepest thanks to Mr. Mukul Seth, Managing Director, Khanna Book Publishing Co. (P) Ltd., Delhi and Mr. Puneet Khanna, Director, Khanna Book Publishing Co. (P) Ltd., Delhi for their valuable cooperation and cordial support and for presenting second edition of the book in this form.

My thanks to Khanna Book Publishing Co. (P) Ltd., team in Delhi for their dedication and timely publication.

It is my pleasant duty to acknowledge my special thanks to all faculty members of MCA Department, dear students and all well wishers, who support, and inspired me through their regards and love directly or indirectly.

No words, No language is ever adequate to express my heartfelt veneration for my parents, dear wife Mrs. Rachna Gupta, loving Aakarsh & Agrim and other family members for their cheerful, enthusiastic support and efforts to cooperate with me in completion of this edition of book.

Above all, I praise the 'Almighty God' for his blessings and for gifted me power of deep thinking and communication skills to present the book for the benefits of readers.

Dr. Brijesh Kr. Gupta

Date: October 13, 2013

Contents

UNIT-II

UNIT-IV

UNIT-I

Mobile computing is a revolutionary technology, born as a result of remarkable advance in the development of computer hardware and wireless communication. It enables us to access information anytime and anywhere even in the absence of physical network connection. With recent performance advancements in computer and wireless communications technologies, advanced mobile wireless computing is expected to see increasingly widespread use and applications.

This unit describes the emerging area of mobile and wireless networking, Cellular Digital Packet Data (CDPD), and Radio Frequency (RF) Technologies, Issues, Constrains, Applications, Protocol, as well as Challenges and Opportunities presented by wireless communication.

Objective of this unit is to understand the basic fundamentals of Mobile Computing. The unit covers the followings:

- Mobile Computing
- Existing Cellular Network Architecture
- Cellular Digital Packet Data (CDPD) Technology
- Radio Frequency (RF) Technology
- Issues In Cellular Networks
- Constrains in Mobile Computing
- Applications of Mobile Computing
- The Future of Mobile Computing
- Generations of Mobile Wireless Technologies and their Services
- Mobile Wireless Protocols
- Bluetooth
- Radio Resource Management in Cellular Systems
- Types of Attacks in Cellular Networks
- Security Issues In Cellular Networks

UNIT 1

Introduction

1.1. INTRODUCTION

Mobile Computing is a technology that allows transmission of data, via a computer, without having to be connected to a fixed physical link. Mobile voice communication is widely established throughout the world and has had a very rapid increase in the number of subscribers to the various cellular networks over the last few years. An extension of this technology is the ability to send and receive data across these cellular networks. ***This is the Principle of Mobile Computing***. Mobile data communication has become a very important and rapidly evolving technology as it allows users to transmit data from remote locations to other remote or fixed locations. This proves to be the solution to the biggest problem of business people on the move - mobility.

Voice telecommunication has already been introduced by the mobile phone and is spreading around all over the world like a contagious virus. Data communication started in the early 80's and has been improving ever since, but with a great drawback. Using the PSDN (Public Switched Data Network), it does not allow mobility at all.

Mobile data communications has become a hotly debated issue. Interest surrounding paging, circuit-switched and packet-switched networks has lit the fire for the debate and the announcement of new-technology networks is adding fuel to the fire.

1.2. EXISTING CELLULAR NETWORK ARCHITECTURE

Mobile telephony took off with the introduction of cellular technology which allowed the efficient utilization of frequencies enabling the connection of a large number of users. During the 1980's analogue technology was used. Among the most well known systems were the NMT900 and 450 (Nordic Mobile Telephone) and the AMPS (Advanced Mobile Phone Service). In the 1990's the digital cellular technology was introduced with GSM (Global System Mobile) being the most widely accepted system around the world. Other such systems are the DCS1800 (Digital Communication System) and the PCS1900 (Personal Communication System).

A cellular network consists of mobile units linked together to switching equipment, which interconnect the different parts of the network and allow access to the fixed Public Switched Telephone Network (PSTN). The technology is hidden from view; it's incorporated in a number of tranceivers called Base Stations (BS). Every BS is located at a strategically selected place and covers a given area or cell - hence the name cellular communications. A number of adjacent cells grouped together form an area and the corresponding BSs communicate through a so called Mobile Switching Centre (MSC). The MSC is the heart of a cellular radio system. It is responsible for routing, or switching, calls from the originator to the destinator. It can be thought of managing the cell, being responsible for set-up, routing control and termination of the call, for management of inter-MSC hand over and supplementary services, and for collecting charging and accounting information. The MSC may be connected to other MSCs on the same network or to the PSTN (See Fig. 1.1).

The frequencies used vary according to the cellular network technology implemented. For GSM, 890-915 MHz range is used for transmission and 935 -960 MHz for reception. The DCS technology uses frequencies in the 1800MHz range while PCS in the 1900MHz range.

Each cell has a number of channels associated with it. These are assigned to subscribers on demand. When a Mobile Station (MS) becomes 'active' it registers with the nearest BS. The corresponding MSC stores the information about that MS and its position. This information is used to direct incoming calls to the MS.

If during a call the MS moves to an adjacent cell then a change of frequency will necessarily occur - since adjacent cells never use the same channels. This procedure is called hand over and is the key to Mobile communications. As the MS is approaching the edge of a cell, the BS monitors the decrease in signal power. The strength of the signal is compared with adjacent cells and the call is handed over to the cell with the strongest signal.

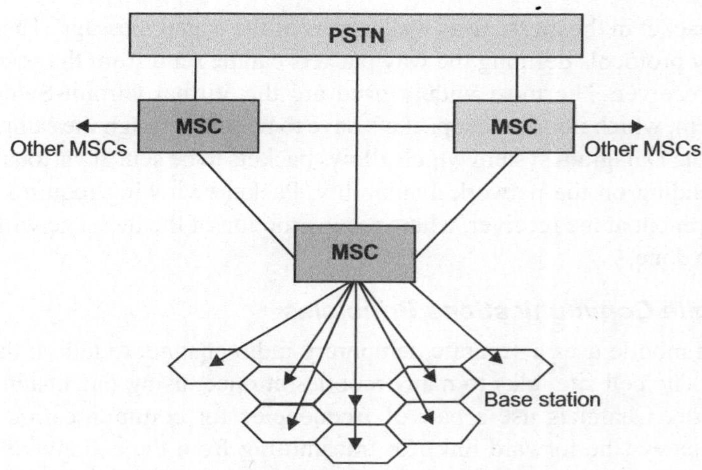

Fig. 1.1: Mobile Switching Centre

During the switch, the line is lost for about 400ms. When the MS is going from one area to another it registers itself to the new MSC. Its location information is updated, thus allowing MSs to be used outside their 'home' areas.

1.2.1. Data Communications

Data Communications is the exchange of data using existing communication networks. The term data covers a wide range of applications including File Transfer (FT), interconnection between Wide-Area-Networks (WAN), facsimile (fax), electronic mail, access to the internet and the World Wide Web (WWW). Data Communications have been achieved using a variety of networks such as PSTN, leased-lines and more recently ISDN (Integrated Services Data Network) and ATM (Asynchronous Transfer Mode)/Frame Relay. These networks are partly or totally analogue or digital using technologies such as circuit - switching, packet - switching etc.

Circuit switching implies that data from one user (sender) to another (receiver) has to follow a pre-specified path. If a link to be used is busy , the message can not be redirected , a property which causes many delays.

Packet switching is an attempt to make better utilization of the existing network by splitting the message to be sent into packets. Each packet contains information about the sender, the receiver, the position of the packet in the message as well as part of the actual message. There are many protocols defining the way packets can be send from the sender to the receiver. The most widely used are the Virtual Circuit-Switching system, which implies that packets have to be sent through the same path, and the Datagram system which allows packets to be sent at various paths depending on the network availability. Packet switching requires more equipment at the receiver, where reconstruction of the message will have to be done.

Mobile Communications Principles

Each mobile uses a separate, temporary radio channel to talk to the cell site. The cell site talks to many mobiles at once, using one channel per mobile. Channels use a pair of frequencies for communication—one frequency (the forward link) for transmitting from the cell site and one frequency (the reverse link) for the cell site to receive calls from the users. Radio energy dissipates over distance, so mobiles must stay near the base station to maintain communications. The basic structure of mobile networks includes telephone systems and radio services. Where mobile radio service operates in a closed network and has no access to the telephone system, mobile telephone service allows interconnection to the telephone network (see Fig. 1.2).

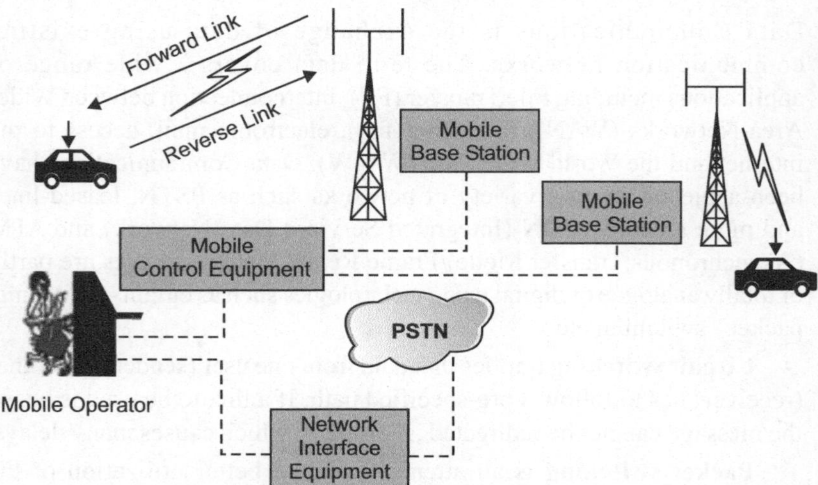

Fig. 1.2: Basic Mobile Telephone Service Network

The introduction of mobility in data communications required a move from the Public Switched Data Network (PSDN) to other networks like the ones used by mobile phones. PCSI has come up with an idea called CDPD (Cellular Digital Packet Data) technology which uses the existing mobile network (frequencies used for mobile telephony).

Mobility implemented in data communications has a significant difference compared to voice communications. Mobile phones allow the user to move around and talk at the same time; the loss of the connection for 400ms during the hand over is undetectable by the user. When it comes to data, 400ms is not only detectable but causes huge distortion to the message. Therefore data can be transmitted from a mobile station under the assumption that it remains stable or within the same cell.

(For Mobile Communication Systems: Historical Background, please see Annexure 1-A)

1.3. CELLULAR DIGITAL PACKET DATA (CDPD) TECHNOLOGY

Today, the mobile data communications market is becoming dominated by a technology called CDPD. There are other alternatives to this technology namely Circuit Switched Cellular, Specialized Mobile Radio and Wireless Data Networks. As it can be seen from the comparative Table 1.0 below the CDPD technology is much more advantageous than the others.

Table 1.0: Comparative Study for Different Technologies

	Cellular Digital Packet Data (CDPD)	Circuit Switched Cellular	Specialized Mobile Radio (Extended)	Proprietary Wireless Data Networks
Speed	best	best	good	good
Security	best	better	good	better
Ubiquity	best	best	good	better
Cost of Service	best	better	better	good
Cost of Deployment	best	best	better	good
Mobility	best	good	better	good
Interoperability	best	good	good	better

CDPD's principle lies in the usage of the idle time in between existing voice signals that are being sent across the cellular networks. The major advantage of this system is the fact that the idle time is not chargeable and so the cost of data transmission is very low. This may be regarded as the most important consideration by business individuals.

CDPD networks allow fixed or mobile users to connect to the network across a fixed link and a packet switched system respectively. Fixed users have a fixed physical link to the CDPD network. In the case of a mobile end user, the user can, if CDPD network facilities are non-existent, connect to existing circuit switched networks and transmit data via these networks. This is known as Circuit Switched CDPD (CS-CDPD) as shown in Fig. 1.3.

Service coverage is a fundamental element of providing effective wireless solutions to users and using this method achieves this objective. Where CDPD is available data is split into packets and a packet switched network protocol is used to transport the packets across the network. This may be of either Datagram or Virtual Circuit Switching form.

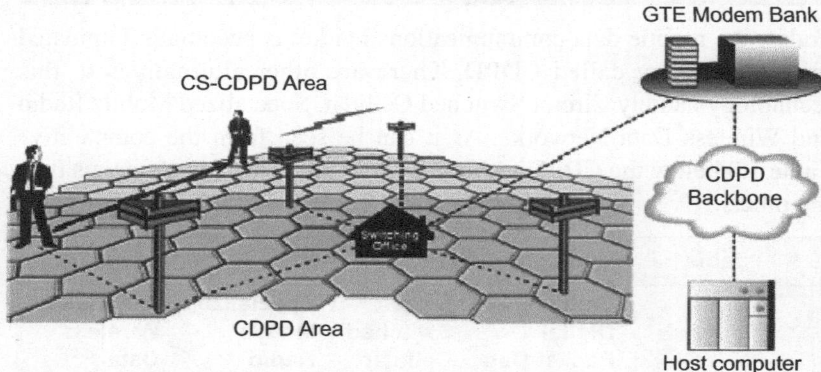

Fig. 1.3: Circuit Switched CDPD

The data packets are inserted on momentarily unoccupied voice frequencies during the idle time on the voice signals. CDPD networks have a network hierarchy with each level of the hierarchy doing its own specified tasks.

The hierarchy consists of the following levels:

1.3.1. Mobile End User Interface

Using a single device such as a Personal Digital Assistant or personal computer which have been connected to a Radio Frequency (RF) Modem which is specially adapted with the antennae required to transmit data on the cellular network, the mobile end user can transmit both data and voice signals. Voice signals are transmitted via a mobile phone connected to the RF Modem Unit. RF Modems transfer data in both forward and reverse channels using Gaussian Minimum Shift Keying (MSK) modulation, a modified form of Frequency Shift Keying (FSK) at modulation index of 0.5 .

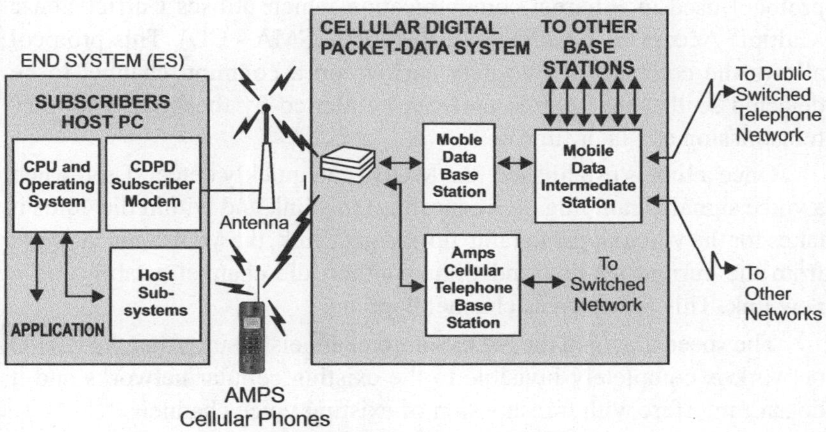

Fig. 1.4: CDPD Overview

1.3.2. Mobile Data Base Station (MDBS)

In each cell of the cellular reception area, there is a Mobile Data Base Station (MDBS) which is responsible for detection of idle time in voice channels, for relaying data between the mobile units and the Mobile Data Intermediate Systems (MDIS), sending of packets of data onto the appropriate unoccupied frequencies as well as receiving data packets and passing them to the appropriate Mobile end user within its domain.

1.3.2.1. Detection of Idle Time

This is achieved using a scanning receiver(also known as sniffer) housed in the MDBS. The sniffer detects voice traffic by measuring the signal strength on a specific frequency, hence detecting an idle channel.

1.3.2.2.1. Relaying Data Packets between Mobile Units and Networks

If the sniffer detects two idle channels then the MDBS establishes two RF air-links between the end user unit and itself. Two channels are required to achieve bidirectional communications. One channel is for forward communication from the MDBS to the mobile units. This channel is unique to each mobile unit and hence contentionless. The reverse channels are shared between a number of Mobile units and as a result, two mobile units sharing a reverse link cannot communicate to each other.

Reverse channels are accessed using a Digital Sense Multiple Access with Collision Detection (DSMA - CD) protocol which is similar to the protocol used in Ethernet communication which utilises Carrier Sense Multiple Access with Collision Detection (CSMA - CD). This protocol allows the collision of two data packets on a common channel to be detected so that the Mobile unit can be alerted by the MDBS to retry transmission at a later time.

Once a link is established, the MDBS can quickly detect if and when a voice signal is ramping up (requesting) this link and within the 40ms it takes for the voice signal to ramp up and get a link, the MDBS disconnects from the current air-link and finds another idle channel establishing a new link. This is known as channel hopping.

The speed at which the MDBS hops channels ensures that the CDPD network is completely invisible to the existing cellular networks and it doesn't interfere with transmission of existing voice channels.

When the situation occurs that all voice channels are at capacity, then extra frequencies specifically set aside for CDPD data can be utilised. Although this scenario is very unlikely as each cell within the reception area has typically 57 channels, each of which has an average of 25 - 30% of idle time.

1.3.3. Mobile Data Intermediate Systems (MDIS)

Groups of MDBS that control each cell in the cellular network reception area are connected to a higher level entity in the network hierarchy, the Mobile Data Intermediate Systems. Connection is made via a wideband trunk cable. Data packets are then relayed by MDBS to and from mobile end users and MDIS.

These MDIS use a Mobile Network Location Protocol (MNLP) to exchange location information about Mobile end users within their domain.

The MDIS maintains a database for each of the M-ES in its serving area. Each mobile unit has a fixed home area but may be located in any area where reception is available. So, if a MDIS unit recieves a data packet addressed to a mobile unit that resides in its domain, it sends the data packet to the appropriate MDBS in its domain which will forward it as required. If the data packet is addressed to a mobile unit in another group of cells, then the MDIS forwards the data packet to the appropriate MDIS using the forward channel. The MDIS units hide all mobility issues from systems in higher levels of the network hierarchy.

In the reverse direction, where messages are from the Mobile end user, packets are routed directly to their destination and not necessarily through the mobile end users home MDIS.

1.3.4. Intermediate Systems (IS)

MDIS are interconnected to these IS which form the backbone of the CDPD system. These systems are unaware of mobility of end-users, as this is hidden by lower levels of the network hierarchy. The ISs are the systems that provide the CDPD interface to the various computer and phone networks.

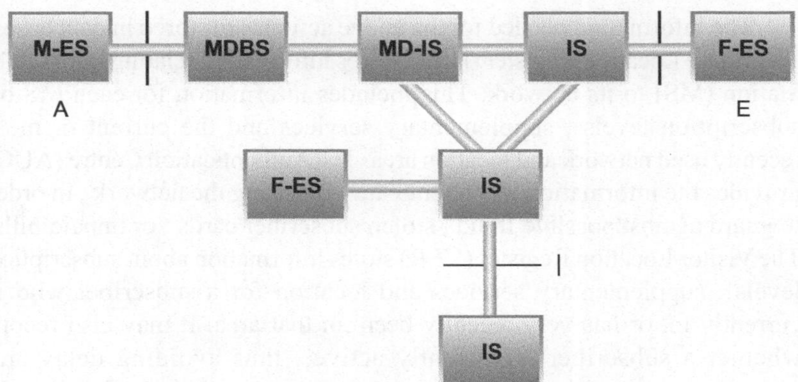

Fig. 1.5: CDPD Network

The IS's relay data between MDIS's and other IS's throughout the network. They can be connected to routers that support Internet and Open Systems Interconnection Connectionless Network Services (OSI-CLNS), to allow access to other cellular carriers and external land-based networks.

1.3.5 CDPD Network Reliability

There are some actions that are necessary in order to obtain reliability over a network:

- **User Authentication**

  The procedure which checks if the identity of the subscriber transferred over the radio path corresponds with the details held in the network.

- **User Anonymity**

  Instead of the actual directory telephone number , the International Mobile Subscriber Identity (IMSI) number is used within the network to uniquely identify a mobile subscriber.

- **Fraud Prevention**

  Protection against impersonation of authorized users and fraudulent use of the network is required.

- **Protection of User Data**

  All the signals within the network are encrypted and the identification key is never transmitted through the air. This ensures maximum network and data security.

The information needed for the above actions are stored in data bases. The Home Location Register (HLR) stores information relating the Mobile Station (MS) to its network. This includes information for each MS on subscription levels , supplementary services and the current or most recently used network and location area. The Authentication Centre (AUC) provides the information to authenticate MSs using the network , in order to guard against possible fraud , stolen subscriber cards , or unpaid bills. The Visitor Location Register (VLR) stores information about subscription levels , supplementary services and location for a subscriber who is currently in, or has very recently been ,in that area. It may also record whether a subscriber is currently active , thus avoiding delay and unnecessary use of the network in trying to call a switched off terminal.

The data packets are transmitted at speeds of typically 19.2 Kilobits/ second to the MDBS, but actual throughput may be as low as 9.6 Kilobits/ second due to the extra redundant data that is added to transmitted packets. This information includes sender address, receiver address and in the case of Datagram Switching, a packet ordering number. Check data is also added to allow error correction if bits are incorrectly received. Each data packet is encoded with the check data using a Reed-Solomon forward error correction code. The encoded sequence is then logically OR'ed with a pseudo-random sequence, to assist the MDBS and mobile units in synchronization of bits. The transmitted data is also encrypted to maintain system security.

CDPD follows the OSI standard model for packet switched data communications. The CDPD architecture extends across layers one, two and three of the OSI layer model. The mobile end users handle the layer 4 functions (transport) and higher layers of the OSI model such as user interface.

1.4. RADIO FREQUENCY (RF) TECHNOLOGY

Electromagnetic waves move through free space and are excellent carriers of information. By attaching an antenna of the appropriate size to an electrical circuit, the electromagnetic waves can be broadcast and can be received by another antenna, which could be located far away. The electromagnetic waves can be categorized on the basis of its frequency. This categorization is called electromagnetic spectrum.

1.4.1. RF (Radio Frequency) Basics and History

These electromagnetic waves can be used for information transmission by amplitude or frequency or phase modulation. Higher frequency waves such as Ultra Violet (UV), X-ray, etc., are even better, however, they are hard to produce and modulate, do not propagate well through physical objects such as buildings, etc., and moreover they are dangerous to living things.

The amount of information that an electromagnetic wave can carry is related to its bandwidth. From telecommunication view point the term bandwidth refers to the capacity of communication equipment or network service in terms of bits per second. For example, a router or communication switch may have a bandwidth of 1.544 Mbps (million bits per second). In wireless, however, bandwidth refers to the range of frequencies available or allowed that could be used for transmission. A bandwidth can be viewed in terms of a diameter of a tube. If the diameter is wider the capacity of the tube to carry larger amount of fluid is larger. Thus a higher bandwidth channel can carry larger amount of information. For example, television has a very wide bandwidth of 6000 KHz because it has to carry audio, video, closed captioning, and other signals. Bandwidths are assigned by the FCC or by the spectrum regulating body.

The radio transmission starts at a Very Low Frequency (VLF) range. These are very long waves. Waves in the Low Frequency (LF) range are used by submarines because they can penetrate water and can follow the earth's surface. The Medium Frequency (MF) and High Frequency (HF) ranges are typical of transmission of hundreds of radio stations either as amplitude modulation (AM) between 520 kHz and 1605.5 kHz, as Short Wave (SW) between 5.9 MHz and 26.1 MHz, or as Frequency Modulation (FM) between 87.5 MHz and 108 MHz. The frequencies limiting these ranges are typically fixed by national regulation and, thus, vary from country to country. Short Waves (SF) are typically used for (amateur) radio transmission around the world, enabled by reflection at the ionosphere. Transmit power is up to 500 kW, which is quite high compared to 1 W of a mobile phone.

Conventional analogue TV is transmitted in ranges of 174-230 MHz and 470-790 MHz using the Very High Frequency (VHF) and Ultra High Frequency (UHF) bands. In this range, Digital Audio Broadcasting (DAB) takes place as well (223-230 MHz and 1452-1472 MHz) and digital TV is planned (470-862 MHz), reusing some of the old frequencies for analog TV. UHF is also used for mobile phones with analog technology (450-465 MHz), the digital GSM (890-960 MHz, 1710-1880 MHz), digital cordless telephones following the DECT standard (1880-1900 MHz) and many more. VHF and especially UHF allow for small antennas and relatively reliable connections for mobile telephony.

Super High Frequencies (SHF) are typically used for directed microwave links (approx. 2-40 GHz) and fixed satellite services in the C-band (4 to 6 GHz), ku-band (11 and 14 GHz), or ka-band (19 and 29 GHz). Some systems are planned in the Extremely High Frequency (EHF) range, which comes close to infrared.

The next step into higher frequencies involves optical transmission, which is not only used for fiber optical links but also for wireless communications. Infrared (IR) transmission is used for direct links, e.g., to connect different buildings via laser links. The most widespread IR technology, Infrared Data Association (IrDA), uses wavelengths of approximately 850-900 nm to connect laptops, PDAs, etc. Finally, visible light is not very reliable due to interference, it is nevertheless useful due to built-in human receivers.

Table 1.1 gives some examples for frequencies used for (analog and digital) mobile phones, cordless telephones, and wireless LANs for countries in the three regions. Older systems like Nordic Mobile Telephone (NMT) are not available all over Europe, and sometimes they have been standardized with different national frequencies. The newer systems (digital) are compatible throughout Europe (standardized by ETSI).

Table 1.1: Examples of Frequency Allocations

	Europe	US	Japan
Mobile Phones	NMT 453-457 MHz, 463-467 MHz; GSM 890-915 MHz, 935-960 MHz, 1710-1785 MHz, 1805-1880 MHz.	AMPS, TDMA, CDMA 824-849 MHz, 869-894 MHz; GSM, TDMA, CDMA 1850-1910 MHz, 1930-1990 MHz;	PDC 810-826 MHz, 940-956 MHz, 1429-1465 MHz, 1477-1513 MHz
Cordless Phones	CT1+ 885-887 MHz, 930-932 MHz; CT2 864-868 MHz; DECT 1880-1900 MHz;	PACS 1850-1910 MHz, 1930-1990 MHz; PACS-UB 1910-1930 MHz;	PHS 1895-1918 MHz; JCT 254-380 MHz;
Wireless LAN	IEEE 802.11 2400-2483 MHz; HIPERLAN 1 5176-5270 MHz.	IEEE 802.11 2400-2483 MHz.	IEEE 802.11 2471-2497 MHz.

Acronyms: NMT (Nordic Mobile Telephone), PDC (Pacific Digital Cellular), PACS (Personal Access Communications System), PHS (Personal Handyphone System), PACS-UB (PACS Unlicensed Band), JCT (Japanese Cordless Telephone).

Europe is heavily dominated by the common fully digital GSM at 900 MHz and 1800 MHz (also known as DCS1800, Digital Cellular System). In contrast to Europe, the US FCC allowed several cellular technologies in the same frequency bands around 850 MHz. Starting from the Analog

Advanced Mobile System (AMPS), this led to the co-existence of several solutions, such as dual mode mobile phones supporting digital Time Division Multiple Access (TDMA) service and analog AMPS according to the standard IS-54. Furthermore, all digital TDMA phones according to IS-136 (also known as NA (North American)-TDMA) and digital Code Division Multiple Access (CDMA) phones according to IS-95 have been developed. Thus the US did not adopt a common mobile phone system but waited for market force to decide. This led to many islands of different systems, and consequently full coverage, as in Europe, is not available in the US. The Personal Digital Cellular (PDC), formerly known as Japanese Digital Cellular (JDC) was established in Japan. The first mobile phones covering all systems around the world were announced for late 1999.

Similar to mobile phone standards, many different cordless telephone standards exist around the world. Some older analog systems such as Cordless Telephone (CT1+) are still in use, but frequently digital technology has been introduced for cordless telephones as well. Examples include CT2 as the first digital cordless telephone introduced in the UK, Digital Enhanced.

Communication Telecommunications (DECT) as a European standard, Personal Access Communications System (PACS) and PACS-Unlicensed Band (PACS-UB) in the US, as well as Personal Handyphone System (PHS) as replacement for the analog Japanese Cordless Telephone (JCT) in Japan.

Channel: A channel represents a frequency and a bandwidth. Usually for wireless communication network designers break the channel bandwidth into two parts (a) uplink channel and (b) downlink channel. In a wireless client/server architecture the server uses downlink channel to communicate with the client and the client uses uplink channel. ARDIS's public shared packet radio network in USA, for example, uses 802-821 MHz for its uplink (terminal to the network) and 851-866 MHz for its downlink (network to terminal). Cordless phone operates in the 46 to 69 MHz frequency range.

***Wideband and Narrowband*:** These terms refer to the width of a band rather than the specific spectrum range allocated to a user. It is a relative term used in the context of a discussion. A bandwidth of 30 MHz allocated for a packet radio networks such as ARDIS or RAM is a wideband compared to the narrowband 30 KHz bandwidth allocated to cellular network. On the other hand, the 30 KHz bandwidth of cellular phones is relatively a wideband compared to, say, the 10 KHz allocated to another use for some other purpose.

Radio waves are used for transmission for the following reasons:

- Easy to generate
- can travel long distance
- can penetrate easily
- can reflect from physical obstacles
- are omni directional

The properties of radio waves are frequency dependent. At low frequencies, radio waves pass through obstacles well, but the power falls off sharply with distance from the source. At high frequencies, radio waves tend to travel in straight lines and bounce off obstacles. They are also absorbed by rain. At all frequencies, radio waves are subject to interference from motors and other electrical equipment.

1.5. ISSUES IN CELLULAR NETWORKS

The infrastructure for Cellular Networks is massive, complex with multiple entities coordinating together, such as the IP Internet coordinating with the core network.

1.5.1. Limitations of Cellular Networks

Compared to Wired Networks, Wireless Cellular Networks have a lot of limitations.

1.5.2. Open Wireless Access Medium

Since the communication is on the wireless channel, there is no physical barrier that can separate an attacker from the network.

1.5.3. Limited Bandwidth

Although wireless bandwidth is increasing continuously, because of channel contention everyone has to share the medium. But still it is a major issue.

1.5.4. System Complexity

Wireless systems are more complex due to the need to support mobility and making use of the channel effectively. By adding more complexity to systems, potentially new security vulnerabilities can be introduced.

1.5.6. Limited Power

Wireless Systems consume a lot of power and therefore have a limited time battery life.

1.5.7. Limited Processing Power

The processors installed on the wireless devices are increasing in power, but still they are not powerful enough to carry out intensive processing.

1.5.8. Relatively Unreliable Network Connection

The wireless medium is an unreliable medium with a high rate of errors compared to a wired network.

1.6. CONSTRAINS IN MOBILE COMPUTING

The recent proliferation of portable computers, in conjunction with nascent high- and low-bandwidth cordless networking technology, provided a pervasive hardware base for mobile computing. The stage is set for hand-held and wearable computing devices of every variety imaginable. Computing will truly be ubiquitous, and no longer an activity restricted to a person's desk. What new challenges will this pose? Mobile computing systems are constrained in important ways, relative to static systems. These constraints are intrinsic to mobility, and are not just artifacts of current technology:

1.6.1. Mobile elements are resource-poor relative to static elements

At any given cost and level of technology, considerations of weight, power, size and ergonomics will render mobile elements less computationally capable than their static counterparts. While mobile elements will undoubtedly improve in absolute ability, they will always be at a disadvantage relative to static elements.

1.6.2. Mobile elements are more prone to loss, destruction, and subversion than static elements

A Wall Street stockbroker is more likely to be mugged on the streets of

Manhattan and have his or her laptop stolen than to have the workstation in a locked office be physically subverted. Even if security isn't a problem, portable computers are more vulnerable to loss or damage.

1.6.3. Mobile elements must operate under a much broader range of networking conditions

A desktop workstation can typically rely on LAN or WAN connectivity. A laptop in a hotel room may only have modem or ISDN connectivity. Outdoors, a laptop with a cellular modem may find itself in intermittent contact with its nearest cell.

These constraints violate many of the assumptions upon which today's distributed systems are based. Further, the ubiquity of portable computers will result in mobile computing systems that are much larger than the distributed systems of today. *Scalability* will thus be a continuing concern. A key requirement of mobile computing systems will be the ability to access critical data regardless of location. Data from shared file systems and databases must be made available to programs running on mobile computers. For example, a technician servicing a jet engine on a parked aircraft needs access to engineering details of that model of engine as well as past repair records of that specific engine. Similarly, a businessman who is continuing his work on the train home from Manhattan needs access to his business records. Yet another example involves emergency medical response to a case of poisoning: the responding personnel will need rapid access to medical databases describing poison symptoms and antidotes, as well as access to the specific patient's medical records to determine drug sensitivity.

The requirement of access to shared data implies interdependence between the elements of a mobile computing system. At the same time, the need to be robust against network and remote site failures requires clients to be as autonomous as possible. Thus mobility exacerbates the tension between *autonomy* and *interdependence* that is characteristic of distributed computing.

Ideally, mobility should be completely *transparent* to users. Transparency relieves users of the need to be constantly aware of the details of their computing environment, thus allowing them to focus on the real tasks at hand. The adaptation necessary to cope with the changing environment should be initiated by the system rather than by users. Of course, perfect transparency is an unattainable ideal. But that should not deter us from exploring techniques that enable us to come as close as possible to the ideal.

1.7. APPLICATIONS OF MOBILE COMPUTING

The question that always arises when a business is thinking of buying a mobile computer is "Will it be worth it?" In many fields of work, the ability to keep on the move is vital in order to utilize time efficiently. Efficient utilization of resources can mean substantial savings in transportation costs and other non quantifiable costs such as increased customer attention, impact of on site maintenance and improved intercommunication within the business.

The importance of Mobile Computers has been highlighted in many fields of which a few are described below:

1.7.1. For Estate Agents

Estate agents can work either at home or out in the field. With mobile computers they can be more productive. They can obtain current real estate information by accessing multiple listing services, which they can do from home, office or car when out with clients. They can provide clients with immediate feedback regarding specific homes or neighborhoods, and with faster loan approvals, since applications can be submitted on the spot. Therefore, mobile computers allow them to devote more time to clients.

1.7.2. Stock Information Collation/Control

In environments where access to stock is very limited e.g. factory warehouses. The use of small portable electronic databases accessed via a mobile computer would be ideal.

Data collated could be directly written to a central database, via a CDPD network, which holds all stock information hence the need for transfer of data to the central computer at a later date is not necessary. This ensures that from the time that a stock count is completed, there is no inconsistency between the data input on the portable computers and the central database.

1.7.3. Credit Card Verification

At Point of Sale (POS) terminals in shops and supermarkets, when customers use credit cards for transactions, the intercommunication required between the bank central computer and the POS terminal, in order to effect verification of the card usage, can take place quickly and securely over cellular channels using a mobile computer unit. This can speed up the transaction process and relieve congestion at the POS terminals.

1.7.4. Emergency Services

Ability to receive information on the move is vital where the emergency services are involved. Information regarding the address, type and other details of an incident can be dispatched quickly, via a CDPD system using mobile computers, to one or several appropriate mobile units which are in the vicinity of the incident.

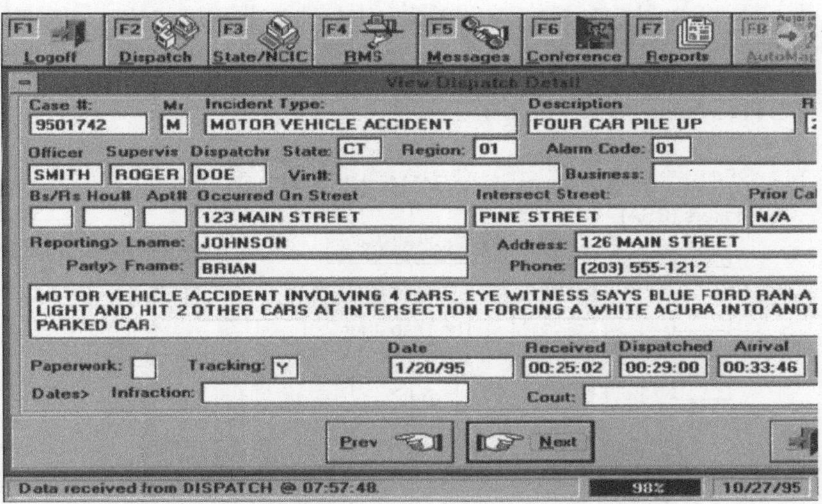

Fig. 1.6: Police Incident Information Screen

1.7.5. In Courts

Defense counsels can take mobile computers in court. When the opposing counsel references a case which they are not familiar, they can use the computer to get direct, real-time access to on-line legal database services, where they can gather information on the case and related precedents. Therefore mobile computers allow immediate access to a wealth of information, making people better informed and prepared.

1.7.6. In Companies

Managers can use mobile computers in, say, critical presentations to major customers. They can access the latest market share information. At a small recess, they can revise the presentation to take advantage of this information. They can communicate with the office about possible new offers and call meetings for discussing responds to the new proposals. Therefore, mobile computers can leverage competitive advantages.

1.7.7. Taxi/Truck Dispatch

Using the idea of a centrally controlled dispatcher with several mobile units (taxis), mobile computing allows the taxis to be given full details of the dispatched job as well as allowing the taxis to communicate information about their whereabouts back to the central dispatch office. This system is also extremely useful in secure deliveries. This allows a central computer to be able to track and receive status information from all of its mobile secure delivery vans. Again, the security and reliability properties of the CDPD system shine through.

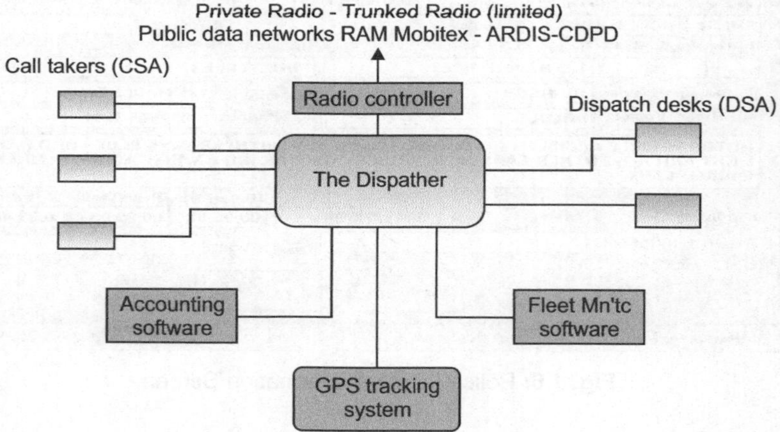

Fig. 1.7: Taxi Dispatch Network

1.7.8. Electronic Mail/Paging

Usage of a mobile unit to send and read emails is a very useful asset for any business individual, as it allows him/her to keep in touch with any colleagues as well as any urgent developments that may affect their work. Access to the Internet, using mobile computing technology, allows the individual to have vast arrays of knowledge at his/her fingertips. Paging is also achievable here, giving even more intercommunication capability between individuals, using a single mobile computer device.

1.8. THE FUTURE OF MOBILE COMPUTING

With the rapid technological advancements in Artificial Intelligence, Integrated Circuitry and increases in Computer Processor speeds, the future of mobile computing looks increasingly exciting. With the emphasis increasingly on compact, small mobile computers, it may also be possible to have all the practicality of a mobile computer in the size of a hand held organizer or even smaller. Use of Artificial Intelligence may allow mobile units to be the ultimate in personal secretaries, which can receive emails and paging messages, understand what they are about, and change the individuals personal schedule according to the message. This can then be checked by the individual to plan his/her day.

The working lifestyle has changed, with the majority of people working from home, rather than commuting. This may be beneficial to the environment as less transportation will be utilized. This mobility aspect may be carried further in that, even in social spheres, people are interacting via mobile stations, eliminating the need to venture outside of the house.

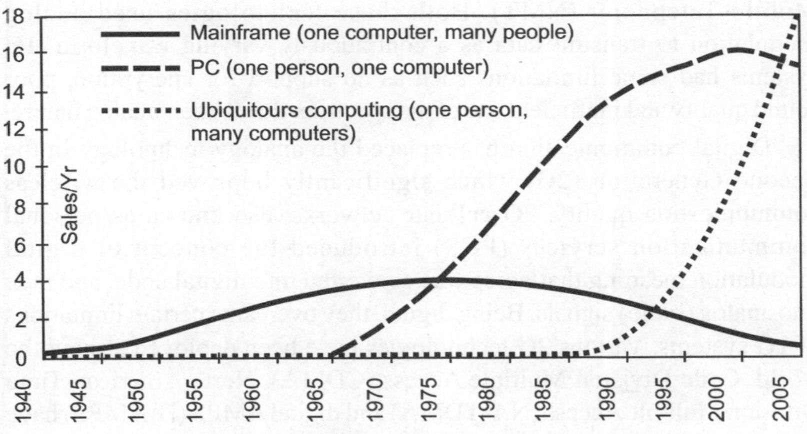

Fig. 1.8: Major Trends in Computing

This scary concept of a world full of inanimate zombies sitting, locked to their mobile stations, accessing every sphere of their lives via the computer screen becomes ever more real as technology, especially in the field of mobile data communications, rapidly improves and, as shown below, trends are very much towards ubiquitous or mobile computing.

Indeed, technologies such as Interactive television and Video Image Compression already imply a certain degree of mobility in the home, ie. home shopping etc. Using the mobile data communication technologies discussed, this mobility may be pushed to extreme.

1.9. GENERATIONS OF MOBILE WIRELESS TECHNOLOGIES AND THEIR SERVICES

Mobile wireless industry has started its technology creation, revelution and evolution since early 1970s. In the past few decades, mobile wireless technologies have experience 4 or 5 generations of technology revolution and evelution, namely from 0G to 4G. The cellular concept was intoduced in the First generation (1G) technology which made the large scale mobile wireless communicaton possible. 1G networks were the first cellular networks introduced in the 1980s. They were only capable of transmitting voice at speeds of about 9.6 kbps max. In the US the system was known Advanced Mobile Phone System (AMPS) and in Europe the Nordic Mobile Telephony (NMT). Both these technologies used analog modulation to transmit data as a continuously varying waveform. 1G systems had some limitations such as no support for encryption, poor sound quality and inefficient use of the spectrum due to their analog nature.

Digital communication has replaced the analogy technology in the Second Generation (2G) which significantly improved the wireless communication quality. 2G cellular networks also known as personal communication services (PCS) introduced the concept of digital modulation meaning that voice was converted into digital code, and then into analog (radio) signals. Being digital, they overcame certain limitations of 1G systems. Various 2G technologies have been deployed around the world. Code Division Multiple Access (CDMA), North American Time Division Multiple Access (NA-TDMA) and digital AMPS (D-AMPS) have been deployed in the US whereas Global System for mobile communication (GSM) has been deployed in Europe and USA and Personal Digital Cellular (PDC) has been deployed in Japan. Although 2G systems were a great improvement from 1G, they were only used for voice communication. 2.5G is a transition step between 2G and 3G (explained later). It is also known as data services over 2G. There have been several deployments of 2.5G across the world. In the USA, they are known as 1xEV-DO and 1xEV-DV. In Europe or places where GSM has been used, 2.5G technologies such as High Speed Circuit Switched Data (HSCSD), General Packet Radio Service (GPRS), Enhanced Data Rate for GSM Evolution (EDGE) have been deployed. Data communication, in addition to the voice communication, has been the main focus in the 3G technologies and a converged network for both voice and data communication is emerging.

The Third Generation (3G) standard is currently being pushed as the next global standard for cellular communications. It will provide services such as fast Internet surfing, advanced value added services and video telephony. Deployments of this technology have already begun and several countries like Austria, Denmark, South Korea and Japan have adopted the 3G network architecture. There are three main technologies that are being applied. In the US CDMA2000, in Europe Wideband CDMA (W-CDMA) and in China Time Division-Synchronous Code Division Multiple Access (TD-SCDMA). Although 3G has not been fully deployed, people have already started talking about the fourth generation (4G) technology. This generation will be designed to have data rates of up to 20Mbps. It will have support for next generation Internet such as IPv6, QoS and Mo-IP, lower system cost and high capacity and capable of supporting communication in moving vehicles with speed up to 250 km/hr.

(For detailed historical developments please see Annexure 1-B)

We briefly listed all the key technologies and protocols used in each generation of the mobile wireless communications in the following Table 1.2.

Table 1.2.	
0G	0G refers to pre-cellular mobile telephony technology in 1970s. These mobile telephones were usually mounted in cars or trucks, though briefcase models were also made.

PTT	Push to talk
MTS	Mobile Telephone System
IMTS	Improved Mobile Telephone Service
AMTS	Advanced Mobile Telephone System
0.5G	0.5G is a group of technologies with improved feature than the basic 0G technologies.
Autotel/PALM	Autotel, or PALM (Public Automated Land Mobile)
ARP	Auto Radio Puhelin, Car Radio Phone
HCMTS	High Capacity Mobile Telephone System
1G	1G (or 1-G) is the first-generation wireless telephone technology, cellphones. These are the analog cellphone standards that were introduced in the 1980s.
NMT	Nordic Mobile Telephone
AMPS	Advanced Mobile Phone System
TAGS	Total Access Communication System (TACS) is the European version of AMPS.
JTAGS	Japan Total Access Communication System
2G	2G (or 2-G) is the second-generation wireless telephone, which is based on digital technologies. 2G networks is basically for voice communications only, except SMS messaging is also available as a form of data transmission for some standards.
GSM	Global System for Mobile Communications
iDEN	Integrated Digital Enhanced Network
D-AMPS	Digital Advanced Mobile Phone System based on TDMA
CDMA-One	Code Division Multiple Access technology defined by IS-95
PDC	Personal Digital Cellular
TDMA	Time Division Multiple Access
2.5G	2.5G is a group of bridging technologies between 2G and 3G wireless communication. It is a digital communication allowing e-mail and simple Web browsing, in addition to voice.
GPRS	General Packet Radio Service
WiDEN	Wideband Integrated Dispatch Enhanced Network
2.75G	2.75G refer to the technologies which don't meet the 3G requirements but are marketed as if they do.

CDMA2000 1xRTT	CDMA-2000 is a TIA standard (IS-2000) that is an evolutionary outgrowth of CDMA-One. CDMA2000 with 1xRTT is slight weaker than 3G requirements.
EDGE	Enhanced Data rates for GSM Evolution
3G	3G stand for the third generation of wireless communication technologies, which support broadband voice, data and multi-media communications over wireless networks.
W-CDMA	Wideband Code Division Multiple Access
UMTS	Universal Mobile Telecommunications System
FOMA	Freedom of Mobile Multimedia Access
CDMA2000 1xEV	More advanced CDMA2000 with 1xEV technology satisfy 3G requirements.
TD-SCDMA	Time Division Synchronous Code Division Multiple Access
3.5G	The 3.5G generally refer to the technologies beyond the well defined 3G wireless/mobile technologies.
HSDPA	High-Speed Downlink Packet Access
3.75G	The 3.75G refer to the technologies beyond the well defined 3G wireless/mobile technologies.
HSUPA	High-Speed Uplink Packet Access
4G	4G is the name of technologies for high-speed mobile wireless communications designed for new data services and interactive TV through mobile network.

1.9.1. Second Generation Wireless Technologies and Services

GSM is the most widely adopted 2G technology in the world. Although it was initially employed in Europe, it has become a global technology with subscribers in about 197 countries. Its specifications were completed in 1990 and service began in 1992. Currently, the second generation (2G) of wireless networks, such as GSM, CDMA (IS-95) and TDMA (IS-136) networks, are widely used in the wireless communications. The 2G networks can provide narrow band (up to 144kbps) voice and data services using circuit switching techniques. To conduct a smooth evolution from the 2G to 3G wireless networks, some transitional technologies, such as GPRS for GSM, 136 high-speed for TDMA or IS-95B for CDMA, are defined, which are sometimes called 2.5G wireless technologies.

Some of the data services which are part of the 2.5G extension are:

- ***Short Messaging Service (SMS):*** Transfer of messages between cell phones. Large messages are truncated and sent as multiple messages.
- ***High-Speed Circuit-Switched Data (HSCSD):*** This was the first attempt at providing data at high speeds data over GSM, with speeds of up to 115 kbps. This technique cannot support large bursts of data. HSCSD was not widely implemented and GPRS became a more popular technique.
- ***General Packet Radio Service (GPRS):*** This technique can support large bursty data transfers. In order to support this two new elements have to be added to existing networks. Service GPRS support node (SGSN) for security mobility and access control and Gateway GPRS support node (GGSN) in order to connect to external packet switched networks.
- ***Enhanced Data Rates for GSM Evolution (EDGE):*** The standard GSM uses GMSK modulation. Edge uses 8-PSK modulation. GPRS and EDGE combined provide data rates of up to 384 kbps.
- ***Cellular Digital Packet Data (CDPD):*** CDPD is a packet based data service. CDPD is able to detect idle voice channels and uses them to transfer data traffic without affecting voice communications.

CDMA is the primary 2G technology in the USA. CDMA-One, also known as IS-95a was the initial technique. This technique allows users to use the entire spectrum and can support more users than TDMA and GSM. Speed between 4.8 and 14.4 kbps can be supported. The CDMATwo extension can provide data rates of up to 115.2 kbps. The 2.5G extension to this technology can be divided into two techniques. 1xEV-DV uses one radio frequency channel for data and voice, whereas 1xEV-DO uses separate channels for data and voice. These are fully compatible with both CDMA One and its 3G replacement CDMA2000, to make the transition as easy as possible.

1.9.2. Third Generation Wireless Technologies and Services

Third Generation Wireless(3G) contains a group of standards to support broadband voice, data and multi-media communications over wireless networks. The aim of 3G is to provide a world wide standard and a common frequency band for mobile networking, please refer Fig. 1.9.

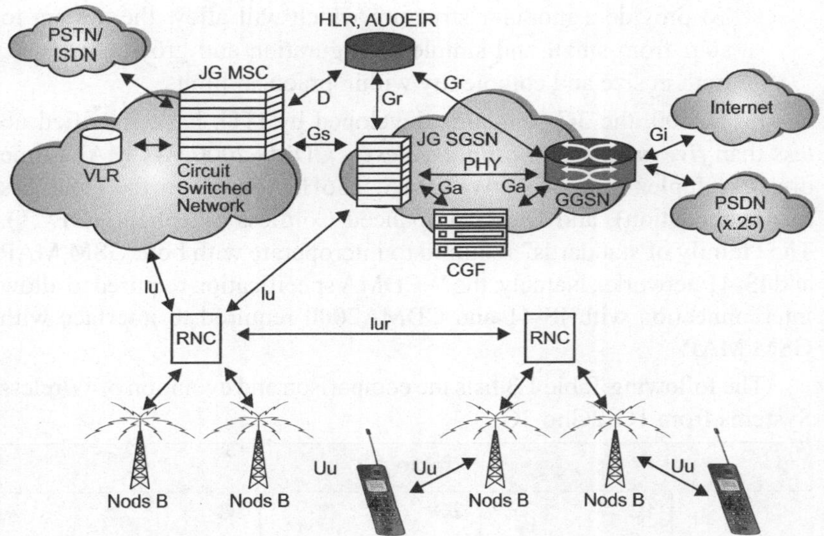

Fig. 1.9: Third Generation Wireless Technologies and Services

The International Telecommunication Union (ITU) started the process in 1992, the result of this effort was a new network infrastructure called International Mobile Telecommunications 2000 (IMT- 2000), with the 2000 signifying that this new technology will be available in 2000, will have data rates of up to 2000 Kbps and will be in the 2000 MHz frequency range.

The following is the list of objectives that IMT-2000 aims to receive:

- To make a wide range of services, both voice and data available to users, irrespective of location.
- To provide services over a wide coverage area.
- To provide the best Quality of Service (QoS) possible.
- To extend the number of services provided subject to constraints like radio transmission, spectrum efficiency and system economics.
- To accommodate a great variety of mobile stations.
- To admit the provision of service by more than one network in any area of coverage.
- To provide an open architecture which will permit the easy introduction of technology advancements as well as different applications.

- To provide a modular structure which will allow the system to start from small and simple configuration and grow as needed, both in size and complexity within practical limits.

IMT-2000, the 3G standards developed by ITU, have specified no less than ***five means of multiple access*** – CDMA2000, WCMA, a time division duplex version of WCDMA, 136HS (based on the UWCC's recommendation), and Digital Enhanced Cordless Telephone (DECT). The "family of standards" required to interoperate with both GSM MAP and IS-41 networks. Namely, the WCDMA specification required to allow interconnection with IS-41 and CDMA2000 required to interface with GSM MAP.

The following Table 1.3 lists the comparison and evolution of Wireless Systems from 1G, 2G to 3G:

Table 1.3

	1G	2G	3G
System	Analogue	Digital	Digital
Major Systems	AMPS, NMT and TACS	GSM, CDMA and TDMA	WCDMA, CDMA-2000 and TD-SCDMA
Application	Voice	Voice + little Circuit-switch Data	Voice + Packet-switch Data
Local Subscriber	Less than 500k	About 5.9M	More than 5M (Estimated)
Speed	Depends on Analogue Signal	9.6kbps - 14.4kbps	384 kbps for mobile and 2 Mbps for stationary
Properties	Unstable, incomplete coverage and poor sound quality	More secure, data services available, broader coverage, more stable, allow more user, better sound quality	Multimedia data, positioning capability, connection to Internet, always connected

1.10. MOBILE WIRELESS PROTOCOLS

1.10.1. Global System for Mobile Communications (GSM)

Groupe Spcial Mobile (GSM) is the Pan European standard for mobile communications defined by the European Telecommunication Standards

Institute (ETSI) and published in 1990. Using GSM technologies and systems, telephony, emergency services, SMS (short message service) and data services can be provided through wireless communications. CDMA, a competing technology developed by Qualcomm, is widely adopted in the US. In a GSM network, there are three functional areas: the Mobile Station such as a mobile phone which is carried by a subscriber, the Base Station Subsystem which controls the radio link with the Mobile Station, and the Network Subsystem which mainly performs the switching of calls between the mobile users, and between mobile and fixed network users.

The signalling protocol in GSM is structured into three general layers as shown in the following Fig. 1.10 and Fig. 1.11.

Layer 1 (the physical layer) uses the data channel structures over the air interface. Layer 2 (the data link layer) is a modified version of the LAPD protocol used in ISDN, called LAPDm. Across the A interface, the Message Transfer Part layer 2 (MTP2) of SS7 is used. Layer 3 is the GSM signalling protocol, which is divided into 3 sub-layers: Radio Resources Management to control the setup, maintenance, and termination of radio and fixed channels, including handovers; Mobility Management to manage the location updating and registration procedures, as well as security and authentication; and Connection Management to handles general call control, similar to CCITT Recommendation Q.931, and manages Supplementary Services and the Short Message Service.

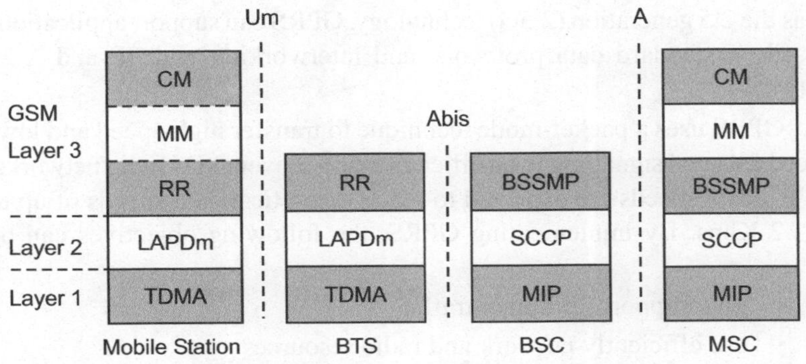

Fig. 1.10: Global System for Mobile Communications

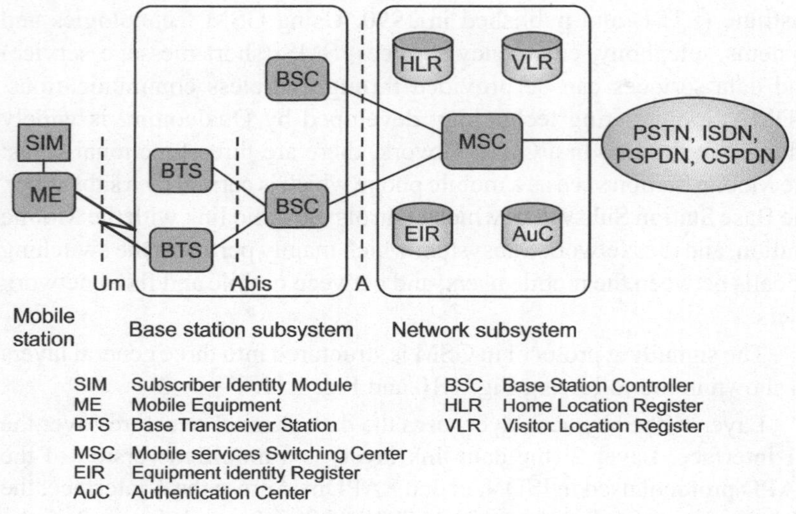

Fig. 1.11: GSM Network Architecture

Signalling between the different entities in the fixed part of the network, such as between the HLR and VLR, uses the Mobile Application Part (MAP), one of protocols in the SS7/C7 stack.

1.10.2. General Packet Radio Service (GPRS)

General Packet Radio Service (GPRS) is a standard designed by ETSI for GSM, DCS, PCS digital cellular networks to enable high-speed wireless Internet and other data communications. Sometimes, it is referred to as the 2.5 generation (2.5G) technology. GPRS can support applications based on standard data protocols, and interworking with IP and X.25 networks.

GPRS uses a packet-mode technique to transfer high-speed and low-speed data and signalling in an efficient manner over GSM radio networks. GPRS data speeds are expected to reach theoretical data speeds of up to 171.2 Kbps. By implementing GPRS, the following objectives can be met:

- give support for bursty traffic
- use efficiently network and radio resources
- provide flexible services at relatively low costs

- possibility for connectivity to the Internet
- provide fast access time
- to have and support flexible co-existence with GSM voice

GPRS architecture consists of Gateway GPRS Support Node (GGSN) and a Serving GPRS Support Node (SGSN) as shown in the Fig. 1.12. The GGSN acts as the gateway to other packet data networks such as the Internet. The SGSN is the serving node that enables virtual connections to the GPRS enabled mobile device and delivery of data. GGSN provides interworking with external packet-switched networks, and is connected with SGSNs via an IP-based GPRS backbone network.

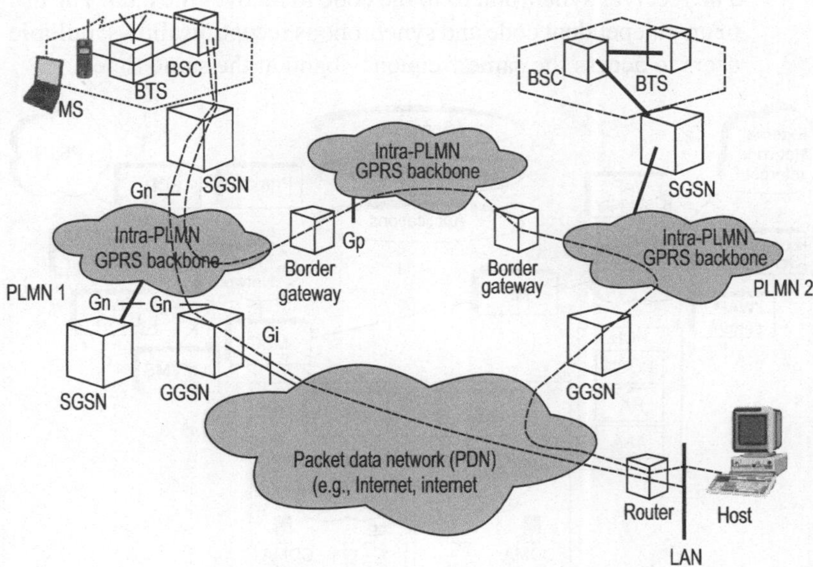

Fig. 1.12: GPRS Network Architecture

GPRS security functionality is equivalent to the existing GSM security. The SGSN performs authentication and cipher setting procedures based on the same algorithms, keys, and criteria as in existing GSM. GPRS uses a ciphering algorithm optimized for packet data transmission.

1.10.3. Code Division Multiple Access (CDMA)

Code Division Multiple Access (CDMA) is a cellular technology defined by Qualcomm in IS-95 and IS-2000. Other widely used multiple access techniques for cellular are Time Division Multiple Access (TDMA) and Frequency Division Multiple Access (FDMA).

CDMA is a form of Direct Sequence Spread Spectrum communications. In general, Spread Spectrum communications is distinguished by three key elements:

- The signal occupies a bandwidth much greater than that which is necessary to send the information, which results in immunity to interference and jamming and multi-user access;
- The bandwidth is spread by means of a code which is independent of the data;
- The receiver synchronizes to the code to recover the data. The use of an independent code and synchronous reception allows multiple users to access the same frequency band at the same time.

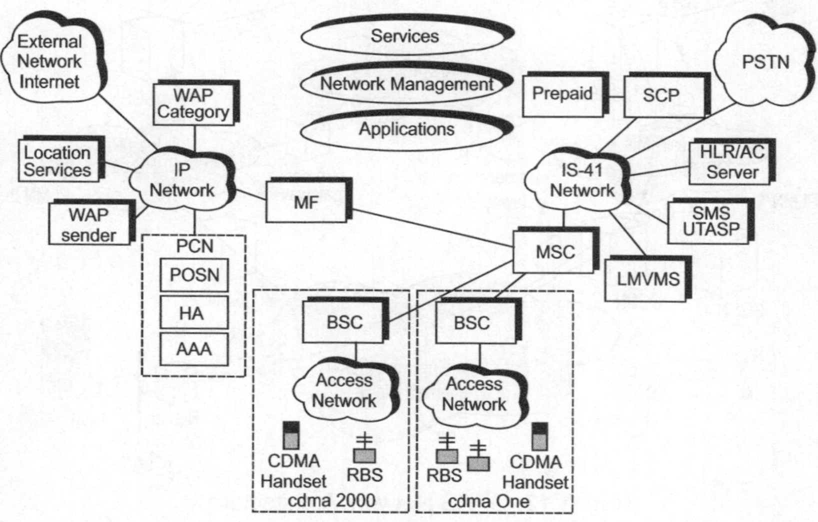

Fig. 1.13: Code Division Multiple Access

Due to increasing market demand for a convered network for both voice and data cpmmunications, CDMA technologies are evolving into CDMA2000 to meet the challenges. CDMA2000 is the 3rd Generation solution based on IS-95. Unlike some 3G standards, it is an evolution of an existing CDMA wireless standard. CDMA2000 supports 3G services as defined by the International Telecommunications Union (ITU) for

IMT-2000. The goal is access to any service, anywhere, anytime from one terminal - true converged, mobile services.

The term Code Division Multiple Access (CDMA) is also widely used to refer to a key technology in the Universal Mobile Telecommunications System (UMTS). The two different uses of this term can be confusing. Actually, the Qualcomm standard CDMA and UMTS have been competing for adoption in many markets.

1.10.3.1. CDMA2000: 3G Standard Based on CDMA IS-95

CDMA2000 is the 3rd Generation solution based on CDMA IS-95, which supports 3G services as defined by the ITU 3G standards IMT-2000. CDMA2000 defines both an air interface and a core network. CDMA-2000 has already been implemented to several networks as an evolutionary step from CDMA-One as CDMA-2000 provides full backward compatibility with IS-95B.

The CDMA-2000 standard is evolving to continually support new services in a standard 1.25 MHz carrier. The first phase of CDMA2000, or CDMA2000 1X will deliver average data rates of 144 kbps. Phase two, labeled CDMA2000 1xEV, will provide for data rates greater than 2Mbps. CDMA2000 1X (or the IS-2000 standard) published by the Telecommunications Industry Association (TIA), offers average data rates of 144 kbps, backward compatibility with cdmaOne networks, and many other performance improvements. CDMA2000 1X can be implemented in existing cdmaOne spectrum (1.25 MHz) or in new spectrum allocations. A CDMA2000 1X network will support simultaneous voice and data services with low latency and improved performance.

The evolution of CDMA2000 beyond 1X is called CDMA2000 1xEV. 1xEV is divided into two steps: 1xEV-DO and 1xEV-DV. 1xEV-DO stands for 1X Evolution Data Only. 1xEV-DV stands for 1X Evolution Data and Voice. Again CDMA2000 1XEV can be implemented in existing cdmaOne spectrum (1.25 MHz) or in new spectrum allocations. 1xEV-DO, requiring a separate carrier for data, will provide for higher data rates on 1X systems. By allocating a separate carrier for data, operators will be able to deliver peak data rates in excess of 2 Mbps at its best effort. 1xEV-DV allows data and voice services for CDMA2000 in one carrier. A 1xEV-DV carrier will provide not only high speed data and voice simultaneously, but will also be capable of delivering real-time packet services.

The standards for a CDMA packet core network are being developed by the TR45.6 working group of the TIA. These standards are being developed by using existing standards from the IETF (Internet Engineering Task Force) on Mobile IP. 3GPP2 is also busy defining the evolution of a CDMA2000 network to All-IP. The CDMA2000 PCN will be the first step in this evolution.

1.10.3.2. Code Division Multiplexing (CDM)

Code Division Multiplexing (CDM) is a technique in which each channel transmits its bits as a coded channel-specific sequence of pulses. This coded transmission typically is accomplished by transmitting a unique time-dependent series of short pulses, which are placed within chip times within the larger bit time. All channels, each with a different code, can be transmitted on the same fiber and asynchronously demultiplxed, Fig. 1.14. Other widely used multiple access techniques are Time Division Multiple Access (TDMA) and Frequency Division Multiple Access (FDMA).

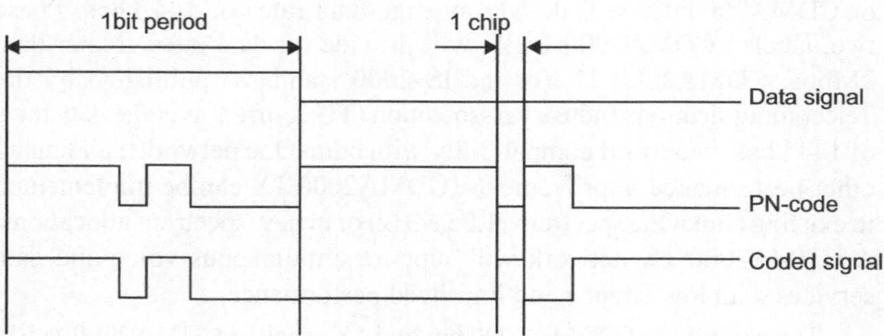

Fig. 1.14: Code Division Multiplexing

Code Division Multiplex techniques are used as an access technology, namely Code Division Multiple Access (CDMA), in Universal Mobile Telecommunications System (UMTS) standard for the third generation (3G) mobile communication identified by the ITU. Another important application of the CDMA is the Global Positioning System (GPS).

However, the term Code Division Multiple access (CDMA) is also widely used to refer to a group of specific implementations of CDMA defined by Qualcomm for use in digital cellular telephony, which include IS-95 and IS-2000. The two different uses of this term can be confusing.

Actually, CDMA (the Qualcomm standard) and UMTS have been competing for adoption in many markets.

1.10.4. Time Division Multiple Access (TDMA)

Time Division Multiple Access (TDMA) is digital transmission technology that allows a number of users to access a single Radio-Frequency (RF) channel without interference by allocating unique time slots to each user within each channel. The TDMA digital transmission scheme multiplexes three signals over a single channel. The current TDMA standard for cellular divides a single channel into six time slots, with each signal using two slots, providing a 3 to 1 gain in capacity over Advanced Mobile-Phone Service (AMPS). Each caller is assigned a specific time slot for transmission.

The wireless industry began to explore converting the existing analog network to digital as a means of improving capacity back in the late 1980s. In 1989, the Cellular Telecommunications Industry Association (CTIA) chose TDMA over Frequency Division Multiple Access (FDMA) (today known as Narrowband Analog Mobile-Phone Service (NAMPS) narrowband standard as the technology of choice for existing 800 MHz cellular markets and for emerging 1.9-GHz markets. With the growing technology competition applied by Qualcomm in favor of Code Division Multiple Access (CDMA) and the realities of the European global system for mobile communications (GSM) standard, the CTIA decided to let carriers make their own technology selection.

The TDMA system is designed for use in a range of environments and situations, from hand portable use in a downtown office to a mobile user traveling at high speed on the freeway. The system also supports a variety of services for the end user, such as voice, data, fax, short message services, and broadcast messages. TDMA offers a flexible air interface, providing high performance with respect to capacity, coverage, and unlimited support of mobility and capability to handle different types of user needs.

1.10.4.1. Working of TDMA

TDMA relies upon the fact that the audio signal has been digitized; that is, divided into a number of milliseconds-long packets. It allocates a single frequency channel for a short time and then moves to another channel.

The digital samples from a single transmitter occupy different time slots in several bands at the same time as shown in Fig. 1.15.

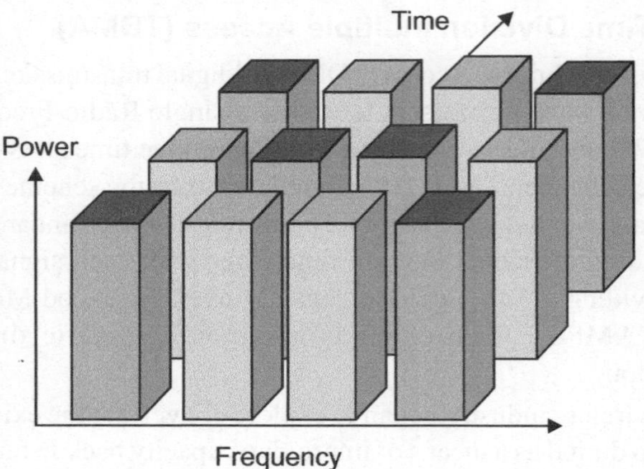

Fig. 1.15: Time Division Multiple Access

The access technique used in TDMA has three users sharing a 30–kHz carrier frequency. TDMA is also the access technique used in the European digital standard, GSM, and the Japanese digital standard, Personal Digital Cellular (PDC). The reason for choosing TDMA for all these standards was that it enables some vital features for system operation in an advanced cellular or PCS environment. Today, TDMA is an available, well-proven technique in commercial operation in many systems.

Effectively, the IS–54 and IS–136 implementations of TDMA immediately tripled the capacity of cellular frequencies by dividing a 30–kHz channel into three time slots, enabling three different users to occupy it at the same time. Currently, systems are in place that allow six times capacity. In the future, with the utilization of hierarchical cells, intelligent antennas, and adaptive channel allocation, the capacity should approach 40 times analog capacity.

1.10.4.2. Advanced TDMA

TDMA substantially improved upon the efficiency of analog cellular. However, like Frequency Division Multiple Access (FDMA), it had the weakness that it wasted bandwidth: the time slot was allocated to a specific conversation whether or not anyone was speaking at that moment. Hughes' enhanced version of TDMA Extended Time Division Multiple

Access (ETDMA) attempts to correct this problem. Instead of waiting to determine whether a subscriber is transmitting, ETDMA assigns subscribers dynamically. ETDMA sends data through those pauses which normal speech contains. When subscribers have something to transmit, they put one bit in the buffer queue. The system scans the buffer, notices that the user has something to transmit, and allocates bandwidth accordingly. If a subscriber has nothing to transmit, the queue simply goes to the next subscriber. So, instead of being arbitrarily assigned, time is allocated according to need. If partners in a phone conversation do not speak over one another, this technique can almost double the spectral efficiency of TDMA, making it almost 10 times as efficient as analog transmission.

1.10.4.3. The Advantages of TDMA

In addition to increasing the efficiency of transmission, TDMA offers a number of other advantages over standard cellular technologies. First and foremost, it can be easily adapted to the transmission of data as well as voice communication. TDMA offers the ability to carry data rates of 64 kbps to 120 Mbps (expandable in multiples of 64 kbps). This enables operators to offer personal communication-like services including fax, voice-band data, and Short Message Services (SMSs) as well as bandwidth-intensive applications such as multimedia and videoconferencing.

Unlike spread-spectrum techniques which can suffer from interference among the users all of whom are on the same frequency band and transmitting at the same time, TDMA's technology, which separates users in time, ensures that they will not experience interference from other simultaneous transmissions.

TDMA also provides the user with extended battery life and talk time since the mobile is only transmitting a portion of the time (from 1/3 to 1/10) of the time during conversations.

TDMA installations offer substantial savings in base-station equipment, space, and maintenance, an important factor as cell sizes grow ever smaller. TDMA is the most cost-effective technology for upgrading a current analog system to digital. TDMA is the only technology that offers an efficient utilization of Hierarchical Cell Structures (HCSs) offering pico, micro, and macrocells. HCSs allow coverage for the system to be tailored to support specific traffic and service needs. By using this approach, system capacities of more than 40-times AMPS can be achieved in a cost-efficient way. Because of its inherent compatibility with FDMA analog systems, TDMA allows service compatibility with the use of dual-mode handsets. Dual band 800/1900 MHz offers the following competitive advantages:

- Identical applications and services are provided to subscribers operating in both bands.
- Carriers can use the same switch for 800– and 1900–MHz services.
- Seamless interworking between 800– and 1900–MHz networks through dual-band/dual-mode phones.
- Using dual-mode, dual-band phones, subscribers on a TDMA 1,900 channel can hand off both to/from a TDMA channel on 800 MHz as well as to/from an analog AMPS channel.

1.10.4.4. Disadvantages of TDMA

One of the disadvantages of TDMA is that each user has a predefined time slot. However, users roaming from one cell to another are not allotted a time slot. Thus, if all the time slots in the next cell are already occupied, a call might well be disconnected. Likewise, if all the time slots in the cell in which a user happens to be in are already occupied, a user will not receive a dial tone.

Another problem with TDMA is that it is subjected to multipath distortion. A signal coming from a tower to a handset might come from any one of several directions. It might have bounced off several different buildings before arriving (see Fig. 1s.16) which can cause interference.

One way of getting around this interference is to put a time limit on the system. The system will be designed to receive, treat, and process a signal within a certain time limit. After the time limit has expired, the system ignores signals. The sensitivity of the system depends on how far it processes the multipath frequencies. Even at thousandths of seconds, these multipath signals cause problems.

All cellular architectures, whether microcell- or macrocell-based, have a unique set of propagation problems. Macrocells are particularly affected by multipath signal loss—a phenomenon usually occurring at the cell fringes where reflection and refraction may weaken or cancel a signal.

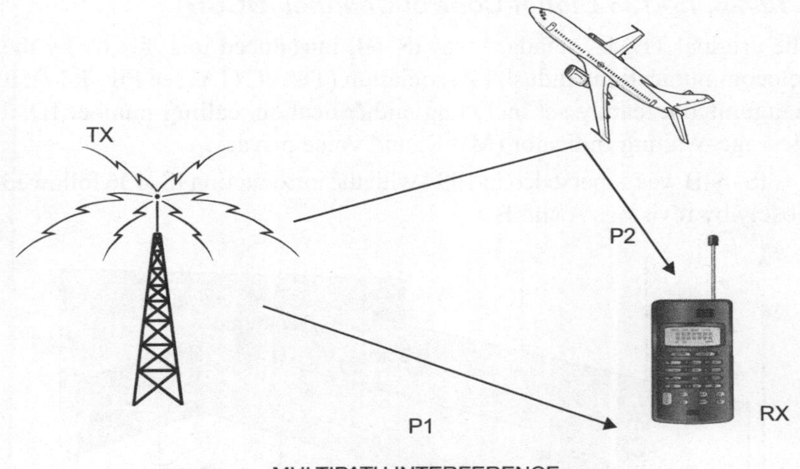

Fig. 1.16: Multipath Interference

1.10.4.5. TDMA Versus CDMA

Since the introduction of CDMA, the wireless world has been occupied by a debate over the relative merits of TDMA and CDMA. The proponents of CDMA have claimed bandwidth efficiency of up to 13 times that of TDMA and between 20 to 40 times that of analog transmission. Moreover, they note that its spread-spectrum technology is both more secure and offers higher transmission quality than TDMA, because of its increased resistance to multipath distortion.

The defenders of TDMA, on the other hand, point out that to date there has been no successful major trial of CDMA technology that support the capacity claims. Moreover, they point out that the theoretical improvements in bandwidth efficiency claimed for CDMA are now being approached by enhancements to TDMA technology. The evolution of TDMA will allow capacity increases of 20 to 40 fold over analog in the near future. This combined with the vastly more expensive technology needed for CDMA ($300,000 per base station compared with $80,000 for TDMA) calls into question what real savings CDMA technology can offer. So far, IS–136 TDMA is the proven leader as the most economical digital migration path for an existing AMPS network.

1.10.4.6. IS–136 Digital-Control Channel (DCCH)

The original TDMA standard was IS–54, introduced in 1988–89 by the Telecommunications Industry Association (TIA)/CTIA (see Fig. 1.17). It inaugurated a feature set including authentication, calling-number ID, a Message-Waiting Indicator (MWI), and voice privacy.

IS–54B was superseded in 1994 with the introduction IS–136 followed closely by revisions A and B.

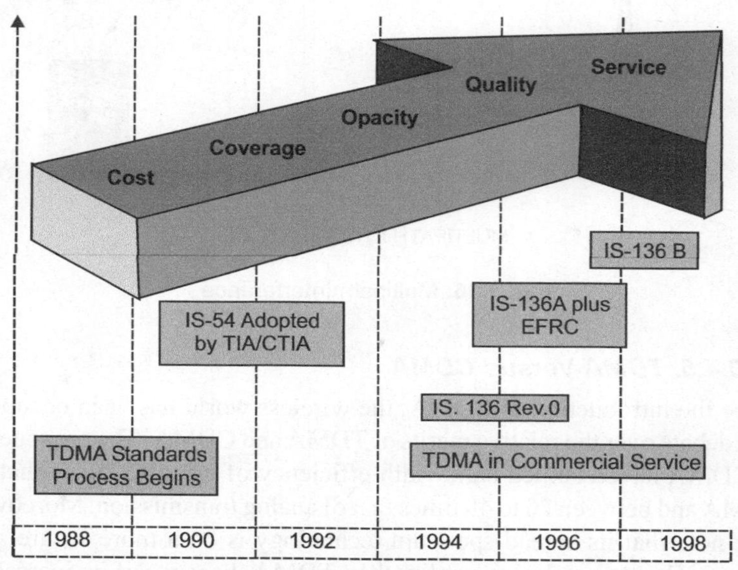

Fig. 1.17: TDMA Standards Evolution

IS–136 was backward compatible to IS–54B and included a DCCH and advanced features.

IS–136A upbanded IS–136 for seamless cellular service between the 800–MHz and 1,900–MHz frequency bands. In addition, it introduced over-the-air activation and programming services.

IS–136B includes a new range of services including broadcast SMS, packet data, etc

1.10.5. Frequency Division Multiple Access (FDMA)

TDMA is basically analog's FDMA with a time-sharing component built into the system. FDMA allocates a single channel to one user at a time as shown in the following Fig. 1.18. If the transmission path deteriorates, the controller switches the system to another channel. Although technically simple to implement, FDMA is wasteful of bandwidth: the channel is assigned to a single conversation whether or not somebody is speaking. Moreover, it cannot handle alternate forms of data, only voice transmissions.

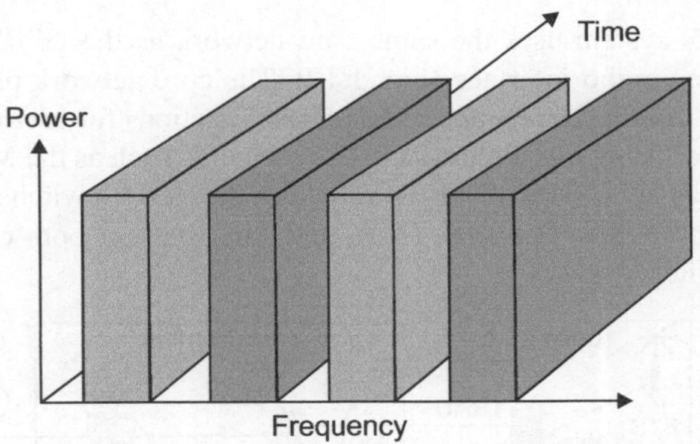

Fig. 1.18: Frequency Division Multiple Access

1.10.6. Universal Mobile Telecommunications System

Universal Mobile Telecommunications System (UMTS) is a key 3G mobile technology identified by the ITU. UMTS is the natural evolutionary choice for operators of GSM networks, a 2G mobile network. Using fresh radio spectrum to support increased numbers of customers in line with industry forecasts of demand for data services over the next decade and beyond, "UMTS" is synonymous with a choice of WCDMA radio access technology that has already been selected by approaching 120 licensees worldwide.

A UMTS network consist of three interacting domains; Core Network (CN), UMTS Terrestrial Radio Access Network (UTRAN) and User Equipment (UE). The main function of the core network is to provide switching, routing and transit for user traffic. Core network also contains the databases and network management functions. The following is a list of key UMTS components:

- UMTS systems (including satellite)
- PublicLand Mobile Network (PLMN)

- MSC/VLR or SGSN
- Location Area
- Routing Area (PS domain)
- UTRAN Registration Area (PS domain)
- Cell
- Sub cell

UMTS system uses the same core network as the GPRS and uses entirely new radio interface (Fig. 1.19). The core network provides the switching, routing, transport, and database functions for user traffic. The core network contains circuit-switched elements such as the MSC, VLR, and gateway MSC (GMSC). It also contains the packet-switched elements SGSN and GGSN. The EIR, HLR, and AuC support both circuit- and packet-switched data.

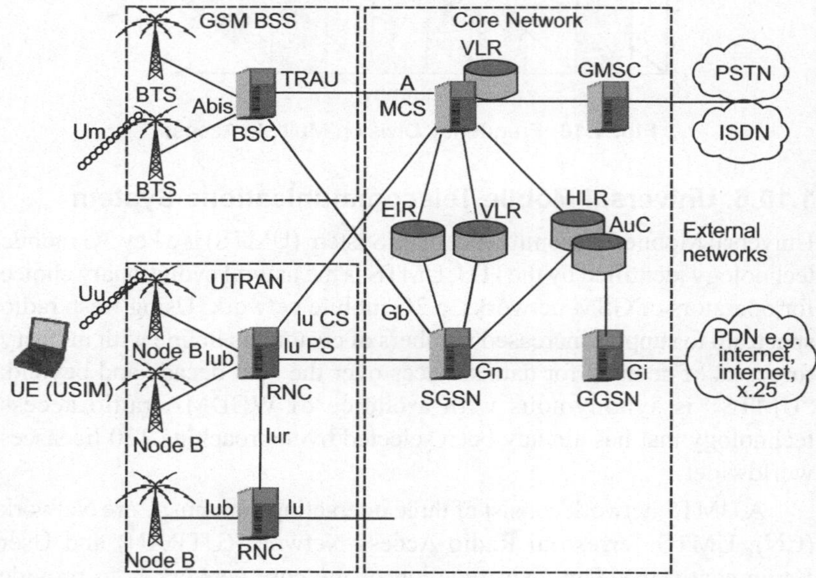

Fig. 1.19: Universal Mobile Telecommunications System

The Asynchronous Transfer Mode (ATM) is the data transmission method used within the UMTS core network. The new radio network in UMTS is called UTRAN (UMTS Terrestrial Radio Access Network) and is connected to the Core Network (CN) of GPRS via Iu interface. The Iu is the UTRAN interface between the Radio network controller RNC and CN.

1.10.7. IP Multimedia Subsystem (IMS) Architecture

The IP Multimedia Subsystem (IMS) is an architectural framework defined by the wireless standards body 3rd Generation Partnership Project (3GPP) for delivering IP multimedia services to mobile users based on the UTMS network. A similar system called Multimedia Domain (MMD) was defined by the 3GPP2 (a different organization) for the CDMA2000 network, which was based on the 3GPP IMS.

For the network access, the user can connect to an IMS network in various ways using IP. Direct IMS terminals (such as mobile phones, Personal Digital Assistants (PDAs) and computers) can register directly on an IMS network, even when they are roaming in another network or country (the visited network). The only requirement is that they can use IPv6 (also IPv4 in early IMS) and run Session Initiation Protocol (SIP) user agents. Fixed access (e.g., Digital Subscriber Line (DSL), cable modems, Ethernet), mobile access (e.g. W-CDMA, CDMA2000, GSM, GPRS) and wireless access (e.g. WLAN, WiMAX) are all supported. Other phone systems like plain old telephone service (POTS — the old analogue telephones), H.323 and non IMS-compatible VoIP systems, are supported through gateways.

The IP Multimedia Core Network Subsystem is a collection of different functions, linked by standardized interfaces, which grouped form one IMS administrative network. The key functions of the core network are:

- Home Subscriber Server (HSS), or User Profile Server Function (UPSF), is a master user database that supports the IMS network entities that actually handle calls. It contains the subscription-related information (user profiles), performs authentication and authorization of the user, and can provide information about the user's physical location.
- Call Session Control Function (CSCF) is used to process SIP signaling packets in the IMS. There are three types of CSCF: Proxy-CSCF (P-CSCF), Serving-CSCF (S-CSCF) and Interrogating-CSCF (I-CSCF).

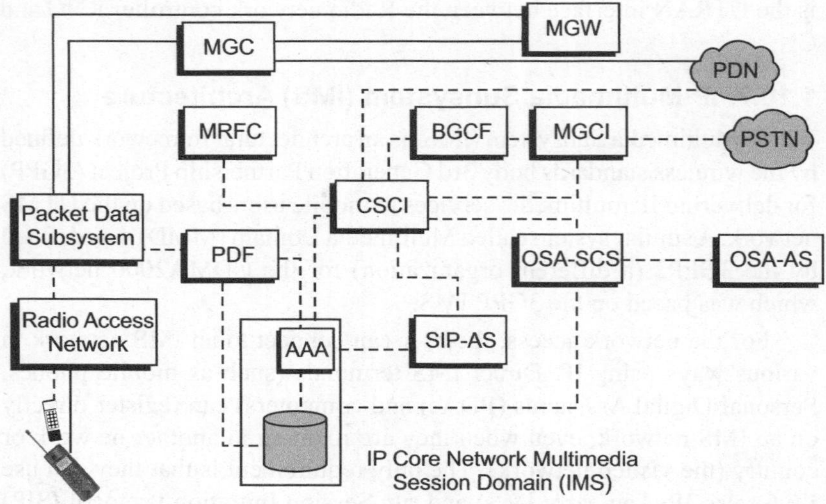

Fig. 1.20: 3GPP/IMS 3GPP2 Common Reference Model

- Application Servers (AS) host and execute services, and interface with the S-CSCF using SIP.
- MRF (Media Resource Function) provides media related functions such as media manipulation (e.g. voice stream mixing) and playing of tones and announcements.
- A BGCF (Breakout Gateway Control Function) is a SIP server that includes routing functionality based on telephone numbers.

Media Resources are those components that operate on the media plane and are under the control of IMS Core functions. Specifically, Media Server (MS) and Media Gateway (MGW).

1.10.8. Wireless Local Loop (WLL)

Wireless Local Loop (WLL) is a technology that connects subscribers to the public switched telephone network (PSTN) using radio signals to substitute the copper wires. The WLL sustem includes cordless access systems, proprietary fixed radio access, and fixed cellular systems. Sometimes WLL is called Radio In The Loop (RITL) or Fixed-Radio Access (FRA). The bandwidth using WLL is much higher than that possible in the copper loop. Wireless local loop is a practical and economical last mile (or first mile) solution for connecting subscribers in areas that do not have the wired infrastructure such as remote rural area and some developing countries.

The WLL system is based on a full-duplex radio network that provides local telephone-like service among a group of users (see Fig. 1.21). The WLL unit consists of a radio transceiver and the WLL interface assembled in one metal box. Two cables and a telephone connector are the only outlets from the box; one cable connects to a directional antenna and a phone receptacle to connect to a common telephone set. A fax or modem could also be connected for fax or computer communication. WLL systems incorporating various types of wireless technologies as summarized as follows:

- TDM/TDMA and P-MP communications equipment: The system uses communications equipment based on time division multiplex/ time division access (TDM/TDMA) technology and a point-to-multipoint (P-MP) system provides service coverage over a wide area encompassing the base station, relay stations and subscriber stations.

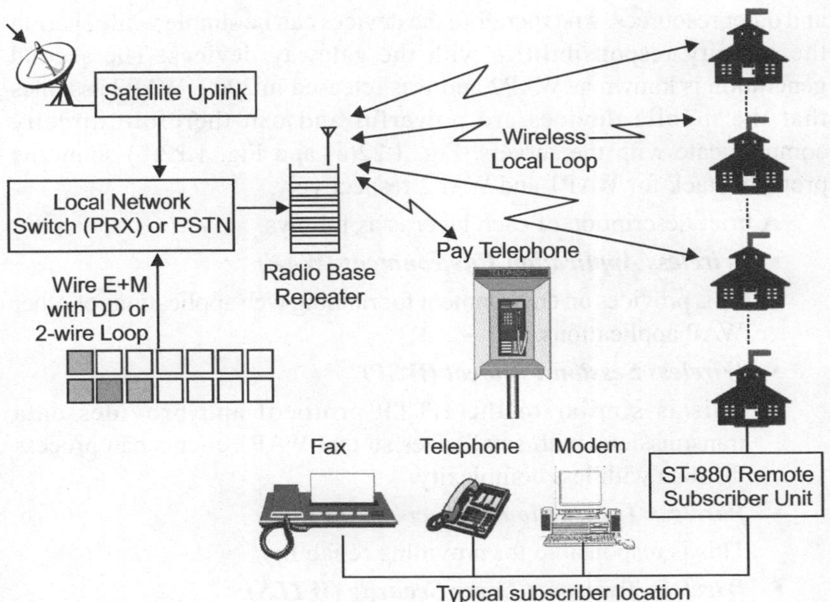

Fig. 1.21: Wireless Local Loop

- Fixed use of cellular systems: This approach uses the wireless equipment of a cellular phone system, thereby curtailing the mobile function. Using cellular phones as the subscriber terminals makes it possible to hold down the system cost.
- PHS-WLL system: The system uses PHS terminal technology and wireless equipment. Since the voice encoding system uses 32 kbps Adaptive Differential Pulse Code Modulation (ADPCM), speech quality on a par with that of fixed telephony is obtained.

1.10.9. Wireless Application Protocol (WAP)

Since one of the most important services provided by 3G systems is access to the Internet, it is important to understand the security mechanisms of the protocol used to access the Internet. WAP is an open specification which enables mobile users to access the Internet. This protocol is independent of the underlying network e.g. WCDMA, CMDA 2000 etc and also independent of the underlying operating system e.g. Windows CE, PALM OS etc. The first generation is known as WAP1 which was released in 1998. WAP1 assumes that the mobile devices are low on power and other resources. And therefore the devices can be simple while sharing the security responsibilities with the gateway devices. The second generation is known as WAP2 and was released in 2002. WAP2 assumes that the mobile devices are powerful and can therefore directly communicate with the servers. Fig. 1.22(a) and Fig. 1.22(b) show the protocol stack for WAP1 and WAP2 respectively.

A brief description of each layer is as follows,

- ***Wireless Application Environment (WAE)***

  This provides an environment for running web applications or other WAP applications.
- ***Wireless Session Protocol (WSP)***

  This is similar to the HTTP protocol and provides data transmissions with small sizes so that WAP1 clients can process the data with less complexity.
- ***Wireless Transaction Protocol (WTP)***

  This is responsible for providing reliability.
- ***Wireless Transport Layer Security (WTLS)***

  This is responsible for providing security features such as

authentication, confidentiality, integrity etc. between a WAP1 client and the WAP gateway.

- ***Wireless Datagram Protocol (WDP)***
  This provides the underlying transport service.
- ***Hypertext Transfer Protocol (HTTP)***
  A standard protocol used to transmit web pages.

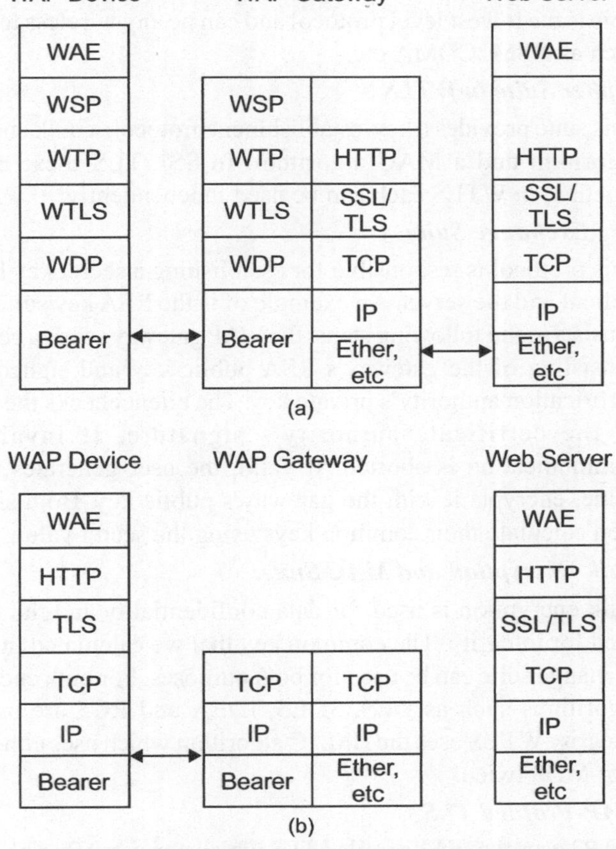

Fig. 1.22: (a) WAP1 Protocol Stack (b) WAP2 Protocol Stack

- ***Transport Layer Security (TLS)***
  This layer provides security features such as authentication, confidentiality, integrity etc. In WAP1, this is between the WAP1

gateway and the server. In WAP2 this is between the WAP2 client and the server.

- **Transport Control Protocol (TCP)**

  Standard transport protocol used to provide reliability over IP.

- **Internet Protocol (IP)**

  Protocol used to route data in a network.

- ***Bearer Protocol***

  This is the lowest level protocol and can be any wireless technique such as GSM, CDMA etc.

- ***Cipher Suite in WTLS***

  This suite provides a key-establishment protocol, a bulk encryption algorithm and a MAC algorithm. In SSL/TLS these are used together, in WTLS each can be used independently.

- ***Key Exchange Suite***

  This protocol is responsible for establishing a secret key between a client and the server. An example of is the RSA key suite, which consists of the following steps: the WAP gateway sends a certificate consisting of the gateway's RSA public key and signed by the certification authority's private key. The client checks the validity of the certificate authority's signature. If invalid, the communication is aborted. If valid, the user generates a secret value, encrypts it with the gateway's public key. Both sides can then calculate their common keys using the secret value.

- ***Bulk Encryption and MAC Suite:***

  Bulk encryption is used for data confidentiality and the MAC is used for integrity. The common key that we calculated in the key exchange suite can be used for both purposes. For bulk encryption, algorithms such as DES, 3DES, IDEA and RC5 are used. For integrity WTLS uses the HMAC algorithm which uses either SHA-1 or MD5 twice.

- ***WAP-Profiled TLS***

  WAP2 uses the WAP profiled TLS which consists of a cipher Suite, authentication suite, tunneling capability and session identification and session resume. Cipher suite consists of key establishment (e.g. RSA), encryption (e.g. DES) and integrity (SHA-1 for MAC calculation). A session identifier is chosen by the server to identify a particular session with the client. Server and Client authentication is done using certificates similar to WTLS. Tunneling is a mechanism set up between the client and the server, so that they can communicate even if the underlying network layers are different.

- ***WAP Identity Module***

  WIM (WAP Identity Module) is a method of identification in WAP. This enables the device to separate its identification from WAP. So a device can be updated without any changes made to the telephone number or billing information. WIM provides operations such as key generation, random numbers, signing, decryption, key exchange, storing certificates etc.

1.11. BLUETOOTH: AN INTRODUCTION

Handheld devices are rapidly becoming an integral part of our daily lives. These devices need to be compatible with data communication interfaces. To achieve this objective but without using all the cumbersome cables there must be a solution which uses wireless links to enable on demand connectivity among devices. In 1998, 5 industrial giants (ERICSSON, NOKIA, IBM, TOSHIBA, INTEL) joined hands to create such a technology. Thus emerged the Bluetooth technology. Bluetooth is a method of data communication that uses Short Range Radio Links to replace cables between computers and their connected units. The aim is to make a technology that optimizes the usage model of all mobile computing and communication devices and providing:

1. Global Usage
2. Voice and Data Handling
3. The ability to withstand interference from other sources in open band
4. Small size
5. Low power consumption

Practically all computerized equipment normally found in a modern office which don't use synchronous communication protocol could be adapted for use with Bleutooth e.g.

1. Modems
2. LAN Access Devices

3. Printers
4. Laptop & Desktop Computers
5. Fax
6. Keyboard /Mouse

Bluetooth is not intended as a wireless extension of ordinary LANs. Both Bluetooth and WLANs are based upon the IEEE 802.11 standard. But there are too many differences for these systems to replace each others:

- WLANs are essentially ordinary LAN-protocols modulated on carrier waves. Bluetooth is more complex than that.
- Bluetooth´s essence is dynamically configured units. That´s not how LANs work.
- Bluetooth hops very fast (1600 hops/second) between frequencies, which does not allow for long datablocks. A Bluetooth channel cannot handle as high data throughput as a WLAN.
- Bluetooth relies on ad-hoc-connectivity. This does not square well with (predominantly) server-based LANs.

1.11.1. Bluetooth Specifications

There are certain Bluetooth specifications , which have two parts:

1.11.1. 1. Profile Specifications

These specify the controller and stack parameter settings as well as the procedures required for intercommunication between Bluetooth devices.

Use Case	Description
Generic Access	Generic procedures for discovery and link management of connecting to Bluetooth devices
Service Delivery	Features and procedures for a Bluetooth device application to discover services in other devices
Cordless Telephone	Features and procedures for inter operability between devices active in a 3-in-1 phone
Intercom	Requirements for supporting Intercom functionality within a 3-in-1 phone
Serial Port	Requirements for setting up emulated serial

	cable connections using RFCOM between two peer devices
Headset	End user service requirements and interoperability features for Bluetooth devices implementing hedsets
Dial up NET	End user service requirements and interoperability features for Bluetooth devices implementing DIAL UP NET
FAX	End user service requirements and interoperability features for bluetooth devices implementing FAX svs
LAN access	Definition of how Bluetooth devices can access LAN services using PPP
Generic object exchange	Requirements for Bluetooth devices tomsupport object exchange usage model
Object push	Application requirements for Bluetooth devices to support the object push usage model
File transfer	Application requirements for Bluetooth devices to support the file transfer usage model
Synchronization	Application requirements for Bluetooth devices to support the object synchronization usage model

1.11.1. 2. Core Specifications

It defines all layers of Bluetooth protocol stack.

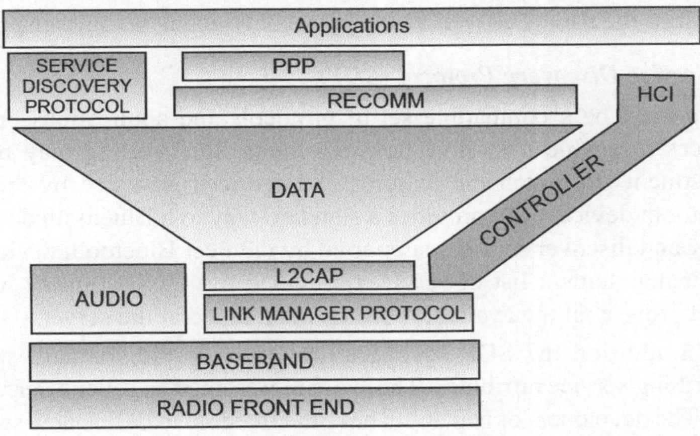

Fig. 1.23: STACK

(a) *Radio Front End (RF)*

It is the lowest layer. Its specification defines the characteristics of the RF, frequency bands , channel arrangements, and receiver sensitivity level.

Radio Front (RF): Bluetooth operates in 2.24 GHZ ISM band .Europe and US allocate allocate 83.5 MHz to this band but France, Spain and Japan allocate less. To accommodate these differences 79 RF channels spread 1MHz are defined for Europe and US and 23 RF channels spread 1MHz are defined for Spain , France and Japan. The radio hops through the full spectrum of 79 or 23 RF channels using random hopping sequence. It has a hopping rate of 1600 bps which prevents it from interference from other sources. The link speed of 1Mbps is achieved using the GFSK (Gaussian Frequency Shift Keying) modulation technique.

(b) Logical Link Control and Adaptation Protocol (L2CAP)

L2CAP is the link layer of Bluetooth. The baseband protocol is small for transporting bigger data products to higher layers. Therefore the Bluetooth SIG defined L2CAP. The L2CAP makes 2 assumptions which significantly simplify the segmentation and optimizes the L2CAP to work in conjunction with the baseband layer.

The different high layer protocols are differentiated by carrying them in different channels .L2CAP channels are connection oriented because they require an explicit phase to establish the channel during which both ends choose a local name and communicate it to the other end. Afterwards each packet send over the channels contains a channel identifier which identifies the source as well as the protocol which is being transported .

(c) Service Discovery Protocol (SDP)

There must be a compatible set of protocols and applications on both devices to enable data flow between them. Such setting may require adjustments to match the features and services provided by the Peer Bluetooth device. SDP provides a standard way to a Bluetooth device to query and discover services supported by the Peer Bluetooth device.The server maintains a list of services provided by it . SDP query helps a client browse all the available records maintained at the server.

In addition the SDP specifications provide the standard way of describing service attributes .These are represented as <identifier,value> pair. The developers of Bluetooth have the freedom to define new sections of standard services or to create new ones . But since such services don't require any coordination with Bluetooth SIG numbering Authority, it is essential that two independent services don't conflict .To prevent such a clash there exist Universally Unique Identifier (UUID) which is generated at the time of services defined which are then included in the assigned numbered documents.

The client browses the list of available services and select from the list .There are 2 search options supported by SDP which has 2 advantages over other IP based SDPs.

1. It is optimized to work with L2CAP.
2. Since most Bluetooth devices are non IP devices they don't support SLPs. SDP provide the mechanism only for retrieving service information from other devices , but invoking these services is outside its scope.

(d) Link Manager Protocol (LMP)

Before two BLUETOOTH devices establish the L2CAP channel the link manager has to carry certain baseband specific actions which include piconet, master slave role assignments and link configuration. For these operations the link manager has to exchange LMP messages over the air link.

Security can also be configured using the LMP messages. The devices should authenticate themselves before a voice or data transfer can take place. Also the transmitted data is in encrypted form. This is possible when there exists a security association between the devices .The LM uses a shared secret key to verify the peer device's authenticity .Only after the successful LMP handshake further data exchange or voice communication takes place.

There is also a method called pairing defined by the baseband and CMP specifications .This means creating a security association using an out of band channel which is then used as a seed to compute a secure shared secret key.

1.11.2. Bluetooth Chips

Bluetooth is unique in offering the front end RF processing integrated with the Base Band Module. On chip integration lowers the cost of network interface ,and the small size makes it easy to embed Bluetooth chips in devices such as cell phones etc. A Bluetooth chip can be connected to its host processor using USB, UART, or PC–interface cards, Fig. 1.24 and Fig. 1.25.

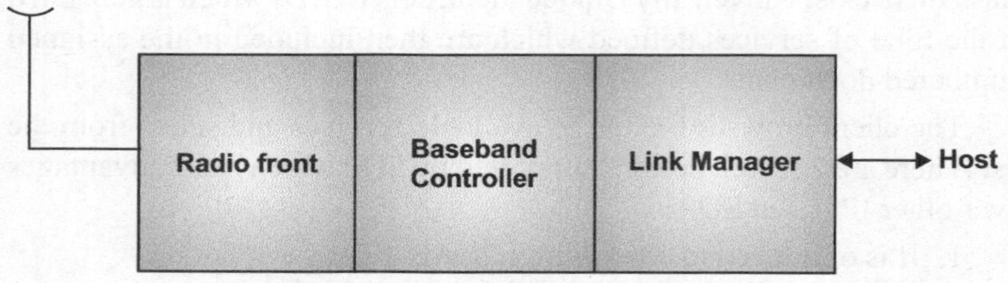

Fig. 1.24: Bluetooth Chip

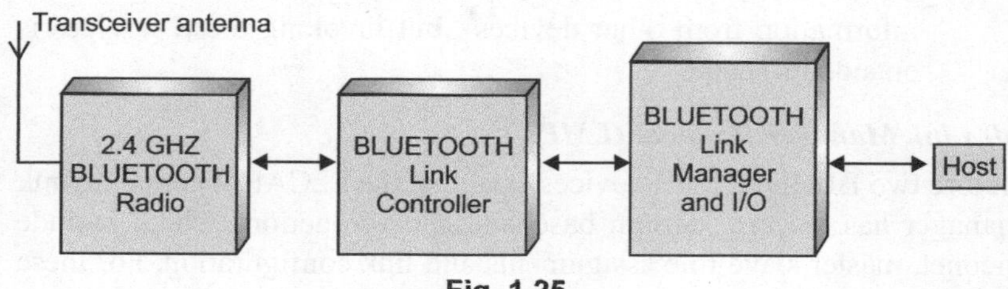

Fig. 1.25

1.11.3. Applications

- Use email while your laptop is still in briefcase .Your mobile beeps when you receive an email see Fig. 1.26.

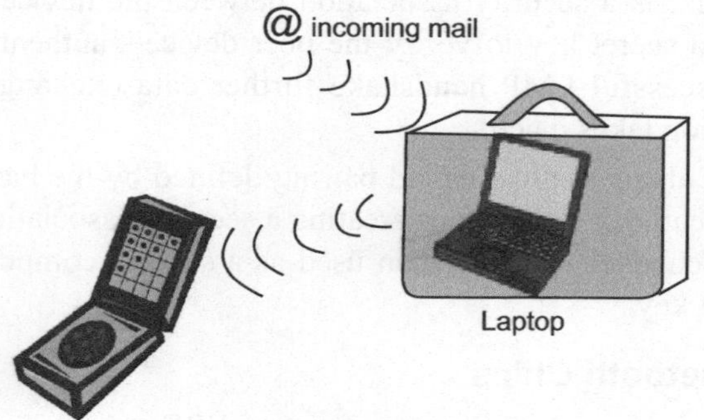

Fig. 1.26

- A Bluetooth keyboard could be used to address more then one computers a dynamic switchable manner.

- A traveling person can search for any near by printers and send printouts to it whenever found.
- Cableless connection to printer and fax

Bluetooth has caught the attention of the consumers because it will enable them to do things which otherwise seem to be cumbersome today: Synchronization data between cell phones laptops and PDA's: using cellphones as cordless when at home. The value propositions is there strong. The challenge is for vendors to meet this expectations. The future of the Bluetooth depends much more on market forces rather then technical issues, e.g.

- unless the initial adoption of Bluetooth is high it will be difficult to meet the low cost objective
- of the technical issues the most important is the security, proper safeguards are required to prevent unauthorized leakage of information

1.12. RADIO RESOURCE MANAGEMENT IN CELLULAR SYSTEMS

The rapid growth in demand for mobile communication has led into intense research and development efforts towards a new generation of cellular systems. The new system must be able to provide Quality-of-Service (QoS), support a wide range of services and improving the system capacity. Small cell systems allow greater spectral reuse, larger capacity. However, small cell systems induce an increasing numbers of handoff. While overlaying cells provide coverage and service for high-speed users. Hierarchical cell architecture can therefore serve all type of user classes with different services and speed. The system performance characteristics include blocking probability, handoff blocking probability, force termination of ongoing calls and total carried traffic. It is helpful to define these system performance parameters. Two types of above mentioned probabilities may be defined as QoS parameters in wireless networks as follows:

- ***Connection / Call Blocking Probability (CBP):*** The Connection/call Blocking Probability (CBP) is the probability that a new connection/call request is rejected. The reason for rejection is generally the unavailability of the sufficient recourses which are required to meet the demands made by the connection/Call.

- ***Forced Termination Probability (FTP):***

  In wireless networks, when a mobile user (MU) travels from one cell to another, the connection handover takes place between the new and previous cell. The Forced Termination Probability (FTP) is the probability that an original call is eventually not completed because of an unsuccessful handover attempt.

  One of the most obvious merits of a wireless network is the total traffic it occurs, which can be define as: total carried traffic.

- ***Total Carried Traffic:***

  It is the amount of traffic admitted to the wireless/cellular network as opposed to the offered load. In light traffic conditions, the carried traffic can be taken to be equal to the offered traffic. However, in general the carried traffic is less than the offered load because of blocking of calls and handover failures.

Efficient utilization of the scare spectrum allocation for cellular communications is certainly one of the major challenges in cellular system design. In radio and transmission subsystems, techniques such as deployment of time and space diversity systems, use of low noise filter and efficient equalizers, and deploy of efficient modulation schemes can be used to suppress interference and extract the desired signal. However, co-channel interference caused by frequency reuse is the most restraining factor on the overall system capacity in wireless networks, and the main idea behind channel assignment strategies is to make use of radio propagation path loss characteristics in order to minimize the Carrier-to-Interference Ratio (CIR) and hence increase the radio spectrum reuse efficiency.

1.12.1. Cellular Architecture

Spectral reuse, system complexity and coverage are some of the most important issues in cellular architecture. Cellular systems with higher spectral efficiency give more complex systems. As the demand for wireless service increases, the numbers of channels assigned to a cell becomes insufficient to support the required number of users. At this point we need to improve capacity in the system be expanded the existing architecture. Techniques such cell splitting, sectoring and adaptive antenna could be use to expand the system capacity.

Other method to increase the spectral efficiency in cellular system is Reuse Partitioning (RUP). In RUP each cell in the system is divided into two or more concentric subcells or zones.

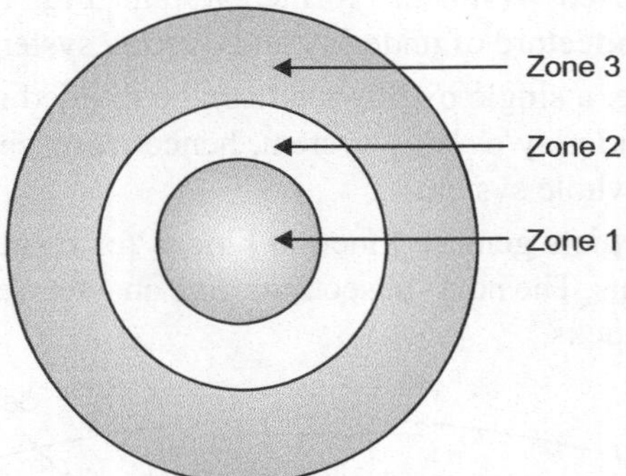

Fig. 1.27: Concentric Subcells

Because the inner zone closest to base station require lower power level to achieve the desired CIR than the outer zone, therefore the minimum reuse distance for the inner zone become smaller than for the outer zone which leads to higher spectrum efficiency. RUP can be divided into fix and adaptive techniques. Another variant of partitioning call Multiple Channel Bandwidth System can be utilised to increase the spectral efficiency. In MCBS the cell is also divided in two are more concentric subcells. To achieve the desired CIR, the inner zone require less bandwidth than the outer zone, thought instead of utilised the same amount of bandwidth throughout the whole cell.

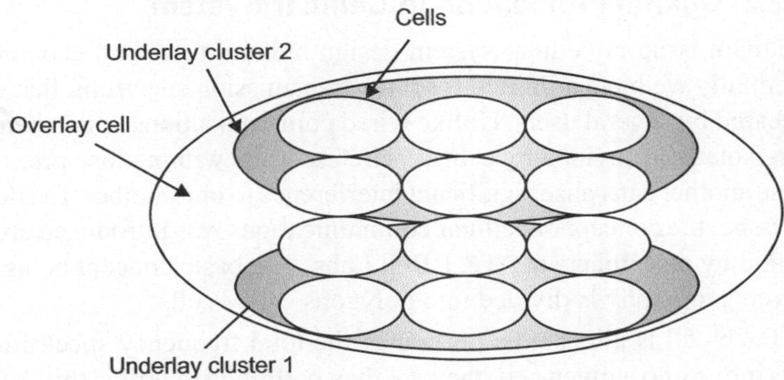

Fig. 1.28: Hierarchical Architecture

Underlay/overlay and overlay/underlay architecture can be use to increase system capacity, performance and coverage. Underlay/overlay system differs from overlay/underlay system in such a way that tighter reuse factor is used within the former system. Fig. 1.28 illustrate the hierarchical architecture of underlay and overlay system.

For example, a single overlay cell can be divided into two underlay clusters in an underlay/overlay system, hence increasing the number of channels in the whole system.

Fig. 1.29 depicts generic function blocks for resource management in cellular systems. The next subsections give an overview and discussion of the generic blocks.

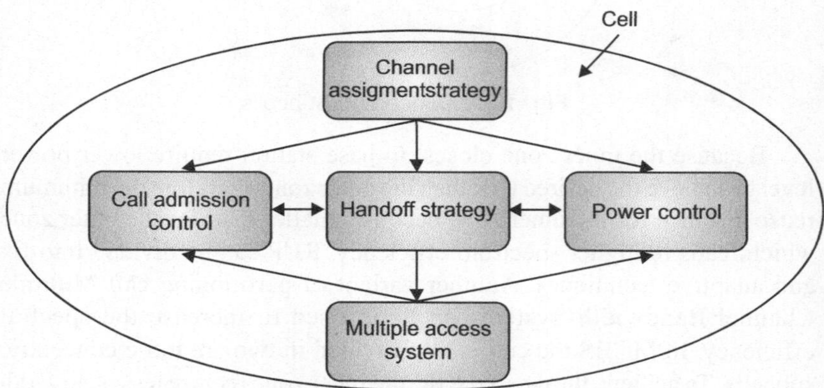

Fig. 1.29: Generic Function Blocks

1.12.2. Channel Allocation in Cellular System

One main issue in cellular system design reduces to one of economics. Essentially we have a limited resource transmission spectrum, that must be shared by several users. Unlike wired communications which benefits from isolation provided by cables, wireless users within close proximity of one another can cause significant interference to one another. To address this issue, the concept of cellular communications was introduced around in 1968 by researchers at AT&T Bell Labs. The basic concept being that a given geography is divided into polygons called cells.

Each cell is allocated a portion of the total frequency spectrum. As users move into a given cell, they are then permitted to utilize the channel allocated to that cell. The virtue of the cellular system is that different cells can use the same channel given that the cells are separated by a minimum distance according to the system propagation characteristics; otherwise, intercellular or cochannel interference occurs. The minimum distance necessary to reduce cochannel interference is called the reuse distance. The reuse distance is defined as the ratio of the distance, *D*, between cells that can use the same channel without causing interference and the cell radius, *R*. Note that *R* is the distance from the center of a cell to the outermost point of the cell in cases when the cells are not circular.

Channel allocation deals with the allocation of channels to cells in a cellular network. Once the channels are allocated, cells may then allow users within the cell to communicate via the available channels. Channels in a wireless communication system typically consist of time slots, frequency bands and/or CDMA pseudo noise sequences, but in an abstract sense, they can represent any generic transmission resource. There are three major categories for assigning these channels to cells (or base-stations). They are

- Fixed Channel Allocation,
- Dynamic Channel Allocation and
- Hybrid Channel Allocation which is a combination of the first two methods.

1.12.2.1. Fixed Channel Allocation (FCA)

The underlying strategy in Fix Channel Assignment / Allocation is the permanent assignment of a set of channels to each cell. Fixed Channel Allocation (FCA) systems allocate specific channels to specific cells. This allocation is static and can not be changed. For efficient operation, FCA systems typically allocate channels in a manner that maximizes frequency reuse. Thus, in a FCA system, the distance between cells using the same channel is the minimum reuse distance for that system. The problem with FCA systems is quite simple and occurs whenever the offered traffic to a network of base stations is not uniform. Consider a case in which two adjacent cells are allocated *N* channels each. There clearly can be situations in which one cell has a need for *N+k* channels while the adjacent cell only requires *N-m* channels (for positive integers *k* and *m*). In such a case, *k* users in the first cell would be blocked from making calls while *m* channels in the second cell would go unused. Clearly in this situation of non-uniform spatial offered traffic, the available channels are not being used efficiently.

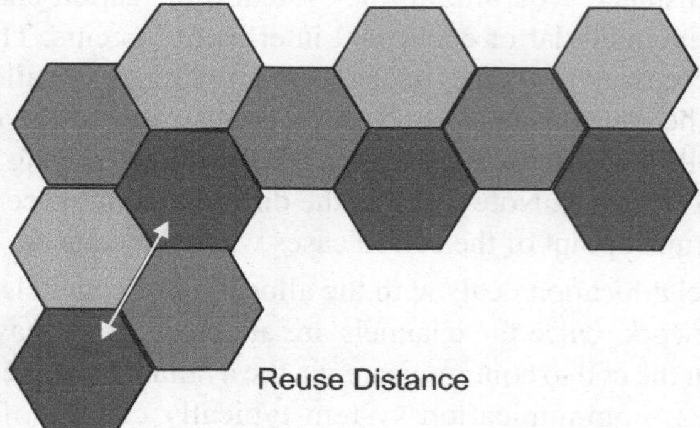

Fig. 1.30: Reuse Distance

FCA has been implemented on a widespread level to data. FCA has distributed network architecture. Many different methods have been proposed as a variation of FCA, channel borrowing methods, channel borrowing with directional locking, and channel borrowing with ordering.

1.12.2.2. Dynamic Channel Allocation (DCA)

Dynamic Channel Allocation (DCA) attempts to alleviate the problem mentioned for FCA systems when offered traffic is non-uniform. In DCA systems, no set relationship exists between channels and cells. Instead, channels are part of a pool of resources. Whenever a channel is needed by a cell, the channel is allocated under the constraint that frequency reuse requirements can not be violated. DCA could be centralized or distributed in nature, channels are dynamically allocated to cells according to interference and service demand. The advantage of DCA is the fact that there is no need for frequency planning. Distributed DCA are less stable than centralized DCA because the former are affected by local changes that could spread out the whole system, hence affecting its performance.

There are two problems that typically occur with DCA based systems.

- First, DCA methods typically have a degree of randomness associated with them and this leads to the fact that frequency reuse is often not maximized unlike the case for FCA systems in which cells using the same channel are separated by the minimum reuse distance.

- Secondly, DCA methods often involve complex algorithms for deciding which available channel is most efficient. These algorithms can be very computationally intensive and may require large computing resources in order to be real-time.

1.12.2.3. Hybrid Channel Allocation Schemes

The third category of channel allocation methods includes all systems that are hybrids of fixed and dynamic channel allocation systems. Several methods have been presented that fall within this category and in addition, a great deal of comparison has been made with corresponding simulations and analyses. We will present several of the more developed hybrid methods below.

Channel Borrowing is one of the most straightforward hybrid allocation schemes. Here, channels are assigned to cells just as in fixed allocation schemes. If a cell needs a channel in excess of the channels previously assigned to it, that cell may borrow a channel from one of its neighboring cells given that a channel is available and use of this channel won't violate frequency reuse requirements. Note that since every channel has a predetermined relationship with a specific cell, channel borrowing (without the extensions mentioned below) is often categorized as a subclass of fixed allocation schemes. The major problem with channel borrowing is that when a cell borrows a channel from a neighboring cell, other nearby cells are prohibited from using the borrowed channel because of co-channel interference. This can lead to increased call blocking over time. To reduce this call blocking penalty, algorithms are necessary to ensure that the channels are borrowed from the most available neighboring cells; i.e., the neighboring cells with the most unassigned channels.

Channel assignment strategies provide the means to efficiently access the resource each cell and how to assign the available resource to achieve the highest spectrum efficiency. CAS strategy is the technique used to make the most efficient and equitable use of available radio spectrum. CAS can be classified into fix, dynamic and flexible.

1.12.2.3.1. Handoff Strategies

Handoff is extreme important in any mobile network because of the cellular architecture employed to maximize spectrum utilization. Handoff is the mechanism that transfers an ongoing call from one cell to another cell as a users move toward the coverage area of the neighboring cell. Each handover require network resource to route the call to next base station. If handover does not occur quickly, the QoS may degrade below an acceptable level and the connection will be dropped.

A hard handoff occurs when users experienced an interruption during the handover process cause by frequency shifting. Soft handover is the ability to select between the instantaneous received signals from different base stations. Handoff can be classified into network-controlled handoff, mobile-controlled handoff and mobile-controlled handoff. When a mobile user move to the edge of the cell boundary, handover process will invoke. Handover initiation occurs dependent on different criteria and strategies used in the system, see Fig. 1.31. The most common criteria are:

- Relative signal strength
- Relative signal strength with threshold
- Relative signal strength with hysteresis
- Relative signal strength with hysteresis and threshold

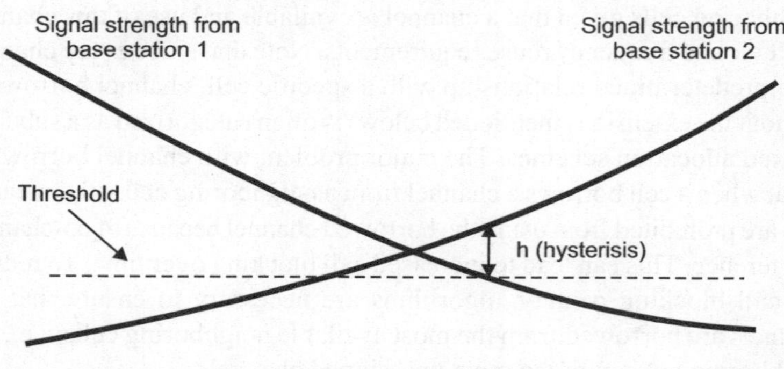

Fig. 1.31: Handoff Scenario

1.12.2.3.2. Various Handover Schemes : A Review

Many handover schemes have been proposed in literature in order to reduce handover failure and call forced termination. The reduction of handover failure, results an increase of new call blocking probability. It becomes a tradeoff between forced termination of ongoing call, and blocking a new originating call. However, the forced termination of ongoing calls is a less desirable event in the performance evaluation of a Cellular Network than blocking new calls. When a call is in progress in a cell, efforts are made to provide continuity to the current call when the user moves from one cell coverage area to another. To deal with initial access and handoff problem, several strategies are reported in the literature as:

Non-prioritized; Reserved Channel; FIFO Priority; Measurement-Based Priority; and Subrating Schemes.

Readers could explore more knowledge from the references given in the end of this chapter.

Queuing of handover [FER00] requests is made possible by the existence of the time interval the Mobile Terminal (MT) spends in the handover area, where it is physically capable of communicating with both the current and next base terminal stations (BTSs). In queuing handover, if all channels of a cell are occupied, calls originating within that cell are blocked and the handover requests to that cell are queued. FIFO is queuing discipline, in which, the call first queued, will be first served. A Measurement-Based Prioritized Scheme is proposed in [TEK92], according to the scheme a queued MT gains a higher priority as its power ratio decreases from the handover threshold to the receiver threshold. The MTs waiting for a channel in the handover queue are sorted continuously according to their priorities. Signal Prediction Priority Queuing (SPPQ)[EBE99], which uses both Received Signal Strength (RSS) and the change in RSS to determine the priority ordering of an MT. In order to optimize the system for the minimum number of dropped handovers, the handover that would be terminated next should be the first to be handed over.

Another scheme called Reserved Channel Scheme (RCS)[KIM99], gives handover calls a higher priority than new calls. In RCS, a number of wireless channels, called guard channels, are exclusively reserved for handover calls, and the remaining channels, called normal channels, can be shared equally between handover and new calls. In [OLI97] the objectives of Dynamic Reserved Channel Scheme (DRCS) are to satisfy a desired dropping of the probability of handover calls, to reduce the blocking probability of new calls, and to improve the channel utilization. Similarly a flexible channel assignment scheme is proposed in [TAJ99]. In the Subrating Scheme (SRS) certain channels are allowed to be temporarily divided into two channels at half the original rate to accommodate handover calls. This subrating occurs when all the channels occupied at the moment of handover arrival. When subrating channel is released, it forms into an original full-rate channel by combining with another subrated channel [KUL99].

In the past, several solutions were studied to reduce the congestion in cellular networks [HON91]. Some of these solutions are in the context of channel assignment algorithms (for example, [TEK91], [CHI92]), which deal with the wireless resource allocation and try to reduce the new call blocking probability while providing high ratio spectrum utilization efficiency. However, they do not impose any explicit control on the admission of new calls in order to reduce the handoff dropping probability [RAM05], [SHI04]. It is important to note that maximizing the utilization efficiency of the wireless network based on availability of wireless spectrum in the cell, where a call is admitted without taking the effect of handoffs into account does not provide connection level QoS [NAG96]. In other words, instead of new call blocking probability, handoff dropping or forced termination probability needs to be taken into account. This is an important factor from the point of view of subscribers of wireless networks who presumably want to guarantee on the availability of wireless resources during their connection, in addition to a low new-call blocking probability. There exist other solutions which treat new calls and handoff calls differently i.e by reserving a number of guard channels at each base station for handoff calls [POS85], [RAP92]. We call this trunk reservation method. These solutions lower the congestion handoff calls probability [HON91], and use only local state information i.e. number of calls in the cell where a new call is initiated for accepting a new call. A wireless call admission technique which limits the ratio state congestion probability has been studied in [ACA94]. This scheme limits the total number of calls in a cell cluster, which is a group of neighboring cells, to a pre-defined threshold, and requires a call controller per cell cluster. In the paper [NAG96], the authors proposed a methodology in which the call admission decision is made in a distributed manner in which each base station makes an admission decision by exchanging state information with the adjacent cells periodically.

1.12.2.3.3. Call Admission Control (CAC)

The challenges in the wireless networks are to guarantee Quality-of-Service (QoS) requirements while taking into account the radio frequency spectrum limitations and radio propagation impairments. Connection admission control is one method to manage radio resource in order to adapt to traffic variations. CAC denotes the process to make a decision for new admission according to the amount of available resource versus users QoS requirements, and the effect upon the QoS of the existing calls imposed by new call.

CAC can be divided into two groups, interference-based CAC and user-based CAC. In interference-based algorithm, admission control is based on carrier-to-interference (C/I) parameter, while user-based algorithms dependent on the number of channels available.

The most traditional CAC algorithm is guard channel algorithm. The guard channel is a concept based on reservation a fractional guard channels for handoff purpose by just considering the status for local cell. Other methods are based on adaptive technique where channels are allocated and reserved in a dynamically way using teletraffic analysis, prediction of injected traffic and prediction of mobile terminal movement. In some prediction scheme, it is sufficient to take care off the radio resource that the mobile will need in the predicted location. In general, the resource reservation mechanism consists of two parts; some of the bandwidth reserved in the next cell the mobile is likely to visit, and a common pool of dynamically adjusted bandwidth used to accommodate other unpredicted flows. The next cell is predicted based on mobility pattern observed in various cells.

Other approach utilized reservation of bandwidth along the predicted path of the mobile, or along some neighbouring of that path. One concept called shadow cluster is introduced. The fundamental idea of the shadow cluster concept is that as an active mobile terminal travels to other cell, the region of influence also moves, following the active mobile terminal to its new location. The base stations currently being influenced are said to form a shadow cluster, because the region of influence follows the movement of the active mobile terminal like a shadow.

Other approach included schemes, which rely on the extended location information (from adjacent cells) to make the CAC decision. The bandwidth reservation could be estimated based upon the nominal cell and neighbouring cells history. Queuing of new calls and handover requests is another approach that reduce the blocking probability and probability of force termination. There is a tradeoff between the increasing in service quality and corresponding decreasing in total carried traffic.

Queuing of handoff request is more sensitive to delay in service than queuing of new call, therefore other preferred queuing of new calls rather than handoff calls. One of the key point of using queuing in CAC is that service differentiation can be manage with modify queuing discipline. Instead of FIFO queuing strategy, other prioritised queuing discipline can be used to maintain priority level in each service class.

1.12.2.4. Multiple Access Scheme (MAS)

Another important part of resource management in cellular system is multiple access scheme. MAS enables dispersed users to share a common transmission medium. The radio resource is in general much more limited than wireline counterpart, it is therefore crucial to have a sophisticated MAS. A good MAS can improve the system capacity. Traditional MAS schemes are TDMA, FDMA, CDMA or a combination of them. MAS can be categorizes in three types, random access, fix assignment and demand assignment.

In random access schemes, the users have to compete for the radio channel, if collision occur, the packet has to be retransmitted. ALOHA and CSMA/CD are to well known random access schemes. In fix assignment, the user transmissions are completely controlled by the base station. Each user is assigned a unique channel for transmission. Simple fix assignment schemes are TDMA and FDMA. In demand assignment, users are assigned a channel on demand. Dynamic TDMA can be used as demand assignment schemes.

In some cellular architecture, it is possible to combine different MAS in one system. For example in hierarchical cellular system, different layer can have their own MAS to support different type of traffic (symmetric/asymmetric) and service classes.

1.12.3. Common Principles of Channel Allocation Schemes

The large array of possible channel allocation systems can become cumbersome. However, all channel allocation methods operate under simple, common principles. On three points, which an efficient channel allocation scheme should address are:

1. Channel allocation schemes must not violate minimum frequency reuse conditions.
2. Channel allocation schemes should adapt to changing traffic conditions.

3. Channel allocation schemes should approach (from above) the minimum frequency reuse constraints so as to efficiently utilize available transmission resources.

As the first requirement suggests, all channel allocation schemes adhere to condition 1. From a frequency reuse standpoint, a fixed channel allocation system distributes frequency (or other transmission) resources to the cells in an optimum manner; i.e., common channels are separated by the minimum frequency reuse distance. Thus, a fixed channel allocation scheme perfectly satisfies condition 3 as well. However, a fixed allocation scheme does not satisfy condition 2.

Philosophically, any dynamic channel allocation scheme will meet the requirements of all of the above three conditions to some degree. At the system architecture level dynamic channel allocation schemes may differ widely, but fundamentally, their only difference is in the degree to which they satisfy condition 3. Different DCA schemes attempt to satisfy condition 3 (in addition to conditions 1 and 2) by approaching the minimum frequency reuse constraint arbitrarily closely, and by doing so in as short a time period as possible. The above three conditions point to the fact that design of dynamic channel allocation schemes falls within the general class of optimization problems. Furthermore, since we can always assume that the available number of base stations is finite and the transmission resources will always be countable then our problem can be reduced to the subclass of combinatorial optimization problems.

1.12.4. Hierarchical Cellular Systems (HCS)

As we are moving towards the third generation mobile systems, the need for improving coverage, systems capacity and service quality becomes more and more important. Different service classes have different QoS requirements. To satisfy these requirements, the network must have enough capacity to serve arriving calls and flexible mechanism to guarantee certain services. With the traditional single layer architecture, it is difficult to implement the flexible mechanism to guarantee QoS.

Moving from a single cell layer towards hierarchical multilayer system can solve many problems related to the single cell architecture. Different cell layers can be dedicated to different user groups based on their mobility and traffic demands. The use of microcells in hierarchical layered structures improves transmission quality, provides flexibility in traffic coverage and significantly increases the system capacity. Overlaying macrocells enhances radio coverage at a low cost.

Conventionally, in a single layer system, supporting prioritized handoff is often done by reserving a numbers of channels in advance, known as guard channels. Allocation of channels can either be dynamic or static, depending on the traffic pattern in the system. Queuing is another method favoring handoff calls. By queuing new call arrivals, available bandwidth can be dedicated to handoff calls.

In hierarchical cellular systems, providing QoS can be improved by having freedom in regulation of injected traffic between the cell layers. Guard channels and queuing can be adopted in HCS, which gives flexible call admission control mechanisms.

1.12.5. Integration of Different Radio Access Systems

The emerge of a variety of mobile data services with variable coverage, bandwidth, handoff strategies and the need to roam among different radio access networks in a hybrid network architecture, has attracted tremendous attention (See Fig. 1.32). The motivation for hybrid networks arises from the fact that no one technology or services can provide ubiquitous coverage, and it will be necessary for a mobile terminal to employ attachment to different networks to maintain connection during the service time.

In the future, software radio will give a mobile terminal many different radio access interfaces without increasing the terminal complexity and the cost. With software radio technology, mobile terminals can access different networks according to their services. In a region with many different independent radio access networks, one cannot explore the optimal use of available frequency resource and distribution of users within different radio access network as in centralized manner. The idea is to integrate different distributed radio access network to centralized network architecture. With a centralized system, we can gain increasing trunking capacity and Grade-of Service (GoS) in the region.

Hybrid networks will take advance of the properties in the existing networks to provide coverage and serve all type of service classes. One solution to exploit hybrid networks is to provide a single integrated handoff and admission control strategy.

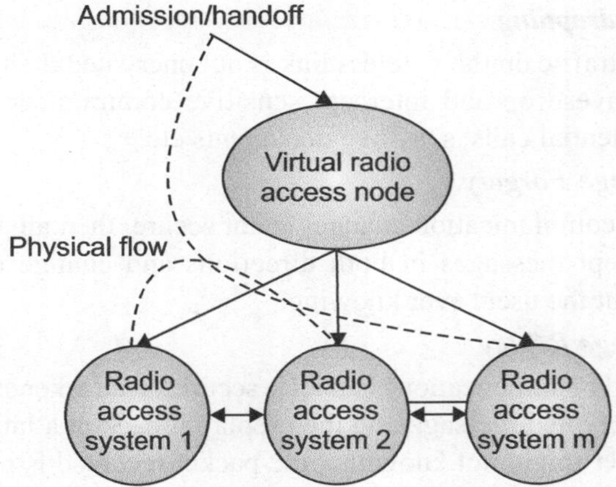

Fig. 1.32: Virtual Access Node

1.13. TYPES OF ATTACKS IN CELLULAR NETWORKS

Due to the massive architecture of a cellular network, there are a variety of attacks that the infrastructure is open to, which could be summarized as follows:

- ***Denial Of Service (DOS)***

  This is probably the most potent attack that can bring down the entire network infrastructure. This is caused by sending excessive data to the network, more than the network can handle, resulting in users being unable to access network resources.

- ***Distributed Denial Of Service (DDOS)***

  It might be difficult to launch a large scale DOS attack from a single host. A number of hosts can be used to launch an attack.

- ***Channel Jamming***

  Channel jamming is a technique used by attackers to jam the wireless channel and therefore deny access to any legitimate users in the network.

- ***Unauthorized Access***

  If a proper method of authentication is not deployed then an attacker can gain free access to a network and then can use it for services that he might not be authorized for.

- ***Eavesdropping***

  If the traffic on the wireless link is not encrypted then an attacker can eavesdrop and intercept sensitive communication such as confidential calls, sensitive documents etc.

- ***Message Forgery***

  If the communication channel is not secure, then an attacker can intercept messages in both directions and change the content without the users ever knowing.

- ***Message Replay***

  Even if communication channel is secure, an attacker can intercept an encrypted message and then replay it back at a later time and the user might not know that the packet received is not the right one.

- ***Man In The Middle Attack***

  An attacker can sit in between a cell phone and an access station and intercept messages in between them and change them.

- ***Session Hijacking***

  A malicious user can highjack an already established session, and can act as a legitimate base station.

1.14. SECURITY ISSUES IN CELLULAR NETWORKS

There are several security issues that have to be taken into consideration when deploying a cellular infrastructure. The importance of which has increased with the advent of advanced networks like 3G.

- ***Authentication***

  Cellular networks have a large number of subscribers, and each has to be authenticated to ensure the right people are using the network. Since the purpose of 3G is to enable people to communicate from anywhere in the world, the issue of cross region and cross provider authentication becomes an issue.

- ***Integrity:***

  With services such as SMS, chat and file transfer it is important that the data arrives without any modifications.

- ***Confidentiality***

  With the increased use of cellular phones in sensitive

communication, there is a need for a secure channel in order to transmit information.

- ***Access Control***

  The Cellular device may have files that need to have restricted access to them. The device might access a database where some sort of role based access control is necessary.

- ***Operating Systems In Mobile Devices***

  Cellular Phones have evolved from low processing power, ad-hoc supervisors to high power processors and full fledged operating systems. Some phones may use a Java Based system, others use Microsoft Windows CE and have the same capabilities as a desktop computer. Issues may arise in the OS which might open security holes that can be exploited.

- ***Web Services***

  A Web Service is a component that provides functionality accessible through the web using the standard HTTP Protocol. This opens the cellular device to variety of security issues such as viruses, buffer overflows, denial of service attacks etc.

- ***Location Detection***

  The actual location of a cellular device needs to be kept hidden for reasons of privacy of the user. With the move to IP based networks, the issue arises that a user may be associated with an access point and therefore their location might be compromised.

- ***Viruses and Malware***

  With increased functionality provided in cellular systems, problems prevalent in larger systems such as viruses and malware arise. The first virus that appeared on cellular devices was Liberty. An affected device can also be used to attack the cellular network infrastructure by becoming part of a large scale denial of service attack.

- ***Downloaded Contents***

  Spyware or Adware might be downloaded causing security issues. Another problem is that of digital rights management. Users might download unauthorized copies of music, videos, wallpapers and games.

- ***Device Security***

  If a device is lost or stolen, it needs to be protected from unauthorized use so that potential sensitive information such as emails, documents, phone numbers etc. cannot be accessed.

ANNEXURE: 1-A

Mobile Communication Systems: Historical Background

1921 Personnel of the Detroit Police Department's radio bureau, began experimentation with a band near 2 MHz for vehicular mobile service. On April 7, 1928 the Department commenced regular one-way radio communication with its patron cars. The system established the practicality of land-mobile radio for police work and led to its adoption throughout the country. Channels in this low-frequency band soon became crowded.

1933 The police department in Bayonne, New Jersey initiated regular two-way communications with its patrol cars, a major advance over previous one-way systems. The very high frequency system placed transmitters in patrol cars to enable patrolmen to communicate with headquarters and other cars instead of just receiving calls. Two-way police radio became standard throughout the country following the success of the Bayonne initiative.

1940 New frequencies allocated between 30-40 MHz leads to substantial buildup of police radio systems. A major advance in police radio occurred when the Connecticut State Police began operating a two-way, frequency modulated (FM) system in Hartford. The statewide system developed by Daniel E. Noble of the University of Connecticut and engineers at the Fred M. Line Company greatly reduced static, the main problem of the amplitude modulated (AM) system. FM mobile radio became standard throughout the country following the success of the Connecticut initiative.

1940 FCC allocates some 40 MHz of spectrum in range between 30 and 500 MHz for a host of mobile services for private individuals, companies, and public agencies.

Late 1940's	Bell System embarked on a program of supplying "public correspondence systems" (communication among a variety of users provided by a common carrier). FCC classified these services as Domestic Public Land Mobile Radio Service (DPLMRS).
1946	First Bell, "urban" DPLMRS inaugurated in St. Louis — three channels near 150 MHz, manually patched.
1947	A 35 to 44 MHz "highway" system between New York and Boston is inaugurated. It was thought that these frequencies would carry further along highways. This was all too true: due to atmospheric skip, unwanted conversations were carried across country.
1956	First manually patched 450 MHz service.
Note	All of these aforementioned services employed push-to-talk (PTT) operation — *i.e.* radio is half duplex which is unfamiliar and awkward for ordinary phone users — and required operator intervention to place a call. In fact, most of these services were not directly part of the PSTN at all, and involved a radio channel patched into a phone line.
1964	First automatic 150 MHz service (called MJ). Free channel is automatically assigned. System was full duplex and customers could do their own dialing.
1969	First automatic 450 MHz service (called MK). Extended MJ to new band. Taken together these two services became the ITMS (Improved Mobile Telephone Service) — the standard until the develop of AMPS.
Late 1970's	In spite of the fact that mobile service was, indeed, a scarce luxury, the demand for service was rising rapidly.
1970-77	FCC debates frequency allocation to common carriers. In 1974 it approved the underlying concepts of wireless cellular phone service and allocated for this purpose 666 duplex (two-way) channels in the 800 - 900 MHz frequency range. authorization granted to Illinois Bell in 1978.
1978	Field trials: AMPS (Advanced Mobile Phone Service) trials begin (850 MHz) in Chicago and ARTS (American Radio Telephone Service) in Washington DC.

1979 *World Administrative Radio Conference* sets up research group to define a common international standard. Leads to *Group Speciale Mobile* (GSM) in 1982.

1981 NMT (Nordic Mobile Telephone System) enters public service in Sweden. Developed by Ericsson using frequencies in the 450 to 470 band.

1984 Initial deployment of AMPS cellular system.

1993 Responding to a spectacular and unexpected rising demand for wireless services, Congress, in the Omnibus Budget Reconciliation Act of 1993, mandated that the FCC reallocate portions of the electro-magnetic spectrum for "Personal Communication" and authorized the FCC to employ competitive bidding procedures in awarding licenses for the use of these new spectral resources. The mandate had several objectives, not the least of which was raising revenue to help balance the federal budget. Furthermore, competitive bidding was deemed to be the most effective means to expedite the licensing process and to open up opportunities for beneficial competition

ANNEXURE: 1-B

UMTS/3G History

The Early Days

- 1770s Luigi Galvani investigated the nature and effects of electrophysiology, and began experiments with muscular stimulation by electrical means.
- 1799 Alessandro Volta discovered the voltaic pile, a forerunner of the electric battery, which produced a steady stream of electricity.
- 1820 Christian Orsted discovered electromagnetism.
- 1830 Joseph Henry transmitted the first practical electrical signal
- 1831 Michael Faraday published his discovery: the principle of electro-magnetical induction.
- 1837 Samuel F.B. Morse developed his fully functional telegraph
- 1842 Joseph Henry discovered that an electrical spark between

two conductors is able to induce magnetism in needles, this effect is detected at a distance of 30 metres

- 1849? - 1857 Antonio Meucci invented a "sound telegraph", a device for transforming electricity to sound. He called his invention a *teletrofono*, or electric telephone. He filed his first patent caveat (notice of intention to take out a patent) in 1871. This provisionary patent lapsed in 1874.
- 1854 The fundamental idea of the electrical transmitting of sound was published by Charles Bourseul first in the magazine "L'Illustration de Paris".
- 1858 Feddersen proves with his experiments the oscillating character of spark-discharges.
- October 1861 Phillip Reis demonstrated his "electric ear" before the Physical Society of Frankfort, Germany. Reis coined the word "*telephony*" in that demonstration.
- 1865 British professor James Clerk Maxwell published a purely mathematical theory in "*On a dynamical Theory of the Electromagnetic Field*".
- 1873 Maxwell shows mathematically that electric waves could be sent over distance in a "*Treatise on Electricity and Magnetism*".
- March 1875 Thomas Alva Edison experimented with "vibrator magnet" oscillating electromagnetic waves.
- March 1876 Alexander Graham Bell made his first successful telephone experiment. Bell filed a for a patent February 14, 1876 beating Elisha Gray by only two hours.
- 1879 David E. Hughes discovered radio waves. He possibly did make the first mobile telephone call.
- In December 1883 Paul Nipkow had thought of a way to send a moving picture by wire
- 1884 Temistocle Caldecchi-Onesti observed that loosely packed metallic powders are bad electricity conductors until subjected to some external forces such as electric sparks generated by the opening and closing of an electrical circuit, or the presence of inductive fields, or by electrostatic induction.
- 1886 German scientist Heinrich Hertz calculated that electro-magnetic waves could be broadcasted by a rapidly alternating current in a short antenna.

- 1888 Hertz proves Maxwell's theories in experiments that transmitted waves in a corner of his physics classroom at the Karlsruhe Polytechnic in Berlin. He demonstrated that these are long, transverse waves that travel at the velocity of light and can be reflected, refracted, and polarized like light.
- Before 1892 Tesla had found the theoretical basis for radio communication and in 1893 he demonstrated radio energy crossing space.
- 1892 First automatic telephone exchange invented by Almon B Strowger entered service in Indiana, USA
- 1894 British physicist Sir Oliver Lodge uses a device called the "coherer" (an electrical device whose function was based on a discovery made in 1890 by a French physicist, Édouard Branly) to detect the presence of radio waves and demonstrates that these waves could be used for signalling.
- November 1894 Jagadish Chandra Bose ignited gunpowder and rang a bell at a distance using electromagnetic waves, proving that communication signals can be sent without using wires.
- 1895 Alexander Stepanovich Popov reported sending and receiving a wireless signal across a 600 yards distance
- 1895 Guglielmo Marconi made his first tentative wireless transmissions, at his family villa in Italy and 1896 he made his first public demonstration of wireless telegraphy
- 1898 First commercial wireless telegram transmitted.
- 1898 Wireless telegraphy is used for the first time in naval manoeuvres - a range of 60 miles.
- 1899 Wireless communication between England and France.
- December 23, 1900 Reginald Fessenden succeeds to transmit voice over radio. Fessenden said into his microphone, "One, two, three, four. Is It snowing where you are Mr. Thiessen? If so telegraph back and let me know." Thiessen replied by telegraph in Morse code that it was indeed snowing.
- December 12, 1901 Marconi's wireless communication across the Atlantic a distance of 3500 kilometres from Cornwall, England to a receiving station on Signal Hill overlooking St. John's Harbour in Newfoundland. (possible the letter "s" in Morse code)

- October 1902, The first Verifiable transatlantic radio transmission was made during from Poldhu, Cornwall to the Italian cruiser Carlos Alberto anchored in the harbour of Sydney, NS with Marconi aboard. The frequency employed was about 272 kHz.
- In 1903, Valdemar Poulsen (Denmark) invented a means of producing continuous waves by "arc transmission", later used to construct high-frequency alternators for sending radio waves
- November 16 1904 John Fleming invented the thermionic two-electrode valve (diode), it was used to sound transmission.
- 1906 American de Lee Forest adds a third electrode to the diode (triode) and produces a sensitive receiver and amplifier. (applied for a patent on October 25, 1906)
- 1906 Reginald Fessenden constructed a high-frequency alternator (2 kW, 100 kHz) and succeeded in transmitting the human voice much longer distance over the radio. On December 24, 1906, at 9 P.M. eastern standard time, Reginald Fessenden transmitted human voices (reading the Bible and poetry, a woman singing, a violin solo and short speech) from Brant Rock near Boston, Massachusetts to several ships at sea owned by the United Fruit Company.
- January 13, 1910, a broadcast from the Metropolitan Opera House in New York City featuring Enrico Caruso was heard 20 km away on a ship at sea.
- 1910 Magnus Ericsson and his wife Hilda used the first "car telephone" hooking two long sticks over a pair of telephone wires and connect to an operator in the telephone exchange.
- 1914 Marconi used the thermionic valve as a radio generator which produces a carrier wave capable of being modulated by speech and transmitted speech over 50 miles.
- Early 1920s First police car radios and walkie-talkies in metropolitan New York area. 1921 Police car radios in Detroit; The first private radio telephone systems.
- 1923, Zworykin demonstrated his television system before officials at Westinghouse and applied for a patent.
- October 30, 1925, John Logie Baird of London was succesful in transmitting his first picture: the head of a dummy.

- December 25, 1926, Kenjito Takayanagi of Tokyo used a cathode-ray tube to transmit an image of Japanese writing.
- 1927 Philo Farnsworth demonstrates the first television for potential investors by broadcasting the image of a dollar sign
- 1941 Hedy Lamarr (born Hedwig Kiesler Markey) with the help of composer George Antheil invented and patented the technology called spread spectrum.
- 1940s and 1950s Spread Spectrum technique for military anti-jam applications
- 1946 First mobile telephone service in St.Louis, USA introduced by AT&T (single-cell, manual operation)
- 1948 Claude Shannon published Shannon-Hartley equation, which states that the capacity for error-free communications is limited and is both proportional to the bandwidth that the signal occupies and to the ratio of the received signal power to the received noise power.

  Capacity = Bandwidth x Log_2 *{1 + Signal to Noise Ratio}*
- 1949 Claude Shannon and Robert Pierce develop basic ideas of CDMA
- December 3 1950 Sture Lauhrén made the world first cellphone call using prototype system developed by Ericsson and The Swedish Telecom
- 1956 RAKE receiver patented
- 1956 Swedish PTT Televerket put a full automatic mobile telephone system into operation.
- 1962 Bell Labs built and launched the first orbiting communications satellite Telstar I.
- June 1969 the Nordic telecommunications conference established the Nordic Mobile Telephone Group which was given the task to develop a new mobile telephone system that would be applied in all the Nordic countries.
- 1970s Several CDMA developments for military systems (e. g. GPS)
- April 3 1973 Motorola vice presidents Marty Cooper and John Mitchell made the first public demonstration of a call from a

handheld wireless phone.

The Analog Cellular Age

- 1979 The first commercial mobile phone network was opened for business in Tokyo. (MCS-L1 introduced by NTT, AMPS based, 25 kHz channels)
- 1979 Pre-commercial operation of Advanced Mobile Phone System (AMPS) in US
- 1981 Commercial operation of NMT450 (early September in Saudi Arabia, 1st October Sweden and week later in Denmark)
- 1982 GSM development started by "Groupe Spécial Mobile" formed by CEPT, the European Conference of Postal and Telecommunications Administrations
- 1982 INMARSAT service started
- March 6 1983 - Motorola introduced the world's first commercial portable cellular phone, the Motorola DynaTAC 8000X
- October 13 1983 First commercial operation of AMPS (AT&T's Illinois Bell, Chicago)
- 1985 C450 system in commercial operation in Germany
- 1985 TACS system (AMPS based) in commercial operation in the UK
- 1985 RadioCom system in commercial operation in France
- 1985 IMT-2000 study began with the establishment of Interim Working Party 8/13 (IWP 8/13) by Decision 69 and work continued in Task Group 8/1. IMT stands for International Mobile Telecommunications and the number 2000 had three meanings. It was supposed to represent the year 2000, when the ITU hoped the system would become available, data rates of 2000 kbps and frequencies in the 2000 MHz region.
- 1986 NMT900 system introduced in Scandinavia
- 1987 European operators and administrators signed GSM MoU agreement and agreed on a launch date of 1 July 1991.The original French name was changed to Global System for Mobile communications.
- 1987 - Early 1990s one UMTS research project in RACE 1, seven projects in RACE2 and fourteen projects in the ACTS Program.

RACE projects were funded by Commission of European Communities (CEC). FAMOUS (Future Advanced Mobile Universal Telecommunications Systems) meetings three times a year between Europe, the United States and Japan.

- 1988 ETSI formed in Europe
- 1986 NMT900 system introduced in Scandinavia
- 1988 ETACS introduced in the UK
- 1989 JTACS introduced in Japan
- 1991 NTACS introduced in Japan

The Digital Cellular Age

- July 1 1991 First GSM network, Radiolinja in Finland was officially opened
- October 1991 the first European roaming call was made between the Finnish PT and Vodafone.
- 1991 - 1995 two CEC funded research projects called Code Division Testbed (CODIT) and Advanced Time Division Multiple Access (ATDMA) were carried out by the major European telecom manufacturers and network operators. The CODIT and ATDMA projects investigated the suitability of wideband Code Division Multiple Access (CDMA) and Time Division Multiple Access (TDMA) based radio access technology for 3G systems. This work was later continued in the FRAMES (Future Radio Wideband Multiple Access System) project and became the basis of the further ETSI UMTS work until decisions were taken in 1998.
- February 1992 World Radio Conference in Malaga (WRC-92) allocated frequencies for future UMTS use. Frequencies 1885 - 2025 and 2110 - 2200 MHz were identified for IMT-2000 use.
- 1992 All major European operators start commercial operation of GSM networks
- 1992 Japanise Digital Cellular (JDC) system introduced
- 1993 First DCS1800 (now called GSM1800) system in commercial operation in UK
- 1993 IS-95 CDMA standard finalised
- 1994 Commercial operation of D-AMPS (IS-54) in US started
- 1994 Commercial operation of PDC in Japan started by NTT

- 1994 Mobile Green Paper (550kb) identified the evolution towards personal communications.
- February 1995 The UMTS Task Force was established, "The Road to UMTS" report.
- 1995 Commercial operation of N-CDMA system (IS-95) in Hong Kong/Korea
- 1995 PCS1900 (D-AMPS in 1900 MHz band, IS-136)
- December 1996 The UMTS Forum was established at the inaugural meeting, held in Zurich, Switzerland. Since 1996, the planned "European" WCDMA standard has been known as the Universal Mobile Telecommunications System (UMTS).
- June 1997 the UMTS Forum produced its first report entitled "A regulatory Framework for UMTS"
- October 1997 ERC decided on UMTS core band.
- January 1998 ETSI SMG meeting in Paris both W-CDMA and TD-CDMA proposals were combined to UMTS air interface specification.
- June 1998 Terrestrial air interface proposals (UTRAN, WCDMA(s), CDMA2000(s), EDGE, EP-DECT, TD-SCDMA) were handed into ITU-R
- September 1998 the first call using a Nokia WCDMA terminal in DoCoMo's trial network was completed at Nokia's R&D unit near Tokyo in Japan.
- December 4 1998 ETSI SMG, T1P1, ARIB TTC, TTA created 3GPP in Copenhagen, Denmark
- December 7 and 8 1998 the first meetings of the 3GPP Technical Specification Groups in Sophia Antipolis, France
- December 14 1998 The decision of the European Parliament and Council of Ministers requires that Member States take all necessary measures to allow the coordinated and progressive introduction of UMTS services by 1st January 2002 at the latest
- February 1999 Nokia Oyj said that it has completed what it claims to be the first WCDMA call through the public switched telephone network in the world. The calls were made from Nokia's test network in Finland using a WCDMA terminal, WCDMA base station subsystem and Nokia GSM Mobile switching centers

connected to the PSTN.

- March 16 1999 Finland gave out the world's first 3G mobile technology licenses. Four licenses awarded to Sonera, Radiolinja, Telia and Suomen Kolmegee. Technically some operators in USA and elsewhere already had the licenses and frequencies to operate third generation networks.
- March 1999 ITU approves radio interfaces for third generation mobile systems in the meeting in Fortaleza, Brazil. Also Ericsson and Qualcomm agreed to share access to each other's technology ending a two-year patent dispute.
- April 27 and 28, 1999 Lucent Technologies, Ericsson and NEC announced that they have been chosen by NTT DoCoMo to supply W-CDMA equipment for NTT DoCoMo's next-generation wireless commercial network in Japan. This was the first announced WCDMA 3G infrastructure deal.
- 1999 World Radio Conference (WRC-99) handled spectrum and regulatory issues for advanced mobile communications applications in the context of IMT-2000. The aim was to identify additional frequency bands to satisfy market demand by 2005-2010.
- December 1999 in Nice ETSI Standardisation finished for UMTS Release 1999 specifications both for FDD and TDD (spec version 3.y.z).
- March 29, 2000 Siemens makes world's first 3G/UMTS call over TD-CDMA (TDD).
- April 2000 World Radio Conference (WRC-2000) finalises the extension of the UMTS/IMT-2000 band.
- Mid 2000 First commercial GPRS networks launched. Several operators and network vendors claim to be the first.
- July 2000 responsibility for maintenance and development of the GSM specifications was transferred from ETSI TC SMG to 3GPP
- October 1, 2000 SK Telecom of Korea launches the first commercial cdma2000 network
- January 1, 2001 was originally planned for first commercial networks operational. No 3G networks were operating in January 1, 2001.

- March 2001 in Palm Springs 3GPP approves UMTS Release 4 specification (spec version 4.y.z).
- April 17, 2001 Ericsson and Vodafone UK claim to have made the world's first WCDMA voice call over commercial network.
- June 28, 2001 NTT DoCoMo launched a trial 3G service; an area-specific information service for i-mode. NTT DoCoMo has announced that it definitely plans to hit its October 1st target for a full commercial launch.
- September 25, 2001 NTT DoCoMo announced that three 3G phone models are commercially available.

The High Speed Cellular Age

- October 1, 2001 NTT DoCoMo launched the first commercial WCDMA 3G mobile network.
- November 1, 2001 Nokia and AT&T Wireless complete first live 3G EDGE call.
- December 1, 2001 Telenor launched in Norway the first commercial UMTS network. UMTS terminals were expected to be available 3Q 2002.
- December 19, 2001 Nortel Networks and Vodafone in Spain (formerly Airtel Movil) completed first live international UMTS 3GPP standard roaming calls between Madrid (Vodafone network) and Tokyo (J-Phone network). Calls were made with a QUALCOMM MSM5200 chipset-based handset and J-Phone SIM technology.
- January 28, 2002 SK Telecom in Korea launched the world's first commercial CDMA2000 1xEV-DO.
- February 8, 2002 Nokia claims to have made the first end-to-end 3G WCDMA standard level 3GPP Release 99 June 2001 packet data calls between its commercial network infrastructure and terminals in its laboratories in Finland. The Nokia 3G WCDMA network and terminal used were based on the commercial version.
- February 18, 2002 Motorola unveils the company's first GSM/GPRS and 3G/UMTS product, the A820. Motorola is "one of the first vendors to introduce a dual-mode enabled UMTS mobile phone"

- February 20, 2002 Nokia and Omnitel Vodafone claims to have made the first rich call in an end-to-end All-IP mobile network at the 3GSM World Congress in Cannes, France.
- March 14, 2002 (Freeze date) UMTS Release 5 (the initial target date was December 2001)
- April 30, 2002 The figures released by the Ministry of Transportation & Communications (MOTC) show that the number of mobile phone users in Taiwan reached 22.6 million at the end of April 2002, representing 100.7 percent of the population in the Taiwan area, meaning that there is more than one phone for each person in Taiwan.
- September 24, 2002 Ericsson announces the first live, dual mode WCDMA/GSM calls with seamless handover between the two modes and high data rate in live networks
- September 25, 2002 Mobilkom Austria launches "Europe's First UMTS-Network" when Boris Nemsic CEO of Mobilkom "video-phoned" the Austrian politican Waltraud Klasnic. [see December 1, 2001 note above]
- September 26, 2002 Nokia introduces the "world's first handset [6650] for WCDMA [UMTS] and GSM networks".
- October 1, 2002 Qualcomm announces world's first Bluetooth WCDMA (UMTS) and GSM Voice Calls.
- October 3, 2002 Nokia and Vodafone Omnitel claims to "have carried out the world's first VoIP call completed in a 3GPP release 4 compliant network that transports circuit-switched voice and data calls through an IP backbone".
- October 10, 2002 Nortel Networks and Qualcomm claim to "completed the industry's first UMTS voice and data calls demonstrating mobility across commercial cell sites using live 1900 MHz radio spectrum, Qualcomm chipsets in commercial-form-factor handsets, and a live, end-to-end 3GPP UMTS network from Nortel Networks".
- October 17, 2002 Nortel Networks claim to have "demonstrated the world's first UMTS calls using an IP-based UTRAN" using form factor handsets and an IP backbone based on Nortel Networks Optical Ethernet equipment. (Announced on October 22, 2002)

- October 31, 2002 Ericsson announced the milestone of 10 000 commercial UMTS/WCDMA macro base stations shipped. Nokia is assumed to have shipped about the same amount.
- November 18, 2002 Nokia introduces the world's first GSM/EDGE 3G mobile phone; Nokia 6200.
- November 29, 2002 Nokia and Vodafone Omnitel carry out 3G WCDMA call handover to commercial GSM network
- January 31, 2003 Ericsson conducts the world's first IPv6 over 3G UMTS/WCDMA network demonstration
- February 10, 2003 LG introduced the world's first dual band, dual mode phone for both CDMA and WCDMA
- February 2003, Korean mobile operator KTF announced plans to begin transmitting TV pictures direct to 3G mobile phones via the CDMA2000 1xEV-DO system
- *June 9, 2003, Samsung Electronics* released mobile phone, SCH-X820, with colour TV function
- July 1, 2003, Cingular Wireless announced the world's first commercial deployment of wireless services using Enhanced Datarate for Global Evolution (EDGE) technology.
- August 27, 2003, Nokia announced that the world's first cdma2000 1xEV-DV high-speed packet data phone call, achieving a peak data rate of 3.09 Mbps, was completed in San Diego.
- March 1, 2004, Nortel Networks announced that it has completed the industry's first 3GPP-compliant UMTS Assisted Global Positioning System (A-GPS) calls at 2100 and 1900 Mhz using mobile equipment provided by Qualcomm and Motorola, and reference satellite data provided by Global Locate.
- October 13, 2004, Nokia and TeliaSonera Finland successfully conduct world's first EDGE-WCDMA 3G packet data handover in commercial network.
- December 16, 2004 (Freeze date) UMTS Release 6 (the initial target date was June 2003)
- February 14, 2005, Ericsson demonstrates 9 Mbps with WCDMA, HSDPA phase 2
- May 10, 2005, Ericsson and 3 Scandinavia demonstrates 1.5 Mbps enhanced uplink in live WCDMAsystem

- August 7, 2006, Ericsson is the first to complete WCDMA calls on all 3GPP-defined frequency bands

REFERENCES

- "Why Mobile Computing? Where can it be used?" Article by Vasilis Koudounas, 1996.
- Network Switching Techniques-Circuit, Packet and Datagram: Halsall, Fred. Data Communications, Computer Networks and Open Systems. 4th edition 1996. pp 424-459.
- Asynchronous Tranfer Mode , Solution for Broadband ISDN, Third edition 1993, By Martin de Prycker.
- Communication Systems, Third edition 1994, By Simon Haykin, pp. 511-540.
- Radio Design Group: Reed-Solomon Forward Error Correction Code Specification
- IEEE Conference Paper, "CDPD - Advanced mobile phone standard network bandwidth contention". 13-15 Dec 1995. New Orleans, LA, USA.
- Network Switching Techniques-Circuit, Packet and Datagram: Halsall, Fred. Data Communications, Computer Networks and Open Systems. 4th edition 1996. pp 424-459.
- "Throughput and Availability of CDPD". Brian D. Woerner; Theodore S.Rappaport; Jeffery H.Reed. Wireless Personal Communications: Research Developments, 1995. pp 227-237.
- "Current and SAR induced in a human head model by the electromagnetic fields irradiated from a cellular phone." Journal Paper. Hsing-Yi Chen; Hou-Hwa Wang. IEEE Transactions on Microwave theory and Techniques Dec 1994. Vol: 42 Iss: 12, pp2249-54.
- "Modeling of hand-held receiving antennas in the presence of a human head" Conference Paper. Thiry X; Mittra R. IEEE Antennas and Propagation Society International Symposium 1995. pp 1116-1119, vol 2.
- "Electromagnetic Energy exposure of Simulated Users of Portable Cellular Telephones". Journal Paper. Balzano Q; Garay O;

Manning T,J. IEEE Transactions on Vehicular Technology Aug 1995. Vol: 44 Iss:3 p 390-403.

- Wireless Communications; Principles and Practice by Theodore S. Rappaport. Prentice Hall, 1996.
- Internerwork Mobility. The CDPD approach, by Mark S. Taylor, William Waung, and Moshen Banan. Prentice Hall, PTR, 1997.
- Mobile Telecommunications Networking by Michael Gallagher and Randall Snyder. McGraw-Hill, 1997.
- Wireless and Mobile Network Architectures, by Yi-Bing Lin and Imrich Chlamtac. John Wiley, 2001.

Channel and Base-Station Allocation Schemes

- Chan, P. T. H., Palaniswami, M. & Everitt, D., "Neural Network-Based Dynamic Channel Assignment for Cellular Mobile Communication Systems," IEEE Transactions on Vehicular Technology, vol. 43, no. 2, May 1994.
- Cox, D.C. and Reudink, D.O., "Dynamic Channel Assignment in High-Capacity Mobile Communications Systems," Bell System Technical Journal, vol. 50, no. 6, July-August 1971.
- Cox, D.C. and Reudink, D.O., "Dynamic Channel Assignment in Two-Dimensional Large -Scale Mobile Radio Systems," Bell System Technical Journal, vol. 51, no. 7, September 1972.
- Cox, D.C. and Reudink, D.O., "Increasing Channel Occupancy in Large-Scale Mobile Radio Systems: Dynamic Channel Reassignment," IEEE Transactions on Communications, vol. 21, no. 11, November 1973.
- Duque-Anton, M., Kunz, D., & Ruber, B., "Channel Assignment for Cellular Radio Using Simulated Annealing," IEEE Transactions on Vehicular Technology, vol. 42, no. 1, February 1993.
- Elnoubi, S. M., Singh, R., and Gupta, S.C., "A New Frequency Channel Assignment Algorithm in High Capacity Mobile Communication Systems," IEEE Transactions on Vehicular Technology, vol. 31, no. 3, August 1982.
- Funabiki N. & Takefuji, Y., "A Neural Network Parallel Algorithm for Channel Assignment Problems in Cellular Radio Networks," IEEE Transactions on Vehicular Technology, vol. 41, no. 4, November 1992.

- Gamst, A., "Homogeneous Distribution of Frequencies in a Regular Hexagonal Cell System," IEEE Transactions on Vehicular Technology, vol. 31, no. 3, August 1982.
- Jakes, W. C., Micr wave Mobile Communication ns, IEEE Press: New Jersey, c. 1993.
- Jiang, H. and Rappaport, S. S., "CBWL: A New Channel Assignment and Sharihng Method for Cellular Communication Systems," IEEE Transactions on Vehicular Technology, vol. 43., no. 2, May 1994.
- Katzela, I., "Channel Assignment Schemes for Cellular Mobile Telecommunication Systems," Unpublished work, Columbia University, December 15, 1992.
- Kunz, D., "Channel Assignment for Cellular Radio Using Neural Networks," IEEE Transactions on Vehicular Technology, vol. 40, no. 1, February 1991.
- Yue, W., "Analytical Methods to Calculate the Performance of a Cellular Mobile Radio Communication with Hybrid Channel Assignment," IEEE Transactions on Vehicular Technology, vol. 40, now. 2, May 1991.
- Zhang, M. and Yum, TS. P., "Comparisons of Channel-Assignment Strategies in Cellular Mobile Telephone Systems", IEEE Transactions on Vehicular Technology, vol. 38, no. 4, November 1989.

Combinatorial Optimization

- Aarts, E. and Korst, J., Simulated Annealing and Boltzmann Machines: A Stochastic Approach to Combinatorial Optimization and Neural Computing, John Wiley & Sons: Chichester, C. 1989.
- Garey, M. R. & Johnson, D. S., Computers and Intractability: A Guide to the Theory of NP-Completeness, W. H. Freeman and Company: New York, c. 1979.

Handover Schemes

- Acampora A.S. and Naghshineh M., "An architecture and methodology for mobile-executed cell hand-off in wireless ATM networks," IEEE J. Select. Areas Commun., vol. 12, no. 8, Oct 1994.

- Acampora, A, "Wireless ATM: A perspective on issues and prospects," IEEE Personal Communications, vol. 3, no. 4, pp. 8-17, Aug. 1996.
- Chia S.T.S., "Mixed cell architecture and handover," in IEE Colloquim 'Mobile Communications in the year 2000', no.139, U.K., June 1992.
- Choi Sunghyun and Shin Kang G., "A Unified Wireless LAN Architecture for Real-Time and Non-Real-Time Communication Services," in IEEE/ACM Trans. On Networking, vol. 8, no. 1, Feb. 2000.
- Cox D., "Wireless network access for personal communications," IEEE Commun. Mag., Dec. 1992.
- Ebersman, H.G., and Tonguz, O.K., "Handoff Ordering Using Signal Prediction Priority queuing in Personal Communication Systems," IEEE Transactions on Vehicular Technol., Vol. 48, no.1, pp. 20-35, Jan. 1999.
- Edwards George and Shankar Ravi, "A Predictive Fuzzy Algorithm for High performance Microcellular Handoff," Proc. IEEE Globecom, Phoenix, Nov. 1997, pp. 987-990, Nov. 1997.
- Edwards George, Kandel Abraham and Shankar Ravi, "Fuzzy handoff algorithms for wireless communication," in Fuzzy Sets and Systems, elsevier, pp. 379-388, Mar. 1998.
- Ender Ayanoglu, Kai Y. Eng and Mark J. Karol, "Wireless ATM: Limits, Challenges and Proposals," IEEE Personal Communications, vol. 3, no. 4, pp. 18-23, Aug. 1996.
- Ferracioli, M., and Verdone, R., "A General Methodology Based on the Handover Rate for Network Planning of Cellular Radio Networks Based on ATM," IEEE JSAC, vol. 18, no. 7, pp. 1313-1325, July 2000.
- Goodman D., "Trends in cellular and cordless communications," IEEE Commun. Mag., Feb. 1991.
- Guerrero, L.O., and Aghvami, A.H., "A Prioritized Handoff Dynamic Channel Allocation Strategy for PCS," IEEE Trans. on Veh. Technol., vol. 48, no. 4, pp. 1203-1215, July 1999.
- Gupta B.K. Sharma, S.C., and Lal, M., "A hybrid scheme for handover in ATM-based personal communication network,"

International Journal on Wireless and optical communications, vol.3, no.1, pp. 69-81, April 2006.

- S. Helal, N. Desai, V. Verma, and C. Lee, "Konark - A Service Discovery and Delivery Protocol for Ad-Hoc Networks," in the Third IEEE Conference on Wireless Communication Networks (WCNC), New Orleans,Louisiana, March 2003.
- Hong,D., and Suda, T., "Congestion control and prevention in ATM networks," IEEE Network Mag., vol. 5, no. 4, pp.10-16, July 1991.
- Hong, D., and Rappaport, S.S., "Traffic model and performance analysis for cellular mobile radio telephone systems with prioritized and nonprioritized handoff procedures," IEEE Trans. on Veh. Technol., Vol. VT-35, no. 3, pp. 77-92, Aug. 1996.
- Huang, Nen-Fu, and Wang, Rui-Chi, "An Efficient Algorithm for ATM-Based Personal Communication Network", Wireless Personal Communications vol.4, pp.257-275, 1997.
- IEEE. Recommended Practice for Multi-Vendor Access Point Interoperability via an Inter-Access Point Protocol Across Distribution Systems Supporting IEEE 802.11 Operation. IEEE Draft 802.1f/D3, January 2002.
- IEEE. Part 11: Wireless LAN Medium Access Control (MAC) and Physical Layer (PHY) Specification. IEEE Standard 802.11, 1999.
- Kim, Y.C., Lee, B.J., Kim, Y.S., and Mukherjee,B., "Dynamic Channel Reservation Based on Mobility in Wireless ATM Networks," IEEE Commun. Mag., vol. 37, no. 11, pp. 47-51, Nov. 1999.
- Kulavaratharasah Mohana Dhamayanthi and A.H. Aghvami, "Teletraffic Performance Evaluation of Microcellular Personal Communication Networks (PCN's) with Prioritized Handoff Procedures", IEEE Transactions on Vehicular Technology, vol. 48, no. 1, pp. 137-152, Jan. 1999.
- Kulavaratharasah Mohana Dhamayanthi and A.H. Aghvami, "Teletraffic Performance Evaluation of Microcellular Personal Communication Networks (PCN's) with Prioritized Handoff Procedures", IEEE Transactions on Vehicular Technology, vol. 37, no. 2, pp. 92-103, May, 1998.

- Lee W.C.Y., "Smaller cells for greater performance," IEEE Commun. Mag., Nov. 1991.
- Lee K.D. and Kim S., "Optimization of adaptive bandwidth reservation in wireless multimedia networks," Computer Networks vol. 38, pp. 631-634.
- Low, C.P., "An Efficient Algorithm for Link Allocation Problem on ATM-Based Personal Communication Network", IEEE journal on selected areas in communications, vol. 18, no. 7, July 2000.
- Marson Marco Ajmone, carolis Giovanni De, Leonrdi Emilio, Cigno Renato Lo and Meo Michela, "Efficient Estimation of call Blocking Probabilities in Cellular Mobile Telephony Networks with Customer Retrials," IEEE Journal on Selected areas in Commun., vol. 19, no. 2, pp. 332-345, Feb. 2001.
- Marsan, M. A., Chiasserini, C.F., Cigno, R.L., and Maurizio, M., "Local and Global Handovers for Mobility Management in wireless ATM Network", IEEE Personal Communication, vol.4, no. 5, pp.16-24, Oct. 1997.
- Naghshineh M., "Distributed contol of wireless/ mobile networks," Doctoral dissertation, Columbia University, New York, 1994.
- Naghshineh M. and Acampora A.S., "Design and control of micro-cellular networks with QOS provisioning for realtime traffic," J. High-Speed Networks, vol. 4, 1996.
- Naghshineh Mahmoud and Schwartz Mischa, "Distributed Call Admission Control in Mobile/Wireless Networks", IEEE Journal on selected areas in comm., vol. 14, no. 4, pp. 711-717, May 1996.
- Oliver, T. W., and Victor, C.M., "Adaptive Resource Allocation for Prioritized Call Admission over an ATM-Based Wireless PCN," IEEE JSAC, vol.15, no. 7, pp. 1208-1225, Sept. 1997.
- Oliveira, C., et al., "An adaptive bandwidth reservation scheme for high-speed multimedia wireless networks," IEEE JSAC, vol. 16, no. 6, pp. 858-873, Aug. 1998.
- Pollini, G.P., "Trends in handover design," IEEE Commun. Magazine, vol. 34, no. 3, pp. 82-90, Mar. 1996
- Posner E.C. and Guerin R., "Traffic policies in cellular radio that minimize blocking of handoff calls," in Proc. 11th Teletraffic Cong. (ITC 11), Kyoto, Japan, Sept. 1985.

- Ramani, S. Savage, "syncscan :Practical Fast handoff for 802.11 Infrastructure Networks," *IEEE INFOCOM* 2005.
- Ramjee, R., et al., "Performance evaluation of connecting rerouting scheme for ATM-based wireless networks," IEEE/ACM Trans. On Networking vol. 6, no. 3, pp. 249-260, June 1998.
- Rappaport S.S., "Models for call hand-off schemes in cellular communication networks," in 3rd WINLAB Workshop: Third Generation Wireless Information Networks, Workshop Record, Apr. 28, 1992.
- Raychaudhari,D., and Wilson, N.D., "ATM-Based Transport Architecture for Multiservices Wireless Personal Communication Networks," IEEE JSAC, vol. 12, no. 8, pp. 1401-1414, Oct.1992.
- Raychaudhuri Dipankar "Wireless ATM Networks: Architecture, System Design and Prototyping," IEEE Personal Communications, vol. 3, no. 4, pp. 42-49, Aug. 1996.
- M. Shin, A. Mishra, and W. Arbaugh, "Improving the latency of 802.11 hand-offs using neighbor graphs," in Proceedings of the ACM MobiSys Conference, Boston, MA, June 2004.
- Sirin Teknay and Bijan Jabbari, "Handover and Channel Assignment in Mobile Cellular Networks", IEEE Communications Magazine, vol. 29, no. 11, pp 42-46, Nov. 1991.
- Tajima, J. and Imamura, K. "A strategy for flexible channel assignment in mobile communication systems," IEEE Transactions on Vehicular Technology, vol. 48, no. 1, pp. 137-152, Jan 1999.
- Tay Y.C and Chua K.C., "A Capacity Analysis for the IEEE 802.11 MAC Protocol" *in Wireless Networks vol 7 p159-171, Kluver Academic Publishers, 2001*
- Tekinay, S.,and Jabbari, B., "Handover and channel assignment in mobile cellular networks," IEEE Commun. Mag., vol. 29, no. 11, pp. 42-46, Nov. 1991, Nov. 1991.
- Tekinay, S.,and Jabbari, B., "A Measurement-Based Prioritization Scheme for Handovers in Mobile Cellular Network," IEEE JSAC, Vol. 10 No. 8, pp. 1343-1350, October 1992, Oct. 1992.
- Tran-Gia P. and Mandjes M., "Modeling of custom metrical Phenomenon in cellular mobile networks," IEEE Journal on Selected areas in Communication,vol. 15, pp.1406-1414, Oct. 1997.

- Yoon, C.H., and Un., C.K., "Performance of personal portable radio telephone system with and without guard channels," IEEE JSAC, vol. 11, no. 6, pp. 911-917, Aug. 1993.
- Zorzi Michele and Rao Ramesh R., "On the Impact of Burst Errors on Wireless ATM," IEEE Personal Communications, vol. 6, no. 4, pp. 65-76, Aug. 1999
- Gupta, B.K., et al., "Effective, Reliable, High Speed Communication Techniques For Earthquake Disaster Mitigation" Proceedings of Symposium on "Seismic Hazard Analysis and Microzonation", Pp. 389- 398, 23rd-24th Sept. 2005, IIT – Roorkee, INDIA.
- Gupta, B.K., Sharma, S.C., and Lal, M, "Trade Offs between Handover Force Termination and Call Blocking Probabilities in Wireless ATM Networks" International Journal of Hybrid Computation Intelligence (IJHCI) , INDIA, Vol. 1(1), pp. 33 – 41, Jan., 2008.
- Gupta, Brijesh Kr.: Ph.D. Thesis on "Congestion Control in Asynchronous Transfer Mode Networks", 2003, Indian Institute of Technology – Roorkee, INDIA.
- Gupta, B.K., Lal, M., and Sharma, S.C. : "Improving Quality Of Service Parameters in Wireless Asynchronous Transfer Mode Network", in Proc. IEE Mobility Conference 2005: The Second Asia Pacific Conference on Mobile Technology, Applications and Systems (2-1 B-8), 15-17 November 2005, Guangzhou, CHINA
- Gupta, B.K., Sharma, S.C. and Lal, M.: "Comparative Simulation Study to Control congestion for Wireless ATM Networks", In Proc. IEE Mobility Conference 2006, 25–27, October, 2006, Bangkok – Thailand.

UNIT-II

Mobile computing paradigm has emerged due to advances in wireless or cellular networking technology. Based on radio and infrared transmission mechanisms, and utilizing such technologies as cellular telephony, personal communications systems, wireless PBXs, and wireless local area networks. These systems have the potential to dramatically change society as workers become "untethered" from their information sources and communications mechanisms. The mobile users can access information independent of their physical location through wireless connections. This rapidly expanding technology poses many challenging research problems in the area of mobile database systems.

While there is a rich body of knowledge associated with radio system engineering, the needed expertise must build upon this to encompass network management, integration of wireless and wireline networks, system support for mobility, computing system architectures for wireless nodes/base stations/servers, user interfaces appropriate for small handheld portable devices, and new applications that can exploit mobility and location information. Mobile data management has been an active area of research for the past many years.

Keeping in mind the above technical issues, we tried to cover the followings to get better solving understanding under this unit.

- Data Communications and Mobility
- Mobile versus Stationary Environment
- Mobile Data Management and Issues
- Mobility Management Issues in 4G Networks
- Data Replication in Mobile Computing
- Clustering for Mobile Wireless Networks
- The Coda File System
- Mobile Computing with the Rover Toolkit

UNIT

2

Mobile Data Management

2.1. DATA COMMUNICATIONS AND MOBILITY

Data Communication is a term used to describe the exchange of data using an existing network. The term data covers a wide range of applications like the fax, File Transfer (FT), interconnection of WANs, the electronic mail (e-mail), access to the internet and the World-Wide Web (www), access to other networks like libraries, banks, air-ticket reservations and so on.

Data communications have been achieved using a variety of networks such as PSTN, leased-lines, Packet switching, and more recently ISDN and ATM/Frame Relay. These networks are partly or totally analogue or digital using technologies such as circuit switching, packet switching etc. Circuit switching, implies that data has to follow a pre-specified path from user A (sender) to user B (receiver). Packet-switching tries to make a better utilization of the existing network by splitting the message into packets each containing information on:

- the sender
- the receiver
- the position of the packet in the message
- the actual message

Packets can be sent form the sender's server either at the same path (virtual circuit switching) or at various paths depending on the network availability (datagram).

Recently fax and data services have been introduced on mobile digital cellular networks at speeds varying from 2400 bits/s to 9600 bits/s. These speeds are much higher than those used for speech.

The introduction of mobility in data communications implies a move from the existing PSDN to other networks like the ones used by mobile phones. Mobility in data communications has a significant difference from the mobility on voice communications. Using mobile phones, one can move around and talk at the same time. Packets of data, though, have to be sent from the same place, that is one can take his/her mobile computer wherever he/she likes and send or receive information from there, but once connected must remain stable until the end of the exchanging of data. As stated at the end of the previous section, during hand over between cells, the line is lost for about 400ms. If it is voice telecommunications this is undetectable but for data communication not only it is detectable but delay is caused since the message will have to be sent again. Furthermore, the channels used for data are of higher speed capability which presents the hand over to other channels either within the same cell or in another cell.

Users of mobile computers, such as palmtops, notebook computers and personal communication systems, now have online access to a large number of databases via wireless networks. The potential market for this activity is estimated to be billions of dollars annually, in access and communication charges. For example, while on the road, passengers will access airline and other carriers schedules, and weather information. Investors will access prices of financial instruments, salespeople will access inventory data, callers will access location dependent data (e.g. where is the nearest taxi-cab, see and route-planning computers in cars will access traffic information.

2.2. MOBILE VERSUS STATIONARY ENVIRONMENT

Designers of applications for mobile environments must address several differences between the mobile environment and the stationary environment. Issues that represent minor inconveniences in stationary distributed systems are significant problems for mobile computers. This requires a rethinking of the classical distributed systems techniques normally used in stationary environments.

Computers in a stationary environment are usually very reliable. Relative to their stationary counterparts, mobile computers are quite fragile: a mobile computer may run out of battery power, be damaged in a fall, be lost, or be stolen. Given these threats, primary ownership of data should reside with stationary computers, not mobile computers. Furthermore, application designers should take special precautions to enhance the resilience of the data stored on mobile computers.

Relative to most stationary computers, a mobile computer has fewer computational resources available. However, the available resources may change dynamically (e.g., a "docked" mobile computer that has access to a larger display, graphic or math coprocessor, additional stationary storage, etc.).

A stationary environment can distribute an application's components and rely upon the use of high-bandwidth, low-latency networks to provide good interactive application performance. Mobile computers operate primarily in a limited bandwidth, high-latency, and intermittently-connected environment; nevertheless, users want the same degree of responsiveness and performance as a fully-connected environment.

Network partitions are an infrequent occurrence in stationary networks; therefore, most applications consider them to be major failures that are exposed to users. In the mobile environment, applications will face frequent, long-duration network partitions. Some of the partitions will be involuntary (e.g., due to a lack of network coverage), while others will be voluntary (e.g., due to high dollar cost). Applications should gracefully, and as transparently as possible, handle such partitions. In addition, users should be able to continue working as if the network was still available (albeit with some limitations). In particular, users should be able to modify local copies of global data.

2.3. MOBILE DATA MANAGEMENT AND ISSUES

Effective data management in today's competitive enterprise environment is an important issue. Data is information; and information is knowledge. Hence, fast and effective access to data is very important. Mobile data management has been an active area of research for the past twenty years. Besides dealing with mobility itself, issues central in data management for mobile computing include low bandwidth, intermittent network connectivity and scarcity of resources with emphasis on power management.

Mobile computing refers to computing using devices that are not attached to a specific location, but instead their position (network or geographical) changes. Mobile computing can be traced back to file systems and the need for disconnected operations in the end of the 80s. With the rapid growth in mobile technologies and the cost effectiveness in deploying wireless networks in the 90s, the goal of mobile computing was to support of AAA (anytime, anywhere and any-form) access to data by users from their portable computers and mobile phones, devices with small displays and limited resources. This led to research in mobile data management including transaction processing, query processing and data dissemination. A key characteristic of all these research efforts was the great emphasis on the mobile computing challenges, including:

2.3.1. Weak and Intermittent Connectivity

This refers to the fact that computation must proceed despite short or long periods of network unavailability.

Wireless networks are more expensive, offer less bandwidth, and are less reliable than wireline networks.

Wireless communications face many obstacles because the surrounding environment interacts with the signal.

Mobile elements may voluntary operate disconnected. Wireless technologies vary on the degree of bandwidth and reliability they provide. There is a high bandwidth broadcast channel from the base station to all mobile clients in its cell.

Furthermore, data transmission over the air is currently monetarily expensive. For some networks (e.g., in cellular telephones), network access is charged per connection-time, while for others (e.g., in packet radio), it is charged per message (packet).

2.3.2. Scarcity of Resources

Due to the small sizes of portable devices, there are implicit restrictions in the availability of storage and computation capacity and mostly of energy.

The growth in wired network bandwidth has been tremendous (in current technology Ethernet provides 10 Mbps, FDDI 100 Mbps and ATM 155 Mbps), products for wireless communication achieve only 19 Kbps for packet radio communications, and 9-14 Kbps for cellular telephony. The typical bandwidth of wireless LANs ranges from 250 Kbps to 2 Mbps and it is expected to increase to 10 Mbps. Since the bandwidth is divided among the users sharing a cell, the deliverable bandwidth per user is even lower. For radio transmission the error rate is so high that the effective bandwidth is limited to less than 10 Kbps. Thus, bandwidth is a scarce resource.

2.3.3. Portability of Mobile Elements

- ***Mobile elements are resource poor when compared to static elements.***
  Mobile elements must be light and small to be easily carried around. Such considerations, in conjunction with a given cost and level of technology, will keep mobile elements having less resources than static elements, including memory, screen size and disk capacity. This results in an asymmetry between static and mobile elements.
- ***Mobile elements rely on battery***
  Even with advances in battery technology, this concern will not cease to exist.
  Concern for power consumption must span various levels in hardware and software design.
- ***Mobile elements are easier to be accidentally damaged, stolen, or lost.***
  Thus, they are less secure and reliable than static elements.

2.3.4. Mobility

The location of mobile elements and therefore their point of attachment to the fixed network change as they move.

The implications of mobility are varying. First, mobility introduces a number of technical challenges at the networking layer. It also offers a number of opportunities at the higher layers for explicitly using location information either at the semantic level (for instance, for providing personalization) or at the performance level (for instance, for data pre-fetching). Finally, it amplifies heterogeneity.

The consequences of mobility are numerous.

- ***The configuration of a system that includes mobile elements is not static. Thus,***
  (a) In designing distributed algorithms, we can no more rely on a fixed topology.

(b) The center of activity, the system load, and locality change dynamically.

- ***Location Management***

(a) The search cost to locate mobile elements is added to the cost of each communication involving them.

(b) Efficient data structures, algorithms, and query execution plans must be devised for representing, managing, and querying the location of mobile elements, which is a fast changing data.

- ***Heterogeneity***

(a) Connectivity becomes highly variant in performance and reliability. For instance, outdoors, a mobile client may have to rely on low and width networks, while inside a building it may be offered reliable high-bandwidth connectivity or even operates connected via wireline connections. Moreover, there may be areas with no adequate coverage resulting in disconnections of various durations.

(b) The number of devices in a network cell changes with time, and so do both the load at the base station and bandwidth availability.

(c) There may be also variability in the provision of specific services, such as in the type of available printers or weather reports.

(d) The resources available to a mobile element vary, for example, a docked computer has more memory or is equipped with a larger screen.

Mobility also raises very important security and authentication issues.

2.4. MOBILITY MANAGEMENT ISSUES IN 4G NETWORKS

Researchers and vendors are expressing a growing interest in 4G wireless networks that support global roaming across multiple wireless and mobile networks—for example, from a cellular network to a satellite-based network to a high-bandwidth wireless LAN. The 4G mobile system is an all IP-based network and provides the user access to different radio access technologies. In this environment, roaming is seamless and users are always connected to the best network.

Traditional phone networks (2G cellular networks) such as GSM, used mainly for voice transmission, are essentially circuit-switched. 2.5G networks, such as GPRS, are an extension of 2G networks, in that they use circuit switching for voice and packet switching for data transmission. Circuit switched technology requires that the user be billed by airtime rather than the amount of data transmitted since that bandwidth is reserved for the user. Packet switched technology utilizes bandwidth much more efficiently, allowing each user's packets to compete for available bandwidth, and billing users for the amount of data transmitted. Thus a move towards using packet-switched, and therefore IP networks, is natural. 3G networks were proposed to eliminate many problems faced by 2G and 2.5G networks, like low speeds and incompatible technologies (TDMA/CDMA) in different countries. Expectations for 3G included increased bandwidth: 128 Kbps in a car, and 2 Mbps in fixed applications. In theory, 3G would work over North American as well as European and Asian wireless air interfaces. In reality, the outlook for 3G is neither clear nor certain. Part of the problem is that network providers in Europe and North America currently maintain separate standards' bodies (3GPP for Europe and Asia; 3GPP2 for North America). The standards' bodies mirror differences in air interface technologies. In addition there are financial questions as well that cast a doubt over 3G's desirability. There is a concern that in many countries, 3G will never be deployed. This concern is grounded, in part, in the growing attraction of 4G wireless technologies. A 4G or 4th generation network is the name given to an IP-based mobile system that provides access through a collection of radio interfaces. A 4G network promises seamless roaming/handover and best connected service, combining multiple radio access interfaces (such as HIPERLAN, WLAN, Bluetooth, GPRS) into a single network that subscribers may use. With this feature, users will have access to different services, increased coverage, the convenience of a single device, one bill with reduced total access cost, and more reliable wireless access even with the failure or loss of one or more networks.

At the moment, 4G is simply an initiative by R&D labs to move beyond the limitations, and deal with the problems of 3G (which is having trouble meeting its promised performance and throughput).

At the most general level, 4G architecture will include three basic areas of connectivity: Personal Area Networking (such as Bluetooth), local high-speed access points on the network including wireless LAN technologies (such as IEEE 802.11 and HIPERLAN), and cellular connectivity. Under this umbrella, 4G calls for a wide range of mobile devices that support global roaming. Each device will be able to interact with Internet-based information that will be modified on the fly for the network being used by the device at that moment. In short, the roots of 4G networks lie in the idea of pervasive computing. The glue for all this is likely to be Software Defined Radio (SDR). SDR enables devices such as cell phones, PDAs, PCs and a whole range of other devices to scan the airwaves for the best possible method of connectivity, at the best price. In an SDR environment, functions that were formerly carried out solely in hardware - such as the generation of the transmitted radio signal and the tuning of the received radio signal - are performed by software. Thus, the radio is programmable and able to transmit and receive over a wide range of frequencies while emulating virtually any desired transmission format.

2.4.1. 4G Characteristics

The defining features of 4G networks are listed below:

- **High Speed:** 4G systems should offer a peak speed of more than 100Mbits per second in stationary mode with an average of 20Mbits per second when traveling.
- **High Network Capacity:** Should be at least 10 times that of 3G systems. This will quicken the download time of a 10-Mbyte file to one second on 4G, from 200 seconds on 3G, enabling high-definition video to stream to phones and create a virtual reality experience on high-resolution handset screens.
- **Fast/Seamless Handover Across Multiple Networks:** 4G wireless networks should support global roaming across multiple wireless and mobile networks.
- **Next-Generation Multimedia Support:** The underlying network for 4G must be able to support fast speed and large volume data transmission at a lower cost than today.

2.4.2. 4G Networks and IPv6

The goal of 4G is to replace the current proliferation of core mobile networks with a single worldwide core network standard, based on IP for control, video, packet data, and voice. This will provide uniform video, voice, and data services to the mobile host, based entirely on IP. The objective is to offer seamless multimedia services to users accessing an all IP-based infrastructure through heterogeneous access technologies. IP is assumed to act as an adhesive for providing global connectivity and mobility among networks. An all IP-based 4G wireless network has inherent advantages over its predecessors. It is compatible with, and independent of the underlying radio access technology. An IP wireless network replaces the old Signaling System 7 (SS7) telecommunications protocol, which is considered massively redundant. This is because SS7 signal transmission consumes a larger part of network bandwidth even when there is no signalling traffic for the simple reason that it uses a call setup mechanism to reserve bandwidth , rather time/frequency slots in the radio waves. IP networks, on the other hand, are connectionless and use the slots only when they have data to send. Hence there is optimum usage of the available bandwidth. Today, wireless communications are heavily biased toward voice, even though studies indicate that growth in wireless data traffic is rising exponentially relative to demand for voice traffic. Because an all IP core layer is easily scalable, it is ideally suited to meet this challenge. The goal is a merged data/voice/multimedia network.

2.4.3. Mobility Management Issues in 4G Networks

Mobility is a critical aspect of 4G. There are three main issues regarding mobility management in 4G networks.

(a) The first issue deals with ***optimal choice of access technology***, or how to be best connected. Given that a user may be offered connectivity from more than one technology at any one time, one has to consider how the terminal and an overlay network choose the radio access technology suitable for services the user is accessing.

There are several network technologies available today, which can be viewed as complementary. For example, WLAN is best suited for high data rate indoor coverage. GPRS or UMTS, on the other hand, are best suited for nation wide coverage and can be regarded as wide area networks, providing a higher degree of mobility. Thus a user of the mobile terminal or the network needs to make the optimal choice of radio access technology among all those available. A handover algorithm should both determine which network to connect to as well as when to perform a handover between the different networks. Ideally, the handover algorithm would assure that the best overall wireless link is chosen. The network selection strategy should take into consideration the type of application being run by the user at the time of handover. This ensures stability as well as optimal bandwidth for interactive and background services (see Fig. 2.1).

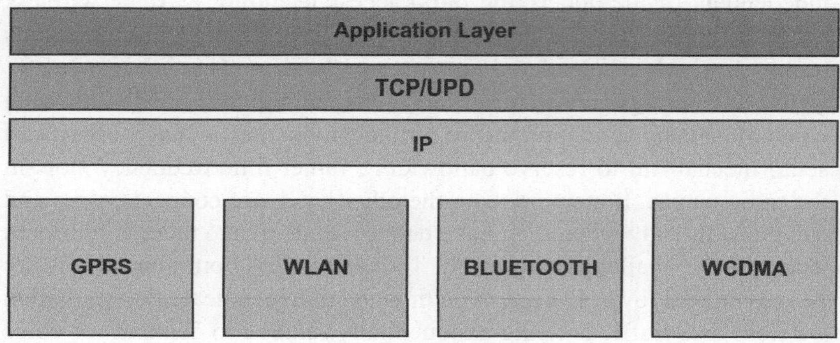

Fig. 2.1

(b) The second issue regards the design of a mobility enabled IP networking architecture, which contains the functionality to deal with ***mobility between access technologies***. This includes fast, seamless vertical (between heterogeneous technologies) handovers (IP micro-mobility), Quality of Service (QoS), security and accounting.

Real-time applications in the future will require fast/seamless handovers for smooth operation. Mobility in IPv6 is not optimized to take advantage of specific mechanisms that may be deployed in different administrative domains. Instead, IPv6 provides mobility in a manner that resembles only simple portability.

To enhance Mobility in IPv6, 'micro-mobility' protocols, Cellular IP and Hierarchical Mobile IPv6 have been developed for seamless handovers i.e. handovers that result in minimal handover delay, minimal packet loss, and minimal loss of communication state.

(c) The third issue concerns the ***adaptation of multimedia transmission*** across 4G networks. Indeed multimedia will be a main service feature of 4G networks, and changing radio access networks may in particular result in drastic changes in the network condition. Thus the framework for multimedia transmission must be adaptive.

In cellular networks such as UMTS, users compete for scarce and expensive bandwidth. Variable bit rate services provide a way to ensure service provisioning at lower costs. In addition the radio environment has dynamics that renders it difficult to provide a guaranteed network service. This requires that the services are adaptive and robust against varying radio conditions.

High variations in the network Quality of Service (QoS) leads to significant variations of the multimedia quality. The result could sometimes be unacceptable to the users. Avoiding this requires choosing an adaptive encoding framework for multimedia transmission. The network should signal QoS variations to allow the application to be aware in real time of the network conditions. User interactions will help to ensure personalized adaptation of the multimedia presentation.

2.4.4. Mobility Management in IPV6

Features of mobility management in Ipv6:

- 128-bit address space provides a sufficiently large number of addresses
- High quality support for real-time audio and video transmission, short/bursty connections of web applications, peer-to-peer applications, etc.
- Faster packet delivery, decreased cost of processing – no header checksum at each relay, fragmentation only at endpoints.
- Smooth handoff when the mobile host travels from one subnet to another, causing a change in its Care-of Address.

2.4.4.1. Enhancements to IPv6 Mobility Management Protocols required by 4G networks

Although the features mentioned in the previous section are suited for 4G networks, recently, there has been almost universal recognition that IPv6 needs to be enhanced to meet the need for future 4G cellular environments. In particular, the absence of a location management hierarchy (IPv6 uses only simple location updates for location management) leads to concerns about the signalling scalability and handoff latency. This is especially significant when we consider that 4G aims at providing mobility support to potentially billions of mobile devices, within the stringent performance bounds associated with real time multimedia traffic.

There are three main areas where IPv6 needs to be enhanced before being used as the core networking protocol in 4G networks:

- **Paging Support**

  The base IPv6 specification does not provide any form of paging support. Hence to maintain connectivity with the backbone infrastructure, the mobile node needs to generate location updates every time it changes its point of attachment, even if it is currently in dormant or standby mode. Excessive signaling caused by frequent motion leads to a significant wastage of the mobile node's battery power, especially in environments with smaller cell areas (such as 802.11 based cellular topologies). It is thus impractical to rely completely on location updates, and essential to define some sort of flexible paging support in the intra-domain mobility management scheme.

- **Scalability**

  IPv6 allows nodes to move within the Internet topology while maintaining reachability and on-going connections between mobile and correspondent nodes. To do this a mobile node sends Binding Updates (BUs) to its Home Agent (HA) and all Correspondent Nodes (CNs) it communicates with, every time it moves. Authenticating binding updates requires approximately 1.5 round trip times between the mobile node and each correspondent node (for the entire return routability procedure in a best case scenario, i.e. no packet losses). In addition, one round trip time is needed to update the HA; this can be done simultaneously while updating CNs.

  These round trip delays will disrupt active connections every time a handoff to a new radio access technology is performed. Eliminating this additional delay element from the time-critical handover period will significantly improve the performance of IPv6. Moreover, in the case of wireless links, such a solution reduces the number of messages sent over the air interface to all CNs and the HA. A local anchor point will allow Mobile IPv6 to benefit from reduced mobility signaling with external networks. For these reasons a new Mobile IPv6 node, called the Mobility Anchor Point (MAP) has been suggested, that can be located at any level in a hierarchical network of routers. Unlike Foreign Agents in IPv4, a MAP is not required on each subnet. The MAP will limit the amount of Mobile IPv6 signaling outside the local domain. The introduction of the MAP provides a solution to the aforementioned problems in the following way:

- The MN sends binding updates to the local MAP rather than the HA (that is typically further away) and CNs
- Only one binding update message needs to be transmitted by the MN before traffic from the HA and all CNs is re-routed to its new location. This is independent of the number of CNs that the MN is communicating with.

Thus, by decreasing signaling traffic, having an intermediate level in the hierarchy helps accommodate a larger number of mobile nodes in the system.

2.4.5. Heterogeneous Access Technologies

A mobile node switches from one network based on an access network technology like GPRS to another network based on a different access technology like WLAN in one of two cases:

(a) When the signal from the network it is currently in starts to become weak, or

(b) When the mobile host detects another network which is better suited to its application compared to its current network.

The decision of the mobile device on the suitability of the network can be based on signal strength, network bandwidth or certain policies which the user might have stored in his profile based on which switching between networks of different access technologies may occur. For example, when a user is streaming a video, she may use WLAN and when she is listening to highly compressed audio, she might switch to GPRS.

Another issue that needs to be resolved is that of informing the source/HA/CH when the MN has moved. In such a situation, the MN does a location update to its HA, which then takes charge of sending IP datagrams to the MN's new location using standard Mobile-IP mechanisms. However, these mechanisms are inadequate.

In line with the 4G vision of bringing together wide-area (such as GPRS) and local-area packet-based (such as 802.11) technologies, mobile terminals are being designed with multiple physical or software-defined interfaces. This is expected to allow users to seamlessly switch between different access technologies, often with overlapping areas of coverage and dramatically different cell sizes. Mobility management protocols should then be capable of handling vertical handoffs.

2.4.6. Scalability Support – Hierachial Mobile IPv6 (HMIPv6)

IPv6 hosts have a home agent and co-located care of address. As they move from domain to domain or subnet to subnet, the send Binding Updates (or BUs) to inform their respective home agent and their corresponding hosts of the change in binding between their permanent IPv6 address and their Co-located Care of Address (CCOA). The HA may then tunnel packets from corresponding hosts to the mobile host at the new CCOA. When the binding updates reach the corresponding hosts, the corresponding hosts may send packets directly to the mobile hosts.

Although this approach provides the convenience of a single IPv6 address that is independent of the point of attachment of the mobile host, it is not scalable. As the number of mobile hosts in a given domain increase, the number of binding updates (which are sent out periodically) increases. This in turn causes more signalling within the domains and across the internet (for hosts that are not within their home domains). This overhead may lead to longer network delays. To work around this problem of IPv6, A shortfall of vanilla IPv6 is that it deals with intra-site mobility and inter-site mobility in the same way. The study in has shown that 69% of user mobility is intra-site, meaning 69% of binding updates are sent to home agents and correspondent hosts. Most of the signaling traffic due to BUs can thus be reduced if local mobility is hidden from correspondent hosts and home agents. The need for a hierarchical mobility management scheme becomes apparent if local and global mobility management are to be handled separately.

2.4.7. Local Mobility Management in HMIPv6

Hierarchical Mobile IPv6 (or HMIPv6) was is an IETF proposal, revised in October 2002.

Networks are divided into domains and subnets, with each administrative domain having a Mobility Anchor Point (MAP) at the highest level. Intra domain mobility of a mobile host is handled separately from inter-domain mobility. When the MH changes points of attachment within the same domain, the MAP of that domain is informed of the change in Care of Address of the MH through binding updates. Binding updates are also sent to correspondent hosts within the same domain. The MAP functions as a foreign agent (in a MIPv4 context) by intercepting IP datagrams destined for the MH and forwarding them to the appropriate care of address (CoA) inside the domain. This way, intra domain handoff can be performed transparent to the MH's Home Agent or external correspondent hosts, that is the MH does not need to send its HA or CHs binding updates. This reduces signalling traffic due to *reduced binding updates*. It also reduces handoff latency as far-off home agents and correspondent hosts need not be updated every time a mobile host changes point of attachment. This may be crucial to ensuring minimal handoff latency to ensure QoS for real-time data. When a mobile host moves between domains, IPv6 mobility management is used, which is represented in the following Fig. 2.2.

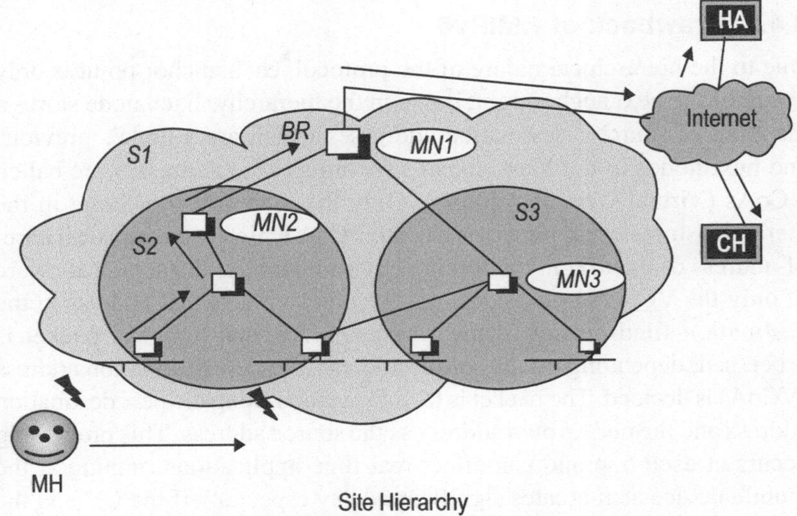

Fig. 2.2: IPV6 Mobility Management

This hierarchical set up can be extended to multiple levels where subnets have MAPs each MH has a virtual care of address associated with it at each level of the hierarchy as shown in Fig. 2.3.

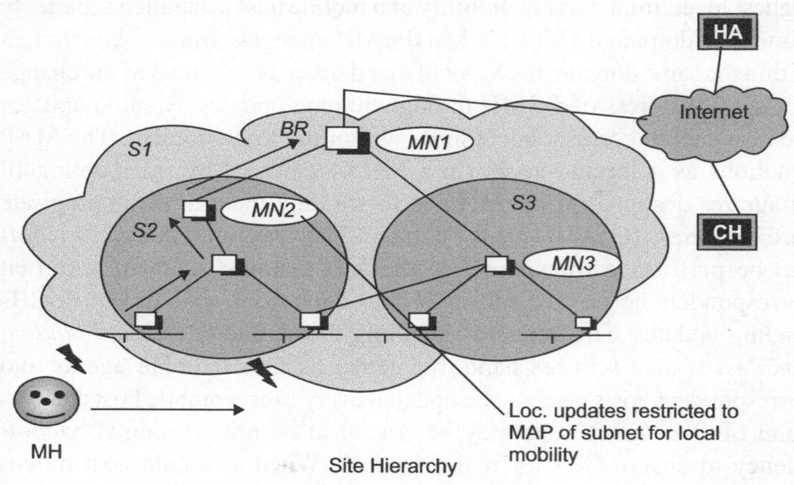

Fig. 2.3: HMIPv6 Mobility Management

2.4.8. Drawback of HMIPv6

Due to the hierarchical nature of the protocol, each anchor point is only aware of the next anchor point down in the hierarchy. Each node stores a mapping of source : destination addresses which are a node's previous and next nodes in the hierarchical structure. These addresses are called VCoAs (Virtual Care of Address). Only the lowest anchor point in the hierarchy stores a mapping of VCoA to PCoA which is the physical care-of-address of the MH in the foreign environment. As the source is aware of only the VCoA of its nearest anchor point , it sets that address in the destination filed header of the IP packet. At each hop, the packet is processed, depending on the source address, the new destination address (VCoA) is decided. The packet is then forwarded using the new destination address and the node's own address as the source address. This processing occurs at each hop and can effect real time applications running at the mobile device as it creates significant delay especially if the CH and the MH are many hops away with the MH part of a big hierarchical structure.

2.4.9. Support for Vertical Handoffs

As mentioned earlier, the current IPv6 specification does not support vertical handoffs. Since IP is the common protocol, everything below it is abstracted from the application. Fro the application, it is always connected as handoffs occur.

To provide this support in IPv6 a daemon can be run at the network layer which takes care of switching between different radio access technologies. The mobile device might be having separate interface cards for each of the networks or may use a single multi-mode card which works in different modes are different times.

The protocol stacks of each of the different radio access technology are stored in the mobile device. The daemon in the network layer will then choose which Radio Access Network (RAN) to use on the basis of network speed, quality of service, cost of usage and other similar criteria. The selection policies are customizable and changes between different RANs are automatic and transparent to the user and depend on coverage and network load conditions.

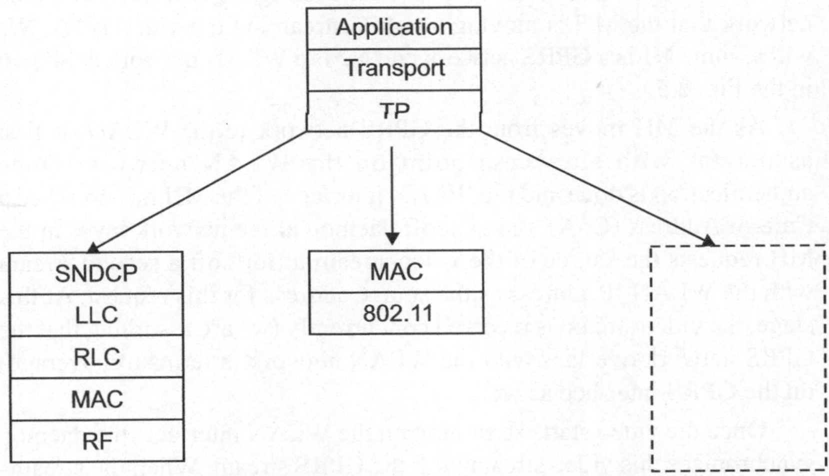

Fig. 2.4: Multiple Protocol Stacks being maintained at the Mobile Host

After selecting the RAN, the daemon then initializes the appropriate protocol stack (GPRS or WLAN etc) before starting to use that interface. This way the IP datagrams being passed down get encapsulated in the correct format of the radio access technology in use. This model allows the device to utilize any interface as long as the hardware is present (or introduced through a flash port or PCMCIA port) by just installing the necessary stack protocols. Other ways such as dynamically downloading the protocol stack from the network were discussed by the group but were discarded due to the complexity and the latency added in the process which made it unsuitable for real time applications. Also, memory not being such a big constraint, it was decided that maintaining multiple protocol stacks at the mobile node itself is a good way of adding vertical handoff functionality to the network layer without introducing much latency. Another enhancement has been suggested by the group to make the application transparent to any kind of delays – due to horizontal or vertical handoffs. This has been suggested in the next subsection.

2.4.10. Soft Handoffs for Real-Time Applications

Ensuring that a real time multimedia application suffers from minimal or no lag, lost frames or jitter while the MH is handed off between two RANs is a steep challenge for the mobility management mechanism.

The network where the MH started streaming the video is N1 and the network that the MH is moving to while streaming the video is N2. We will assume N1 is a GPRS network and N2 is a WLAN network as shown in the Fig. 2.5.

As the MH moves from the GPRS network to the WLAN, it first associates with an access point on the WLAN network. Once authentication is done and the WLAN interface of the MH has obtained a Care-of Address (CoA), the handoff daemon at the network layer in the MH requests the source of the video stream to fork off a second stream with the WLAN IP address as the source address for this request. At this stage, the video stream is received concurrently (we are assuming that the GPRS network overlaps with the WLAN network in terms of coverage) on the GPRS interface as well.

Once the video starts streaming on the WLAN interface, the daemon synchronizes this video stream with the GPRS stream. When the streams are synchronized, the daemon will send the WLAN stream to the application running on the MH while asking the GGSN of the GPRS network to inform the source of the video stream to stop streaming on the GPRS network. It then updates the GGSN of its new location and continues streaming the video on the WLAN network. The handoff procedure would have then completed, totally transparent to the user (apart from a change in say the resolution of the video being adjusted to the available bandwidth of the RAN).

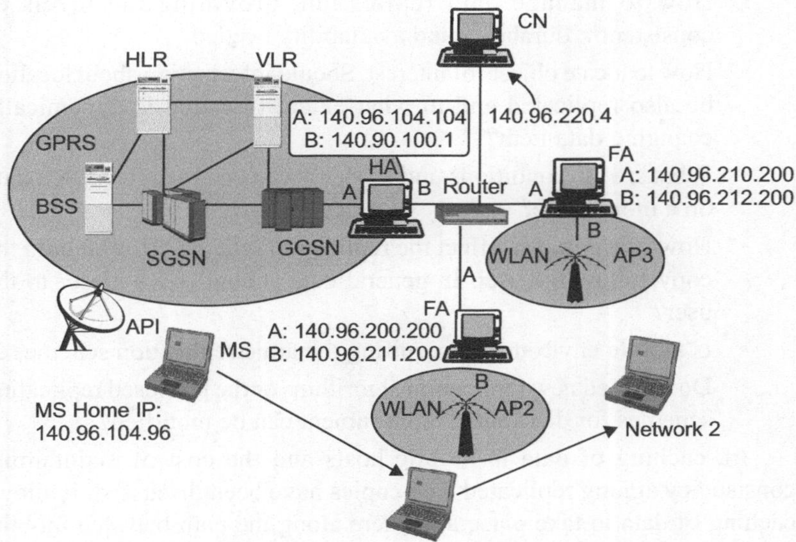

Fig. 2.5: GPRS – WLAN Handoff

2.5. DATA REPLICATION IN MOBILE COMPUTING

The ability to replicate the data objects is essential in mobile computing to increase availability and performance. Shared data items have different synchronization constraints depending on their semantics and particular use.

These constraints should be enforced on an individual basis. Replicated systems need to provide support for disconnected mode, data divergence, application defined reconciliation procedures, optimistic concurrency control, etc. Replication is a way by which the system ensures transparency for mobile users. A user who has relocated and has been using certain files and services at the previous location wants to have his environment recreated at the new location.

Mobility of users and services and its impact on data replication and migration will be one of the main technical problems to be resolved. There are many issues raised by the relocated data and mobility of users and services:

- How to manage data replication, providing the levels of consistency, durability and availability needed?
- How to locate objects of interest. Should information about location be also replicated and to what extent (location is dynamically changing data item?
- What are the conditions under which we need to replicate the data on a mobile site?
- How users' moves affect the replication scheme? How should the copy follow the user. In general data should move closer to the user?
- Is mobile environment requiring dynamic replication schemes ?
- Do we need new replication algorithms or the proposed replication schemes for distributed environment can be modified?

In, caching of data in mobile hosts and the cost of maintaining consistency among replicated data copies have been discussed. It allows caching of data to take place anywhere along the path between mobile/ fixed servers and clients. It determines via simulations which caching policy best suits given mobility and read/write patterns.

Data is replicated at multiple network nodes for performance and availability. ***Eager Replication*** keeps all replicas exactly synchronized at all nodes by updating all the replicas as part of one atomic transaction. Eager replication gives serializable execution – there are no concurrency anomalies. But, eager replication reduces update performance and increases transaction response times because extra updates and messages are added to the transaction.

Eager replication is not an option for mobile applications where most nodes are normally disconnected. Mobile applications require ***Lazy Replication*** algorithms that asynchronously propagate replica updates to other nodes after the updating transaction commits. Some continuously connected systems use lazy replication to improve response time.

Lazy replication also has shortcomings, the most serious being stale data versions. When two transactions read and write data concurrently, one transaction's updates should be serialized after the other's. This avoids concurrency anomalies. Eager replication typically uses a locking scheme to detect and regulate concurrent execution. Lazy replication schemes typically use a multi-version concurrency control scheme to detect non-serializable behavior. Most multi-version isolation schemes provide the transaction with the most recent committed value. Lazy replication may allow a transaction to see a very old committed value. Committed updates to a local value may be "in transit" to this node if the update strategy is "lazy".

Eager replication delays or aborts an uncommitted transaction if committing it would violate serialization. Lazy replication has a more difficult task because some replica updates have already been committed when the serialization problem is first detected. There is usually no automatic way to reverse the committed replica updates, rather a program or person must ***reconcile*** conflicting transactions. Fig. 2.6 shows two ways to propagate updates to replicas.

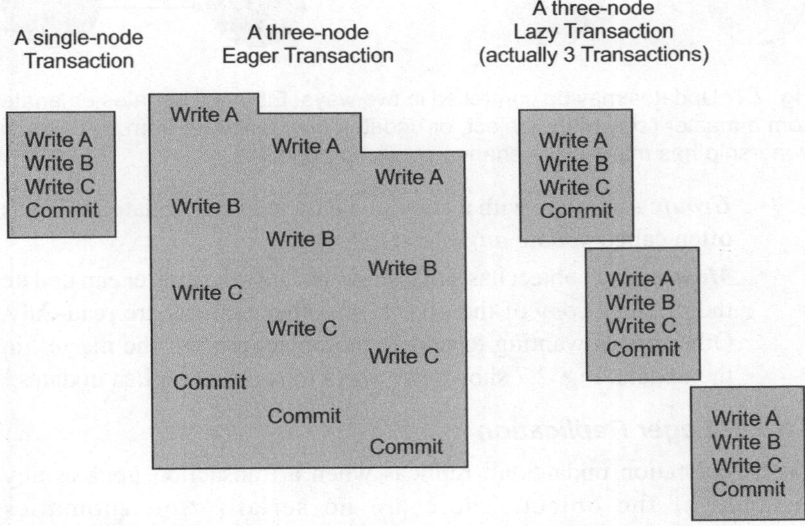

Fig. 2.6: When replicated, a simple single-node transaction may apply its updates remotely either as part of the same transaction (eager) or as separate transactions (lazy). In either case, if data is replicated at N nodes, the transaction does N times as much work

2.5.1. Replication Models

- ***Eager***: Updates are applied to all replicas of an object as part of the original transaction.

- ***Lazy:*** One replica is updated by the originating transaction. Updates to other replicas propagate asynchronously, typically as a separate transaction for each node.

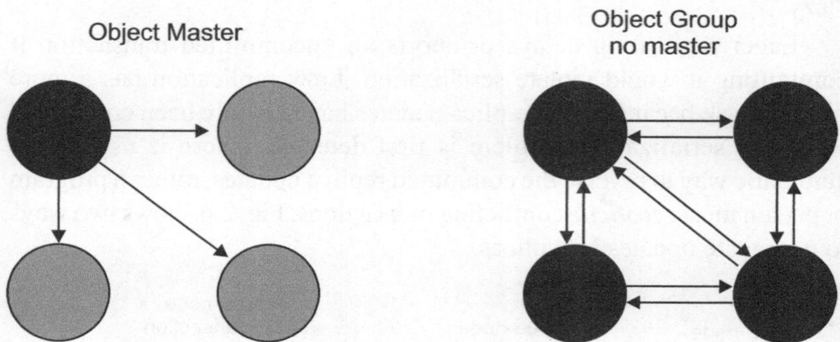

Fig. 2.7: Updates may be controlled in two ways. Either all updates emanate from a master copy of the object, or updates may emanate from any. Group ownership has many more chance conflicting updates.

- ***Group***: Any node with a copy of a data item can update it. This is often called *update anywhere.*
- ***Master***: Each object has a master node. Only the master can update the *primary copy* of the object. All other replicas are read-only. Other nodes wanting to update the object request the master do the update. Fig. 2.7 shows two ways to regulate replica updates.

2.5.1.1. Eager Replication

Eager replication updates all replicas when a transaction updates any instance of the object. There are no serialization anomalies (inconsistencies) and no need for reconciliation in eager systems. Locking detects potential anomalies and converts them to waits or deadlocks.

With eager replication, reads at connected nodes give current data. Reads at disconnected nodes may give stale (out of date) data. Simple eager replication systems prohibit updates if any node is disconnected. For high availability, eager replication systems allow updates among members of the quorum or cluster. When a node joins the quorum, the quorum sends the new node all replica updates since the node was disconnected.

Even if all the nodes are connected all the time, updates may fail due to deadlocks that prevent serialization errors. Having a master for each object helps eager replication avoid deadlocks. Suppose each object has an owner node. Updates go to this node first and are then applied to the replicas. If, each transaction updated a single replica, the object-master approach would eliminate all deadlocks.

Eager replication has two major problems:

1. Mobile nodes cannot use an eager scheme when disconnected.
2. The probability of deadlocks, and consequently failed transactions rises very quickly with transaction size and with the number of nodes. A ten-fold increase in nodes gives a thousand-fold increase in failed transactions (deadlocks).

It is observed that, there is no solution to this problem. If replica updates were done concurrently, the action time would not increase with N then the growth rate would *only* be quadratic.

2.5.1.2. Lazy Group Replication

Lazy group replication allows any node to update any local data. When the transaction commits, a transaction is sent to every other node to apply the root transaction's updates to the replicas at the destination node (Fig. 2.8). It is possible for two nodes to update the same object and race each other to install their updates at other nodes. The replication mechanism must detect this and reconcile the two transactions so that their updates are not lost.

Timestamps are commonly used to detect and reconcile lazy-group transactional updates. Each object carries the timestamp of its most recent update. Each replica update carries the new value and is tagged with the old object timestamp. Each node detects incoming replica updates that would overwrite earlier committed updates. The node tests if the local replica's timestamp and the update's old timestamp are equal. If so, the update is safe. The local replica's timestamp advances to the new transaction's timestamp and the object value is updated. If the current timestamp of the local replica does not match the old timestamp seen by the root transaction, then the update may be "dangerous". In such cases, the node rejects the incoming transaction and submits it for *reconciliation*.

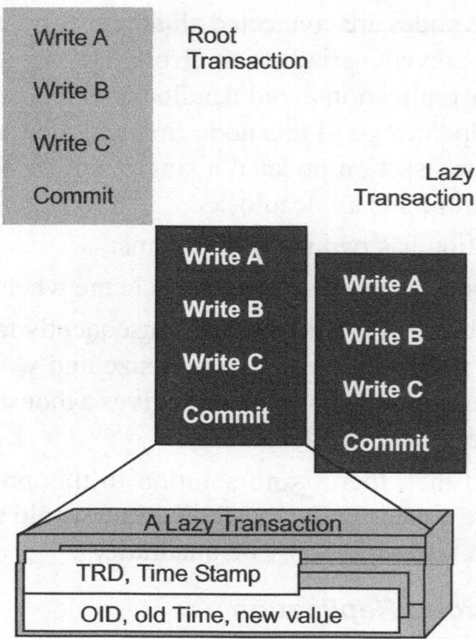

Fig. 2.8: A lazy transaction has a root execution that updates either master or local copies of data. Then subsequent transactions update replicas at remote nodes—one lazy transaction per remote replica node. The lazy updates carry timestamps of each original object. If the local object timestamp does not match, the update may be dangerous and some form of reconciliation is needed

2.5.1.3. Lazy Master Replication

Master replication assigns an owner to each object. The owner stores the object's correct current value. Updates are first done by the owner and then propagated to other replicas. Different objects may have different owners.

When a transaction wants to update an object, it sends an RPC (Remote Procedure Call) to the node owning the object. To get serializability, a read action should send read-lock RPCs to the masters of any objects it reads.

To analysis the scheme, we assume the node originating the transaction broadcasts the replica updates to all the slave replicas after the master transaction commits. The originating node sends one slave transaction to each slave node (as in Fig. 2.6). Slave updates are timestamped to assure that all the replicas converge to the same final state. If the record timestamp is newer than a replica update timestamp, the update is "stale" and can be ignored. Alternatively, each master node sends replica updates to slaves in sequential commit order. Lazy-Master replication is not appropriate for mobile applications. A node wanting to update an object must be connected to the object owner and participate in an atomic transaction with the owner.

As with eager systems, lazy-master systems have no reconciliation failures; rather, conflicts are resolved by waiting or deadlock. Ignoring message delays, the deadlock rate for a lazy-master replication system is similar to a single node system with much higher transaction rates. Lazy master transactions operate on master copies of objects. But, because there are *Nodes* times more users, there are *Nodes* times as many concurrent master transactions and approximately $Nodes^2$ times as many replica update transactions. The replica update transactions do not really matter, they are background housekeeping transactions. They can abort and restart without affecting the user. So the main issue is how frequently the master transactions deadlock.

Lazy-master replication sends fewer messages during the base transaction and so completes more quickly. Nevertheless, all of these replication schemes have troubling deadlock or reconciliation rates as they grow to many nodes.

In summary, lazy-master replication requires contact with object masters and so is not useable by mobile applications. Lazy-master replication is slightly less deadlock prone than eager-group replication primarily because the transactions have shorter duration.

2.5.1.4. Non-Transactional Replication Schemes

Certainly, there are replicated databases: bibles, phone books, check books, mail systems, name servers, and so on. But updates to these databases are managed in interesting ways — typically in a lazy-master way. Further, updates are not record-value oriented; rather, updates are expressed as transactional transformations such as "Debit the account by $50" instead of "change account from $200 to $150".

One strategy is to abandon serializabilty for the ***convergence property***: if no new transactions arrive, and if all the nodes are connected together, they will all converge to the same replicated state after exchanging replica updates. The resulting state contains the committed appends, and the most recent replacements, but updates may be lost.

Lotus Notes gives a good example of convergence. Notes is a lazy group replication design (update anywhere, anytime, anyhow). Notes provides convergence rather than an ACID transaction execution model. The database state may not reflect any particular serial execution, but all the states will be identical. As explained below, timestamp schemes have the lost-update problem.

Lotus Notes achieves convergence by offering lazy-group replication at the transaction level. It provides two forms of update transaction:

- ***Append*** adds data to a Notes file. Every appended note has a timestamp. Notes are stored in timestamp order. If all nodes are in contact with all others, then they will all converge on the same state.
- ***Timestamped replace a value*** replaces a value with a newer value. If the current value of the object already has a timestamp greater than this update's timestamp, the incoming update is discarded.

If convergence were the only goal, the timestamp method would be sufficient. But, the timestamp scheme may lose the effects of some transactions because it just applies the most recent updates. Applying a timestamp scheme to the checkbook example, if there are two concurrent updates to a checkbook balance, the highest timestamp value wins and the other update is discarded as a "stale" value. Concurrency control theory calls this the *lost update problem*. Timestamp schemes are vulnerable to lost updates.

Convergence is desirable, but the converged state should reflect the effects of all committed transactions. In general this is not possible unless global serialization techniques are used.

In certain cases transactions can be designed to commute, so that the database ends up in the same state no matter what transaction execution order is chosen. Timestamped Append is a kind of commutative update but there are others (e.g., adding and subtracting constants from an integer value). It would be possible for Notes to support a third form of transaction:

- ***Commutative Updates*** that are incremental transformations of a value that can be applied in any order.

Lotus Notes, the Internet name service, mail systems, Microsoft Access, and many other applications use some of these techniques to achieve convergence and avoid delusion.

Microsoft Access offers convergence as follows. It has a single design master node that controls all schema updates to a replicated database. It offers update-anywhere for record instances. Each node keeps a version vector with each replicated record. These version vectors are exchanged on demand or periodically. The most recent update wins each pairwise exchange.

The examples contrast with a simple update-anywhere-anytime-anyhow lazy-group replication offered by some systems. If the transaction profiles are not constrained, lazy-group schemes suffer from unstable reconciliation described in earlier sections. Such systems degenerate into system delusion as they scale up.

Lazy group replication schemes are emerging with specialized reconciliation rules. Oracle 7 provides a choice of twelve reconciliation rules to merge conflicting updates. In addition, users can program their own reconciliation rules. These rules give priority certain sites, or time priority, or value priority, or they merge commutative updates. The rules make some transactions commutative. A similar, transaction-level approach is followed in the two-tier scheme described next.

2.5.1.5. Two-Tier Replication

An ideal replication scheme would achieve following four goals:

Availability and Scalability: Provide high availability and scalability through replication, while avoiding instability.

Mobility: Allow mobile nodes to read and update the database while disconnected from the network.

Serializability: Provide single-copy serializable transaction execution.

Convergence: Provide convergence to avoid system delusion.

The safest transactional replication schemes, (ones that avoid system delusion) are the eager systems and lazy master systems. They have no reconciliation problems (they have no reconciliation). But these systems have other problems. As shown earlier:

- Mastered objects cannot accept updates if the master node is not accessible. This makes it difficult to use master replication for mobile applications.
- Master systems are unstable under increasing load. Deadlocks rise quickly as nodes are added.

- Only eager systems and lazy master (where reads go to the master) give ACID serializability.

Circumventing these problems requires changing the way the system is used. We believe a scaleable replication system must function more like the check books, phone books, Lotus Notes, Access, and other replication systems we see about us.

Lazy-group replication systems are prone to reconciliation problems as they scale up. Manually reconciling conflicting transactions is unworkable. One approach is to *undo* all the work of any transaction that needs reconciliation — backing out all the updates of the transaction. This makes transactions atomic, consistent, and isolated, but not durable — or at least not durable until the updates are propagated to each node. In such a lazy group system, every transaction is tentative until all its replica updates have been propagated. If some mobile replica node is disconnected for a very long time, all transactions will be tentative until the missing node reconnects. So, an undo-oriented lazy-group replication scheme is untenable for mobile applications.

The solution seems to require a modified mastered replication scheme. To avoid reconciliation, each object is mastered by a node — much as the bank owns your checking account and your mail server owns your mailbox. Mobile agents can make tentative updates, then connect to the base nodes and immediately learn if the tentative update is acceptable.

The ***two-tier replication*** scheme begins by assuming there are two kinds of nodes:

***Mobile* Nodes** are disconnected much of the time. They store a replica of the database and may originate tentative transactions. A mobile node may be the master of some data items.

Base Nodes are always connected. They store a replica of the database. Most items are mastered at base nodes.

Replicated data items have two versions at mobile nodes:

Master Version: The most recent value received from the object master. The version at the object master is *the* master version, but disconnected or lazy replica nodes may have older versions.

Tentative Version: The local object may be updated by tentative transactions. The most recent value due to local updates is maintained as a tentative value.

Similarly, there are two kinds of transactions:

Base Transaction: Base transactions work only on master data, and they produce new master data. They involve at most one connected-mobile node and may involve several base nodes.

Tentative Transaction: Tentative transactions work on local tentative data. They produce new tentative versions. They also produce a base transaction to be run at a later time on the base nodes.

Tentative transactions must follow a ***scope rule***: they may involve objects mastered on base nodes and mastered at the mobile node originating the transaction (call this the transaction's *scope*). The idea is that the mobile node and all the base nodes will be in contact when the tentative transaction is processed as a "real" base transaction — so the real transaction will be able to read the master copy of each item in the scope.

Local transactions that read and write *only* local data can be designed in any way you like. They cannot read-or write any tentative data because that would make them tentative.

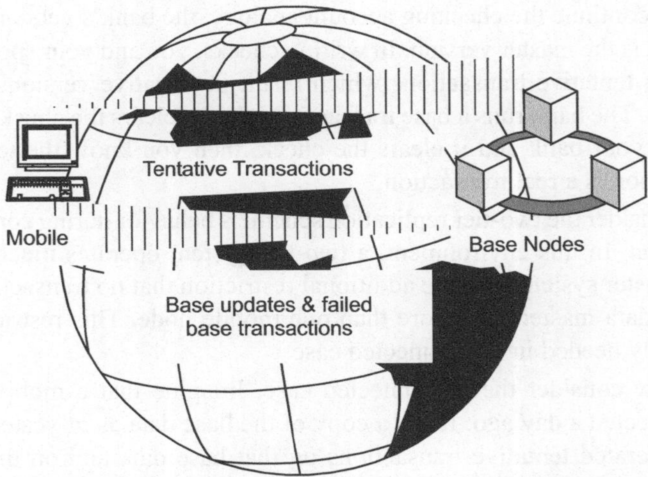

Fig. 2.9: The two-tier-replication scheme. Base nodes store replicas of the database. Each object is mastered at some node. Mobile nodes store a replica of the database, but are usually disconnected. Mobile nodes accumulate tentative transactions that run against the tentative database stored at the node. Tentative transactions are reprocessed as base transactions when the mobile node reconnects to the base. Tentative transactions may fail when reprocessed.

The base transaction generated by a tentative transaction may fail or it may produce different results. The base transaction has an ***acceptance criterion***: a test the resulting outputs must pass for the slightly different base transaction results to be acceptable. To give some sample acceptance criteria:

- The bank balance must not go negative.
- The price quote can not exceed the tentative quote.
- The seats must be aisle seats.

If a tentative transaction fails, the originating node and person who generated the transaction are informed it failed and why it failed. Acceptance failure is equivalent to the reconciliation mechanism of the lazy-group replication schemes. The differences are:

(a) The master database is always converged — there is no system delusion, and

(b) The originating node need only contact a base node in order to discover if a tentative transaction is acceptable.

To continue the checking account analogy, the bank's version of the account is the master version. In writing checks, you and your spouse are creating tentative transactions which result in tentative versions of the account. The bank runs a base transaction when it clears the check. If you contact your bank and it clears the check, then you know the tentative transaction is a real transaction.

Consider the two-tier replication scheme's behavior during connected operation. In this environment, a two-tier system operates much like a lazy-master system with the additional restriction that no transaction can update data mastered at more than one mobile node. This restriction is not really needed in the connected case.

Now consider the disconnected case. Imagine that a mobile node disconnected a day ago. It has a copy of the base data as of yesterday. It has generated tentative transactions on that base data and on the local data mastered by the mobile node. These transactions generated tentative data versions at the mobile node. If the mobile node queries this data it sees the tentative values. For example, if it updated documents, produced contracts, and sent mail messages, those tentative updates are all visible at the mobile node.

When a mobile node connects to a base node, the mobile node:

1. Discards its tentative object versions since they will soon be refreshed from the masters,
2. Sends replica updates for any objects mastered at the mobile node to the base node "hosting" the mobile node,
3. Sends all its tentative transactions (and all their input parameters) to the base node to be executed in the order in which they committed on the mobile node,
4. Accepts replica updates from the base node (this is standard lazy-master replication), and
5. Accepts notice of the success or failure of each tentative transaction.

The "host" base node is the other tier of the two tiers. When contacted by a mobile note, the host base node:

1. Sends delayed replica update transactions to the mobile node.
2. Accepts delayed update transactions for mobile-mastered objects from the mobile node.
3. Accepts the list of tentative transactions, their input messages, and their acceptance criteria. Reruns each tentative transaction in the order it committed on the mobile node. During this reprocessing, the base transaction reads and writes object master copies using a lazy-master execution model. The scope-rule assures that the base transaction only accesses data mastered by the originating mobile node and base nodes. So master copies of all data in the transaction's scope are available to the base transaction. If the base transaction fails its acceptance criteria, the base transaction is aborted and a diagnostic message is returned to the mobile node. If the acceptance criteria requires the base and tentative transaction have identical outputs, then subsequent transactions reading tentative results written by T will fail too. On the other hand, weaker acceptance criteria are possible.
4. After the base node commits a base transaction, it propagates the lazy replica updates as transactions sent to all the other replica nodes. This is standard lazy-master.
5. When all the tentative transactions have been reprocessed as base transactions, the mobile node's state is converged with the base state.

The key properties of the two-tier replication scheme are:

1. Mobile nodes may make tentative database updates.
2. Base transactions execute with single-copy serializability so the master base system state is the result of a serializable execution.
3. A transaction becomes durable when the base transaction completes.
4. Replicas at all connected nodes converge to the base system state.
5. If all transactions commute, there are no reconciliations.

This comes close to meeting the four goals outlined at the start of this section.

When executing a base transaction, the two-tier scheme is a lazy-master scheme. If a base transaction deadlocks, it is resubmitted and reprocessed until it succeeds, much as the replica update transactions are resubmitted in case of deadlock.

The reconciliation rate for base transactions will be zero, if all the transactions commute. The reconciliation rate is driven by the rate at which the base transactions fail their acceptance criteria.

Processing the base transaction may produce results different from the tentative results. This is acceptable for some applications. It is fine if the checking account balance is different when the transaction is reprocessed. Other transactions from other nodes may have affected the account while the mobile node was disconnected. But, there are cases where the changes may not be acceptable. If the price of an item has increased by a large amount, if the item is out of stock, or if aisle seats are no longer available, then the salesman's price or delivery quote must be reconciled with the customer.

These acceptance criteria are application specific. The replication system can do no more than detect that there is a difference between the tentative and base transaction. This is probably too pessimistic a test. So, the replication system will simply run the tentative transaction. If the tentative transaction completes successfully and passes the acceptance test, then the replication system assumes all is well and propagates the replica updates as usual.

Users are aware that all updates are tentative until the transaction becomes a base transaction. If the base transaction fails, the user may have to revise and resubmit a transaction. The programmer must design the transactions to be commutative and to have acceptance criteria to detect whether the tentative transaction agrees with the base transaction effects.

2.6. CLUSTERING FOR MOBILE WIRELESS NETWORKS

Wireless communications is enjoying is fastest growth period in history, due to enabling technologies which permit widespread deployment. Historically, growth in the mobile communication field has come slowly, and has been coupled closely to technological improvements. The rapid worldwide growth in cellular telephone subscribers has demonstrated conclusively that wireless communication is a robust, viable voice and data transport mechanism. The widespread success of cellular has led to the development of newer wireless systems and standards for many other types of telecommunications traffic besides mobile voice telephone calls. For example, next generation cellular networks are being designed to facilitate high-speed data communications traffic in addition to voice calls. New standards and technologies are being implemented to allow wireless networks to replace fiber optic or copper lines between fixed points several kilometers apart (fixed wireless access). Similarly, wireless networks have been increasingly used as a replacement for wires within homes, buildings, and office settings through the deployment of Wireless Local Area Networks (WLANs).

Personal Communication Network (PCN) is an emerging wireless network that promises many new services. With the availability of interface cards, mobile users are no longer required to be confined within a static network premise to get network access. Mobile users may move from one place to another and yet maintain transparent network access through wireless links. Information exchanged between users, may be bi-directional, which includes but not limited to voice, data, and image, irrespective of location and time while permitting users to be mobile. PCN and mobile computing require a wireless network infrastructure which is fast deployable, possibly multihop, and capable of multimedia service support. The *first* infrastructure of this type was the *Packet Radio Network (PRNET)*, developed in the 70's to address the battlefield and disaster recovery communication requirements. PRNET was totally asynchronous and was based on a completely distributed architecture. It handled datagram traffic reasonably well, but did not offer efficient multimedia support.

Recently, under the WAMIS (Wireless Adaptive Mobile Information Systems) and Glomo ARPA programs several mobile, multimedia, multihop (*M*3) wireless network architectures have been developed, which require some form of synchronous, time division infrastructure. The synchronous time frame leads to efficient multimedia support implementations. However, it introduces more complexity and is less robust in the face of mobility and channel fading. Clearly there are complexity vs performance tradeoffs in introducing various degrees of synchronization into the network, from the completely asynchronous PRNET to the tightly synchronized cluster TDMA solution.

2.6.1. Basic Concepts of Single-hop and Multi-hop

In general, one can distinguish between single-hop and multi-hop underlying infrastructures. In *single hop* infrastructures, each mobile device communicates with a stationary host, which corresponds to its point of attachment to the network. The rest of the routing is the responsibility of a stationary infrastructure, e.g., the Internet. On the other hand, in *multi-hop* wireless communication, an ad-hoc wireless network is formed in which, wireless hosts participate in routing messages among each other. In both infrastructures, the hosts between the source (or sources) that holds the data and the requester of data (or data sink) form a dissemination tree. The hosts (mobile or stationary) that form the dissemination tree may store data and take part in the computation towards achieving *in network* processing (e.g., aggregation). Locally caching or replicating data at the wireless host or at the intermediate nodes of the dissemination tree are important for improving system performance and availability.

Multihopping is the ability of the radios to relay packets from one to another without the use of base stations. Most of the nomadic computing applications today are based on a single hop radio connection to the wired network (Internet or ATM).

Fig. 2.10 shows the cellular model commonly used in the wireless networks. A, B, C, and *D* are fixed base stations connected by a wired backbone. Nodes 1 through 8 are mobile nodes. A mobile node is only one hop away from a base station. Communications between two mobile nodes must be through fixed base stations and the wired backbone.

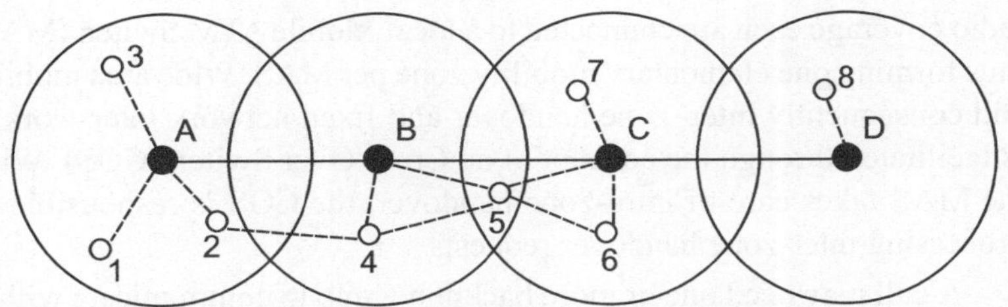

Fig. 2.10: Conventional Cellular Networks (Single-hop)

Brijesh Kr. Gupta et al, 2006 proposed a Hybrid Scheme for ATM – Based Personal Communication Network, in which authors extended fixed guard channel method to the nodes in the ATM based backbone network for link bandwidth allocation to enable prioritized handover admission control. To make easy understanding the role of ATM as a backbone description is given in the following sections:

2.6.1.1. Backbone Handover

The physical network underlying the assumed connection architecture is shown in Fig. 2.11. The Radio Access Points (RAP) providing the physical

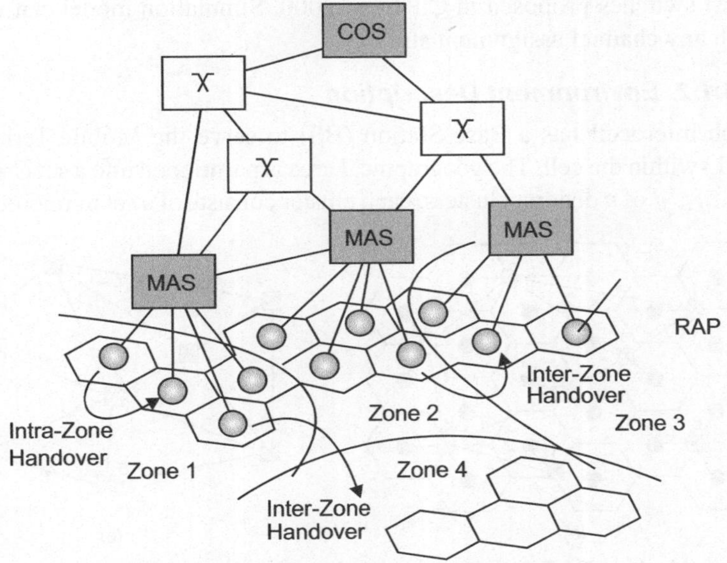

Fig. 2.11: Handover requires Backbone Link

radio coverage each are connected to a local Mobile ATM Switch (MAS), thus forming one elementary mobility zone per MAS. Wide area mobility and consequently inter–zone handover and fixed network inter-working is facilitated through the concept of an Cross Over Switch (COS). While the MAS takes care of intra-zone handover, the COS is responsible for processing inter-zone handover requests.

A call may need one or more backbone link, to communicate with its destination. The number of links depends on the network topology and the destination of the call. The cost of a call is associated with the number of links, so efforts are made to optimize the number of links to the minimum. A partition methodology is proposed, in which the set of cells are divided into subsets so that the base stations of the cells belonging to the same subset are connected to the same ATM switch. The optimum partition, which gives the minimum number of handover requires a change in the ATM switch. This methodology is based on handover rate between cells, which allows the choice of the best partition by taking mobility, radio, and fixed network aspect into account.

In the simulation model, multiple cells are connected by MAS. The cells are connected by fixed backbone network. PCN architecture based ATM switches proposed in C.P.Low, 2000. Simulation model can work with any channel assignment strategy.

2.6.1.2. Environment Description

Each microcell has a Base Station (BS) to serve the Mobile Terminal (MT) within the cell. The geographical area is partitioned into a set $C=\{C_1, C_2, ..., C_n\}$ of n disjoint clusters, each cluster consists of a set of microcells.

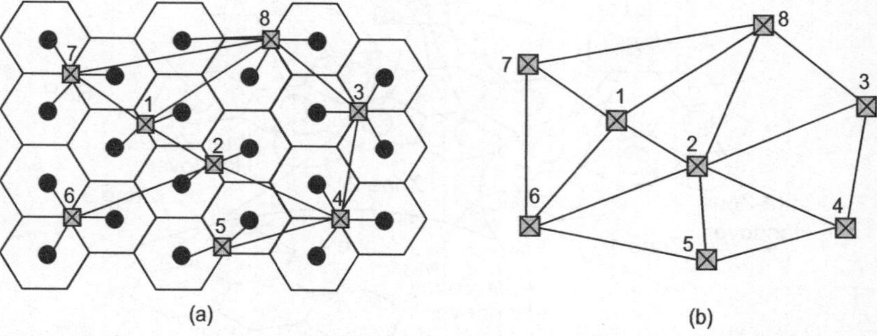

Fig. 2.12: An ATM Based Cellular Network (a) An ATM Based Architecture (b) Corresponding H Graph of the PCN Architecture

An ATM switch is allocated within each cluster and each BS in this cluster is connected to one of the ports of this switch. The ATM switch offers the services of establishing / releasing channels for the MTs in the cluster, also this switch should have routing/rerouting capabilities. Two neighboring clusters can be interconnected via the associated ATM switches. The links between ATM switches are called backbone links, and the links between ATM switch and BS are called local links.

An ATM-based topology could be represented by an undirected graph $H = (V,F)$; where each vertex v_i in V stand for a cluster C_i (or an ATM switch) and an edge $e_{i,j}$ is in F if clusters C_i and C_i are adjacent in the given network. Fig. 2.12 shows an ATM based PCN topology, which consist of 21 cells, attached to 8 ATM switches, which connected by 9 backbone links. Corresponding H graph of Fig. 2.12 (a) is shown in Fig. 2.12(b).

Constructing a backbone network between MASs could be done in different ways. Depending on the geographical area, the cost of the backbone link, and traffic patterns. Figs 2.13 (a) and 2.13(b) show different possible backbone network for Fig. 2.12 (b).

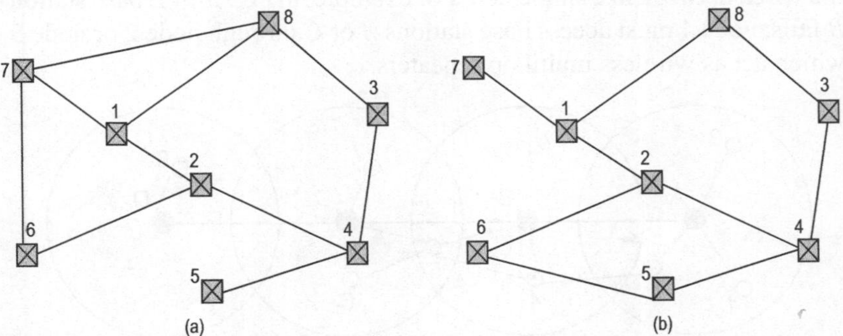

Fig. 2.13: (a) & (b) Different Possible Backbone Network Connections

MT engaged in a call or data transfer within the same cluster will consume two local links, one for each local link between base station and the associated switch. For intercluster communication, backbone links will be allocated in addition to local links. The channel occupied will depend on the communication path being assigned.

Multihopping

In parallel with (and separately from) the single hop cellular model, another type of model, based on radio to radio packet ***multihopping,*** has been emerging to serve a growing number of applications which rely on a fast deployable, wireless infrastructure. The classic examples are battlefield communications and (in the civilian sector) disaster recovery (fire, earthquake) and search and rescue. A recent addition to this set is the "ad hoc" personal communications network, which could be rapidly deployed on a campus, for example, to support collaborative computing and access to the Internet during special events (concerts, festivals etc). Multihopping through wireless repeaters strategically located on campus permits to reduce battery power and to increase network capacity. More precisely, by carefully limiting the power of radios, we conserve battery power. Furthermore, we also cause less interference to other transmissions further away; this gives the additional benefit of "spatial reuse" of channel spectrum, thus increasing the capacity of the system.

Interestingly, the multihop requirement may also arise in cellular networks. If a base station fails, a mobile node may not be able to access the wired network in a single hop. For example, in Fig. 2.14 if base station *B* fails, node 4 must access base stations *A* or *C* through node 2 or node 5 which act as wireless multihop repeaters.

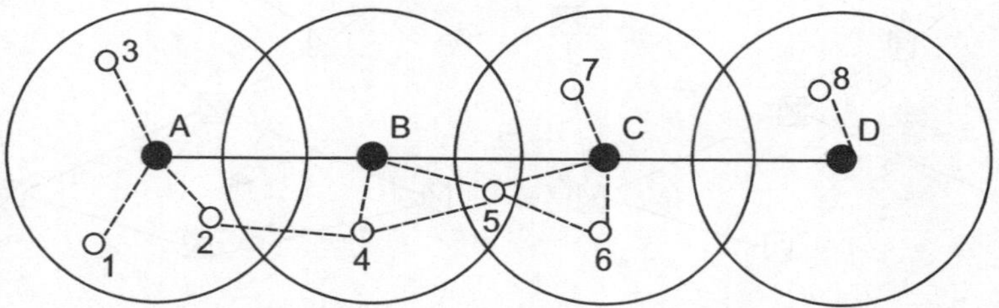

Fig. 2.14: A Multihop situation occurs when Base Station B fails

2.6.2. Multicluster Architecture

A major challenge in multihop, multimedia networks is the ability to account for resources so that bandwidth reservations (in a deterministic or statistical sense) can be placed on them. It is observed that in cellular (single hop) networks such accountability is made easy by the fact that all stations learn of each other's requirements, either directly, or through a control station (e.g. base station in cellular systems). This advantage can be extended to multihop networks by creating clusters of radios, in such a way that access can be controlled and bandwidth can be allocated in each cluster. The notion of cluster has been used also in earlier Packet Radio nets, but mainly for hierarchical routing rather than for resource allocation.

Most hierarchical clustering architectures for mobile radio networks are based on the concept of *clusterhead*. The clusterhead acts as a local coordinator of transmissions within the cluster. It differs from the base station concept in current cellular systems, in that it does not have special hardware and in fact is dynamically selected among the set of stations. However, it does extra work with respect to ordinary stations, and therefore it may become the bottleneck of the cluster.

2.7. THE CODA FILE SYSTEM

Coda (Constant Data Availability) has been developed at Carnegie Mellon University (CMU) in the 1990s, and is now integrated with a number of popular UNIX-based operating systems such as Linux. Coda was designed to be a scalable, secure, and highly available distributed file system.

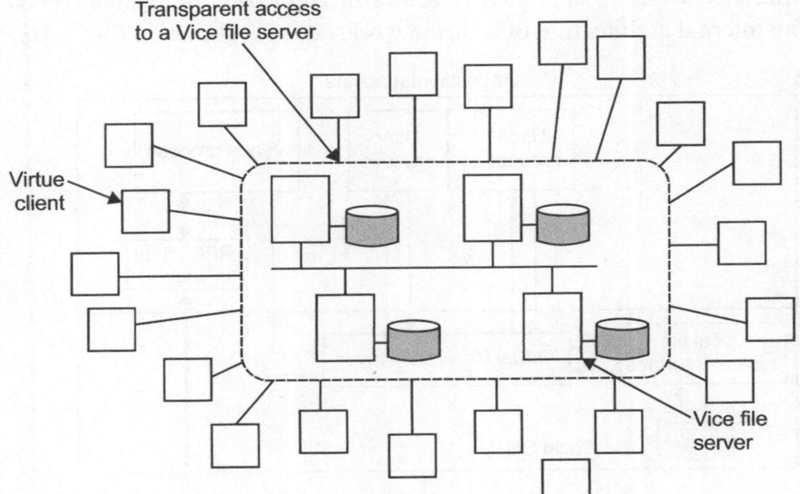

Fig. 2.15: The Overall Organization of AFS

An important goal was to achieve a high degree of naming and location transparency so that the system would appear to its users very similar to a pure local file system. By also taking high availability into account, the designers of Coda have also tried to reach a high degree of failure transparency. Coda is a descendant of version 2 of the ***Andrew File System (AFS),*** which was also developed at CMU, and inherits many of its architectural features from AFS. AFS was designed to support the entire CMU community, which implied that approximately 10,000 workstations would need to have access to the system. To meet this requirement, **AFS** nodes are partitioned into two groups. One group consists of a relatively small number of dedicated ***Vice*** file servers, which are centrally administered. The other group consists of a very much larger collection of ***Virtue*** workstations that give users and processes access to the file system, as shown in Fig. 2.15.

Coda follows the same organization as AFS. Every Virtue workstation hosts a user-level process called ***Venus,*** whose role is similar to that of an NFS client. A Venus process is responsible for providing access to the files that are maintained by the Vice file servers. In Coda, Venus is also responsible for allowing the client to continue operation even if access to the file servers is (temporarily) impossible. This additional role is a major difference with the approach followed in ***Network File System(NFS).*** The internal architecture of a Virtue workstation is shown in Fig. 2.16.

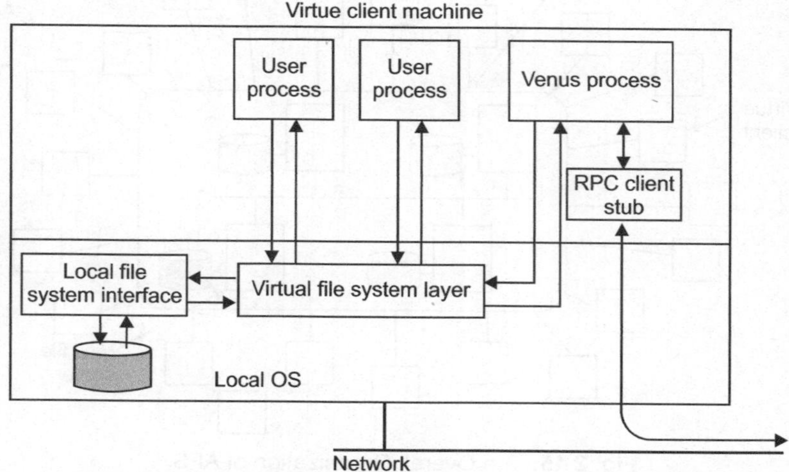

Fig. 2.16: The Internal Organization of a Virtue Workstation

The important issue is that Venus runs as a user-level process. Again, there is a separate Virtual File System (VFS) layer that intercepts all calls from client applications, and forwards these calls either to the local file system or to Venus, as shown in Fig. 2.16. This organization with VFS is the same as in NFS. Venus, in turn, communicates with Vice file servers using a user-level RPC system. The RPC system is constructed on top of UDP datagrams and provides at-most-once semantics. There are three different server-side processes. The great majority of the work is done by the actual Vice file servers, which are responsible for maintaining a local collection of files. Like Venus, a file server runs as a user-level process. In addition, trusted Vice machines are allowed to run an authentication server, which we discuss in detail later. Finally, update processes are used to keep meta information on the file system consistent at each Vice server.

Unlike NFS, Coda provides a globally shared name space that is maintained by the Vice servers. Clients have access to this name space by means of a special subdirectory in their local name space, such as */afs*. Whenever a client looks up a name in this subdirectory, Venus ensures that the appropriate part of the shared name space is mounted locally.

2.7.1. Communication

Interposes communication in Coda is performed using RPCs. However, the **RPC2** system for Coda is much more sophisticated than traditional RPC systems such as ONC RPC, which is used by NFS. RPC2 offers reliable RPCs on top of the (unreliable) UDP protocol. Each time a remote procedure is called, the RPC2 client code starts a new thread that sends an invocation request to the server and subsequently blocks until it receives an answer. As request processing may take an arbitrary time to complete, the server regularly sends back messages to the client to let it know it is still working on the request. If the server dies, sooner or later this thread will notice that the messages have ceased and report back failure to the calling application. An interesting aspect of RPC2 is its support for side effects. A **side effect** is a mechanism by which the client and server can communicate using an application-specific protocol. Consider, for example, a client opening a file at a video server. What is needed in this case is that the client and server set up a continuous data stream with an isochronous transmission mode. In other words, data transfer from the server to the client is guaranteed to be within a minimum and maximum end-to-end delay.

RPC2 allows the client and the server to set up a separate connection for transferring the video data to the client on time. Connection setup is done as a side effect of an RPC call to the server. For this purpose, the RPC2 runtime system provides an interface of side-effect routines that is to be implemented by the application developer. For example, there are routines for setting up a connection and routines for transferring data. These routines are automatically called by the RPC2 runtime system at the client and server, respectively, but their implementation is otherwise completely independent of RPC2. This principle of side effects is shown in Fig. 2.17.

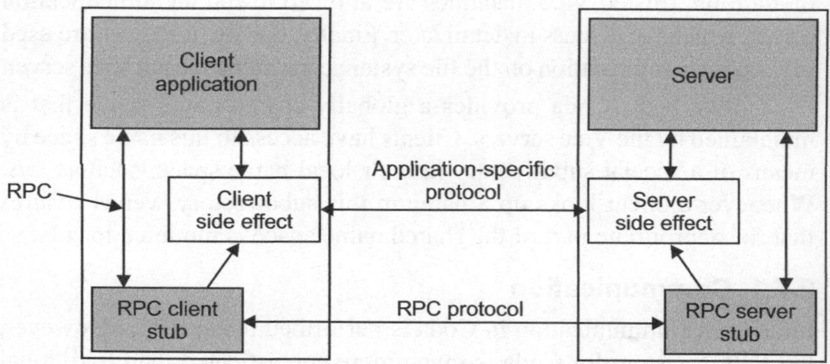

Fig. 2.17: Side Effects in Coda's RPC2 System

Another feature of RPC2 that makes it different from other RPC systems, is its support for multicasting. As we explain in detail below, an important design issue in Coda is that servers keep track of which clients have a local copy of a file. When a file is modified, a server invalidates local copies by notifying the appropriate clients through an RPC. Clearly, if a server can notify only one client at a time, invalidating all clients may take some time, as illustrated in Fig. 2.18(a).

The problem is caused by the fact that an RPC may fail. Invalidating files in a strict sequential order may be delayed considerably because the server cannot reach a possibly crashed client, but will give up on that client only after a relatively long expiration time. Meanwhile, other clients will still be reading from their local copies.

A better solution is shown in Fig. 2.18(b). Instead of invalidating each copy one-by-one, the server sends an invalidation message to all

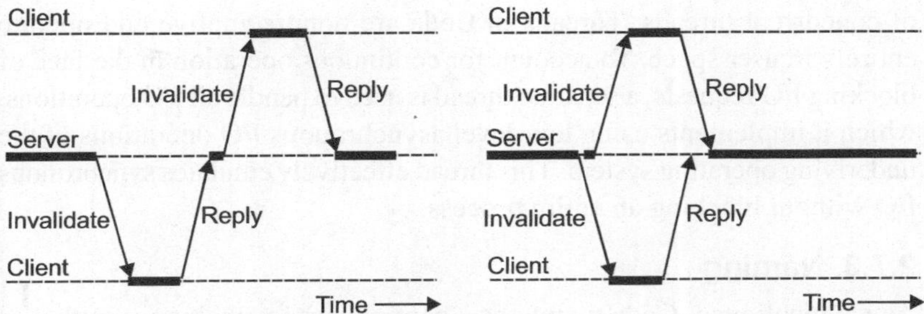

Fig. 2.18: (a) Sending an Invalidation Message one at a Time (b) Sending Invalidation Messages in Parallel.

clients in parallel. As a consequence, all nonfailing clients are notified in the same time as it would take to do an immediate RPC. Also, the server notices within the usual expiration time that certain clients are failing to respond to the RPC, and can declare such clients as being crashed.

Parallel RPCs are implemented by means of the ***MultiRPC*** system which is part of the RPC2 package. An important aspect of MultiRPC is that the parallel invocation of RPCs is fully transparent to the callee. In other words, the receiver of a MultiRPC call cannot distinguish that call from a normal RPC. At the caller's side, parallel execution is also largely transparent. For example, the semantics of MultiRPC in the presence of failures are much the same as that of a normal RPC. Likewise, the side-effect mechanisms can be used in the same way as before. MultiRPC is implemented by essentially executing multiple RPCs in parallel. This means that the caller explicitly sends an RPC request to each recipient. However, instead of immediately waiting for a response, it defers blocking until all requests have been sent. In other words, the caller invokes a number of one-way RPCs, after which it blocks until all responses have been received from the nonfailing recipients. An alternative approach to parallel execution of RPCs in MultiRPC is provided by setting up a multicast group, and sending an RPC to all group members using IP multicast.

2.7.2. Processes

Coda maintains a clear distinction between client and server processes. Clients are represented by Venus processes; servers appear as Vice processes. Both type of processes are internally organized as a collection of concurrent threads. Threads in Coda are nonpreemptive and operate entirely in user space. To account for continuous operation in the face of blocking I/O requests, a separate thread is used to handle all I/O operations, which it implements using low-level asynchronous I/O operations of the underlying operating system. This thread effectively emulates synchronous I/O without blocking an entire process.

2.7.3. Naming

As we mentioned, Coda maintains a naming system analogous to that of UNIX. Files are grouped into units referred to as ***volumes***. A volume is similar to a UNIX disk partition (i.e., an actual file system), but generally has a much smaller granularity. It corresponds to a partial subtree in the shared name space as maintained by the Vice servers. Usually a volume corresponds to a collection of files associated with a user. Examples of volumes include collections of shared binary or source files, and so on. Like disk partitions, volumes can be mounted. Volumes are important for two reasons. First, they form the basic unit by which the entire name space is constructed. This construction takes place by mounting volumes at mount points. A mount point in Coda is a leaf node of a volume that refers to the root node of another volume. The second reason why volumes are important, is that they form the unit for server-side replication. We return to this aspect of volumes below.

Considering the granularity of volumes, it can be expected that a name lookup will cross several mount points. In other words, a path name will often contain several mount points. To support a high degree of naming transparency, a Vice file server returns mounting information to a Venus process during name lookup.

This information will allow Venus to automatically mount a volume into the client's name space when necessary. This mechanism is similar to crossing mount points as supported in NFS version 4. It is important to note that when a volume from the shared name space is mounted in the client's name space, Venus follows the structure of the shared name space. To explain, assume that each client has access to the shared name space by means of a subdirectory called */afs*. When mounting a volume, each Venus process ensures that the naming graph rooted at */afs* is always a subgraph of the complete name space jointly maintained by the Vice servers, as shown in Fig. 2.19. In doing so, clients are guaranteed that shared files indeed have the same name, although name resolution is based on a locally-implemented name space. Note that this approach is fundamentally different from that of NFS.

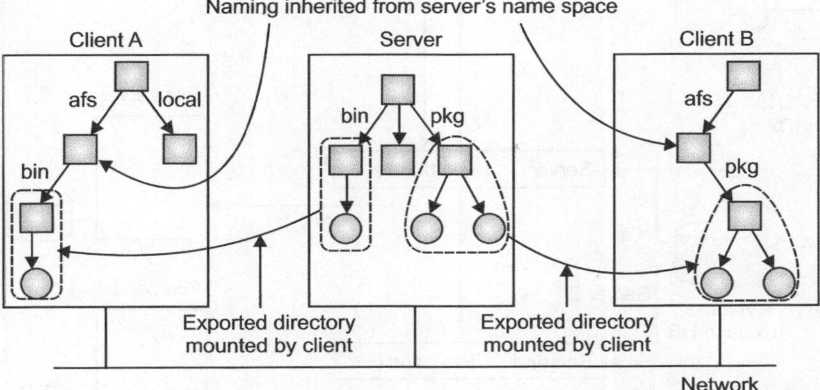

Fig. 2.19: Clients in Coda have access to a Single Shared Name Space

File Identifiers

Considering that the collection of shared files may be replicated and distributed across multiple Vice servers, it becomes important to uniquely identify each file in such a way that it can be tracked to its physical location, while at the same time maintaining replication and location transparency. Each file in Coda is contained in exactly one volume. As we mentioned above, a volume may be replicated across several servers. For this reason, Coda makes a distinction between logical and physical volumes. A logical volume represents a possibly replicated physical volume, and has an associated ***Replicated Volume Identifier (RVID).*** An RVID is a location and replication independent volume identifier. Multiple replicas may be associated with the same RVID. Each physical volume has its own ***Volume Identifier (VID),*** which identifies a specific replica in a location independent way. The approach followed in Coda is to assign each file a 96-bit file identifier. A file identifier consists of two parts as shown in Fig. 2.20.

The first part is the 32-bit RVID of the logical volume that the file is part of. To locate a file, a client first passes the RVID of a file identifier to a **Volume Replication Database**, which returns the list of VIDs associated with that RVID. Given a VID, a client can then look up the server that is

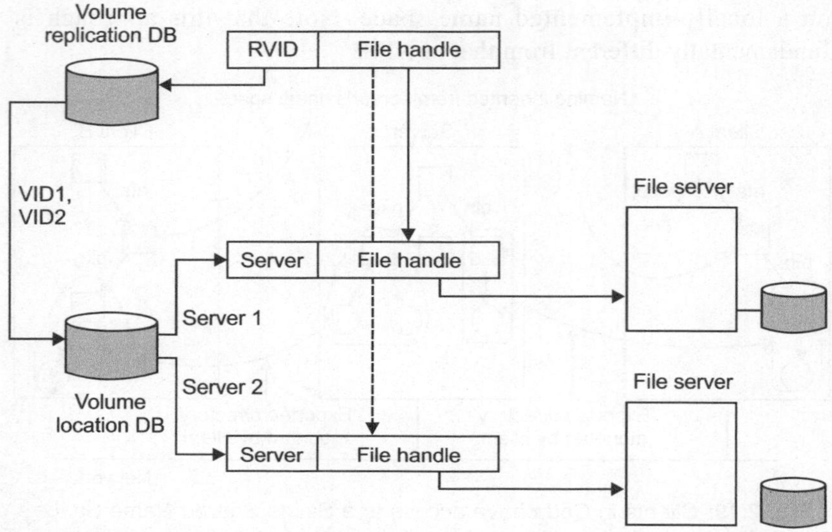

Fig. 2.20: The Implementation and Resolution of a Coda File Identifier

currently hosting the particular replica of the logical volume. This lookup is done by passing the VID to a **Volume Location Database** which returns the current location of that specific physical volume. The second part of a file identifier consists of a 64-bit file handle that uniquely identifies the file within a volume. In reality, it corresponds to the identification of an index node as represented within VFS. Such a **vnode** as it is called, is similar to the notion of an inode in UNIX systems.

2.7.4. Synchronization

Many distributed file systems, including Coda's ancestor, AFS, do not provide UNIX file-sharing semantics but instead support the weaker session semantics. Given its goal to achieve high availability, Coda takes a different approach and makes an attempt to support transactional semantics, albeit a weaker form than normally supported by transactions. The problem that Coda wants to solve is that in a large distributed file system it may easily happen that some or all of the file servers are temporarily unavailable. Such unavailability can be caused by a network or server failure, but may also be the result of a mobile client deliberately disconnecting from the file service. Provided that the disconnected client has all the relevant files cached locally, it should be possible to use these files while disconnected and reconcile later when the connection is established again.

Sharing Files in Coda

To accommodate file sharing, Coda uses a special allocation scheme that bears some similarities to share reservations in NFS. To understand how the scheme works, the following is important. When a client successfully opens a file *f*, an entire copy of *f* is transferred to the client's machine. The server records that the client has a copy of *f*. So far, this approach is similar to open delegation in NFS.

Now suppose client *A* has opened file *f* for writing. When another client *B* wants to open *f* as well, it will fail. This failure is caused by the fact that the server has recorded that client *A* might have already modified *f*. On the other hand, had client *A* opened *f* for reading, an attempt by client *B* to get a copy from the server for reading would succeed. An attempt by *B* to open for writing would succeed as well.

Now consider what happens when several copies of *f* have been stored locally at various clients. Given what we have just said, only one client will be able to modify *f*. If this client modifies *f* and subsequently closes the file, the file will be transferred back to the server. However, each other client may proceed to read its local copy despite the fact that the copy is actually outdated. The reason for this apparently inconsistent behavior, is that a session is treated as a transaction in Coda. Consider Fig. 2.21, which shows the time line for two processes, *A* and *B*. Assume

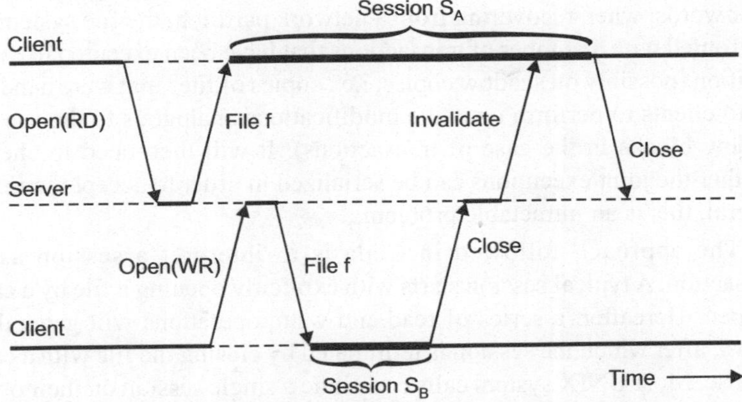

Fig. 2.21: The Transactional behavior in Sharing Files in Coda

A has opened *f* for reading, leading to session *SA*. Client *B* has opened *f* for writing, shown as session *SB*. When *B* closes session *SB*, it transfers the updated version of *f* to the server, which will then send an invalidation message to *A*. *A* will now know that it is reading from an older version of *f*. However, from a transactional point of view, this really does not matter because session *SA* could be considered to have been scheduled before session *SB*.

Transactional Semantics

In Coda, the notion of a network partition plays a crucial role in defining transactional semantics. A **partition** is a part of the network that is isolated from the rest and which consists of a collection of clients or servers, or both. The basic idea is that series of file operations should continue to execute in the presence of conflicting operations across different partitions. Recall that two operations are said to conflict if they both operate on the same data, and at least one is a write operation. Let us first examine how conflicts may occur in the presence of network partitions. Assume that two processes *A* and *B* hold identical replicas of various shared data items just before they are separated as the result of a partitioning in the network. Ideally, a file system supporting transactional semantics would implement **one-copy serializability**, which is the same as saying that the execution of operations by *A* and *B*, respectively, is equivalent to a joint serial execution of those operations on nonreplicated data items shared by the two processes. The main problem in the face of partitions is to *recognize* serializable executions after they have taken place within a partition. In other words, when recovering from a network partition, the file system is confronted with a number of transactions that have been executed in each partition (possibly on shadow copies, i.e., copies of files that were handed out to clients to perform tentative modifications analogous to the use of shadow blocks in the case of transactions). It will then need to check whether the joint executions can be serialized in order to accept them. In general, this is an intractable problem.

The approach followed in Coda is to interpret a session as a transaction. A typical session starts with explicitly opening a file by a call to open. Hereafter, a series of read and write operations will generally follow, after which the session is terminated by closing the file with a call to close. Most UNIX system calls constitute a single session on their own and are also considered by Coda to be independent transactions. Coda recognizes different types of sessions. For example, each UNIX system call is associated with a different session type. More complex session types are the ones that start with a call to open. The type of a session is automatically deduced from the system calls made by an application. An important advantage of this approach is that applications that use the standardized VFS interface need not be modified. For each session type, it is known in advance which data will be read or modified.

As an example, consider the **store** session type, which starts with opening a file *f* for writing on behalf of a specific user *u*, as explained above. Fig. 2.22 lists the meta-data associated with *f* and user *u* that are affected by this session type, and whether they are only read or also modified. For example, it will be necessary to read the access rights that user *u* has with respect to file *f*. By explicitly identifying the metadata that are read and modified for a specific session, it becomes much easier to recognize conflicting operations.

File-associated data	Read?	Modified?
File identifier	Yes	No
Access rights	Yes	No
Last modification time	Yes	Yes
File length	Yes	Yes
File contents	Yes	Yes

Fig. 2.22: The metadata read and modified for a store session type in Coda.

From this point on, session processing is fairly straightforward. Let us start by considering a series of concurrent sessions that take place within a single network partition. To simplify matters, assume that there is a single server contained in the partition. When a client starts a session, the Venus process on the client machine fetches all data contained in the session's read set and write set from the server, provided that the rules for file sharing as explained above are not violated. In doing so, it effectively acquires the necessary read and write locks for those data. There are two important observations to make at this point. First, because Coda can automatically infer the type of a session from the (first) system call made by an application, and knows the metadata that are read and modified for each session type, a Venus process knows which data to fetch from a server at the start of a session. As a consequence, it can acquire the necessary locks at the start of a session. The second observation is that because file sharing semantics are effectively the same as acquiring the necessary locks in advance, the approach followed in this case is the same as applying a two-phase locking (2PL) technique. An important property of 2PL, is that all resulting schedules of read and write operations of concurrent sessions are serializable.

Now consider processing sessions in the face of partitions. The main problem that needs to be solved is that conflicts across partitions need to be resolved. For this purpose, Coda uses a simple versioning scheme. Each file has an associated version number that indicates how many updates have taken place since the file was created. As before, when a client starts a session, all the data relevant to that session are copied to the client's machine, including the version number associated with each data element.

Assume that while one or more sessions are being executed at the client, a network partition occurs by which the client and server are disconnected. At that point, Venus will allow the client to continue and finish the execution of its sessions as if nothing happened, subject to the transactional semantics for the single partition case described above. Later, when the connection with the server is established again, updates are transferred to the server in the same order as they took place at the client.

When an update for file *f* is transferred to the server, it is tentatively accepted if no other process has updated *f* while the client and server were disconnected. Such a conflict can be easily detected by comparing version numbers. Let *Vclient* be the version number of *f* acquired from the server when the file was transferred to the client. Let *Nupdates* be the number of updates in that session that have been transferred and accepted by the server after reintegration. Finally, let *Vnow* denote the current version number of *f* at the server. Then, a next update for *f* from the client's session can be accepted if and only if :

$$Vnow + 1 = Vclient + Nupdates$$

In other words, an update from a client is accepted only when that update would lead to the *next* version of file *f*. In practice, this means that only a single client will eventually win having the effect that the conflict is resolved. Conflicts arise if *f* is being updated in concurrently executed sessions. When a conflict occurs, the updates from the client's session are undone, and the client is, in principle, forced to save its local version of *f* for manual reconciliation. In terms of transactions, the session cannot be committed and conflict resolution is left to the user.

2.7.5. Caching and Replication

Caching and replication play an important role in Coda. In fact, these two approaches are fundamental for achieving the goal of high availability as set out by the developers of Coda. In the following, we first take a look at client-side caching, which is crucial in the face of disconnected operation. We then take a look at server-side replication of volumes.

Client Caching

Client-side caching is crucial to the operation of Coda for two reasons. First, and in line with the approach followed in AFS, caching is done to achieve scalability. Second, caching provides a higher degree of fault tolerance as the client becomes less dependent on the availability of the server. For these two reasons, clients in Coda always cache entire files. In other words, when a file is opened for either reading or writing, an entire copy of the file is transferred to the client, where it is subsequently cached. Unlike many other distributed file systems, cache coherence in Coda is maintained by means of callbacks. For each file, the server from which a client had fetched the file keeps track of which clients have a copy of that file cached locally. A server is said to record a **callback promise** for a client. When a client updates its local copy of the file for the first time, it notifies the server, which, in turn, sends an invalidation message to the other clients. Such an invalidation message is called a **callback break,** because the server will then discard the callback promise it held for the client it just sent an invalidation. The interesting aspect of this scheme is that as long as a client knows it has an outstanding callback promise at the server, it can safely access the file locally. In particular, suppose a client opens a file and finds it is still in its cache. It can then use that file provided the server still has a callback promise on the file for that client. The client will have to check with the server if that promise still holds. If so, there is no need to transfer the file from the server to the client again.

This approach is illustrated in Fig. 2.23, which is an extension of Fig. 2.21. When client *A* starts session S_A, the server records a callback promise. The same happens when *B* starts session S_B. However, when *B* closes S_B, the server breaks its promise to callback client *A* by sending *A* a callback break. Note that due to the transactional semantics of Coda,

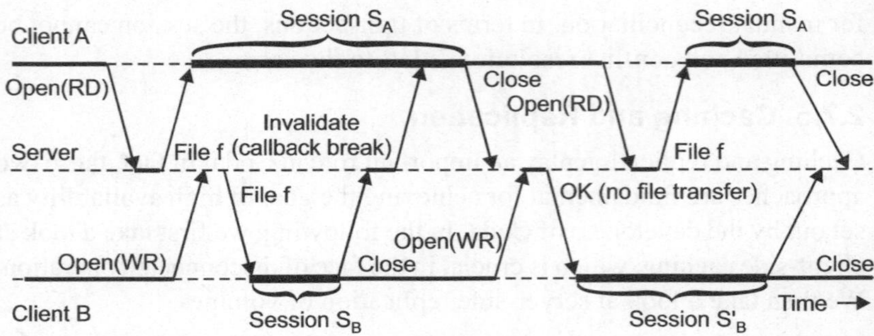

Fig. 2.23: The use of local copies when opening a session in Coda

when client *A* closes session S_A, nothing special happens; the closing is simply accepted as one would expect.

The consequence is that when *A* later wants to open session S'_A , it will find its local copy of *f* to be invalid, so that it will have to fetch the latest version from the server. On the other hand, when *B* opens session S'_B , it will notice that the server still has an outstanding callback promise implying that *B* can simply re-use the local copy it still has from session *SB*.

Server Replication

Coda allows file servers to be replicated. As we mentioned, the unit of replication is a volume. The collection of servers that have a copy of a volume, are known as that volume's **Volume Storage Group**, or simply **VSG**. In the presence of failures, a client may not have access to all servers in a volume's VSG. A client's **Accessible Volume Storage Group (AVSG)** for a volume consists of those servers in that volume's VSG that the client can contact. If the AVSG is empty, the client is said to be **disconnected**.

Coda uses a replicated-write protocol to maintain consistency of a replicated volume. In particular, it uses a variant of Read-One, Write-All (ROWA). When a client needs to read a file, it contacts one of the members in its AVSG of the volume to which that file belongs. However, when closing a session on an updated file, the client transfers it in parallel to each member in the AVSG. This scheme works fine as long as there are no failures, that is, for each client, that client's AVSG of a volume is the same as its VSG. However, in the presence of failures, things may go wrong. Consider a volume that is replicated across three servers *S*1, *S*2, and *S*3. For client *A*, assume its AVSG covers servers *S*1 and *S*2 whereas client *B* has access only to server *S*3, as shown in Fig. 2.24.

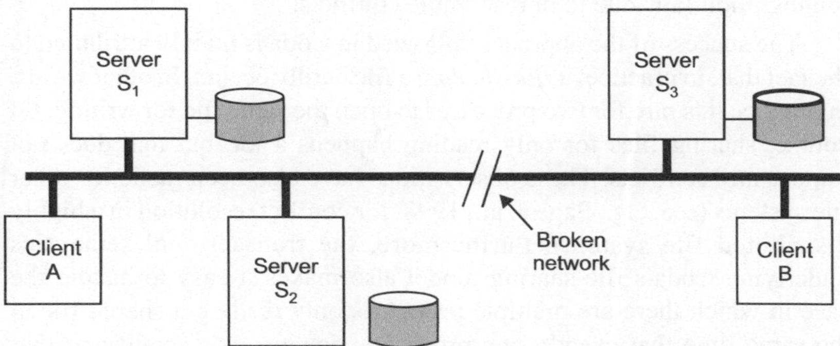

Fig. 2.24: Two clients with a different AVSG for the same replicated file.

Coda uses an optimistic strategy for file replication. In particular, both *A* and *B* will be allowed to open a file, *f*, for writing, update their respective copies, and transfer their copy back to the members in their AVSG. Obviously, there will be different versions of *f* stored in the VSG.

2.7.6. Fault Tolerance

Coda has been designed for high availability, which is mainly reflected by its sophisticated support for client-side caching and its support for server replication. An interesting aspect of Coda that needs further explanation is how a client can continue to operate while being disconnected, even if disconnection lasts for hours or days.

2.7.7. Disconnected Operation

As we mentioned above, a client is said to be disconnected with respect to a volume, if its AVSG for that volume is empty. In other words, the client cannot contact any of the servers holding a copy of the volume. In most file systems (e.g., NFS), a client is not allowed to proceed unless it can contact at least one server. A different approach is followed in Coda. There, a client will simply resort to using its local copy of the file that it had when it opened the file at a server. Closing a file (or actually, the session in which the file is accessed) when disconnected will always succeed. However, it may be possible that conflicts are detected when modifications are transferred to a server when connection is established again. In case automatic conflict resolution fails, manual intervention will be necessary. Practical experience with Coda has shown that disconnected operation generally works, although there are occasions in which reintegration fails due to unresolvable conflicts.

The success of the approach followed in Coda is mainly attributed to the fact that, in practice, *write-sharing* a file hardly occurs. In other words, in practice it is rare for two processes to open the same file for writing. Of course, sharing files for only reading happens a lot, but that does not impose any conflicts. These observations have also been made for other file systems (see, e.g., Page et al., 1998, for conflict resolution in a highly distributed file system). Furthermore, the transactional semantics underlying Coda's file-sharing model also makes it easy to handle the case in which there are multiple processes only reading a shared file at the same time that exactly one process is concurrently modifying that file. The main problem that needs to be solved to make disconnected operation a success, is to ensure that a client's cache contains those files that will be accessed during disconnection. If a simple caching strategy is followed, it may turn out that a client cannot continue as it lacks the necessary files. Filling the cache in advance with the appropriate files is called **hoarding**. The overall behavior of a client with respect to a volume (and thus the files in that volume) can now be summarized by the state-transition diagram shown in Fig. 2.25.

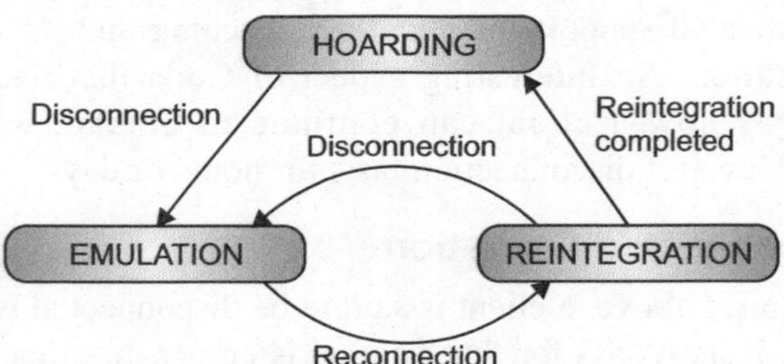

Fig. 2.25: The State-Transition Diagram of a Coda Client with respect to a Volume

Normally, a client will be in the *HOARDING* state. In this state, the client is connected to (at least) one server that contains a copy of the volume. While in this state, the client can contact the server and issue file requests to perform its work. Simultaneously, it will also attempt to keep its cache filled with useful data (e.g., files, file attributes, and directories). At a certain point, the number of servers in the client's AVSG will drop to zero, bringing it into an *EMULATION* state in which the behavior of a server for the volume will have to be emulated on the client's machine. In practice, this means that all file requests will be directly serviced using the locally cached copy of the file. Note that while a client is in its *EMULATION* state, it may still be able to contact servers that manage other volumes. In such cases, disconnection will generally have been caused by a server failure rather than that the client has been disconnected from the network.

Finally, when reconnection occurs, the client enters the *REINTEGRATION* state in which it transfers updates to the server in order to make them permanent. It is during reintegration that conflicts are detected and, where possible, automatically resolved. As shown in Fig. 2.25, it is possible that during reintegration the connection with the server is lost again, bringing the client back into the *EMULATION* state.

Crucial to the success of continuous operation while disconnected is that the cache contains all the necessary data. Coda uses a sophisticated priority mechanism to ensure that useful data are indeed cached. First, a user can explicitly state which files or directories he finds important by storing pathnames in a **hoard database**. Coda maintains such a database per workstation. Combining the information in the hoard database with information on recent references to a file allows Coda to compute a current priority on each file, after which it fetches files in priority such that the following three conditions are met:

- There is no uncached file with a higher priority than any cached file.
- The cache is full, or no uncached file has nonzero priority.
- Each cached file is a copy of the one maintained in the client's AVSG.

If all three conditions are met, the cache is said to be in **equilibrium**. Because the current priority of a file may change over time, and because cached files may need to be removed from the cache to make room for other files, it is clear that cache equilibrium needs to be recomputed from time to time. Reorganizing the cache such that equilibrium is reached is done by an operation known as a **hoardwalk**, which is invoked once every 10 minutes.

The combination of the hoard database, priority function, and maintaining cache equilibrium has shown to be a vast improvement over traditional cache management techniques, which are generally based on counting and timing references. However, the technique cannot guarantee that a client's cache will always contain the data the user will need in the near future. Therefore, there are still occasions in which an operation in disconnected mode will fail due to inaccessible data.

Recoverable Virtual Memory

Besides providing high availability, the AFS and Coda developers have also looked at simple mechanisms that help in building fault-tolerant processes. A simple and effective mechanism that makes recovery much easier, is **Recoverable Virtual Memory (RVM)**. RVM is a user-level mechanism to maintain crucial data structures in main memory while being ensured that they can be easily recovered after a crash failure.

The basic idea underlying RVM is relatively simple: data that should survive crash failures are normally stored in a file that is explicitly mapped into memory when needed. Operations on that data are logged, similar to the use of a writeahead log in the case of transactions. In fact, the model supported by RVM is close to that of flat transactions, except that no support is provided for concurrency control.

Once a file has been mapped into main memory, an application can perform operations on that data that are part of a transaction. RVM is unaware of data structures. Therefore, the data in a transaction is explicitly set by an application as a range of consecutive bytes of the mapped-in file. All (in-memory) operations on that data are recorded in a separate writeahead log that needs to be kept on stable storage. Note that due to the generally relatively small size of the log, it is feasible to use a battery power-supplied part of main memory, which combines durability with high performance.

2.7.8. Security

Coda inherits its security architecture from AFS, which consists of two parts. The first part deals with setting up a secure channel between a client and a server using secure RPC and system-level authentication. The second part deals with controlling access to files.

Secure Channels

Coda uses a secret-key cryptosystem for setting up a secure channel between a client and a server. The protocol followed in Coda is derived from the Needham-Schroeder authentication protocol. A user is first required to obtain special tokens from an Authentication Server (AS), these tokens are somewhat comparable to handing out a ticket in the Needham-Schroeder protocol in the sense that they are used to subsequently set up a secure channel to a server. All communication between a client and server is based on Coda's secure RPC mechanism, which is shown in Fig. 2.26. If Alice (as client) wants to talk to Bob (as server), she sends her identity to Bob, along with a challenge R_A, which is encrypted with the secret key $K_{A,B}$ shared between Alice and Bob. This is shown as message 1.

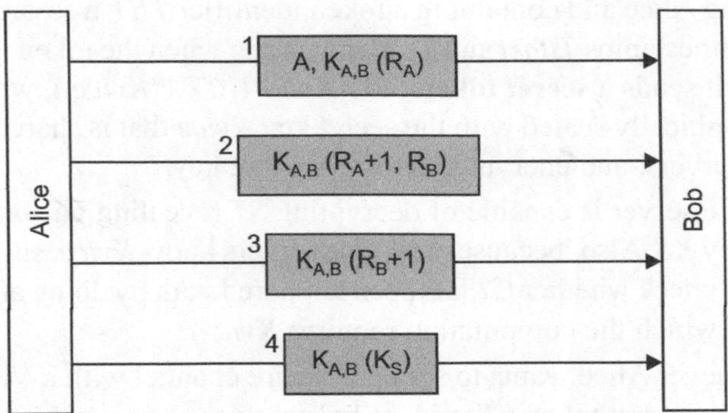

Fig. 2.26: Mutual Authentication in RPC2

Bob responds by decrypting message 1 and returning $R_A + 1$, proving that he knows the secret key and thus that he is Bob. He returns a challenge R_B (as part of message 2), which Alice will have to decrypt and return as well (shown as message 3). When mutual authentication has taken place, Bob generates a session key K_S that can be used in further communication between Alice and Bob. Secure RPC in Coda is used only to set up a secure connection between a client and a server; it is not enough for a secure login session that may involve several servers and which may last considerably longer. Therefore, a second protocol is used that is layered on top of secure RPC, in which a client obtains authentication tokens from the AS as briefly mentioned above.

An **authentication token** is somewhat like a ticket in Kerberos. It contains an identifier of the process that obtained it, a token identifier, a session key, timestamps telling when the token becomes valid and when it expires. A token may be cryptographically sealed for integrity. For example, if T is a token, *Kvice* a secret key shared by all Vice servers, and H a hash function, then $[T,H(Kvice, T)]$ is a cryptographically sealed version of T. In other words, despite the fact that T is sent as plaintext over an insecure channel, it is impossible for an intruder to modify it such that a Vice server would not notice the modification.

When Alice logs into Coda, she will first need to get authentication tokens from the AS. In this case, she does a secure RPC using her password to generate the secret key K_A, as she shares with the AS, and which is used for mutual authentication as explained before. The AS returns two authentication tokens. A **clear token** $CT = [A, TID, K_S, Tstart, Tend]$ identifying Alice and containing a token identifier *TID*, a session key K_S, and two timestamps *Tstart* and *Tend* indicating when the token is valid. In addition, it sends a **secret token** $ST = Kvice\ ([CT\ ]^*Kvice\ )$, which is *CT* cryptographically sealed with the secret key *Kvice* that is shared between all Vice servers, and encrypted with that same key.

A Vice server is capable of decrypting *ST* revealing *CT* and thus the session key *KS*. Also, because only Vice servers know *Kvice*, such a server can easily check whether *CT* has been tampered with by doing an integrity check (of which the computation requires *Kvice*).

Whenever Alice wants to set up a secure channel with a Vice server, she uses the secret token *ST* to identify herself as shown in Fig. 2.27. The session key K_S that was handed to her by the AS in the clear token is used to encrypt the challenge R_A she sends to the server.

The server, in turn, will first decrypt *ST* using the shared secret key *Kvice* , giving *CT*. It will then find K_S, which it subsequently uses to

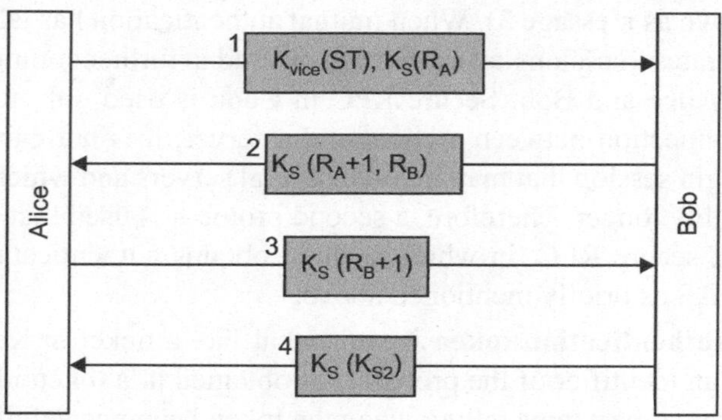

Fig. 2.27: Setting up a Secure Channel between a (Venus) Client and a Vice Server in Coda.

complete the authentication protocol. Of course, the server will also do an integrity check on *CT* and proceed only if the token is currently valid.

A problem occurs when a client needs to be authenticated before it can access files, but is currently disconnected. Authentication cannot be done because the server cannot be contacted. In this case, authentication is postponed and access is tentatively granted. When the client reconnects to the server(s), authentication takes place before entering the *REINTEGRATION* state.

Access Control

Let us briefly consider protection in Coda. As in AFS, Coda uses access control lists to ensure that only authorized processes have access to files. For reasons of simplicity and scalability, a Vice file server associates an access control list only with directories and not with files. All normal files in the same directory (i.e., excluding subdirectories) share the same protection rights. Coda distinguishes access rights with respect to the types of operations shown in Fig. 2.28. Note that there is no right with respect to executing a file. There is simple reason for this omission: execution of files takes place at clients and is thus out of the scope of a Vice file server. Once a client has downloaded a file there is no way for Vice to even tell whether the client is executing it or just reading it. Coda maintains information on users and groups. Besides listing the rights a user or group has, Coda also supports the listing of negative rights. In other words, it is possible to explicitly state that a specific user is *not* permitted certain access rights. This approach has shown to be convenient in the light of immediately revoking access rights of a misbehaving user, without having to first remove that user from all groups.

Operation	Description
Read	Read any file in the directory
Write	Modify any file in the directory
Lookup	Look up the status of any file
Insert	Add a new file to the directory
Delete	Delete an existing file
Administer	Modify the ACL of the directory

Fig. 2.28: Classification of file and directory operations recognized by Coda with respect to access control

2.8. MOBILE COMPUTING WITH THE ROVER TOOLKIT

The mobile computing environment presents application designers with a unique set of communication and data integrity constraints that are absent in traditional distributed computing settings. For example, although mobile communication infrastructures are becoming more common, network bandwidth in mobile environments is often severely limited or unavailable. Mobile application designers therefore require system facilities that minimize dependence upon continuous network connectivity; provide tools to optimize the utilization of available network bandwidth; minimize dependence on data stored on remote servers; and allow for dynamic division of work between clients and servers.

Rover is a software toolkit that supports the construction of both mobile-transparent and mobile-aware applications. The objective of the mobile-transparent approach is to develop proxies for system services that hide the mobile characteristics of the environment from applications. Since applications can be run without alteration, the mobile-transparent approach is appealing. However, to excel, applications operating in the harsh conditions of a mobile environment must often be aware of and take an active part in mitigating those conditions.

The Rover toolkit supports a set of programming and communication abstractions that enable the construction of both mobile-transparent and mobile-aware applications. Using the Rover abstractions, applications obtain increased availability, concurrency, resource allocation efficiency, fault tolerance, consistency, and adaptation. Experimental evaluation of a suite of mobile applications built with the toolkit demonstrates that such application-level control can be obtained with relatively little programming overhead and allows correct operation, increases interactive performance, and dramatically reduces network utilization under intermittently connected conditions.

2.8.1. The Argument for Mobile-Aware Computing

The attributes of the typical stationary environment have guided the development of classical distributed computing techniques for building client-server applications. These applications are usually unaware of the environment; therefore, they make certain assumptions about the location and availability of resources.

Such mobile-transparent applications can be used unmodified in mobile environments by having the system shield or hide the differences between the stationary and mobile environments from applications. Coda used this approach by providing a file system interface to applications. The systems consist of a local proxy for some service (the file system) running on the mobile host and providing the standard service interface to the application, while attempting to mitigate any adverse effects of the mobile environment. The proxy on the mobile host cooperates with a remote server on a well-connected, stationary host.

However, the mobile-transparent approach sacrifices functionality and performance. While the system hides mobility issues from the application, it usually requires manual intervention by the user (i.e., having the user indicate which data to prefetch onto the user's computer). Similarly, conflict resolution is complicated because the interface between the application and its data was designed for a stationary environment. Consider an application writing records into a file shared among stationary and mobile hosts. While disconnected, the application on the mobile host inserts a new record. The local file system proxy records the write in a log. Meanwhile, an application on a stationary host alters another record in the same file. Upon reconnection, the file system can detect that conflicting updates have occurred. However, the file system alone cannot resolve the conflict.

Coda recognizes this limitation and provides for the use of Application-Specific Resolvers (ASRs). However, ASRs alone are insufficient. In the above example, there is no way for the ASR to use the file system interface to determine whether the mobile host inserted a new record or the stationary host deleted an old one. The cause of this confusion is that Coda changes the contract between the application and the file system in order to hide the condition of the underlying network. The read/write interface no longer applies to a single file, but to possibly inconsistent replicas of the file. Therefore, any applications that depend on the standard read/write interface for synchronization and ordering may fail.

So, although the mobile-transparent approach is appealing (in that it offers to run existing applications without alteration), it is fundamentally limited in that the functionality needed to create correct, well-performing applications in an intermittently-connected environment often requires the cooperation of both application and user. The alternative to hiding environmental information from applications is to expose the information to the applications and involve them in decision-making. This yields the class of mobile-aware applications.

A mobile-aware application can store not only the value of a write, but also the operation associated with the write. This adds a significant amount of application-specific semantic information; for example, it allows for "on-the-fly" dynamic construction of conflict resolution procedures.

Unlike previous systems, the Rover toolkit is designed to support both mobile-aware and mobile-transparent approaches. For mobile-aware applications, the Rover toolkit provides the components and architecture necessary for operation in a mobile environment. Our hypothesis is that running mobile applications efficiently and correctly often requires making applications and users aware of the environment in which they are running.

The mobile-aware argument can be viewed as applying the end-to-end argument to mobile applications: "Communication functionality can be implemented only with the knowledge and help of the application standing at the endpoints of the communications system." The file system example described above illustrates that applications need to be aware of intermittent network connectivity to achieve consistency. Similar arguments can be made with respect to performance, reliability, low-power operation, etc.

The mobile-aware argument does not require that every application use its own, ad hoc approach to mobile computing. On the contrary, it allows the underlying communication and programming systems to define an application programming interface that optimizes common cases and supports the transfer of appropriate information between the layers. Since mobile-aware applications share common design goals, they will need to share design features and techniques. The Rover toolkit provides exactly such a mobile-aware application programming interface.

2.8.2. Rover: The Toolkit Approach

The Rover toolkit offers applications a distributed object system based on a client/server architecture (Fig. 2.29). Clients are Rover applications that typically run on mobile hosts, but could run on stationary hosts as well. Servers, which may be replicated, typically run on stationary hosts and hold the long term state of the system. Communication between clients is limited to peer-to-peer interactions within a mobile host (using the local object cache for sharing) and mobile host-server interactions; there is no support for remote peer-to-peer or mobile host-mobile host interactions.

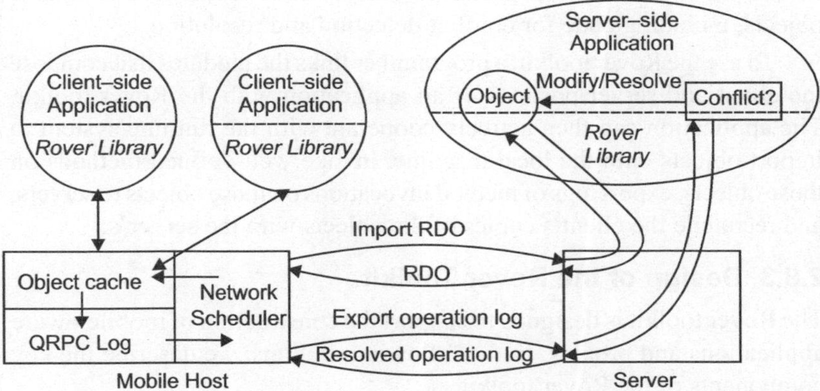

Fig. 2.29: Rover offers applications a client/server distributed object system with client caching and optimistic concurrency control. Rover applications employ a primary-copy, tentative-update optimistic-consistency-based distributed object model of data sharing: they call into the Rover library to import RDOs, and to export logs of operations that mutate RDOs. Client-side applications invoke operations directly on locally cached RDOs. Server-side applications are responsible for resolving conflicts and notifying clients of resolutions. A network scheduler drains the stable QRPC log, which contains the RPCs that must be performed at the server.

The Rover toolkit provides mobile communication support based on two ideas:

- Relocatable Dynamic Objects (RDOs), and
- Queued Rremote Procedure Call (QRPC).

A relocatable dynamic object is an object (code and data) with a well-defined interface that can be dynamically loaded into a client computer from a server computer, or vice versa, to reduce client-server communication requirements. Queued remote procedure call is a communication system that permits applications to continue to make non-blocking remote procedure calls even when a host is disconnected - requests and responses are exchanged upon network reconnection.

The key task of the programmer when building a mobile-aware application with Rover is to define RDOs for the data types manipulated by the application, and for data transported between client and server.

The programmer then divides the program into portions that run on the client and portions that run on the server; these parts communicate by means of QRPC. The programmer then defines methods that update objects, including code for conflict detection and resolution.

To use the Rover toolkit, a programmer links the modules that compose the client and server portions of an application with the Rover toolkit. The application can then actively cooperate with the runtime system to import objects onto the local machine, invoke well-defined methods on those objects, export logs of method invocations on those objects to servers, and reconcile the client's copies of the objects with the server's.

2.8.3. Design of the Rover Toolkit

The Rover toolkit is designed to support the construction of mobile-aware applications and proxies. In the following sections, we describe the key components of the Rover toolkit.

2.8.3.1. Object Design and QRPC

As the central structures about which all Rover design decisions revolve, Relocatable Dynamic Objects (RDOs) provide the key point of control in Rover applications. All application code and all application-touched data are written as RDOs. RDOs may execute at either clients or servers. All RDOs have a "home" server that maintains the primary, canonical copy. Clients import secondary copies of RDOs into their local caches and export tentatively updated RDOs back to their home servers.

RDOs may vary in complexity from simple calendar items with a small set of operations to modules that encapsulate a significant part of an application (e.g., the graphical user interface for an e-mail browser). Complex RDOs may create a thread of control when they are imported. The safe execution of RDOs is ensured by authentication and by execution of RDOs in a controlled environment. These safety measures are appropriate for the sharing of objects between mobile hosts and servers in the framework of specific applications. However, there are several safety issues relating to the general use of mobile code that are not addressed.

At the level of RDO design, application builders have semantic knowledge that is extremely useful in attaining the goals of mobile computing. By tightly coupling data with program code, applications can manage resource utilization more carefully than is possible with a replication system that handles only generic data. Rover's object model makes this coupling extremely natural. For example, an RDO can include compression and decompression methods along with compressed data in order to obtain application-specific and situation-specific compression, reducing both network and storage utilization.

Rover clients use QRPC to lazily fetch RDOs from servers (see Fig. 2.29). When an application issues a QRPC, Rover stores the QRPC in a local stable log and immediately returns control to the application. If the application has registered a callback routine, then when the requested RDO has arrived, Rover will invoke the callback to notify the application. Alternatively, applications may simply block to wait for critical data (although this is an undesirable action, especially when the mobile host is disconnected). When the mobile host is connected, the Rover network scheduler drains the log in the background, forwarding any queued QRPCs to the server.

When a Rover application modifies a locally cached RDO, the cached copy is marked tentatively committed. Updates are committed by using QRPC to lazily propagate the mutating operations to the Rover server, where they are applied to the canonical copies. In the meantime, the application may choose to use tentatively committed RDOs. This allows the application to continue execution even if the mobile host is disconnected.

2.8.3.2. Communication Scheduling

The Rover network scheduler may deliver QRPCs out of order (i.e., non-FIFO), depending upon any associated priorities and the dollar costs. It also may reorder logged requests based on consistency requirements and application-specified operation priorities. Reordering is important to usability in an environment with intermittent connectivity, as it allows the user (through applications) to identify the important operations. For example, a user may choose to send urgent updates as soon as possible while delaying other sends until inexpensive communication is available.

QRPC supports split-phase operation; thus, if a mobile host is disconnected between sending the request and receiving the reply, a Rover server will periodically attempt to contact the mobile host and deliver the reply. The split-phase communication model enables Rover to use different communication channels for the request and the response and to close channels during the intervening period. Several wireless technologies offer asymmetric communication options, such as receive-only pagers and PCS phones that can initiate calls, but cannot receive them. By splitting the request and response pair, communication can be directed over the most efficient, available channel. Closing the channel while waiting is particularly useful when the waiting period is long and the client must pay for connection time.

The combination of the split-phase and stable nature of QRPCs allows a mobile host to be completely powered-down while waiting for pending operation. When the mobile host resumes normal operation, the results of the RDO invocation will be relayed reliably from the server. Thus, long-lived computation can occur at the server while the mobile host conserves power.

2.8.3.3. Computation Relocation

Rover gives applications control over the location where computation will be performed. In an intermittently connected environment, the network often separates an application from the data upon which it is dependent. By moving RDOs across the network, applications can move data and/or computation from client to server and vice versa. Computation relocation is useful when a large body of data can be distilled down to a small amount of data or code that actually transits the network or when remote functionality is needed during periods of disconnection.

For example, migrating a GUI (Graphical User Interface) to the client serves both these purposes. The code to implement a GUI is small compared to the graphical display updates it generates. At the same time, the GUI together with the application's RDOs can locally process user actions, avoiding additional network traffic and enabling disconnected operation.

Clients can also use RDOs to export computation to servers. Such RDOs are particularly useful for two operations: performing filtering actions against a dynamic data stream and performing complex actions against a large amount of data. With RDOs, the desired processing can be performed at the server, with only the processed results returned to the client.

2.8.3.4. Notification

Since the mobile environment is dynamic, it is important to present the user and the application with information about the current environment. The Rover toolkit provides applications with environmental information for use in dynamic decision making or for presentation to the user. Applications may use either polling or callback models to determine the state of the mobile environment.

Applications can forward notifications to users or use them for silent policy changes. For example, in our calendar application (see Section V), appointments that have been modified but not propagated to the server are displayed in a distinctive color. This informs users that the appointment might be canceled due to a conflict.

2.8.3.5. Object Replication and Consistency

An essential component to accomplishing useful work while disconnected is having the necessary information locally available. RDO replica caching is the chief technique available in Rover to achieve high availability, concurrency, and reliability. In the following section, we discuss strategies for selecting objects to replicate and for reducing consistency-related-costs.

2.8.3.5.1. Replication

RDO replication is accomplished during periods of network connectivity by filling the mobile host's cache with useful RDOs. Applications should decide which objects to prefetch. The usability of applications will be critically dependent upon simple user interface metaphors for indicating collections of objects to be prefetched. Requiring users to directly list the names of objects that they wish to prefetch is inherently confusing and error-prone. Instead, Rover applications can provide prioritized prefetch lists based upon high-level user actions. For example, Rover Exmh automatically generates prefetch operations for the user's inbox folder, recently received messages, as well as folders the user visits or selects.

While replication can bring great benefits, application designers must be careful to avoid unnecessary communication, increased latencies, and dead-lock. Applications should not replicate any more data than absolutely necessary and should strive to keep update messages small.

2.8.3.5.2. Consistency

When clients are allowed to perform concurrent updates on shared RDOs, most applications require consistency control. The Rover toolkit provides significant flexibility in the choice of mechanism, ranging from application-level locking to application-specific algorithms for resolving uncoordinated updates to a single RDO. Since no single scheme is appropriate for all applications, Rover leaves the selection of consistency scheme to the application. However, only a limited number of methodologies lend themselves naturally to mobile environments. Therefore, Rover provides substantial but not exclusive support for primary-copy, tentative-update optimistic consistency.

Many applications will continue to use a variety of approaches, including ad hoc approaches such as hand editing or requiring all data replicas to converge to the same values. Certain applications will be structured as a collection of independent atomic actions, where the importing action uses application-level locks, version vectors, or dependency-set checks to implement fully-serializable transactions within Rover method calls. Of course, pessimistic concurrency control may cause long blocking periods in the mobile environment.

Rover directly supports primary-copy, tentative-update optimistic consistency control. Since optimistic concurrency control schemes allow updates by any host on any local data, this approach to be widely used. Therefore, the Rover library support for operation logging, rollback, and replay; log manipulation functions; and automatically maintained RDO consistency vectors. So far, all Rover applications built to date use primary-copy consistency control.

The server is responsible for maintaining the consistent view of the system. Update conflicts are detected and resolved by the server, and the results of reconciliation are always treated by clients as overriding the tentative state stored at the client. Thus, the client only needs to submit tentative operations to the server to reconcile the system state and to assure that any updates are durable.

Rover automatically logs method invocations, rather than only new data values, to increase flexibility in resolving conflicts. For example, a financial account object with debit, credit, and balance methods provides a great deal more semantic information to the application than a simple account file containing only the balance. Debit and credit operations from multiple clients could be arbitrarily interleaved as long as the balance never becomes negative. In contrast, consistently updating a balance value by overwriting the old value would require use of an exclusive lock on the global balance.

When the QRPC for a mutating operation arrives at a server, the server invokes the requested method on the primary copy. Typically a method call first checks whether the RDO has changed since it was imported by a mobile host. The definition of conflicting modifications is strongly application- and data-specific. Therefore, Rover does not try to detect conflicts directly, although it maintains version vectors for each RDO to aid conflict detection.

In the event of an update-update conflict, the conflict must be resolved. Since the submitted operation is tentative and was originally performed at the client on tentative data, the result of performing the operation at the server may not be exactly what the client expected. However, since Rover can employ type-specific concurrency control, many conflicts can be avoided. Note that conflict detection may depend not only on the application, but on the data or even the operation involved.

2.8.4. Implementation of the Rover Toolkit

As shown in Fig. 2.30 the Rover toolkit consists of four key components: the access manager, the object cache (client-side only), the operation log, and the network scheduler; we discuss each component in turn.

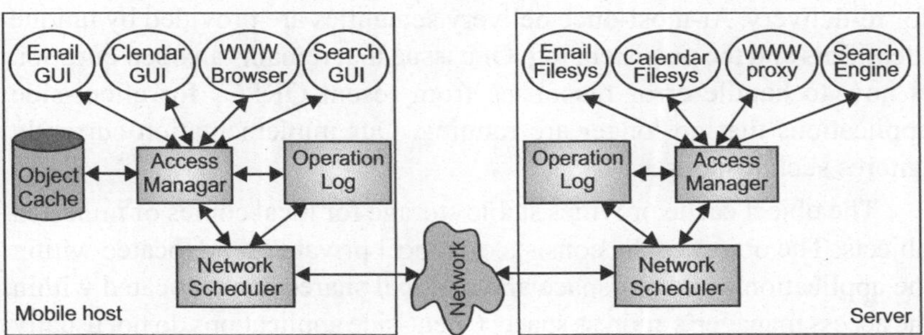

Fig. 2.30: The Rover architecture consists of four key components at clients and servers: access manager, object cache (client-side only), operation log, and network scheduler.

Each machine has a local Rover access manager, which is responsible for handling all interactions between client-side and server-side applications and among client-side applications. The access manager services requests for objects (RDOs), mediates network access, logs modifications to objects, and, at clients, manages the object cache. Client-side applications communicate with the access manager to import objects from servers and cache them locally. Server-side applications are invoked by the access manager to handle requests from client-side applications. Applications invoke the methods provided by the objects and, using the access manager, make changes globally visible by exporting them back to the servers.

Within the access manager, RDOs are imported into the object cache, while QRPCs are exported to the operation log. The access manager routes invocations and responses between applications, the cache, and the operation log. The log is drained by the network scheduler, which mediates between the various communication protocols and network interfaces.

Rover starts as a minimal "kernel" that imports functionality on demand. This feature is particularly important for mobile hosts with limited resources: small memory or small screen versions of applications may be loaded by default. However, if the application finds more hardware and network resources available (e.g., if the mobile host is docked) further RDOs may be loaded to handle these cases.

Failure recovery is also handled by the access manager. This task is eased somewhat by our use of both a persistent cache and an operation log. After a failure, the access manager re-queues any incomplete QRPCs for re-delivery. At-most-once delivery semantics are provided by unique identifiers and the persistent log. One issue that remains an open question is how to handle error responses from resent QRPCs for client-side applications that no longer are running. Our implementation currently ignores such responses.

The object cache provides stable storage for local copies of imported objects. The object cache consists of a local private cache located within the application's address space and a global shared cache located within the access manager's address space. Client-side applications do not usually interact directly with the object cache. When a client-side application issues an import or export operation, the toolkit satisfies the request based upon whether the object is found in a local cache and the consistency option specified for the object.

Once an object has been imported into the client-side application's local address space, method invocations without side effects are serviced locally by the object. At the application's discretion, method invocations with side effects may also be processed locally, inserting tentative data into the object cache. Operations with side effects also insert a QRPC into a stable operation log located at the client. Each insert is a synchronous action.

The stable log is implemented as an ordinary UNIX file. Rover performs both a flush and a synchronize operation to force new QRPCs to the log. Thus, the log update is on the critical path for message sending.

Support for intermittent network connectivity is accomplished by allowing the log to be incrementally flushed back to the server. Thus, as network connectivity comes and goes, the client will make progress towards reaching a consistent state.

One issue Rover addresses with an application-specific approach is operation log growth during disconnected operation. The ability to convey application-level semantics directly to servers is an important functional advantage, especially in the presence of intermittent connectivity. However, it may lead to an operation log that grows in size at a rate exceeding that of a simple write-ahead log. The traditional approach is log compaction. Rover takes a different approach by directly involving applications in log compaction. Applications can download procedures into the access manager to manipulate their log records. For example, an application can filter out duplicate requests (e.g., duplicate QRPCs to verify that an object is up-to-date can be reduced to a single QRPC). In addition, applications can apply their own notion of "overwriting" to the operations in the log.

The network scheduler groups operations destined for the same server for transmission and selects the appropriate transport protocol and medium over which to send them. Rover is capable of using a variety of network transports. Rover supports both connection-based protocols (e.g., HTTP over TCP/IP networks) and connectionless protocols (e.g., SMTP over IP or non-IP networks). Different protocols have different strengths. For example, while SMTP has extremely high latency, it is fundamentally a queued background process; it is more appropriate than more interactive protocols for fetching extremely large documents, such as stored video, which require large amounts of time regardless of the protocol. Another advantage is that the IP networks required for HTTP or TCP are not always available, whereas SMTP often reaches even the most obscure locations.

The network scheduler leverages the queuing of QRPCs performed by the log to gain transmission efficiency. The result is a potentially significant reduction in per-operation transmission overhead and an increase in connection efficiency through amortization of connection setup and teardown across multiple requests and responses. This amortization is especially important when connection setup is expensive (either in terms of added latency or dollar cost). For example, the latency for a null RPC over a 9.6 Kbit/s Cellular CSLIP link is 2.23 seconds; batching offers a substantial performance benefit. Scheduler sent a request as soon as it was received from a client application. The new extended scheduler uses the following heuristic to batch requests that are destined for the same server: when a request is received from one client application, the scheduler uses the access manager to check all the client applications (including the one that sent the original request) to see if any are in the process of sending a request (this is the dashed arrow in Fig. 2.30). If there are additional requests pending, the scheduler delays sending the original request. Upon receipt of the next request, the scheduler repeats the pending request check. When there are no pending requests from client applications, the scheduler batches the requests and sends them on the same connection; the results are also received on the same connection.

This heuristic imposes a small delay on requests (the time for the access manager to check each client application for pending requests and to receive the requests). However, this is a small penalty to pay relative that incurred by a high roundtrip time, since it allows the scheduler to automatically batch requests. Thus, an application that issues several requests in a series will have the requests automatically batched and sent to the server using a single connection. We are also investigating alternatives that rely upon applications to specify the set of requests that should be batched together.

The network scheduler also applies compression to the headers associated with requests and, in the absence of application-specified compression, applies compression to application data. This offers significant performance advantages, especially when combined with batching. Typical compression ratios for the applications we have studied are 1.5 - 9.7 to one. The combination of batching and compression yields (on average) a two- to four-fold reduction in execution times.

2.8.5. Mobile Computing using Rover

In this section, we discuss the steps involved with implementing mobile-aware applications (or porting existing applications to a mobile-aware environment), the programming interface provided by the Rover toolkit, and the set of sample applications that we constructed using the toolkit.

2.8.5.1.Using Objects Instead of Files

There are several steps involved in porting an existing application to Rover or creating a new Rover-based application. Each step requires the application developer to make one of several implementation choices. The choices are used in developing the initial set of Rover applications is presented in Fig. 2.31. While Rover does not provide any mechanical tools for building applications, it does provide a consistent framework.

Issue	Choice
Object Design	Use RDOs that encapsulate sufficient state to effectively service local requiests, but are small enough to easily prefetch
Computation Migration	Use RDOs to migrate computation that requires high bandwidth access
Notification	Use colors and text to notify users of tentative information
Replication	Use RDOs to replicate information
Consistancy	Use logs of operations to detecgt conflicts and help resolve them
Object Prefetching	Tradeoff of RDO size versus easier prefetching, but have to avoid overly aggressive prefetching

Fig. 2.31: Implementation choices for the initial application set built using the Rover toolkit.

The first step is to split the application into components and identify which components should be present on each side of the network link. It is very important that application developers think carefully about how application functions should be divided between a client and a server. The division will be mostly static, as most of the file system components will remain on the server and most of the GUI components will remain on the client. However, those components that are dependent upon the computing environment (network or computational resources) or are infrequently used may be dynamically generated. For example, the search operation performed by a client could be dynamically customized to the current link attributes: over a low-latency link, more work could be done at the client and less at the server, and vice versa for a high-latency link. Likewise, the main portion of an application's help information could be prefetched by a client, but less frequently referenced portions could be loaded on demand.

Once the application has been split into components, the next step is to appropriately encapsulate the application's state within objects that can be replicated and sent to multiple clients. For example, a user's electronic mail consists of messages and folders. In a traditional distributed computing environment, one encapsulation is to store each message in an individual file and use directories to group the messages into folders. Information about the size or modification date of a message is determined by using file system status operations. In the mobile computing environment, the corresponding encapsulation stores messages as objects and folders as objects containing references to message objects. Each object encapsulates both the message or folder data and the appropriate metadata.

In migrating to the mobile environment, the application's reading of files is replaced by the importing of objects and its writing of files is replaced by the exporting of changes to objects. The file system interface still exists in the server-side of the application. However, inserted between the two halves of the application is an object layer.

One of the primary purposes of the object layer is to provide a means of reducing the number of network messages that must be sent between the client and server; this is done by migrating computation. Consider the e-mail folder scan operation, which returns a list of messages and information about the messages in a folder. Using a file system-based approach means scanning the directory for the folder, opening each message, and extracting the relevant information. This is an appropriate operation for a well-connected host, but would be very expensive and time-consuming over a high-latency link. Using an object-based approach, the server-side application constructs a folder object containing the metadata for the messages contained in the folder. The client-side application can then import the folder object in a single roundtrip request and avoid multiple roundtrip requests. The multiple requests are replaced by local computation - querying the folder object about the messages it contains.

The next step is to add support for interacting with the environment. For example, in the e-mail example, one of the important pieces of message metadata that a folder object contains is the message's size and the size of any attachments. This information can be used by the application and conveyed to the user to allow useful decisions to be made. Support for prefetching is another environment interaction issue. Also, the application developer must decide which mechanisms to use for notifying users of the status of displayed data.

The final important step is the addition of application-specific conflict resolution. For most stationary environments, conflicts are infrequent. For the mobile environment, they will be more common. Fortunately, application developers can leverage the additional semantic information that is available with Rover's operation-based (instead of value-based) approach to object updating.

2.8.5.2. Toolkit Programming Interface

The programming interface between Rover and its client applications contains four primary functions: create session, import, invoke, and export. Client applications call create session once with authentication information to set up a connection with the local access manager and receive a session identifier. The authentication information is used by the access manager to authenticate client requests sent to Rover servers.

To import an object, an application calls import and provides the object's unique identifier, the session identifier, a callback, and arguments. In addition, the application specifies a priority that is used by the network scheduler to reorder QRPCs. The import function immediately returns a promise to the application. The application can then wait on this promise or continue execution. Rover transparently queues QRPCs for each import operation in the stable log. When the requested object is received by the access manager, the access manager updates the promise with the returned information. In addition, if a callback was specified, the access manager invokes it.

The current implementation also has a load operation that is an import combined with a call to create a process. Applications use the load operation to import RDOs that need a separate thread of control. When the access manager receives an RDO that was requested by a load, it creates a separate process and executes the RDO. The reason for a separate load operation is historical. At the time that the prototype was implemented, the underlying target operating systems (the y

and SunOS operating systems) did not support multiple threads per address space and only provided limited support for dynamic linking. In a future implementation, load may be directly incorporated within import.

Once an object is imported, an application can invoke methods on it to read and/or change it. Applications export each local change an object back to servers by calling the export operation and providing the object's unique identifier, the session identifier, a callback, and arguments. Like import, export immediately returns a promise. When the access manager receives responses to exports, it updates the affected promises and invokes any application-specified callbacks.

2.8.5.3. Rover Application Suite

This section provides examples of how those issues are addressed in several mobile-transparent and mobile-aware applications that have been developed using the Rover toolkit.

The two mobile-transparent applications are: *Rover NNTP proxy*, a USENET reader proxy; and *Rover HTTP proxy*, a proxy for Web browsers. The mobile-aware applications are: *Rover Exmh*, an e-mail browser; *Rover Webcal*, a distributed calendar tool; *Rover Irolo*, a graphical rolodex tool; *Rover Stock Market Watcher,* a tool that obtains stock quotes.

Two of the mobile-aware applications are based upon existing UNIX applications. Rover Exmh is a port of Brent Welch's Exmh Tcl/Tk-based e-mail browser. Rover Webcal is a port of Ical, a Tcl/Tk and C++ based distributed calendar and scheduling program written by Sanjay Ghemawat. Rover Irolo and the Rover Stock Market Watcher were built from scratch.

The application suite was chosen to test several hypotheses about the ability to reasonably meet users' expectations in a mobile, intermittently-connected environment. These applications represent a set of applications that mobile users are likely to use. Because RDOs affect the structure of applications, it is important to qualitatively test the ideas contained in the Rover toolkit with complete applications in addition to using standard quantitative techniques.

As can been seen in Fig. 2.32, porting these file system-based workstation applications to a mobile-aware Rover applications requires varying amounts of work. Some applications were written/ported in a few weeks, while others required several person-months of work. For example, porting Exmh and Ical to Rover required simple changes to approximately 10% of the lines of code. Most of these changes came from replacing file system calls with object invocations; these modifications in Rover Exmh and Rover Webcal were made almost independently of the rest of the code.

Rover program	Base code	New Rover client code	New Rover server code
Rover Exmh	24,000Tel/Tk	1,700 Tel/Tk 220 C	140 Tel/Tk 2,700 C
Webcal	26,000 C++ and Tel/Tk	2,600 C++ and Tel/Tk	1,300 C++ and Tel/Tk
Rover HTTP proxy	none	250 Tel/Tk 1,500 C	740 C
Rover Irolo	470 Tel/Tk	400 Tel/Tk 220 C	280 Tel/Tk
Rover NNTP proxy	none	525 Tel/Tk 476 C	350 C
Rover Stock Watcher	none	84 Tel/Tk 220 C	260 Perl 65 Tel/Tk

Fig. 2.32: Lines of code changed or added in porting Exmh and Webcal and implementing the Rover HTTP Proxy, Rover Irolo, Rover NNTP Proxy, and the Rover Stock Watcher

The Rover HTTP and NNTP proxies demonstrate how Rover mobile-aware proxies support existing applications (e.g., Netscape and XRN) without modification. Creating these proxies for these services is far easier than modifying all the applications that use these services.

2.8.5.3.*1. Mobile-Transparent Applications*

Rover NNTP proxy.

Using the Rover NNTP proxy, users can read USENET news with standard news readers while disconnected and receive news updates even over very slow links. Whereas most NNTP servers download and store all available news, the Rover proxy cache is filled on a demand-driven basis. When a user begins reading a newsgroup, the NNTP proxy loads the headers for that newsgroup as a single RDO while articles are prefetched in the background. As the user's news reader requests the header of each article, the NNTP proxy provides them by using the local newsgroup RDO. As new articles arrive at the server, the server-side of the proxy constructs operations to update the newsgroup-header object. Thus, when a news reader performs the common operation of rereading the headers in a newsgroup, the NNTP proxy can service the request with minimal communication over the slow link.

Rover HTTP proxy.

This is a unique application that interoperates with most of the popular Web browsers. It allows users of existing Web browsers to "click ahead" of the arrived data by requesting multiple new documents before earlier requests have been satisfied. The proxy intercepts all web requests and, if the requested item is not locally cached, returns a null response to the browser and enqueues the request in the operation log. When a connection becomes available, the page is automatically requested. In the meantime, the user can continue to browse already available pages and issue additional requests for pages without waiting. The granularity of RDOs is individual pages and images.

The client and server cooperate in prefetching. The client specifies the depth of prefetching for pages, while the server automatically prefetches in-lined images.

The proxy uses a separate window (from the browser) to display the status of a page (loaded or pending). If an uncached file is requested and the network is unavailable, an entry is added to the window. As pages arrive, the window is updated to reflect the changes. This window exposes the object cache and operations log directly to the user and allows the user limited control over them.

The proxy can also directly control NCSA's Mosaic and NCC's Netscape Navigator browsers using their remote control interfaces.

2.8.5.3.2. *Mobile-Aware Applications*

Rover Exmh.

Rover Exmh uses three types of RDOs: mail messages, mail folders, and lists of mail folders. By using this level of granularity, many user requests can be handled locally without any network traffic. Upon startup, Rover Exmh prefetches the list of mail folders, the mail folders the user has recently visited, and the messages in the user's inbox folder. Alternatively, using a finer-level of granularity (e.g., header and message body) would allow for more prefetching, but could delay servicing of user requests (especially during periods of disconnection). In the other direction, using a larger granularity (e.g., entire folders) would seriously affect usability and response times for slow links.

Some computation can be migrated to servers. For example, instead of performing a glimpse search of mail folders locally at the client (and thus having to import the index across a potentially low bandwidth link), the client can construct a query request RDO and send it to the server.

The GUI indicates that an operation is tentative using color coding. Conflict detection is based upon a log of changes to RDOs; this allows the server to detect and resolve a conflict such as one user adding a message to a folder and another user deleting it. Unresolvable conflicts are reflected back to the user.

Rover Webcal.

This distributed calendar tool uses two types of RDOs: items (appointments, daily todo lists, and daily reminders) and calendars (lists of items). At this level of granularity, the client can fetch calendars and then prefetch items using a variety of strategies (e.g., plus or minus one week, a month at a time, etc.).

Rover Webcal uses color coding to aid the user in identifying those objects that have been locally modified but not yet propagated to a server. Conflict detection is based upon a log of changes to RDOs; this allows the server to detect and resolve a conflict such as one user adding an item to a calendar and another user deleting it.

Rover Irolo.

This graphical rolodex application uses two types of RDOs: entries and indices (lists of entries). The GUI displays the last time an entry was updated and indicates whether the item is committed or tentative. Conflict detection is based upon a log of changes to RDOs; this allows the server to detect and resolve a conflict such as one user adding an entry to an index and another user deleting it.

Rover Stock Market Watcher.

This application uses both computation migration and fault-tolerance techniques. The client constructs RDOs for stocks that are to be monitored and sends them to the server. The server uses fault-tolerant techniques to store the real-time information retrieved from stock ticker services.

REFERENCES

- S. Acharya, M. J. Franklin, and A. B. Zdonik. Balancing push and pull for data broadcast. In SIGMOD Conference, pages 183–194, 1997.
- S. Acharya, M. J. Franklin, and S. B. Zdonik. Disseminating updates on broadcast disks. In VLDB, pages 354–365, 1996.
- R. Alonso, D. Barbara, and H. Garcia-Molina. Data Caching Issues in an Information Retrieval System. ACM Transactions on Database Systems (TODS), 15(3):359–384, September 1990.
- D. Barbar´a and T. Imielinski. Sleepers and workaholics: Caching strategies in mobile environments. VLDB J., 4(4):567–602, 1995.
- H. Berenson, P. Bernstein, J. Gray, J. Melton, E. O'Neil., and P. O'Neil. A Critique of ANSI SQL Isolation Levels. In Proceedings of the ACM SIGMOD Conference, pages 1–10, 1995.
- P. A. Bernstein, A. Fekete, H. Guo, R. Ramakrishnan, and P. Tamma. Relaxed-currency serializability for middle-tier caching and replication. In SIGMOD Conference, pages 599–610, 2006.
- M. Cherniack, E. F. Galvez, M. J. Franklin, and S. B. Zdonik. Profile-Driven Cache Management. In Proceedings of the ICDE Conference, pages 645–656, 2003.
- S. B. Davidson, H. Garcia-Molina, and D. Skeen. Consistency in Partitioned Networks. ACM Computing Surveys, 17(3):341–370, September 1985.
- M. J. Franklin, M. J. Carey, and M. Livny. Transactional client-server cache consistency: Alternatives and performance. ACM Trans. Database Syst., 22(3):315–363, 1997.
- P. K. Chrysanthis G. Santhanakrishnan, A. Amer. Towards universal mobile caching. In Proc. of the 4th ACM Int'l Workshop on Data Engineering for Wireless and Mobile Access, June 2005.
- H. Garcia-Molina and G. Wiederhold. Read-Only Transactions in a Distributed Database. ACM Transactions on Database Systems, 7(2):209–234, June 1982.
- J. Gray, P. Helland, P. O' Neil, and D. Shasha. The Dangers of Replication and a Solution. In Proceedings of the ACM SIGMOD Conference, pages 173–182, Montreal, Canada, 1996.

- S. Weissman Lauzac and P. K. Chrysanthis. Personalizing Information Gathering for Mobile Database Clients. In Proceedings of the ACM Annual Symposium on Applied Computing, pages 49–56, 2002.
- Q. Lu and M. Satyanarayanan. Improving Data Consistency in Mobile Computing Using Isolation-Only Transactions. In Proceedings of the Fifth Workshop on Hot Topics in Operating Systems, Orcas Island, Washington, May 1995.
- S. Mazumdar and P. K. Chrysanthis. Localization of Integrity Constraints in Mobile Databases and Specification in PRO-MOTION. ACM Mobile Networks, 9(5):481–490, October 2004.
- K. Petersen, M. Spreitzer, D. B. Terry, M. Theimer, and A. J. Demers. Flexible update propagation for weakly consistent replication. In SOSP, pages 288–301, 1997.
- E. Pitoura and B. Bhargava. Data Consistency in Intermittently Connected Distributed Systems. IEEE Transactions on Knowledge and Data Engineering, 11(6):896–915, November 1999.
- E. Pitoura and P. K. Chrysanthis. Exploiting versions for handling updates in broadcast disks. In VLDB, pages 114–125, 1999.
- E. Pitoura and P. K. Chrysanthis. Scalable processing of read-only transactions in broadcast push. In ICDCS, pages 432–439, 1999.
- E. Pitoura and P. K. Chrysanthis. Multiversion data broadcast. IEEE Trans. Computers, 51(10):1224–1230, 2002.
- E. Pitoura, P. K. Chrysanthis, and K. Ramamritham. Characterizing the temporal and semantic coherency of broadcast-based data dissemination. In ICDT, pages 410–424, 2003.
- E. Pitoura and G. Samaras. Data Management for Mobile Computing. Kluwer Academic Publishers, 1998.
- Y. Saito and M. Shapiro. Optimistic Replication. ACM Computing Surveys, 37(1):42–81, March 2005.
- M. Satyanarayanan. The evolution of coda. ACM Trans. Comput. Syst., 20(2):85–124, 2002.
- M. A. Sharaf, J. Beaver, A. Labrinidis, and P. K. Chrysanthis. Balancing energy efficiency and quality of aggregate data in sensor networks. pages 13(4): 384 – 403, December 2004.

- D. Terry, A. Demers, K. Petersen, M. Spreitzer, M. Theimer, and B.Welch. Session Guarantees for Weakly Consistent Replicated Data. In Proceedings of the International Conference on Parallel and Distributed Information Systems, pages 140–149, September 1994.
- D. B. Terry, M.MTheimer, K. Petersen, A. J. Demers, M. J Spreitzer, and C. H. Hauser. Managing Update Conflicts in Bayou, a Weakly Connected Replicated Storage System. In Proceedings of the 15th ACM Symposium on Operating Systems Principles, December 1995.
- G. Walborn and P. K. Chrysanthis. PRO-MOTION: Support for Mobile Database Access. Personal and Ubiquitous Computing, 1(3), September 1997.
- D. Zeinalipour-Yazti, P. Andreou, P. K. Chrysanthis, and G. Samaras. Mint views: Materialized in-network top-k views in sensor networks. In Proceedings of the 7th International Conference in Mobile Data Management, pages 182–189, May 2007.
- Y. Zhuge, H. Garcia-Molina, and J. Wiene. Consistency Algorithms for Multi-Source Warehouse View Maintenance. Distributed and Parallel Databases, 4(4), 1997.
- Alwan, R. Bagrodia, N. Bambos, M. Gerla, L. Kleinrock, J. Short and J. Villasenor, "Adaptive mobile multimedia networks", IEEE Personal Communications, pp. 34-51, April 1996.
- R. Bagrodia and W. Liao, "Maisie: A language for the design of efficient discrete-event simulations", IEEE Transaction on Software Engineering, pp.225-38, 1994.
- D.J. Baker and A. Ephremides, "The architectural organization of a mobile radio network via a distributed algorithm", IEEE Transactions on Communications, pp. 1694-1701, Nov. 1981.
- D.J. Baker, J. Wieselthier and A. Ephremides, "A distributed algorithm for scheduling the activation of links in a self-organizing, mobile, radio network", IEEE ICC'82, pp. 2F.6.1-2F.6.5.
- N. Bambos, S.C. Chen, and G.J. Pottie, "Radio link admission algorithms for wireless networks with power control and active link quality protection," Proceedings of IEEE INFOCOM'95, 1995.

- I. Chlamtac and S. S. Pinter, "Distributed nodes organization algorithm for channel access in a multihop dynamic radio network," IEEE Transactions on Computers, pp. 728-737, June 1987.
- M. Gerla and J.T.-C. Tsai, "Multicluster, mobile, multimedia radio network," ACM-Baltzer Journal of Wireless Networks, Vol. 1, No. 3, pp. 255-265, 1995.
- D. Goodman and R.A. Valenzuela, K.T. Gayliard and B. Ramamurthi, "Packet reservation multiple access for local wireless communications," IEEE Transactions on Communications, pp. 885-890, Aug. 1989.
- T. Hou and V. Li, "Transmission range control in multihop packet radio networks," IEEE Transactions on Communications, pp. 38-44, Jan. 1986.
- L. Hu, "Topology control for multihop packet radio networks," IEEE Transactions on Communications, pp. 1474-1481, Oct. 1993.
- L. Hu, "Distributed code assignments for CDMA packet radio networks," IEEE/ACM Transactions on Net- working, pp. 668-677, Dec. 1993.
- K. Keeton, B.A. Mah, S.Seshan, R.H. Katz, and D. Ferrari, "Providing connection-oriented network services to mobile hosts," Proceedings of USENIX ASSOCIATION Mobile and Location-Independent Computing System, pp. 83-102, August 1993.
- C.R. Lin and M. Gerla, "A distributed architecture for multimedia in a multihop dynamic packet radio network," Proceedings of IEEE Globecom '95, pp. 1468-1472, November, 1995.
- C.R. Lin and M. Gerla, "Asynchronous multimedia multihop wireless networks," Proceedings of IEEE INFOCOM '97, April, 1997.
- C.E. Perkins and P. Bhagwat, "Highly dynamic destination-sequenced distance-vector routing (DSDV) for mobile computers," Proceedings of ACM SIGCOMM '94, pp. 234-244, 1994.
- J. Jubin and J.D. Tornow, "The DARPA packet radio network protocols," Proceedings of the IEEE, January, 1987.
- N. Shacham, E.J. Craighill and A.A. Poggio, "Speech transport in packet-radio networks with mobile nodes," IEEE Journal on Selected Areas in Communications, pp. 1084-1097, Dec. 1983.

- K. Coale. Mobile Workers Need Connectivity Info World 14(10):59-62, March 2, 1992.
- D. Comer and J. Griffoen, A New Design for Distributed Systems: The Remote Memory Model. In Proc. 1990 Summer USENIX Technical Conf., pages 127-135. USENIX, June, 1990.
- J. Ioannidis, D. Duchamp, and G. Q. Maguire, Jr. IP-based Protocols for Mobile Internetworking.In Proc. SIGCOMM'91, pages 235-245. ACM, September, 1991.
- J. J. Kistler and M. Satyanarayanan, Disconnected Operation in the Coda File System. In Proc. Thirteenth ACM Symp. on Operating System Principles, pages 213-225. ACM, October, 1991.
- A. Leff, P. S. Yu, and J. L. Wolf. Policies for Efficient Memory Utilization in a Remote Caching Architecture. In Proc. First Intl. Conf. on Parallel and Distributed Information Systems, pages 198-207. IEEE, December, 1991.
- M. N. Nelson, B. B. Welch, J. K. Ousterhout, Caching in the Sprite Network File System. ACM Trans. Computer Systems 6(1):134-154, February, 1988.
- B. N. Schilit and D. Duchamp. Adaptive Remote Paging for Mobile Computers Technical Report CUCS-004-91, Columbia Univ. Computer Science Dept., February, 1991.
- C. Tait and D. Duchamp, Service Interface and Replica Consistency Algorithm for Mobile File System Clients. In Proc. First Intl. Conf. on Parallel and Distributed Information Systems, pages 190-197. IEEE, December, 1991.
- C. Tait and D. Duchamp, Detection and Exploitation of File Working Sets. In Proc. Eleventh Intl. Conf. on Distributed Computing Systems, pages 2-9. IEEE, May, 1991.
- C. Tait and D. Duchamp, An Efficient Variable Consistency Replicated File Service. March, 1992.
- F. Teraoka, Y. Yokote, and M. Tokoro, A Network Architecture Providing Host Migration Transparency, In Proc. SIGCOMM '91, pages 209-220. ACM, September, 1991.
- Alwan, R. Bagrodia, N. Bambos, M., L. Kleinrock, J. Short and J. Villasenor, ..Adaptive mobile multimedia networks, IEEE Personal Communications, pp. 34-51, April 1996.

- J. Broch, D. Maltz, D. Johnson, Y. Hu, and J. Jetcheva. A performance comparison of multi-hop wireless ad hoc routing protocols. In Proceedings of the Fourth Annual ACM/IEEE International Conference on Mobile Computing and Networking,October 1998.
- S. Das, R. Castaneda, J. Yan, and R. Sengupta. Comparative performance evaluation of routing protocols for mobile, ad hoc networks. In Proceedings of 7th Annual ICCCN, October 1998.
- Murthy, S. , and Garcia-Luna-Aceves, J.J. A Routing Protocol for Packet Radio Networks. Proc. of ACM Mobile Computing and Networking Conference, MOBICOM.95, Nov. 14- 15, 1995.
- D. Johnson and D. Maltz. Dynamic source routing in ad hoc wireless networks. In T. Imielinski and eds. H. Korth, editors, Mobile Computing. Kluwer Academic Publications, 1996.
- M.S. Corson and A. Ephremides. A distributed routing algorithm for mobile wireless networks. ACM-Baltzer Journal of Wireless Net-works,1:61-81, January 1995.
- Z. J. Haas and M. Perlman. The performance of query control schemes for the zone routing protocol. In Proceedings of ACM Sigcomm'98, October 1998.
- M. Jiang, J. Li and Y.C. Tay. Cluster-Based Routing Protocol (CBRP), Internet-Draft, draft-ietf-manet-zone-zrp-02.txt, August 1999.
- C.-C. Chiang. Routing in Clustered Multihop, Mobile Wireless Networks with Fading Channel. Proc. IEEE SICON'97, Apr.1997, pp.197-211.
- M. Gerla and J.T.-C. Tsai, .Multicluster, mobile, multimedia radio network,.. ACM Baltzer Journal of *Wireless Networks,* Vol. 1, No. 3, pp. 255-265, 1995.
- C. R. Lin and M. Gerla. Adaptive clustering for mobile wireless networks. IEEE Journal on Selected Areas in Communications, 15(7), September 1997.
- A.B. McDonald and T.F. Znati. A mobility-based framework for adaptive clustering in wireless ad hoc networks, IEEE J. Selected Areas in Communications, 17, 8, August 1999, 1466-1487.

- L. Ismail, D. Hagimont. A Performance Evaluation of the Mobile Agent Paradigm. Proc. of the Communications of the ACM, Volume 41, Num. 10. ACM Press. October 1998. pp 44 - 52.
- T. White, A. Bieszczad and B. Pagurek, Distributed Fault Location in Networks Using Mobile Agents. In Proceedings of the Second International Workshop on Agents in Telecommunications Applications (IATA '98), pp. 130-141, July 4th-7th, 1998.
- A. Bieszczad, B. Pagurek, and T. White. Mobile Agents for Network Management. IEEE Communications Surveys, September 1998.
- Robert Sugar, Sandor Imre. Dynamic Agent Domains in Mobile Agent Based Network Management. IEEE International Conference on Networking, 2001.
- Bernstein, P.A., V. Hadzilacos, N. Goodman, Concurrency Control and Recovery in Database Systems, Addison Wesley, Reading MA., 1987.
- Berenson, H., Bernstein, P.A., Gray, J., Jim Melton, J., O'Neil, E., O'Neil, P., "A Critique of ANSI SQL Isolation Levels," Proc. ACM SIGMOD 95, pp. 1-10, San Jose CA, June 1995.
- Garcia Molina, H. "Performance of Update Algorithms for Replicated Data in a Distributed Database," TR STAN-CS-79-744, CS Dept., Stanford U., Stanford, CA., June 1979.
- Garcia Molina, H., Barbara, D., "How to Assign Votes in a Distributed System," J. ACM, 32(4). Pp. 841-860, October, 1985.
- Gifford, D. K., "Weighted Voting for Replicated Data," Proc. ACM SIGOPS SOSP, pp: 150-159, Pacific Grove, CA, December 1979.
- Gray, J., Reuter, A., *Transaction Processing: Concepts and Techniques,* Morgan Kaufmann, San Francisco, CA. 1993.
- Gray, J., Homan, P, Korth, H., Obermarck, R., "A Strawman Analysis of the Probability of Deadlock," IBM RJ 2131, IBM Research, San Jose, CA., 1981.
- Gupta Brijesh Kr., Sharma, S.C., and Lal, M.., "A hybrid scheme for handover in ATM-based personal communication network," International Journal on Wireless and optical communications, vol.3, no.1, pp. 69-81, April 2006.
- Low, C.P "An Efficient Algorithm for Link Allocation Problem

on ATM-Based Personal Communication Network", IEEE journal on selected areas in communications, vol. 18, no. 7, July 2000

- Hammond, Brad, "Wingman, A Replication Service for Microsoft Access and Visual Basic", Microsoft White Paper, bradha@microsoft.com
- Herman, G., Gopal, G, Lee, K., Weinrib, A., "The Datacycle Architecture for Very High Throughput Database Systems," Proc. ACM SIGMOD, San Francisco, CA. May 1987.
- Kawell, L.., Beckhardt, S., Halvorsen, T., Raymond Ozzie, R., Greif, I.,"Replicated Document Management in a Group Communication System," Proc. Second Conference on Computer Supported Cooperative Work, Sept. 1988.
- Bernstein, P.A., V. Hadzilacos, N. Goodman, Concurrency Control and Recovery in Database Systems, Addison Wesley, Reading MA., 1987.
- Berenson, H., Bernstein, P.A., Gray, J., Jim Melton, J., O'Neil, E., O'Neil, P., "A Critique of ANSI SQL Isolation Levels," Proc. ACM SIGMOD 95, pp. 1-10, San Jose CA, June 1995.
- Garcia Molina, H. "Performance of Update Algorithms for Replicated Data in a Distributed Database," TR STAN-CS-79-744, CS Dept., Stanford U., Stanford, CA., June 1979.
- Garcia Molina, H., Barbara, D., "How to Assign Votes in a Distributed System," J. ACM, 32(4). Pp. 841-860, October, 1985.
- Gifford, D. K., "Weighted Voting for Replicated Data," Proc. ACM SIGOPS SOSP, pp: 150-159, Pacific Grove, CA, December 1979.
- Gray, J., Reuter, A., *Transaction Processing: Concepts and Techniques,* Morgan Kaufmann, San Francisco, CA. 1993.
- Gray, J., Homan, P, Korth, H., Obermarck, R., "A Strawman Analysis of the Probability of Deadlock," IBM RJ 2131, IBM Research, San Jose, CA., 1981.
- Hammond, Brad, "Wingman, A Replication Service for Microsoft Access and Visual Basic", Microsoft White Paper, bradha@microsoft.com
- Herman, G., Gopal, G, Lee, K., Weinrib, A., "The Datacycle Architecture for Very High Throughput Database Systems," Proc. ACM SIGMOD, San Francisco, CA. May 1987.

- Kawell, L.., Beckhardt, S., Halvorsen, T., Raymond Ozzie, R., Greif, I.,"Replicated Document Management in a Group Communication System," Proc. Second Conference on Computer Supported Cooperative Work, Sept. 1988.
- H. T. Kung and J. T. Robinson, "On Optimistic Methods for Concurrency Control," ACM Transactions on Database Systems, vol. 6, no. 2, pp. 213-226, June 1981.
- J. J. Kistler and M. Satyanarayanan, "Disconnected operation in the Coda file system," ACM Transactions on Computer Systems, vol. 10, pp. 3-25, Feb. 1992.
- P. Kumar, Mitigating the Effects of Optimistic Replication in a Distributed File System, Ph.D. thesis, School of Computer Science, Carnegie Mellon University, Dec. 1994.
- J. H. Saltzer, D. P. Reed, and D. D. Clark, "End-to-end arguments in system design," ACM Transactions on Computer Systems, vol. 2, no. 4, pp. 277-28, Nov. 1984.
- A. Joseph, A. F. deLespinasse, J. A. Tauber, D. K. Gifford, and F. Kaashoek, "Rover: A toolkit for mobile information access," in Proc. of the Fifteenth Symposium on Operating Systems Principles (SOSP), Copper Mountain Resort, CO, Dec. 1995, pp. 156-171.
- A.D. Birrell and B.J. Nelson, "Implementing remote procedure calls," ACM Transactions on Computer Systems, vol. 2, no. 1, pp. 39-59, Feb. 1984.
- A. Joseph and F. Kaashoek, "Building reliable mobile-aware applications using the rover toolkit," in Proc. of the Second International Conference on Mobile Computing and Networking (MOBICOM '96), Rye, NY, Nov. 1996, pp. 117-129.
- R. H. Katz, "Adaptation and mobility in wireless information systems," IEEE Personal Communications, vol. 1, pp. 6-17, 1994.
- N. Davies, G. Blair, K. Cheverst, and A. Friday, "Supporting adaptive services in a heterogeneous mobile environment," in Proc. of the Workshop on Mobile Computing Systems and Applications, Santa Cruz, CA, Dec. 1994.
- A. Demers, K. Petersen, M. Spreitzer, D. Terry, M. Theimer, and B. Welch, "The Bayou architecture: Support for data sharing among mobile users," in Proc. of the Workshop on Mobile

Computing Systems and Applications, Santa Cruz, CA, Dec. 1994, pp. 2-7.

- M.G. Baker, "Changing communication environments in MosquitoNet," in Proc. of the Workshop on Mobile Computing Systems and Applications, Santa Cruz, CA, Dec. 1994, pp. 64-68.
- M. Satyanarayanan, J. J. Kistler, L. B. Mummert, M. R. Ebling, P. Kumar, and Q. Lu, "Experience with disconnected operation in a mobile environment," in Proc. of the First USENIX Symposium on Mobile & Location-Independent Computing, Cambridge, MA, Aug. 1993, pp. 11-28.
- L. B. Mummert, M. R. Ebling, and M. Satyanarayanan, "Exploiting weak connectivity for mobile file access," in Proc. of the Fifteenth Symposium on Operating Systems Principles (SOSP), Copper Mountain Resort, CO, Dec. 1995, pp. 143-155.
- P. Reiher, J. Heidemann, D. Ratner, G. Skinner, and G. J. Popek, "Resolving file conflicts in the Ficus file system," in Proc. of the USENIX Summer 1994 Technical Conference, Boston, MA, 1994, pp. 183-195
- L. B. Huston and P. Honeyman, "Disconnected operation for AFS," in Proc. of the First USENIX Symposium on Mobile & Location-Independent Computing, Cambridge, MA, Aug. 1993, pp. 1-10.
- L. Huston and P. Honeyman, "Partially connected operation," in Proc. of the Second USENIX Symposium on Mobile & Location-Independent Computing, Ann Arbor, MI, Apr. 1995, pp. 91-97.
- T. Watson and B. Bershad, "Local area mobile computing on stock hardware and mostly stock software," in Proc. of the First USENIX Symposium on Mobile & Location-Independent Computing, Cambridge, MA, Aug. 1993, pp. 109-116.
- T. Watson, "Application design for wireless computing," in Proc. of the Workshop on Mobile Computing Systems and Applications, Santa Cruz, CA, Dec. 1994, pp. 91-94.
- J. Landay, "User interface issues in mobile computing," in Proc. of the Fourth Workshop on Workstation Operating Systems (WWOS-IV). IEEE, Oct. 1993, pp. 40-47.
- D. B. Terry, M. M. Theimer, K. Petersen, A. J. Demers, M. J. Spreitzer, and C. H. Hauser, "Managing update conflicts in a

weakly connected replicated storage system," in Proc. of the Fifteenth Symposium on Operating Systems Principles (SOSP), Copper Mountain Resort, CO, Dec. 1995, pp. 172-183.

- M. Theimer, A. Demers, K. Petersen, M. Spreitzer, D. Terry, and B. Welch, "Dealing with tentative data values in disconnected work groups," in Proc. of the Workshop on Mobile Computing Systems and Applications, Santa Cruz, CA, Dec. 1994, pp. 192-195.
- D. B. Terry, A. J. Demers, K. Petersen, M. J. Spreitzer, M. M. Theimer, and B. B. Welch, "Session guarantees for weakly consistent replicated data," in Proc. of the 1994 Symposium on Parallel and Distributed Information Systems, Sept. 1994, pp. 140-149.
- M.T. Le, F. Burghardt, S. Seshan, and J. Rabaey, "InfoNet: the networking infrastructure of InfoPad," in Proc. of the Spring COMPCON Conference, 1995, pp. 163-168.
- S. Narayanaswamy, et. al., "Application and network support for InfoPad," IEEE Personal Communications, vol. 3, no. 2, pp. 4-17, Apr. 1996.
- L. Kawell Jr., S. Beckhardt, T. Halvorsen, R. Ozzie, and I. Greif, "Replicated document management in a group communication system," Presented at the Second Conference on Computer-Supported Cooperative Work, Portland, OR, Sept. 1988.
- J. Gray, P. Helland, P. O'Neil, and D. Shasha, "The dangers of replication and a solution," in Proc. of the 1996 SIGMOD Conference, Montreal, Quebec, Canada, June 1996.
- W. Weihl and B. Liskov, "Implementation of Resilient, Atomic Data Types," ACM Transactions on Programming Languages and Systems, vol. 7, no. 2, pp. 244-269, Apr. 1985.
- D. H. Crocker, Standard for the Format of ARPA Internet Text Messages, Internet RFC 822, Aug. 1982.
- Information Sciences Institute, Transmission Control Protocol: DARPA Internet Program Protocol Specification, Internet RFC 793, Sept. 1981.

UNIT-III

Recent advances in communication technology have created the opportunity for mobile terminals to receive many services that were, until not long ago, only available to tethered terminals. The first system to support large scale mobility was the Advanced Mobile Phone System(AMPS), a 900 MHz analog system. A new digital system, Personal Communication Services (PCS) provides voice as well as limited data services to wireless users. PCS works in the 1900 MHz spectrum. There are competitive standards for analog, digital, and PCS systems throughout the world. One of the challenging tasks in a PCS environment is to efficiently maintain the location of the PCS subscribers who move around freely with their Mobile Unit (MU).

The location of mobile user is of prime importance in wireless computing. In a mobile computing, the location of a user can be regarded as a data item whose value changes with every move. In the mobile computing, the location management is a data management problem. Primary issues here are how to know the current position of the MU? Where to store the location information and who should be responsible for determining and updating of information? The unit presents the followings:

- Location Management
- Location Based Services
- General Issues in Location Management
- Location Management in Wireless Networks
- Recent Research on Location Management
- Future LM Developments and E911
- Mobile Networking Through Mobile IP
- Wireless LANs and IEEE 802.11
- TCP over Wireless

UNIT

3

Location Management

3.1. LOCATION MANAGEMENT

3.1.1. Introduction

Mobile wireless devices with wireless connection facilities are changing the way people think about the use of computing and communication. These wireless devices can communicate with one another even though the user is mobile. People carrying a mobile computer will be able to access information regardless of the time and their current position.

Significant growth is expected in specialized mobile services such as driving directions, traffic report, tour guides, and commerce services such as mobile shopping. However, Location Management (LM) will be an important issue in these situations because wireless devices can change location while connected to a wireless network. New strategies must be introduced to deal with the dynamic changes of a mobile device's network address.

The ability to change locations while connected to the network creates a dynamic environment. This means that data, which is static for stationary computing, becomes dynamic for mobile computing. There are a few questions that must be answered when looking at a LM scheme.

- What happens when a mobile user changes location?
- Who should know about the change?
- How can you contact a mobile host?
- Should you search the whole network or does anyone know about the mobile users moves?

Cellular networks are spreading rapidly, leading to overloaded systems, unacceptable delays, and increasing computational costs due to inefficient Location Management (LM). LM schemes are essentially based on users' mobility and incoming call rate characteristics. The main task of LM is to keep track of a users' location all the time while operating and on the move so that incoming messages (calls) can be routed to the intended recipient.

3.1.2. Location Management Schemes

The following sections presents recent theoretical proposals to overcome current flaws, indicates probable trends towards future cellular LM, and covers the Enhanced 911 (E911) service and its use of LM. Future LM developments and real-world example demonstrating applications of LM and its importance.

3.1.2.1. Static Location Management

Presently, most LM schemes are static, where Location Updates (LUs) occur on either periodic intervals or upon every cell change. However, static Location Areas (LAs) incur great costs with the ping-pong effect. When users repetitively move between two or more LAs, updates are continuously performed unnecessarily. In these static LAs, cells are constant in size, uniform, and identical for each user. The current static LM standards are IS-41 and y

which use a hierarchical database structure and are described in next part of the chapter.

3.1.2.1.1. Static Location Update

Three simple static Location Update schemes exist in static LM, being always-update, never-update, and static interval-based. The third of these is the most commonly used in practical static LM systems. One scheme involves the user updating its location upon every inter-cell movement, and is named always-update. This will incur significant energy and computational costs to both the network and the user, especially to the most mobile users. This may be particularly wasteful, as if a user makes frequent, quick movements within an LA, beginning and ending at the same location, many LUs will occur that might be unnecessary, especially if few or no calls are incoming. However, the network will always be able to quickly locate a user upon an incoming call, and extensive paging will not be necessary. The converse method would be to never require the user to inform the network of inter cell movements, only updating on LA changes, and is named never-update. In this scheme, resources are saved as constant updates are not required, but paging costs rise substantially. This occurs as every cell within the user's LA may need to be checked during paging due to the lack of information, which causes excessive overhead for users. These two schemes are generally unused in real-world systems, but help to provide an illustration to network administrators as to the costs of LM, the problems that occur when thoughtless LU methods are used, and a baseline that every newly developed LU scheme must show improvements over. The final static LM technique discussed requires each user within the network to update at static, uniform intervals. This attempts to provide a balance between the extremes of the previous schemes, as the network will neither be overwhelmed with LUs nor wholly unaware of users' locations. However, users with rapid rates of movement may move into new LAs between updates, which causes locating that user to be very difficult. Conversely, an inactive user will not move at all, but will still regularly be sending unneeded LUs.

3.1.2.1.2. Static Location Areas

Location Areas in static LM are themselves static as well. They are effectively the easiest solution to physically dividing a network, providing the same LA to every user, without any customization. These function as static LU schemes do: suboptimally, but sufficiently for most networks. However, their perhaps most egregious flaw is their vulnerability to the ping-pong effect. Given that these static LAs are set and cannot change, users may repetitively move between two or more adjacent LAs, which for many LU schemes will cause a large number of LUs with a small or zero absolute cell distance moved.

3.1.2.1.3. Static LM Standards/Implementation

In current cellular telephone usage, there are two common standards:

- The Electronic and Telephone Industry Associations (EIA/TIA) Interim Standard IS-41
- The Global System for Mobile Communications (GSM) Mobile Application Part (MAP).

Both of these are quite similar, having two main tasks of Location Update and Call Delivery. Currently, a two level hierarchical database scheme is used. The Home Location Register (HLR) contains the records of all users' services, in addition to location information for an entire network, while Visitor Location Registers (VLRs) download data from the HLR concerning current users within the VLR's specific service areas. Each LA has one VLR servicing it, and each VLR is designed to only monitor one LA. Additionally, each VLR is connected to multiple Mobile Switching Centers (MSCs), which operate in the transport network in order to aid in handoffs and to locate users more easily. For LUs, IS- 41 and GSM both use a form of the always-update method.

All inter-cell movements cause an update to the VLR, while the HLR does not need any modification, as both the MSC and VLR that the user resides in remains constant. Inter-MSC movements within the same LA cause the VLR to be updated with the new cell address, and also cause an update to the HLR to modify the stored value of the user's MSC. Finally, Inter-VLR movements cause the new VLR to create a record for the user, as well as causing an update to the HLR where both MSC and VLR fields are updated. After this occurs, the old VLR's record for the user is removed.

Fig. 3.1 displays a symbolic high-level view of the HLR/VLR architecture, as well as demonstrating the methods of communication on a call. In Call Delivery, the system database is queried to determine the LA or registration area of the user. This is split into two steps; a fixed network interrogation is performed to find a region of cells containing the target, in which the HLR is queried to obtain the VLR of the called user. Next, paging is used to poll cells within this region until the user is found.

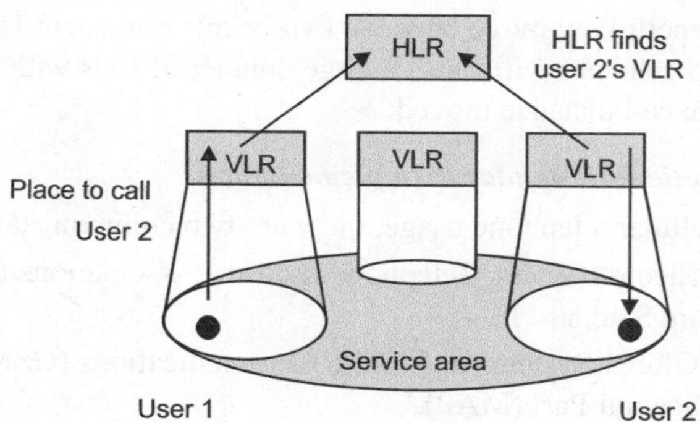

Fig. 3.1: HLR/VLR Architecture

Currently, a system called Signaling System 7 (SS7) is used to transmit these locating messages. In this system, Signal Transfer Points (STPs) route messages through the network (as the HLR), while Service Control Points (SCPs) maintain the databases and information (as VLRs), and Service Switching Points (SSPs) help route calls (as MSCs). Fig. 3.2 provides an illustration that demonstrates how SS7 further aids the HLR/ VLR architecture.

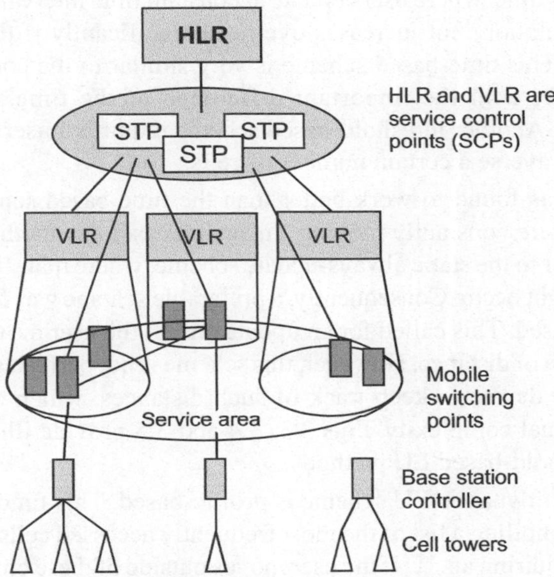

Fig. 3.2: HLR/VLR Architecture with SS7

3.1.2.2. Dynamic Location Management

Dynamic Location Management is an advanced form of LM where the parameters of LM can be modified to best fit individual users and conditions. Theories have been and continually are being proposed regarding dynamic LUs and LAs. Additionally, many are reexamining paging and mobility parameters based upon these developments. Many of these proposals in dynamic LM attempt to reduce computational overhead, paging costs, and the required number of LUs. However, many of these proposals are excessively theoretical and complex, and are difficult to implement on a large scale.

3.1.2.2.1. Dynamic Location Update

Many dynamic LU schemes exist, in order to improve upon excessively simple and wasteful static LU schemes. Additionally, these schemes are intended to be customizable, such that each user will have their own optimal LU standard, greatly reducing the overall number of LU updates. One of these dynamic LU formats is threshold-based, where updates occur each time a parameter goes beyond a set threshold value. One possible threshold is time, where users update at constant time intervals. This saves user computation, but increases overhead significantly if the user does not move. This time-based scheme is very similar to the common static LU scheme, with the important difference of the time value being modifiable. Another threshold-based scheme requires a user update each time they traverse a certain number of cells.

This was found to work better than the time-based scheme, unless the users were constantly moving. In such a case, this method becomes quite similar to the static always-update scheme, where many unnecessary updates might occur. Consequently, a preferable scheme was found, called distance-based. This called for an update only if the user moved a certain radial length of distance. However, this scheme is not perfect, as it requires the cellular device to keep track of such distances, which added much computational complexity. Figs 3.3, 3.4 and 3.5 provide illustrations of these threshold-based LU methods.

Another dynamic LU scheme is profile-based. This functions by the network compiling a list of the most frequently accessed cells by the user, and only requiring an LU if the user moves outside of these common cells.

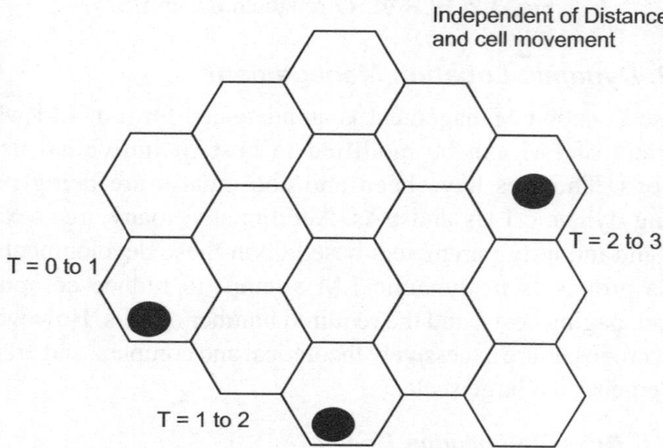

Fig. 3.3: Time-based Threshold Location Update

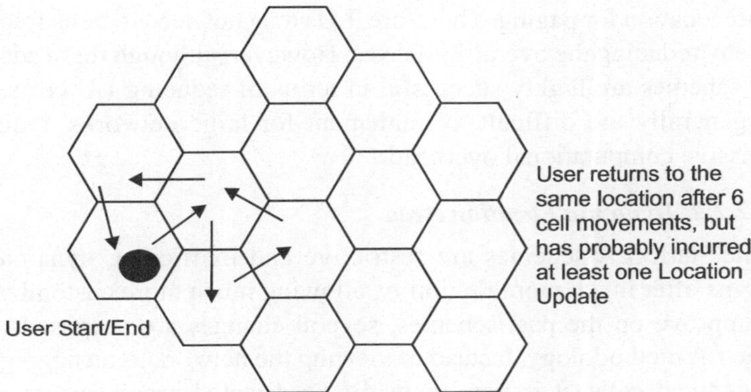

Fig. 3.4: Cell -based Threshold Location Update

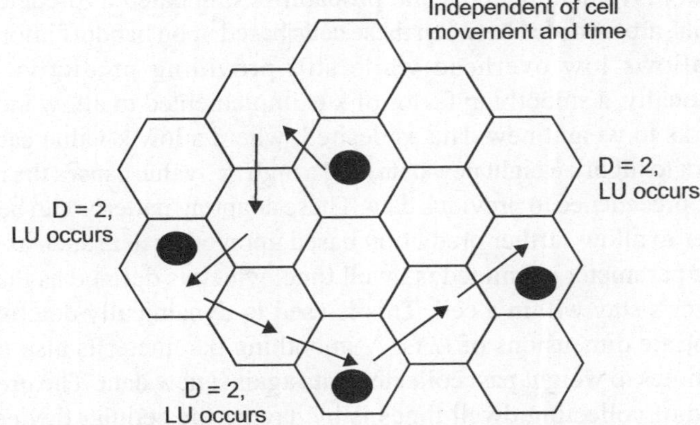

Fig. 3.5: Distance - based Threshold Location Update

As would be expected, this scheme is only effective if these predictions can be made accurately and without excessive overhead, but is otherwise inefficient. Additionally, this list must be relatively small, or else paging will become costly. A more advanced scheme, built upon the efforts of previous methods, is called adaptive. Adaptive LU schemes are very flexible and even may differ from each other, as such schemes are designed to take multiple parameters, such as velocity and mobility patterns, to determine the most efficient LAs. In such an example, having knowledge of a user's past movements combined with the user's current speed and direction allows strong predictive power when determining a possible future location for paging. Therefore, LUs may not need to be as frequent, thereby reducing the overall LM costs. However, although these adaptive LM schemes are highly successful in terms of reducing LU costs, they are generally too difficult to implement for large networks, requiring excessive computational overhead.

3.1.2.2.2. Dynamic Location Area

While static LA schemes are restrictive and inefficient, dynamic LA designs offer much more flexibility, allowing much more customization. To improve on the past schemes, several changes are proposed to the static LA methodology. Instead of viewing the network as an aggregation of identical cells, it is now viewed as a directed graph, where nodes represent cells, with physical adjacency shown through graph edges. General movement patterns and probabilities, updated at predetermined intervals, are recorded between these cells based upon handoff information. This allows low overhead while still providing predictive power. Additionally, a smoothing factor of k is implemented to allow individual networks to weight new data as desired, where a low k value causes the network to highly weight new data, and a high 'k'-value causes the network to give precedence to previous data. These adapting patterns can be stored, in order to allow further prediction based upon other data such as time. A similar parameter examined is dwell time, which is defined as the length of a user's stay within a cell. This is used to dynamically determine the appropriate dimensions of LAs. A smoothing parameter is also used for dwell times to weight past collected data against new data. The preferable method of collecting dwell times is by having the cellular device report its dwell time to the network upon a handoff. Within a dynamic scheme, LAs, instead of being constant and circular, can be diverse and may take different shapes, in order to be optimal for individual user parameters and network characteristics. As well, cells are organized within these LAs based upon frequency of use, with the most freq uently visited cells being placed in an ordered array. This array can be used in conjunction with known physical topology to design optimal user LAs, constructed such that the users will change LAs and make handoffs as infrequently as possible. To further optimize service for the individual user, call interval times and relative mobility rates are calculated to make low-overhead predictions concerning when LA and cell changes will occur.

3.1.2.2.3. User Characterization

The primary goal of dynamic LM is to provide LU and LA algorithms to each individual user that minimizes the costs for them. To do this, call rate and movement factor estimations must be made. To determine the call rate, the network first determines the call interval, by taking the average interval between calls (in seconds), and adding new call intervals in a weighted manner. The call rate, is then calculated by dividing 3600 by the call interval, in order to obtain the number of calls per hour. Given that cells will be of different sizes and covering different types of areas in dynamic LA, it is incorrect to base user movement properties on raw user cell dwell times. Instead, the movement factor is used, where this factor specifies a user's movement speed relative to other users.

3.1.2.2.4. Cost Analysis

As seen before, the total cost of LM is equal to the LU cost added to the paging cost. This equation is always true, regardless of which system is used. However, different systems will have different values for these, and the goal is to find an implementable system that minimizes the total. The paging cost can be fairly simply defined, as the previously calculated call rate, multiplied by the number of cells in the paging area, multiplied by a constant representing the cost per paging message. Consequently, reducing any of these parameters will reduce the overall paging cost.

3.1.3. Location Management Parameters/Analysis

While evaluating schemes to design LAs or determining the optimal updating standard of LUs for users may seem of higher importance, paging and user mobility can also be briefly examined to assist in improving LM and refining models. Although LU costs are generally higher than paging costs, these paging costs are not insignificant. Additionally, poor paging procedures and ineffective mobility modeling and prediction may lead to either significantly delayed calls or decreased QoS, neither of which are acceptable to a user.

3.1.3.1. Paging

In the attempt to locate recipients of calls as quickly as possible, multiple methods of paging have been created. The most basic method used is Simultaneous Paging, where every cell in the user's LA is paged at the same time in order to find the user. Unless there are a relatively low number of cells within the LA, this will cause excessive amounts of paging. Although this method will find the user quicker than the following scheme of Sequential Paging, the costs make Simultaneous Paging rather inefficient. An alternative scheme is Sequential Paging, where each cell within an LA is paged in succession, with one common theory suggesting the polling of small cell areas in order of decreasing user dwelling possibility. Unfortunately, this was found to have poor performance in some situations, as if the user was in an infrequently occupied location,not only might every cell be paged, but a large delay could occur in call establishment. Additionally, this method requires accurate data gathering concerning common user locations, which necessitates more frequent LUs and thereby increased costs.

Consequently, most real-world Sequential Paging methods simply poll the cells nearest to the cell of the most recent LU, and then continue outward if the user is not immediately found. However, such a method will still be inefficient if the user's velocity is high or an LM scheme is used which specifies infrequent LUs.

As an attempt to improve on previous models, another design called Intelligent Paging was introduced, which calculates specific paging areas to sequentially poll based upon a probability matrix. This method is essentially an optimized version of Sequential Paging. However, this scheme has too much computational overhead incurred through updating and maintaining the matrix, and although perhaps optimal in theory, is effectively impossible for commercial cellular network implementation. Therefore, most current schemes use one of the first two methods presented.

3.1.3.2. User Mobility

For aid in effectively predicting the user's next location, user movement patterns are analyzed and mobility models are designed. Many such mobility models exist and can be used by networks in LM. The simplest of these models is random-walk, where user movements are assumed to be entirely random. While this is clearly going to lead to inaccurate predictions, it does require no knowledge of the individual user, and can be effective as a simulation tool. Frequently, random-walk is used to demonstrate the improvements a given scheme makes in comparison to this random method. A very general scheme, ignoring individual users but considering the network as a whole, is called ***fluid-flow***. This method aggregates the movement patterns of users, and consequently can help optimize the network's utilization and design at a macroscopic level. However, fluid-flow provides no insight on a smaller scale, nor will it give any predictions as to specific user movements for any specific user. Markovian mobility models also exist, where user movements are predicted through past movements. At large computational cost, every inter-cell movement probability is defined for each user. An extension of the Markovian model, created at perhaps even greater cost, is the activity-based model. In this model, parameters such as time of day, current location, and predicted destination are also stored and evaluated to create movement probabilities. However, for all the resource expenditures required in implementing these methods, in a test of a simple activity-based scheme, unstable results were returned. An even more complex activity-based scheme might provide better results, but would not be implementable on a large scale due to its immense costs.

3.2. LOCATION BASED SERVICES

Although Location Based Services (LBS) have been an issue in the field of mobile communications for many years, no common definition has been devised for it. The terms *location- based service, location-aware service, location-related service*, and *location service* have been used interchangeably. These various terms have lead to several definitions of LBS. As per one of the definitions, LBS as services that integrate a mobile device's location or position with other information so as to provide added value to a user. he GSM association has defined LBS as services that use the location of the target for adding value to the service, where the target is the entity to be located (this entity is not necessarily the user of the service). The 3rd *Generation Partnership Project (3GPP)* defines LBS as a service provided by a service provider that utilizes the available information of the terminal. One of the most traditional examples of LBS is Global Positioning System (GPS). GPS was used by the US Department of Defense since the 1970s. However, in the 1980s, GPS became available freely for the industry worldwide. Not only does user location allow companies to conceive completely new service concepts (e.g. tracking applications), but it also has the potential to make many messaging and mobile Internet services more relevant to customers as information is adjusted to context (e.g. weather information adjusted to the region one is in). Finally, location information can considerably improve service Location Area (LA) Paging Area (PA)

3.2.1. Classification of LBSs

LBSs can be classified as Reactive LBSs and Proactive LBSs:

3.2.1.1. Reactive LBSs

Reactive LBSs are always explicitly activated by the user. The interaction between LBS and users is roughly as follows: the user first invokes the service and establishes a service session, either via a mobile device or a desktop PC. The user then requests for certain functions or information whereupon the service gathers location data (either of the user or of another target person), processes it, and returns the location-dependent result to the user. This request/response cycle may be repeated several times before the session is finally terminated. Thus, a reactive LBS is characterized by a synchronous interaction pattern between user and service.

3.2.1.2. Proactive LBSs

Proactive LBSs are automatically initialized as soon as a predefined location event occurs, for example, if a user enters, approaches, or leaves a certain point of interest or if he/she approaches, meets, or leaves another target. Thus, proactive services are not explicitly requested by the user, but the interaction between them happens asynchronously. In contrast to reactive LBSs where the user is only located once, proactive LBSs require to permanently track a user in order to detect location events.

3.2.2. Applications of LBSs

LBSs are often used via web browsers and are considered a particular type of web services. A representative application example of LBSs is that of Personalized Web Services for the Olympic Games in Beijing in 2008. LBSs are mainly used in three areas: military and government industries, emergency services, and the commercial sector.

As was mentioned earlier, the first location system in use was the satellite based GPS that allows for precise localization of people and objects of up to 3 meters accuracy. GPS is an example of the first area of LBSs, i.e. military and government industries.

Besides the military use of location data, emergency services have turned out to be an important field. Every day, 170000 emergency calls are made in the USA, and 1/3 of these originate from mobile phones, and in most cases, from people who don't know their exact location so as to guide the emergency provider with directions. As a result, the US Federal Communications. Commission (FCC) set an October 2001 deadline for commercial wireless carriers to provide the caller.s location information in a 911 emergency call. This means that when placing an emergency call from a mobile device, a caller.s device position is automatically transmitted to the closest emergency station. Consequently, people in such situations don.t have to explain at length where they are but rather are located in seconds. However, none of the carriers were able to meet the deadline of the FCC, and the deadline date was left open. It is expected for a few more years before the entire system is implemented with full coverage.

The third and final application area of LBSs is commercial. For some time, marketers have been unsure whether lower levels of accuracy as they are obtained from well Cell-ID (a mobile positioning system) would be sufficient to launch compelling consumer and business services. Yet, early service examples show that the accuracy level required depends very much on the service. Even with Cell-ID, location information can successfully be integrated by operators into many existing and new applications that enhance current value propositions and usability.

3.3 GENERAL ISSUES IN LOCATION MANAGEMENT

Current issues for LM involve database architecture design, transmission of signaling between various components of a signaling network, security, dynamic database updates, querying delays, terminal paging methods, and paging delays. The following are some issues in LM schemes:

3.3.1. Without Location Management

- Is referred to as the *Level 0 method.*
- The system doesn't track any mobile devices.
- Searching for a user is done over the complete radio coverage area and within a specific time limit.
- Is also referred to as the *Flooding Algorithm.*
- It is used in:
  (a) Paging systems because of the lack of uplink channel allowing mobile hosts to inform their whereabouts to the network.

(b) Small private mobile wireless networks because of their small coverage areas and user populations.

- Its main advantage is that it is simple to implement because of the absence of a special database.
- Its main disadvantage is that it does not fit into large networks dealing with high number of users and high incoming data exchange rates.

3.3.2. Manual Registration in Location Management

- Is referred to as the *Level 1 method.*
- The system is relatively simple to manage because it only requires the management of an indicator that stores the current location of the user.
- The mobile is relatively simple since its task is limited to scanning the channels to detect paging messages. An example of such a system is telepoint cordless systems.
- The main disadvantage of this method is that users have to re-register each time they move.

3.3.3. Automatic Location Management using LAs

- Is referred to as the *Level 2 method.*
- Widely used and deployed in 1G and 2G cellular systems.
- Since this method is a LA based method, a home database and several visitor databases are included in the network architecture.

3.3.4. Memory less-Based Location Management Methods

These methods depend mainly on the processing capabilities of the system. They are based on algorithms and the network architecture.

3.3.5 Memory-Based Location Management Methods

The design of memory-based location management methods has been motivated by the fact that systems perform many repetitive actions that can be avoided if predicted.

3.3.6. Security

As LM may be viewed as a specific service discovery mechanism, any attack on it is consequently an attack on service discovery. In advanced research S-PALMA is a security mechanism that protects the LM messages. It provides security services such as access control, authentication, message integrity and authentication, confidentiality, and anti-replay. It is intended to cope with identity usurpation, man-in-the-middle, and replay attacks at the edge of the overlay network. It relies on the P2P distributed architecture to provide additional availability.

The S-PALMA architecture consists of a set of Distributed Lookup Servers (DLS), interconnected via heterogeneous networks. These DLSs are organized into an overlay network to publish location information to each other for storage, and to collaboratively resolve queries from mobile hosts.

Applicative interconnections are maintained using Tapestry node insertion and neighbor notification algorithms. In this new virtual space, each DLS is assigned a new identifier generated from its IP address using a hash function (SHA-1). Mobile nodes communicate with DLSs to advertise their presence or submit queries. When a node issues a query to a DLS, it receives the response from that particular DLS. The secure messages are designed in such a way to cope with mobility constraints (particularly delay) by avoiding heavy public-key operations.

3.3.7. Group-Based Location (GBL) Management

It is based on the assumption that the number of high cost location update messages from mobile hosts to the location server can be reduced by clustering mobile hosts with similar mobility into a set of groups. A single location report for the whole group is sent to the location server. A leader will be selected to perform location updating on behalf of the whole group to the moving object database. A positive consequence is that mobile hosts no longer need to possess the long-range communication capability with the remote server; location information can be reported via the group leader. Owing to the dynamic movement of mobile hosts, some of them will occasionally leave their current group and join other groups. These changes in group membership dictate a group management mechanism for a group leader or cluster-head to handle the leave and join events for a mobile host. The more interesting step lies in the selection of an appropriate group and its leader for a wandering mobile host before triggering a join event. This is referred to as the *group finding process*, and the mobile host looking for a group to join as the *group seeker*. Based on this observation,

In the GBL scheme, there are two levels of location update occurring local update and group update. The first level, termed as *local location update*, is about the strategy for reporting location and movement information to the leader of the group by its members. The second level, termed as *group location update*, is about the strategy for reporting the group location information to the stationary location server via the uplink channel.

3.4 LOCATION MANAGEMENT IN WIRELESS NETWORKS

Location Management (LM) is a key factor for wireless mobile networks. Without a good strategy for LM, mobile communication and computing cannot exist. Location Based Services are services that integrate a mobile device's location or position with other information so as to provide added value to a user. LBS are classified as Reactive and Proactive. Applications of LBS are classified as military and government industries, emergency services, and the commercial sector.

LM functions such as location updating and paging have to fulfill services and the requirements of users and operators. One of these requirements is cost efficiency, which could be reached by minimizing the signaling traffic both on radio links and on fixed network links. Current research in LM for wireless data networks includes Wireless Networks, Ad-hoc networks, and WiFi. Not much research is done for LM in Bluetooth. Integration of IPv6 and Mobile IP into LM is another interesting research topic that has a promising future.

In heterogeneous wireless networks, mobile users are able to move from one subsystem to another while maintaining access capability to their subscribed services, which refers to global mobility or global roaming. One of the most challenging problems in global roaming management is LM that consists of keeping track of mobile users who leave their home network and roam into foreign networks that use different protocols. In this context, locating a user requires interoperability between several fixed and mobile subsystems that do not necessarily implement the same technology, which may increase the signaling traffic and decrease the network performance.

3.4.1. LM in Wireless Mobile Ad-hoc Networks

A major challenge faced in Mobile Ad-hoc Networks (MANET) is locating devices for communication, especially with high node mobility and sparse node density. Present solutions provided by Ad-hoc routing protocols range from flooding the entire network with route requests, to deploying a separate LM scheme to maintain a device location database. LM in wireless Ad-hoc networks can be classified mainly as *Soft LM* and *Hard LM*. Soft LM schemes do not require strict LM strategies and is thus computationally less expensive than standard *Hard LM* schemes.

3.4.2. LM in WiFi (802.11)

The widespread deployment of wireless LANs and the increasing popularity of light-weight mobile computing devices have lead to an increased interest in location-aware applications and services. The goal of these applications and services is to enable the user to interact more effectively with his environment. Examples of such value added service include services like displaying the map of the immediate surroundings and guiding a user inside a building.

3.4.3. LM in Bluetooth

LM in 802.15 devices such as Bluetooth, Zigbee, and Infrared hasn't been much of a research issue because these devices operate in areas of less than 1 m radius. In addition, these technologies were initially designed without any location sensing in mind. Another issue to mention here is that there is a signaling interference between 802.11 devices and 802.15 devices since both operate in the 2.4 GHz unlicensed frequency band.

Some enhancements that Bluetooth would have to undergo so that it is best suited for indoor location sensing. Some of these enhancements include:

1. Reducing the time taken by a Bluetooth device to detect other Bluetooth devices in its vicinity.
2. The Bluetooth core specifications do not require that signal strength values be available to higher-level software. If this information is made available, it can greatly aid in accurate location sensing.
3. The Bluetooth specifies 3 power levels at which Bluetooth devices can operate. The minimum power level (1 mW in class 1) gives a coverage range of roughly 10 m. If future implementations can give a shorter range, then location sensing can be made more accurate.

Since Bluetooth devices are expected to be cheaper in the future, we can use more sensors covering very short area thus improving accuracy.

3.4.4. LM and IP

The integration of IP, Mobile IP, IPv6, and Mobile IPv6 into next generation LM systems has been an active area of research for the past 2 decades. The idea of locating users using Mobile IP has been more of a dream a few years ago. However, researchers are getting there, and the dream is becoming more of a reality. Mobile IP is a common standard to support global mobility of mobile hosts. One of the major problems for the Mobile IP is frequent location update and high signaling overhead.

3.5. RECENT RESEARCH ON LOCATION MANAGEMENT

3.5.1. Location Registration and Call Delivery

Location registration involves updating location databases when current location information is available. On the other hand, call delivery involves the querying of location databases to determine the current location of a called MT. These can be costly processes, especially when the MT is located far from its assigned HLR. For example, if the MT is currently roaming in San Francisco and its HLR is in Atlanta, a location registration message is transmitted from San Francisco to Atlanta whenever the MT moves to a new RA that belongs to a different VLR. Under the same scenario, when a call for the MT is originated from a nearby MT in San Francisco, the MSC of the calling MT must first query the HLR in Atlanta before it finds out that the called MT is located in the same area as the caller. This may not be a significant problem in today's cellular network since the penetration is relatively low. As the number of mobile subscribers keeps increasing, the volume of signaling traffic generated by location management is becoming extremely high. Methods for reducing the signaling traffic are therefore needed.

Research in this area generally falls into two categories

First, extensions to the IS-41 location management strategy are developed which aim to improve the IS-41 scheme while keeping the basic database network architecture unchanged. This type of solution has the advantage of easy adaptation to the current PCS networks without major modification. These schemes are based on the centralized database architecture inherited from the IS-41 standard. Another category of research results in completely new database architectures which require a new set of schemes for location registration and call delivery. Most of these schemes are based on Distributed Database Architectures.

In Centralized Database Architectures, the basic idea is that the volume of signaling and database access traffic for locating an MT can be reduced by maintaining a cache of location information at a nearby STP. Whenever the MT is accessed through the STP, an entry is added to the cache which contains a mapping from the ID of the MT to that of its serving VLR. When another call is initiated for an MT, the STP first checks if a cache entry exists for the MT. If no cache entry for the MT exists, the IS-41 call delivery scheme described earlier is used to locate the MT. If a cache entry exists, the STP will query the VLR as specified by the cache. If the MT is still residing under the same VLR, a *hit* occurs, and the MT is found. If the MT has already moved to another location which is not associated with the same VLR, a *miss* occurs, and the IS-41 call delivery scheme is used to locate the MT.

Fig. 3.6 demonstrates the operation of per-user location caching. When a call is initiated from MT 1 to MT 2, as indicated in Fig. 3.6, the system can locate MT 2 by using the cached information at STP1. As a result, MT 2 is successfully located without querying the HLR of MT 2. As compared to the IS-41 scheme demonstrated in Fig. 3.4, per-user location caching allows the STP to location the VLR of the called MT after only one cache database lookup. This is true, however, only when the

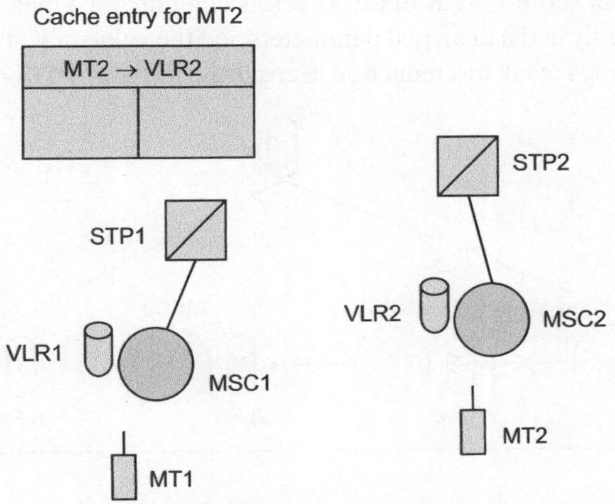

Fig. 3.6: Per-user Location Caching Scheme

cached location information of the called MT is valid (a hit). The cost of per-user location caching is higher than the IS-41 scheme when a miss occurs. Based on the system parameters, the minimum hit ratio required to produce a performance gain using per-user location caching needs to be determined.

In pointer forwarding strategy, the basic idea is that instead of reporting a location change to the HLR every time the MT moves to an area belonging to a different VLR, the reporting can be eliminated by simply setting up a forwarding pointer from the old VLR to the new VLR. When a call for the MT is initiated, the network locates the MT by first determining the VLR at the beginning of the pointer chain and then follows the pointers to the current serving VLR of the MT. To minimize the delay in locating an MT, the length of the pointer chain is limited to a predefined maximum value, K. When the length of the pointer chain reaches K, additional forwarding is not allowed, and location change must be reported to the HLR when the next movement occurs.

Fig. 3.7 demonstrates the operation of pointer forwarding. Pointers are set up from VLR 1 to VLR 2 and from VLR 2 to VLR 3 as the MT moves from MSC 1 to MSC 2 and from MSC 2 to MSC 3, respectively. For $K = 2$, the pointer chain cannot be extended any further. An additional movement from MSC 3 to MSC 4 will result in a location registration at the HLR. The original pointers are deleted, and the HLR records the ID of the current serving VLR of the MT. It is demonstrated that, depending on the mobility and call arrival parameters and the value of K, this scheme may not always result in a reduction in cost from the original IS-41 scheme.

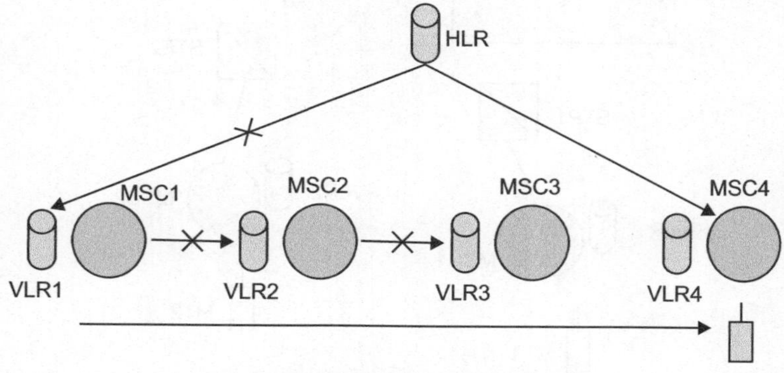

Fig. 3.7: Pointer Forwarding Strategy

In Distributed Database Architectures, two-level HLR/VLR database architecture as described in the IS-41 standard is replaced by a large number of location databases. These location databases are organized as a tree with the root at the top and the leaves at the bottom. The MTs are associated with the leaf (lowest-level) location databases, and each location database contains location information for the MTs residing in its subtree. Fig. 3.8 demonstrates the operation of the proposed scheme. Given that an MT, MT 1, is located at RA 1, an entry exists for MT 1 in each database along the path from its current location to the root of the tree.

The entries for MT 1 at these databases are as shown in Fig. 3.8. When a call is initiated, the network locates the called MT by following its database entries; for example, if a call for MT 1 is initiated by MT 2, as shown in Figure 3.8. The call request is received by node A. Since the database of node A does not have an entry for MT 1, the call request is forwarded to node B and so on. When the request finally reaches node D, an entry for MT 1 is found and the location of MT 1 determined after another three database lookups, as demonstrated in Figure 8. When an MT moves to an RA that belongs to a different leaf database, the corresponding databases are updated to indicate the correct location of the MT. When compared to schemes based on a centralized database architecture, such as the IS-41 scheme, the proposed scheme reduces the distance traveled by signaling messages. However, this scheme increases the number of database updates and queries, and thus increases the delay in location registration and call delivery.

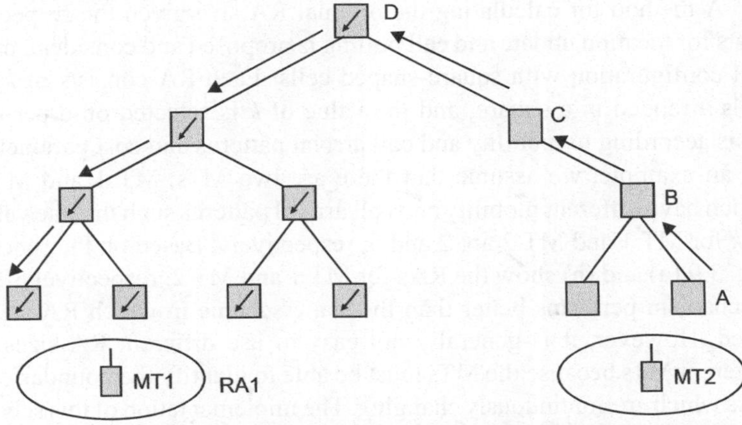

Fig. 3.8: Distributed Hierarchical Tree-Based Database Architecture

3.5.2. Location Update and Terminal Paging

As discussed previously, current PCS networks partition their coverage areas into a number of Registration Areas (RAs). Each RA consists of a group of cells, and each MT performs a location update when it enters an RA. When an incoming call arrives, the network locates the MT by simultaneously paging all cells within the RA.

There are a number of inefficiencies associated with this location update and paging scheme:

- Excessive location updates may be performed by MTs that are located around RA boundaries and make frequent movements back and forth between two RAs.
- Requiring the network to poll all cells within the RA each time a call arrives may result in an excessive volume of wireless broadcast traffic.
- The mobility and call arrival patterns of MTs vary, and it is generally difficult to select an RA size that is optimal for all users. An ideal location update and paging mechanism should be able to adjust on a per-user basis.

The RA-based location update and paging scheme is a static scheme because it cannot be adjusted based on the parameters of an MT from time to time. Recent research efforts focuses primarily on dynamic location update mechanisms which perform location update based on the mobility of the MTs and the frequency of incoming calls.

A method for calculating the optimal RA size given the respective costs for location update and cell polling is proposed and consider a mesh cell configuration with square-shaped cells. Each RA consists of k x k cells arranged in a square, and the value of k is selected on a per-user basis according to mobility and call arrival patterns and cost parameters. As an example, we assume that there are two MTs, MT 1 and MT 2, which have different mobility and call arrival patterns such that the values of k for MT 1 and MT 2 are 2 and 4, respectively. Based on the scheme, Fig. 3.9 (a) and (b) show the RAs for MT 1 and MT 2, respectively. This mechanism performs better than the static scheme in which RA size is fixed. However, it is generally not easy to use different RA sizes for different MTs because the MTs must be able to identify the boundaries of RAs which are continuously changing. The implementation of this scheme is complicated when cells are hexagonal or, in the worst case, when irregular cells are used.

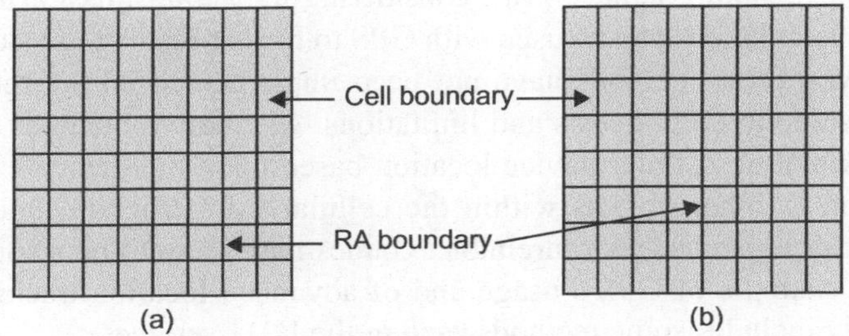

Fig. 3.9: Registration area for a) k = 2; and b) k = 4.

3.6. FUTURE LM DEVELOPMENTS AND E911

The world of cellular networks and LM is certainly not static. Even the most recent theories and developments may become outdated within months. With the increased use of 3G Cellular Networks, and the E911 service providing a national standard in which LM is absolutely essential, it is critical to observe what is to come.

3.6.1. Location Tracking Evolution

Currently, the market standard for location tracking uses the cell ID to track cellular devices through many of the methods as described previously, primarily including the HLR/VLR architecture. However, it is not as precise as many would desire, as this system is not always able to locate users to within a few meters. Future possibilities for location tracking in cellular systems include Global Positioning Systems (GPS), which use line-of-sight satellite position calculation, giving five-meter range precision, but encounter problems when physical obstructions block the connection. Another possibility is Assisted Global Positioning Systems (AGPS), which is similar to normal GPS, but uses advanced searching techniques to determine user position. Unfortunately, AGPS is quite expensive, and still requires line-of-sight. Finally, there is the potential to use Broadband Satellite Networks, which use the low-earth-orbit satellites to create a global network. These give relatively high precision without line-ofsight, but are very complex to manage. An example of a current commercial use for GPS is cellular phone games. These games are a larger part of the industry than might be expected. In order to approximate the true location of the call, these networks generally use Time of Arrival (TOA) measurements and examine the difference of arrival times for multiple incoming signals, while considering signal transmission location. These calculations can be used with GPS to further resolve user location. However, these methods have not been implemented on a large scale, mainly due to GPS's costs and limitations. Alternative methods include approximating cellular device location based upon the device's relative location to other objects within the cellular infrastructure, but this is generally imprecise and unreliable. Games may seem to be a somewhat trivial example of GPS's usage and of advanced location tracking, but actually includes some methods used in the E911 service.

Regardless, these are future plans, currently only used for military, private, and small network settings, and may not fully enter the cellular phone marketplace in the near future. Most of these are excessively expensive or are too difficult to maintain for a large number of cellular subscribers at this point in time. Still, for users willing to pay additional fees for Location-Based Services, these technologies can be of great use and entertainment value. As technology improves and the transition to 3G continues, perhaps such services will become common.

3.6.2. E911

Enhanced 911 is an emergency calling system that uses advanced LM techniques to find the physical location of a user in distress. Public Safety Answering Points (PSAPs), specific physical locations designed to center E911 activities around, are staffed by 911 operators who use AGPS or TDOA to aid in locating users in need of assistance. Additionally, Wireless Location Signatures (WLS) are used with path loss and shadow fading data, and are combined with Geographical Predicted Signature Databases (PSD) and statistical analysis to make the most accurate predictions of user locations possible.

In E911, calls follow this process: the BS forwards the call to the MSC, where a voice path is set up to the access point. The MSC requests the BS locate the caller, which forwards the location request to the Serving Mobile Location Center (SMLC). The SMLC uses network measurement reports to approximate the location of the user, and then forwards the approximation to the Gateway Mobile Location Center (GMLC), which then finally transfers a refined estimate to the PSAP. It is a very complex process, unusable for normal communication, but essential in these extreme cases. However, as recent a development as E911 is, may already be in the process of being phased out. The National Emergency Number Association (NENA) report states that E911 must be upgraded to a Next Generation 911 (NG911) scheme in the near future. New devices must implement systems to handle NG911 calls, and LM must continue to be improved. The new NG911 must be expanded to VoIP architecture, and better integration of national databases and stations must occur. However, E911 still stands as an example of the importance of LM as well as the rapidity of change within cellular networks.

3.7. MOBILE NETWORKING THROUGH MOBILE IP

Mobile Computing is becoming increasingly important due to the rise in the number of portable computers and the desire to have continuous network connectivity to the Internet irrespective of the physical location of the node. The Internet infrastructure is built on top of a collection of protocols, called the TCP/IP protocol suite. Transmission Control Protocol (TCP) and Internet Protocol (IP) are the core protocols in this suite. IP requires the location of any host connected to the Internet to be uniquely identified by an assigned IP address. This raises one of the most important issues in mobility, because when a host moves to another physical location, it has to change its IP address. However, the higher level protocols require IP address of a host to be fixed for identifying connections. The Mobile Internet Protocol (Mobile IP) is an extension to the Internet Protocol proposed by the Internet Engineering Task Force (IETF) that addresses this issue. It enables mobile computers to stay connected to the Internet regardless of their location and without changing their IP address. More precisely, Mobile IP is a standard protocol that builds on the Internet Protocol by making mobility transparent to applications and higher level protocols like TCP.

In the following sections design, mobility support, advantages, and other technical issues related with Mobile IP have been discussed.

3.7.1. Mobile IP: An Introduction

Mobile-IP is a means by which mobile computers can use Internet protocols (IP) to communicate data with network resources transparently to application software. The mobile client supplies information to a router, called its home agent, about its current whereabouts using a simple registration protocol. The mobile client uses the same IP address as it moves from place to place, and the problem of enabling mobility for IP clients is translated into the problem of allowing a home agent to determine a current path to the unchanging destination address of its mobile client. Subsequently, the home agent delivers data to the mobile client at its current location by a tunneling mechanism. Since the mobile-IP protocol does not depend on the characteristics of any particular sub network protocol, the same mechanism works for every wireless medium, as well as existing wired media like Ethernet.

The next version of IP, IPv6 is designed to be an evolutionary step from IPv4. IPv6 addresses are 128 bits long. Mobility support in IPv6 solves many of the problems of basic Mobile IP. Some advantages of Mobile IPv6 over Mobile IPv4 are:

- Route Optimization is built as a fundamental part of Mobile IPv6 unlike Mobile IPv4 where it is an optional set of extensions that may not be supported by all nodes.
- Foreign Agents are not needed in Mobile IPv6. The enhanced features of IPv6 like Neighbour Discovery and Address Auto-configuration enable mobile nodes to function in any location without the services of any special router in that location.
- In Mobile IPv4, when a mobile node communicates with a correspondent node, it puts its home address as the source address of the packet. Thus " ingress filtering routers " used to filter out the packets as the source address of the packet is different from the network from which the packet originated. This problem is tackled in Mobile IPv6 by putting the care-of address as the source address and having a Home Address Destination option, allowing the use of the care-of address to be transparent over the IP layer.

3.7.2. Motivation for the Mobile IP Design

The IP address of a host consists of two parts:

- The higher order bits of the address determine the network on which the host resides;
- The remaining low-order bits determine the host number.

IP decides the next-hop by determining the network information from the destination IP address of the packet. On the other hand, higher level layers like TCP maintain information about connections that are indexed by a quadruplet containing the IP addresses of both the endpoints and the port numbers. Thus, while trying to support mobility on the Internet under the existing protocol suite, we are faced with two mutually conflicting requirements:

- a mobile node has to change its IP address whenever it changes its point of attachment, so that packets destined to the node are routed correctly,
- to maintain existing TCP connections, the mobile node has to keep its IP address the same. Changing the IP address will cause the connection to be disrupted and lost.

Mobile IP, the standard proposed by IETF, is designed to solve the problem by allowing each mobile node to have two IP addresses and by transparently maintaining the binding between the two addresses. One of the IP addresses is the permanent home address that is assigned at the home network and is used to identify communication endpoints. The other is a temporary care-of address that represents the current location of the host. The main goals of Mobile IP are to make mobility transparent to the higher level protocols and to make minimum changes to the existing Internet infrastructure.

3.7.3. Overview of the Protocol

Mobile IP supports mobility by transparently binding the home address of the mobile node with its care-of address. This mobility binding is maintained by some specialized routers known as mobility agents. Mobility agents are of two types - home agents and foreign agents. The home agent, a designated router in the home network of the mobile node, maintains the mobility binding in a *mobility binding table* where each entry is identified by the tuple <permanent home address, temporary care-of address, association lifetime>. Fig. 3.10 shows a mobility binding table. The purpose of this table is to map a mobile node's home address with its care-of address and forward packets accordingly.

Foreign agents are specialized routers on the foreign network where the mobile node is currently visiting. The foreign agent maintains a **visitor list** which contains information about the mobile nodes currently visiting that network. Each entry in the visitor list is identified by the tuple: < permanent home address, home agent address, media address of the mobile node, association lifetime>. Fig. 3.11 shows an instance of a visitor list.

Home Address	Care-of Address
131.193.171.4	128.172.23.28
131.193.171.2	119.123.56.28

Fig. 3.10: Mobility Binding Table

Home Address	Home Agent	Media Address	Lifetime Address (in s)
131.193.44.13	131.193.44.7	00-60-08-95-66-E1	150
131.193.33.19	131.193.33.1	00-60-08-68-A2-56	200

Fig. 3.11: Visitor List

The basic Mobile IP protocol has four distinct stages. These are:

- **Agent Discovery:** Agent Discovery consists of the following steps:
  1. Mobility agents advertise their presence by periodically broadcasting Agent Advertisement messages. An Agent Advertisement message lists one or more care-of addresses and a flag indicating whether it is a home agent or a foreign agent.
  2. The mobile node receiving the Agent Advertisement message observes whether the message is from its own home agent and determines whether it is on the home network or a foreign network.
  3. If a mobile node does not wish to wait for the periodic advertisement, it can send out Agent Solicitation messages that will be responded by a mobility agent.
- **Registration:** Registration consists of the following steps as shown in Fig. 3.12.
  1. If a mobile node discovers that it is on the home network, it operates without any mobility services.
  2. If the mobile node is on a new network, it registers with the foreign agent by sending a Registration Request message which includes the permanent IP address of the mobile host and the IP address of its home agent.

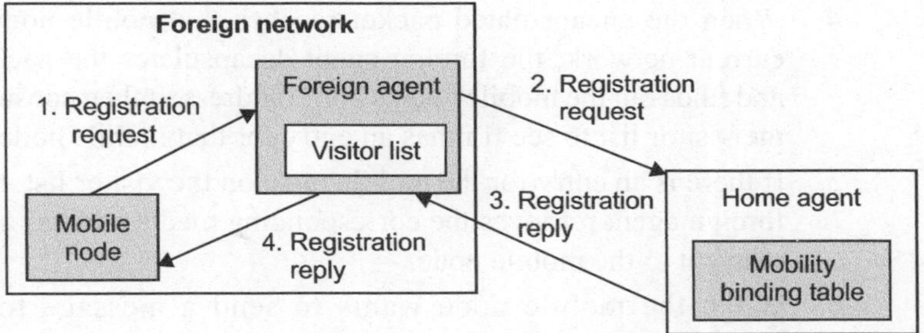

Fig. 3.12: Registration process in Mobile IP

3. The foreign agent in turn performs the registration process on behalf of the mobile host by sending a Registration Request containing the permanent IP address of the mobile node and the IP address of the foreign agent to the home agent.
4. When the home agent receives the Registration Request, it updates the mobility binding by associating the care-of address of the mobile node with its home address.
5. The home agent then sends an acknowledgement to the foreign agent.
6. The foreign agent in turn updates its visitor list by inserting the entry for the mobile node and relays the reply to the mobile node.

- **In Service:** This stage can be subdivided into the following steps:
  1. When a correspondent node wants to communicate with the mobile node, it sends an IP packet addressed to the permanent IP address of the mobile node.
  2. The home agent intercepts this packet and consults the mobility binding table to find out if the mobile node is currently visiting any other network.
  3. The home agent finds out the mobile node's care-of address and constructs a new IP header that contains the mobile node's care-of address as the destination IP address. The original IP packet is put into the payload of this IP packet. It then sends the packet. This process of encapsulating one IP packet into the payload of another is known as **IP-within-IP** encapsulation, or **tunneling** as represented in Fig. 3.13.

4. When the encapsulated packet reaches the mobile node's current network, the foreign agent decapsulates the packet and finds out the mobile node's home address. It then consults the visitor list to see if it has an entry for that mobile node.
5. If there is an entry for the mobile node on the visitor list, the foreign agent retrieves the corresponding media address and relays it to the mobile node.
6. When the mobile node wants to send a message to a correspondent node, it forwards the packet to the foreign agent, which in turn relays the packet to the correspondent node using normal IP routing.
7. The foreign agent continues serving the mobile node until the granted lifetime expires. If the mobile node wants to continue the service, it has to reissue the Registration Request.

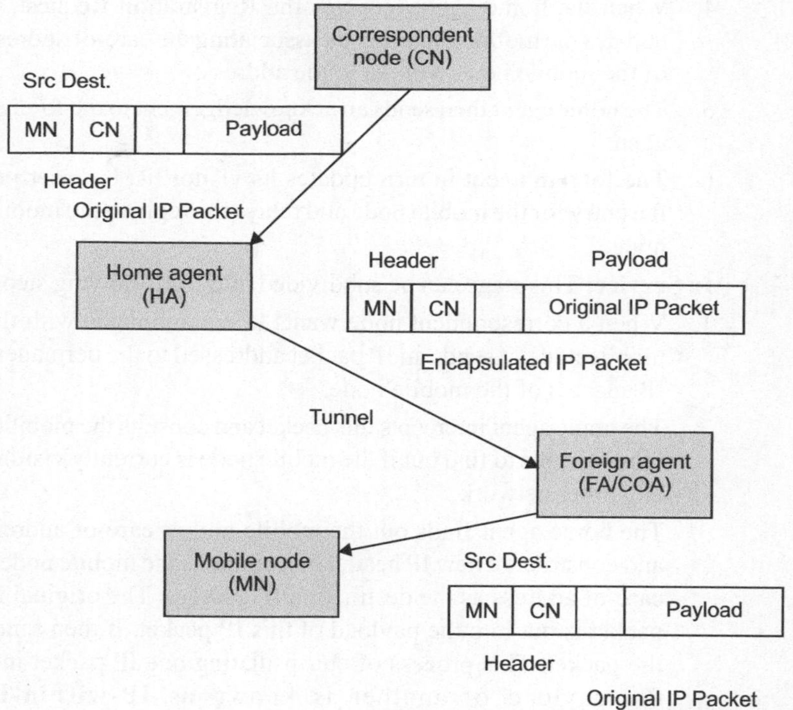

Fig. 3.13: Tunneling operation in Mobile IP

- **Deregistration:** If a mobile node wants to drop its care-of address, it has to deregister with its home agent. It achieves this by sending a Registration Request with the lifetime set to zero. There is no need for deregistering with the foreign agent as registration automatically expires when lifetime becomes zero. However if the mobile node visits a new network, the old foreign network does not know the new care-of address of the mobile node. Thus datagrams already forwarded by the home agent to the old foreign agent of the mobile node are lost.

3.7.4. Security Considerations

Security is very important in Mobile IP as mobile nodes are often connected to the Internet via wireless links which are very vulnerable to security attacks. For example, during registration procedure the home agent should be convinced that it is getting authentic Registration Request from a mobile node and not receiving information from a bogus node. Mobile IP solves this problem by specifying a security association between the home agent and the mobile node. This security association is at present manually configured. Every registration message should contain a mobile node-home agent authentication extension which contain an Security Parameters Index(SPI) followed by an authenticator. The SPI is an index into the mobility security association and it defines the security context (i.e., the algorithm and the secret) used to compute and check the authenticator. The default algorithm is keyed MD5 with a key size of 128 bits. Also each registration contains unique data to avoid valid registration recording by malicious nodes. Two methods are used to generate the unique data:

- ***timestamps*** - The node generating the message inserts the time-of-day, and the node receiving the message checks whether it is sufficiently close to its time-of-day.
- ***nonces*** - Node A generates a new random number in every message to node B, and checks whether node B returns the same number in its next message to node A. Both messages use an authentication code to protect against alteration by an outsider. Node B can also generate random numbers and use them in its messages.

3.7.5. Route Optimization

In the basic Mobile IP protocol, IP packets destined to a mobile node that is outside its home network are routed through the home agent. However packets from the mobile node to the correspondent nodes are routed directly. This is known as triangle routing. Fig. 3.14 illustrates triangle routing.

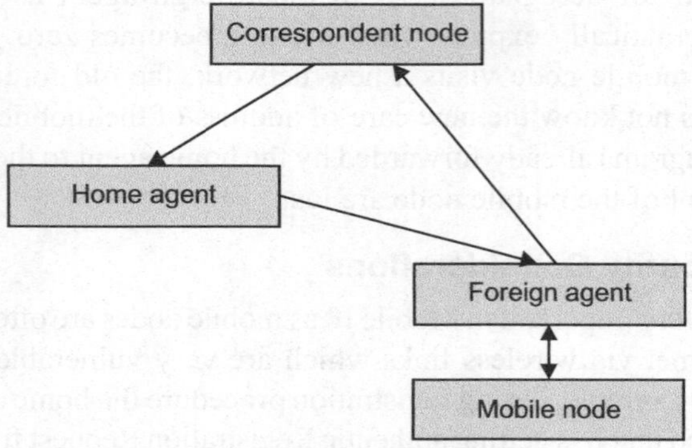

Fig. 3.14: Triangle Routing

This method may be inefficient in many cases. Consider the case when the correspondent host and the mobile host are in the same network, but not in the home network of the mobile host. In this case the messages will experience unnecessary delay since they have to be first routed to the home agent that resides in the home network. One way to improve this is *Route Optimization*.

Route Optimization is an extension proposed to the basic Mobile IP protocol. Here messages from the correspondent node are routed directly to the mobile node's care-of address without having to go through the home agent. Route Optimization provides four main operations. These are:

- Updating binding caches,
- Managing smooth handoffs between foreign agents,
- Acquiring registration keys for smooth handoffs,
- Using special tunnels.

3.7.5.1. Updating Binding Caches

Binding caches are maintained by correspondent nodes for associating the home address of a mobile node with its care-of address. A binding cache entry also has an associated lifetime after which the entry has to be deleted from the cache. If the correspondent node has no binding cache entry for a mobile node, it sends the message addressed to the mobile node's home address. When the home agent intercepts this message, it encapsulates it and sends it to the mobile node's care-of address. It then sends a Binding Update message to the correspondent node informing it of the current mobility binding.

3.7.5.2. Managing Smooth Handoffs Between Foreign Agents

When a mobile node registers with a new foreign agent, the basic Mobile IP does not specify a method to inform the previous foreign agent. Thus the datagrams in flight which had already tunneled to the old care-of address of the mobile node are lost. This problem is solved in Route Optimization by introducing smooth handoffs. Smooth handoff provides a way to notify the previous foreign agent of the mobile node's new mobility binding.

If a foreign agent supports smooth handoffs, it indicates this in its Agent Advertisement message. When the mobile node moves to a new location, it requests the new foreign agent to inform its previous foreign agent about the new location as part of the registration procedure. The new foreign agent then constructs a Binding Update message and sends it to the previous foreign agent of the mobile node. Thus if the previous foreign agent receives packets from a correspondent node having an out-of-date binding, it forwards the packet to the mobile node's care-of address. It then sends a Binding Warning message to the mobile node's home agent. The home agent in turn sends a Binding Update message to the correspondent node. This notification also allows datagrams sent by correspondent nodes having out-of-date binding cache entries to be forwarded to the current care-of address. Finally this notification allows any resources consumed by the mobile node at the previous foreign agent to be released immediately, instead of waiting for the registration lifetime to expire.

3.7.5.3. Acquiring Registration Keys For Smooth Handoffs

For managing smooth handoffs, mobile nodes need to communicate with the previous foreign agent. This communication needs to be done securely as any careful foreign agent should require assurance that it is getting authentic handoff information and not arranging to forward in-flight datagrams to a bogus destination. For this purpose a registration key is established between a foreign agent and a mobile node during the registration process. The following methods for establishing registration keys have been proposed in the order of declining preference:

- If the home agent and the foreign agent share a security association, the home agent can choose the registration key.
- If the foreign agent has a public key, it can again use the home agent to supply the registration key.
- If the mobile node includes its public key in its Registration Request, the foreign agent can choose the new registration key.
- The mobile node and its foreign agent can execute the Diffie-Hellman key exchange protocol as part of the registration protocol.

This registration key is used to form a security association between the mobile node and the foreign agent.

3.7.5.4. Using Special Tunnels

When a foreign agent receives a tunneled datagram for which it has no visitor list entry, it concludes that the node sending the tunneled datagram has an out-of-date binding cache entry for the mobile node. If the foreign agent has a binding cache entry for the mobile node, it should re-tunnel the datagram to the care-of address indicated in its binding cache entry. On the other hand, when a foreign agent receives a datagram for a mobile node for which it has no visitor list or binding cache entry, it constructs a special tunnel datagram. The special tunnel datagram is constructed by encapsulating the datagram and making the outer destination address equal to the inner destination address. This allows the home agent to see the address of the node that tunneled the datagram and prevent sending it to the same node. This avoids a possible routing loop that might have occurred if the foreign agent crashed and lost its state information.

3.7.6. Minimal Encapsulation Scheme

Encapsulation in Mobile IP is carried out by putting the original datagram (=IP header + payload) inside another IP envelope. The fields in the outer IP header add too much overhead to the final datagram - several fields are duplicated from the inner IP header. To prevent this waste of space a Minimal Encapsulation Scheme has been defined where instead of inserting a new header, the original header is modified to reflect the care-of address and a minimal forwarding header is inserted to store the original source and destination address. Thus the care-of address of the mobile node becomes the destination address of the IP packet and the home agent's address becomes the source address. The minimal forwarding header stores the original source and destination addresses. When the foreign agent tries to decapsulate, it simply restores the fields in the forwarding header to the IP header and removes the forwarding header. Fig. 3.15 illustrates the Minimal Encapsulation scheme.

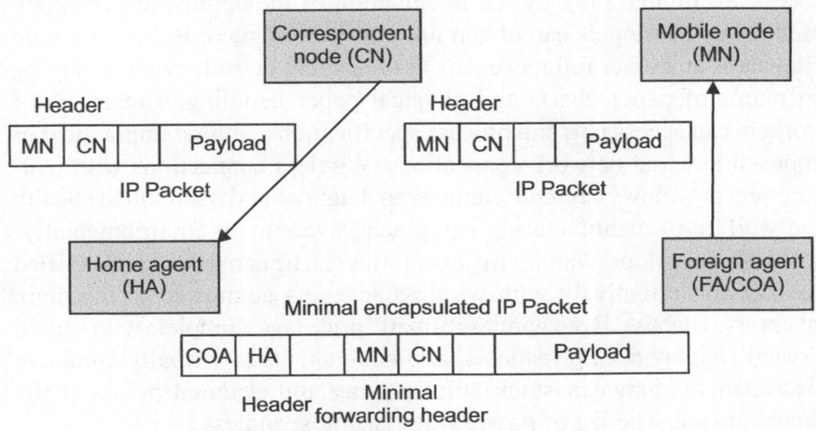

Fig. 3.15: Minimal Encapsulation

It is evident that Mobile IP has great potential. Mobile IP is a standard protocol that builds on the Internet Protocol by making mobility transparent to applications and higher level protocols like TCP.

3.8. WIRELESS LANS AND IEEE 802.11

Over recent years, the market for wireless communications has enjoyed tremendous growth. Wireless technology now reaches or is capable of reaching virtually every location on the face of the earth. Hundreds of millions of people exchange information every day using pagers, cellular telephones, and other wireless communication products. With tremendous success of wireless telephony and messaging services, it is hardly surprising that wireless communication is beginning to be applied to the realm of personal and business computing. No longer bound by the harnesses of wired networks, people will be able to access and share information on a global scale nearly anywhere they venture. This article will try to answer some basic questions of why and where wireless local area networks can be used, and present a brief description of some protocols that have been developed, with emphasis on IEEE 802.11.

The major motivation and benefit from wireless LANs is increased mobility. Untethered from conventional network connections, network users can move about almost without restriction and access LANs from nearly anywhere. Examples of the practical uses for wireless network access are limited only by the imagination of the application designer. Medical professionals can obtain not only patient records, but real-time vital signs and other reference data at the patient bedside without relying on reams of paper charts and physical paper handling. Factory floor workers can access part and process specifications without impractical or impossible wired network connections. Wireless connections with real-time sensing allows a remote engineer to diagnose and maintain the health and welfare of manufacturing equipment, even on an environmentally-hostile factory floor. Warehouse inventories can be carried out and verified quickly and effectively with wireless scanners connected to the main inventory database. Even wireless "smart" price tags, complete with Liquid Crystal Display (LCD) readouts, allow merchants to virtually eliminate discrepancies between stock-point pricing and scanned prices at the checkout lane. The list of possibilities is almost endless.

In addition to increased mobility, wireless LANs offer increased flexibility. Again, imagination is the limiting parameter. One can visualize without too much difficulty a meeting in which employees use small computers and wireless links to share and discuss future design plans and products. This "ad hoc" network can be brought up and torn down in a very short time as needed, either around the conference table and/or around the world. Some car rental establishments already use wireless networks to help facilitate check-ins. Traders on Wall Street are able to use wireless terminals to make market trades. Even students of university campuses have been known to access lecture notes and other course materials while wandering about campus.

Sometimes it is more economical to use a wireless LAN. For instance, in old buildings, the cost of asbestos cleanup or removal outweighs the cost of installing a wireless LAN solution. In other situations, such as a factory floor, it may not be feasible to run a traditional wired LAN. Wireless LANs offer the connectivity and the convenience of wired LANs without the need for expensive wiring or rewiring.

3.8.1. IEEE 802.11

IEEE 802.11 is still in the process of being adopted as a standard by the

IEEE standards body. Although 802.11 provides a reliable means of wireless data transfer, some improvements to it have been proposed. For example, at Virginia Tech, research is being performed into ways in which the 802.11 network parameters can be dynamically adjusted to improve throughput. The use of wireless LANs is expected to increase dramatically in the future as businesses discover the enhanced productivity and the increased mobility that wireless communications can provide in a society that is moving towards more connectionless connections.

3.8.1.1. IEEE 802.11 Layers

The IEEE 802.11 standard places specifications on the parameters of both the physical (PHY) and Medium Access Control (MAC) layers of the network. The PHY layer, which actually handles the transmission of data between nodes, can use either direct sequence spread spectrum, frequency-hopping spread spectrum, or infrared (IR) pulse position modulation. IEEE 802.11 makes provisions for data rates of either 1 Mbps or 2 Mbps, and calls for operation in the 2.4 - 2.4835 GHz frequency band (in the case of spread-spectrum transmission), which is an unlicensed band for industrial, scientific, and medical (ISM) applications, and 300 - 428,000 GHz for IR transmission. Infrared is generally considered to be more secure to eavesdropping, because IR transmissions require absolute line-of-sight links (no transmission is possible outside any simply connected space or around corners), as opposed to radio frequency transmissions, which can penetrate walls and be intercepted by third parties unknowingly. However, infrared transmissions can be adversely affected by sunlight, and the spread-spectrum protocol of 802.11 does provide some rudimentary security for typical data transfers.

The MAC layer is a set of protocols which is responsible for maintaining order in the use of a shared medium. The 802.11 standard specifies a Carrier Sense Multiple Access with Collision Avoidance (CSMA/CA) protocol. In this protocol, when a node receives a packet to be transmitted, it first listens to ensure no other node is transmitting. If the channel is clear, it then transmits the packet. Otherwise, it chooses a random "backoff factor" which determines the amount of time the node must wait until it is allowed to transmit its packet. During periods in which the channel is clear, the transmitting node decrements its backoff counter. (When the channel is busy it does not decrement its backoff counter.) When the backoff counter reaches zero, the node transmits the packet. Since the probability that two nodes will choose the same backoff factor is small, collisions between packets are minimized. Collision detection, as is employed in Ethernet, cannot be used for the radio frequency transmissions of IEEE 802.11. The reason for this is that when a node is transmitting it cannot hear any other node in the system which may be transmitting, since its own signal will drown out any others arriving at the node.

3.9. TCP OVER WIRELESS

A wireless network consists of mobile stations and various intermediate nodes. Some type of intermediate node is required to connect a wireless network with a wireline network. A cellular telephony network, for example, is connected to a wireline network by an inter-working unit, and a wireless local area network (WLAN) is interconnected with an access point (also called base station). Wireless links are not as robust as wireline links, since the radio quality may vary considerably over time, the bandwidth is usually lower, and transmission errors occur more frequently. Sending signals over an omnidirectional radio based medium gives rise to more errors than in a guided medium such as fiber or coax. Signal strength weakens with the distance between the mobile station and the base station, and radio waves bounce off objects, giving rise to interference and multi-path effects.

In order to shield upper protocol layers from transmission errors both error correction, interleaving and retransmissions can be used at lower layers. In many wireless networks, the data link layer performs error recovery according to some Automatic Repeat re Quest (ARQ) protocol. Link ARQ protocols are categorized according to the level of reliability provided to upper layers. An ARQ protocol is defined as perfectly persistent or reliable, if it retransmits frames until they are acknowledged or, after a very large number of retransmission attempts, disconnects the link and notices upper layers.

If the maximum number of retransmissions (or the maximum time spent retransmitting a frame) is limited, to tens of retransmissions, then the ARQ protocol is defined as highly persistent or highly reliable. A low persistent or partially reliable ARQ protocol, on the other hand, retransmits a frame 2-5 times before it gives up and transmits the next frame instead.

Due to the low loss nature of wired links, TCP assumes that packet losses mostly occur due to congestion. TCP reacts to congestion by decreasing its congestion window thus reducing network utilization. In wireless networks, however, losses may occur due to the high bit-error rate of the transmission medium or due to fading and mobility. TCP still reacts to losses according to its congestion control scheme, thus unnecessarily reducing the network utilization.

The typical wireless network system model is shown in Fig. 3.16. This model can represent both Wireless Local Area Networks (WLANs) such as 802.11 networks, and Wireless Wide Area Networks (WWANs) such as CDPD and GPRS networks. In ad hoc networks, on the other hand, there is no required infrastructure (such as base stations (BSs)), and nodes can organize themselves to establish communication routes. Satellite networks allow various configurations with potentially several wireless hops.

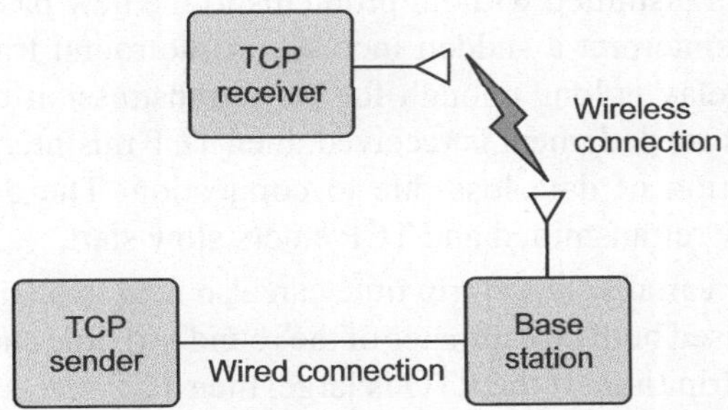

Fig. 3.16: Typical Model of a TCP-Wireless Connection

Handling wireless losses may or may not be transparent to the sender. In other words, the sender implementation may be modified to be aware of losses due to wireless links, or local recovery can be used to handle such losses. The latter method shields the sender from knowing about the wireless link. A special case of this method terminates the TCP connection at the wireless interface, namely, the base station, which in turn uses some other reliable connection to connect to the destination. This solution is referred to as split-connection.

3.9.1. Issues with TCP in Wireless Networks

The performance of TCP is generally lower in wireless networks than in fixed. This is explained by the fact that TCP cannot distinguish problems that typically occur in wireless networks from congestion. The congestion control algorithms in TCP are based on the assumptions that data is lost mainly due to congestion and that data loss due to transmission errors is rare. Therefore, data loss is interpreted as a signal of congestion in the network. Even in a wireless network, where data loss may not be related to congestion, data loss still signals congestion to the sender.

TCP segments may be lost if the radio conditions are poor and the link layer protocol provides a low reliability. After some retransmission attempts the link layer protocol gives up and leaves further error recovery to TCP. Handover events may also lead to data loss. A whole window of data may be lost due to handover. Data loss due to an unreliable link layer or a handover, may cause a timeout event followed by slow start or three dupacks followed by fast retransmit and fast recovery. In either case, the congestion control action taken by TCP is unnecessary. Directly after the loss event, the radio quality may become high again, and after handover data may be transmitted without problems to the new base station. TCP may also misinterpret a sudden increase in the round trip time as data loss. If the delay is long enough for the retransmission timer to expire before an acknowledgment is received, then TCP misinterprets the delay as an indication of data loss due to congestion. The delayed data is unnecessarily retransmitted and TCP enters slow start.

A highly variable round trip time can also lead to a large RTO, since the RTO is based both on estimates of the round trip time and on variations in the round trip time. If the RTO is large, then TCP reacts slowly to data loss. Variations in the round trip time can be caused by link level retransmissions of a wireless link. If the link layer frames that contain a TCP segment must be retransmitted because of a poor radio environment, then the whole segment is delayed. Round trip time variations may also be caused by handover or competing traffic. Queuing in routers, base stations, and other intermediate nodes may also lead to a long round trip time. A long round trip time may cause low throughput and underutilization of the network, since it takes a number of round trip times before the congestion window reaches the capacity of the network. TCP performance is degraded, especially for short lived flows, which transmits a small amount of data.

As TCP is one of the reasons for the success of the Internet, it is desirable to use TCP also in wireless networks. However, TCP performance is degraded more than necessary due to non-congestion related packet loss and varying round trip times, incurred by the properties of wireless networks. Therefore, a number of optimizations have been proposed to increase the performance of TCP over wireless networks. The optimization proposals all have the same goal, to improve TCP performance over wireless networks, but different approaches are used to reach the goal. For example, some link layer optimizations try to emulate the behavior of wired links by reducing the probability of non-congestion related loss, while optimizations that use explicit notifications aim for the opposite, that the end points should be aware of the network heterogeneity. Some of the optimization proposals may improve TCP performance in many types of wireless networks, while others are intended for WLANs or for a specific WWAN.

In the future, wireless network technologies will provide a higher capacity. Even so, TCP performance will not automatically become optimal. Problems inherent to wireless networks related to variable radio conditions and to handover will still be crucial to the performance of TCP.

REFERENCES

- EIA/TIA, "Cellular Radio-Telecommunications Intersystem Operations," Tech. Rep. IS-41 Revision C, 1995.
- M. Mouly and M. B. Pautet, *The GSM System for Mobile Communications*, M. Mouly, 49 rue Louise Bruneau, Palaiseau, France, 1992.
- Y. B. Lin and S. K. DeVries, "PCS Network Signaling Using SS7," *IEEE Commun. Mag*, June 1995., pp. 44-p;55.
- A. R. Modarressi and R. A. Skoog, "Signaling System 7: A Tutorial," *IEEE Commun. Mag.*, vol. 28, no. 7, July 1990, pp. 19-p;35.
- D. R. Wilson, "Signaling System No. 7, IS-41 and Cellular Telephony Networking," *Proc. IEEE*, vol. 80, no. 4, Apr. 1992, pp. 664-p;52.
- S. Mohan and R. Jain, "Two User Location Strategies for Personal Communications Services," *IEEE Pers. Commun.*, 1st Qtr. 1994, pp. 42-p;50.
- C. N. Lo, S. Mohan, and R. S. Wolff, "Performance Modeling and Simulation of Data Management for Personal Communications Applications," *Proc. IEEE PIMRC '92*, Nov. 1992, pp. 1210-p;14.

- C. N. Lo, R. S. Wolff, and R. C. Bernhardt, "An Estimate of Network Database Transaction Volume to Support Personal Communications Services," *Proc. Int'l. Conf. on Universal Pers. Commun.*, 1992, pp. 236-p;41.
- R. Jain, Y. B. Lin, and S. Mohan, "A Caching Strategy to Reduce Network Impacts of PCS," *IEEE JSAC*, vol. 12, no. 8, Oct. 1994, pp. 1434-p;44.
- Y. B. Lin, "Determining the User Locations for Personal Communications Services Networks," *IEEE Trans. Vehicular Tech.*, vol. 43, no. 3, Aug. 1994, pp. 466-p;73.
- N. Shivakumar and J. Widom, "User Profile Replication for Faster Location Lookup in Mobile Environments," *Proc. ACM MOBICOM '95*, Nov. 1995, pp. 161-69
- R. Jain and Y. B. Lin, "An Auxiliary User Location Strategy Employing Forwarding Pointers to Educe Network Impact of PCS," *ACM-Baltzer J. Wireless Networks*, vol. 1, no. 2, July 1995, pp. 197-p;210.
- J. S. M. Ho and I. F. Akyildiz, "Local Anchor Scheme for Reducing Location Tracking Costs in PCNs," *IEEE/ACM Trans. Networking*, Oct. 1996.
- J. Z. Wang, "A Fully Distributed Location Registration Strategy for Universal Personal Communication Systems," *IEEE JSAC*, vol. 11, no. 6, Aug. 1993, pp. 850-p;60.
- B. R. Badrinath, T. Imielinski and A Virmani, "Locating Strategies for Personal Communication Network," *Proc. Workshop on Networking of Pers. Commun. Applications*, Dec. 1992.
- V. Anantharam *et al.*, "Optimization of a Database Hierarchy for Mobility Tracking in a Personal Communications Network," *Performance Evaluation*, vol. 20, no. 1-p;3, May 1994, pp. 287-p;300.
- H. Xie, S. Tabbane and D. Goodman, "Dynamic Location Area Management and Performance Analysis," *Proc. IEEE VTC '93*, May 1993, pp. 536-p;39.
- A. Bar-Noy, I. Kessler and M. Sidi, "Mobile Users: To Update or Not to Update?" *ACM-Baltzer J. Wireless Networks*, vol. 1, no. 2, July 1995, pp. 175-p;86.

- U. Madhow, M. L. Honig and K. Steiglitz, "Optimization of Wireless Resources for Personal Communications Mobility Tracking," *Proc. IEEE INFOCOM '94*, June 1994, pp.577-p;84.
- I. F. Akyildiz and J. S. M. Ho, "Dynamic Mobile User Location Update for Wireless PCS Networks," *ACM-Baltzer J. Wireless Networks*, vol. 1, no. 2, July 1995, pp. 187-p;96
- J. S. M. Ho and I. F. Akyildiz, "A Mobile User Location Update and Paging Mechanism Under Delay Constraints," *ACM-Baltzer J. Wireless Networks*, vol. 1, no. 4, Dec. 1995, pp. 413-p;25.
- C. Rose and R. Yates, "Minimizing the Average Cost of Paging Under Delay Constraints," *ACM-Baltzer J. Wireless Networks*, vol. 1, no. 2, July 1995, pp. 211-p;19
- I. F. Akyildiz, J. S. M. Ho and Y. B. Lin, "Movement Based Location Update and Selective Paging Schemes," *IEEE/ACM Trans. Networking*, Aug. 1996.
- Amitava Mukherjee, Somprakash Bandyopadhyay, Debashis Saha, .Location Management and Routing in Mobile Wireless Networks., Artech House, 2003, pp. 69-113
- Axel Kupper, .Location-based Services: Fundamentals and Operation., John Wiley and Sons Ltd, 2005
- Jochen Schiller, Agnes Voisard, .Location-Based Services., Morgan Kaufmann, 2004
- Xinwei Luo, Tracy Camp, William Navidi, .Predictive Methods for Location Services in Mobile Ad-hoc Networks., IEEE, 2005, 6 pages
- Hassan A. Karimi, Xiong Liu, .A Predictive Location Model for Location-Based Services., ACM, 2003, pp. 126-133
- Kaouthar Sethom, Khaled Masmoudi, Hossam Afifi, .A Secure P2P Architecture for Location Management., ACM, May 2005, pp. 22-26
- Gary Hoi Kit Lam, Hong Va Leong, Stephen Chi Fai Chan, Reducing Group Management in Group-based Location Management., Proceedings of the 15th International Workshop on Database and Expert Systems Applications (DEXA .04), 2004, 5 pages

- Kaouthar Sethom, Hossam Afifi, Guy Pujolle, .A Distributed Architecture for Location Management in Next Generation Networks., IEEE, 2005, pp. 1181-1186
- Kevin Lee, Hong Wing Lee, Sanjay Jha, Nirupama Bulusu, .Adaptive, Distributed Location Management in Mobile, Wireless Networks., IEEE Communications Society, 2004, pp. 4077-4081
- Abdoul D. Assouma, Ronald Beaubrun, Samuel Pierre, .A Location Management Scheme for Heterogeneous Wireless Networks., IEEE, 2005, pp. 51-56
- San-Yih Hwang, Jeng-Kuen Chiu, .Toward Optimal Replication for Hierarchical Location Management in Wireless Systems., 2005, 12 pages
- Joy Ghosh, Sumesh Philip, Chunming Qiao, .Acquaintance Based Soft Location Management (ABSLM) in MANET., IEEE Communications Society, 2004, pp. 166-171
- Sumesh Philip, Joy Ghosh, Swapnil Khedekar, Chunming Qiao, .Scalability Analysis of Location Management Protocols for Mobile Ad-hoc Networks., IEEE Communications Society, 2004, pp. 183-188
- Sumesh Philip, Chunming Qiao, .MobiHoc Poster: Hierarchical Grid Location Management for Large Wireless Ad hoc Networks., IEEE Communications Society, 2004, pp. 33-34
- Artur Ziviani, Serge Fdida, Jose F. de Rezende, Otto Carlos Duarte, .A TCP-Tailored Approcah to Location Management in Mobile Ad-hoc Networks., IEEE, 2005, pp. 1043-1045
- Ankur Agiwal, Parakram Khandpur, Huzur Saran,. LOCATER. Location Estimation for Wireless LANs., ACM, 2004, pp. 102-109
- Andrei Oliveira da Silva, Paulo Henrique de Souza Schneider, Fabricio D.Avila Cabral, Ana Cristina da Silva, Joao Batista de Oliveira, Eduardo Augusto Bezerra, .Towards Service and User Discovery on Wireless Networks., ACM, 2004, pp. 79-82
- Travis Calvert, Steven Case, .Wireless Location Determination: Using Existing 802.11 Wireless networks to Determine a User.s Location., 2005, 8 pages
- Song Li, Gang Zhao, Lin Liao, .User Location Service over an 802.11 Ad-hoc Network., 13 pages

- Abhishek Patel, Dan Kim, Lionel Ni, .A Study of Frequency Interference and Indoor Location Sensing with 802.11b and Bluetooth Technologies., IEEE, 2005, 10 pages
- F.J. Gonzalez-Castano, J. Garcia-Reinoso, .Survivable Bluetooth Location Networks., IEEE, 2003, pp. 1014-1018
- Ha Won Kim, Sung Je Hong, Jong Kim, .Adaptive Location Management Scheme for Mobile IP., IEEE, 2005, 5 pages
- Aurbin Sharma, A. L. Ananda, .A Protocol for Micromobility Management in Next Generation IPv6 Networks., ACM, October 2004, pp. 72-78
- James Cowling, "Dynamic Location Management in Heterogeneous Cellular Networks," MIT Thesis.
- K. Kyantakya and K. Jobmann, "Wireless Networks – Location Management in Cellular Networks: Classification of the Most Important Paradigms, Realistic Simulation Framework, and Relative Performance Analysis."IEEE transactions on vehicular technology 2005: v.54, no.2 687-708.
- Navid Toosizadeh and Hadi Bannazadeh, "Location Management in Mobile Networks: Comparison and Analysis," University of Toronto Report.
- Emir Halepovic and Carey Williamson, "Characterizing and Modeling User Mobility in a Cellular Data Network," University of Calgary.
- Shi-Wu Lo, Tei-Wei Kuo, Kam-Yiu Lam, Guo-Hui Li, "Efficient location area planning for cellular networks with hierarchical location databases," Computer Networks.
- Y. Xiao, Y. Pan, J. Li, "Design and analysis of location management for 3G cellular networks," IEEE Transactions on Parallel and Distributed Systems, v.15 i.4 April 2004 p.339-349.
- Vicenete Casares Giner and Pablo Garcia-Escalle, "On the Fractional Movement-Distance Based Scheme for PCS Location Management with Selective Paging," Lecture Notes in Computer Science, Volume 3427, Jan 2005, Pages 202 - 218.
- Yang Xiao "Optimal fractional movement-based scheme for PCS location management ," Communications Letters, IEEE, v.7 i.2 Feb 2003 p.67-69.

- Kevin Lee, Hong Wing Lee, Sanjay Jha, and Nirupama Bulusu, "Adaptive, Distributed Location Management in Mobile, Wireless Networks."
- Kam-Yiu Lam, BiYu Liang, ChuanLin Zhang, "On Using Handoff Statistics and Velocity for Location Management in Cellular Wireless Networks," The Computer Journal Jan 2005: 48, 1.
- Bharat Rao, Lous Minakakis, "Evolution of Mobile Location-Based Services."
- Omer Rashid, Ian Mullins, Paul Coulton, Reuben Edwards, "Extending Cyberspace: Location Based Games Using Cellular Phones."
- Jahan Hassan and Sanjay Jha, "Cell Hopping: A Lightweight Architecture for Wireless Communications," IEEE Wirelesss Communications October 2003.
- Guangbin Fan, Ivan Stojmenovic, and Jingyuan Zhang, "A Triple Layer Location Management Strategy for Wireless Cellular Networks."
- F. Yu, V.W.S. Wong, and V.C.M. Leung, "Performance Enhancement of Combining QoS Provisioning and Location Management in Wireless Cellular Networks," IEEE transactions on wireless communications 2005: v.4 no.3 943-953.
- Upkar Varshney, "Location Management for Mobile Commerce Applications in Wireless Internet Environment."
- Johnson,D. and Perkins,C. Internet Draft - Mobility Support in IPv6. March 2000.
- Perkins,C. and Johnson,D. Internet Draft - Route Optimization in Mobile IP. February 2000.
- Tanenbaum, Andrew S. Computer Networks - Third Edition. Prentice Hall, Inc., Upper Sadle River, New Jersey.
- Sharma V., Gupta Brijesh Kr., Sharma S.C.,and Qamar, S.: "Mobile Networking through Mobile IP : A Survey", In Proceedings National Conference on Emerging Technologies in Computer Science (ETCS – 2007), pp. 63 – 71, 22nd –23rd Sept., 2007, Meerut, INDIA
- S. Acharya, R. Alonso, M. Franklin, S. Zdonik, Broadcast disks: data management for asymmetric communication environments, in: Proceedings of the ACM SIGMOD Conference, CA, 1995.

- R. Alonso, H.F. Korth, Database system issues in nomadic computing, in: Proceedings of ACM SIGMOD Conference on Management of Data, 1993, pp. 388-392.
- R. Alonso, S. Ganguly, Query optimisation for energy efficiency in mobile environments, in: Proceedings of the 1993 International Workshop on Foundations of Models and Languages for Data and Objects, Aigen, Austria, 1993.
- B. Awerbuch, D. Peleg, Online tracking of mobile users, Journal of ACM 42 (5) (1995) 1021- 1058.
- V. Anantharaman, M.L. Honig, U. Madhow, V.K. Wei, Optimisation of a database hierarchy for mobility testing in a personal communication network, Performance Evaluation 20 (13), 1994.
- R.K. Ahuja, T.L. Magnanti, J.B. Orlin, Network Flows, Prentice-Hall, Englewood Cliffs, NJ, 1993.
- B. Daniel, Mobile computing and databases: a survey, IEEE Transactions on Data and Knowledge Engineering 1999.
- D. Barbara, Certification reports: supporting transactions in wireless systems, in: Proceedings of 17th International Conference on Distributed Computing Systems, 1997, pp. 466- 473.
- B.R. Badrinath, A. Acharya, T. Imielinski, Structuring distributed algorithms for mobile hosts, in: 14th IEEE International Conference on Distributed Computing Systems, June, 1994, pp. 21-28.
- B. Bruegge, B. Benninington, Applications of mobile computing and communications, IEEE Personal Communications 3 (1), (1996).
- B.R. Badrinath, T. Imielinski, Replication and mobility, in: 2nd IEEE Workshop on the Management of Replicated Data, November, 1992, pp. 9-12.
- B. Bhargava, S.B. Kamisetty, S. Madria, Fault tolerant authentication in mobile computing, Special Session, New Paradigms in Computer Security, in: International Conference on Internet Computing (IC'2000), Las Vegas, USA, pp. 395-402.
- D. Barbara, T. Imielinski, Sleepers and workaholics: caching strategies in mobile environments, VLDB Journal, 1995.

- B.R. Badrinath, T. Imielinski, A. Virmani, Locating strategies for personal communication networks, in: IEEE GLOBECOM workshop on Networking for Personal Communications Applications, December, 1992.
- N. Barghouti, G. Kaiser, Concurrency control in advanced database applications, ACM Computing Surveys 23 (3) (1991) 269-317.
- P.K. Chrysanthis, Transaction processing in a mobile computing environment, in: Proceedings of IEEE workshop on Advances in Parallel and Distributed Systems, October, 1993, pp. 77- 82.
- Chung, B. Bhargava, S. Madria, Taxonomy of data management via broadcasting in a mobile computing environment, in: Mobile Computing: Implementing Pervasive Information and Communication Technologies, Kluwer Academic Publishers, Dordrecht, 2001.
- G. Cho, L.F. Marshall, An efficient location and routing scheme for mobile computing environments, IEEE Journal on Selected Areas in Communications 13 (5) (1995).
- *J. Cai, K.L. Tan, B.C. Ooi, On* incremental cache coherency schemes in mobile computing environment, in: Proceedings of IEEE International Conference on Data Engineering (ICDE), 1997.
- G. Dong, M. Mohania, Algorithms for view maintenance in mobile databases, in: Proceedings of the First Australian Workshop on Mobile Computing and Databases and Applications (MCDA'96), Melbourne, Australia, 1996.
- S. Dolev, D.K. Pradhan, Modified tree structure for location management in mobile environments, Computer Communications 19 (1997) 335-345.
- M.R. Ebling, Evaluating and improving the effectiveness of caching for availability, Ph.D. Thesis, Department of Computer Science, Carnegie Mellon University, 1997.
- M.H. Eich, A. Helal, A mobile transaction model that captures both data and movement behaviour, ACM/Baltzer Journal on Special Topics on Mobile Networks and Applications 1997.
- Y. Fu, S. Madria, Multi-layered databases for intelligent query answering in mobile environments, in: International Workshop on Reliable and Secure Applications in Mobile Environments, New Orleans (also invited paper in NSF workshop), October, 2001.

- M. Faiz, A. Zaslavsky, Database replica management strategies in multidatabase systems with mobile hosts, in: 6th International Hong Kong Computer Society Database Workshop, 1995.
- D.J. Goodman, Trends in cellular and cordless communications, IEEE Communication Magazine, 1991.
- M. Gaedke, M. Beigl, G. Hans-Werner, C. Segor, Web content delivery to heterogeneous mobile platforms, in: ER Workshops Proceedings as Lecture Notes in Computer Science, vol. 1552, Springer, Berlin, 1998.
- J. Gray, P. Helland, P. O'Neil, D. Shasha, The dangers of replication and a solution, in: Proceedings of ACM SIGMOD International Conference on Management of Data, 1996, pp. 173-182.
- J.S.M. Ho, F. Akyildiz, Dynamic hierarchical database architecture for location management in ocs networks, IEEE Transactions on Networking 5 (5) (1997).
- Y. Huang, P. Sistla, O. Wolfson, Data replication for mobile computers, in: Proceedings of the ACM SIGMOD International Conference on Management of Data, 1994.
- Y. Huang, P. Sistla, O. Wolfson, Divergence caching in client-sever architectures, in: Proceedings of the Third International Conference on Parallel and Distributed Systems (PDIS), Austin, TX, September, 1994, pp. 131-139.
- T. Imielinksi, B.R. Badrinath, Wireless mobile computing: challenges in data management, Communications of ACM 37 (10) (1994).
- T. Imielinksi, B.R. Badrinath, Querying in highly distributed environments, in: Proceedings of the 18th VLDB, August, 1992, pp. 41-52.
- J. Ioannidis, G.Q. Maquire, The design and implementation of a mobile networking architecture, in: USENIX Winter 1993 Technical Conference, January, 1993.
- R. Jain, Reducing traffic impacts of PCS using hierarchical user location databases, in: Proceedings of the IEEE International Conference on Communications, 1996.
- J. Jing, O. Bukhres, A. Elmagarmid, Distributed lock management for mobile transactions, in: Proceedings of the 15th International

Conference on Distributed Computing Systems, Vancouver, Canada, June, 1995.

- R. Jain, Y. Lin, C. Lo, S. Mohan, A caching strategy to reduce network impacts of (PCS), IEEE Journal on Selected Areas in Communications 12 (8) (1994).
- Lee Sang-keun, Hwang Chong-Sun, Yu HeonChang, Supporting transactional cache consistency in mobile database systems, in: ACM International Workshop on Data Engineering for Wireless and Mobile Data Access, 1999.
- M. Krishnamurthi, M. Azizoglu, A.K. Somani, Optimal location management algorithms for mobile networks, in: Proceedings of the Fourth ACM International Conference on Mobile Computing and Networking (MOBICOM'98), 1998, pp. 223-232.
- J. Kisler, M. Satyanarayanan, Disconnected operation in the coda file system, ACM Transactions on Computer Systems 10 (1) (1992).
- P. Krishna, N.H. Vaidya, D.K. Pradhan, Static and dynamic location management in mobile wireless networks, Journal of Computer Communications 19 (4) (1996) (special issue on Mobile Computing).
- Y. Lin, Reducing location update cost in PCS network, IEEE Transactions on Networking 5 (1997) 25-33.
- Q. Lu, M. Satyanaraynan, Improving data consistency in mobile computing using isolationonly transactions, in: Proceedings of the Fifth Workshop on Hot Topics in Operating Systems, Orcas Island, Washington, May, 1995.
- S.K. Madria, Transaction models for mobile computing, in: Proceedings of 6th IEEE International Conference on Network (ICON'98), World Scientific, Singapore, July, 1998.
- S.K. Madria, B. Bhargava, Improving availability in mobile computing using prewrite operations, Distributed and Parallel Database Journal (2001).
- S.K. Madria, B. Bhargava, A transaction model for mobile computing, in: Proceedings 2nd IEEE International Database and Engineering Application Symposium (IDEAS'98), Cardiff, UK, 1998.
- S.K. Madria, B. Bhargava, On the correctness of a transaction

model for mobile computing, in: 9th International Conference on Database and Expert System Applications (DEXA'98), Vienna, Austria, Lecture Notes in Computer Science, vol. 1460, Springer, Berlin, 1998.

- S.K. Madria, B. Bhargava, E. Pitoura, V. Kumar, Data organization issues in location dependent query processing in mobile computing environment, in: Proceedings of 4th East- European Symposium on Advances in Databases and Information Systems (in co-operation with ACM-SIGMOD), Prague, Czech Republic, 2000.
- S. Mohan, R. Jain, Two user location strategies for PCS, IEEE Personal Communications Magazine 1 ((1), 1st quarter) (1994).
- S.K. Madria, M. Mohania, J. Roddick, A query processing model for mobile computing using concept hierarchies and summary databases, in: Proceedings of the 5th International Conference on Foundation for Data Organization (FODO'98), Japan, November, 1998
- A. Massari, S. Weissman, P.K. Chrysanthis, Supporting mobile database access through query by icons, Distributed and Parallel Databases: An International Journal (1996).
- E. Pitoura, Transaction-based co-ordination of software agents, in: 9th International Conference on Database and Expert System Applications (DEXA'98), Vienna, Austria, Lecture Notes in Computer Science, vol. 1460, Springer, Berlin, August, 1998.
- E. Pitoura, B. Bhargava, Building Information Systems for Mobile Environments, in: Proceedings of 3rd International Conference on Information and Knowledge Management, 1994, pp. 371-378.
- E. Pitoura, B. Bhargava, Maintaining consistency of data in mobile computing environments, in: Proceedings of 15th International Conference on Distributed Computing Systems, June, 1995
- E. Pitoura, B. Bhargava, Dealing with mobility: issues and research challenges, Technical Report TR-93-070, Department of Computer Sciences, Purdue University, 1993.
- E. Pitoura, B. Bhargava, Revising transaction concepts for mobile computing, in: Proceedings of the 1st IEEE Workshop on Mobile Computing Systems and Applications, December, 1994, pp. 164-168.

- E. Pitoura, P.K. Chrysanthis, Scalable processing of read-only transactions in broadcast push, in: Proceedings of IEEE International Conference on Distributed Computing Systems, 1999.
- E. Pitoura, P.K. Chrysanthis, Exploiting versions for handling updates in broadcast disks, in: Proceedings of VLDB, 1999.
- E. Pitoura, I. Fudos, An efficient hierarchical scheme for locating highly mobile users, in: ACM Proceedings for International Conference on Information and Knowledge Management (CIKM), 1998.
- C. Pu, G. Kaiser, Hutchinson, Split-transactions for open-ended activities, in: Proceedings of the 14th VLDB Conference, 1988.
- E. Pitoura, G. Samaras, Locating objects in mobile computing, TKDE 13 (4) (2001) 571 - 592.
- K. Ramamritham, P.K. Chrysanthis, A taxonomy of correctness criterion in database applications, Journal of Very Large Databases 4 (1) (1996).
- K. Ravindran, K. Shah, Casual broadcasting and consistency of distributed data, in: 14th International Conference on Distributed Computing Systems, June, 1994, pp. 40-47.
- A. Rasheed, A. Zaslavsky, Ensuring database availability in dynamically changing mobile computing environment, in: Proceedings of the 7th Australian Database Conference, Melbourne, Australia, 1996.
- M. Satyanarayanan, Mobile information access, IEEE Personal Communications 3 (1) (1996).
- I. Stanoi, D. Agarwal, A. El Abbadi, S.H. Phatak, B.R. Badrinath, Data warehousing alternatives for mobile environments, in: Proceedings of ACM International Workshop on Data Engineering for Wireless and Mobile Access, Seattle, Washington, 1999.
- M. van Steen, F.J. Hauck, P. Homburg, A.S. Tanenbaum, Locating objects in wide-area systems, IEEE Communication Magazine (1998) 2-7.
- J. Shanmugasundaram, A. Nithrakashyap, R. Sivasankaran, K. Ramamritham, Efficient concurrency control for broadcast environments, in: Proceedings of the ACM SIGMOD Conference, 1999.

- N. Shivakumar, J. Widom, User profile replication for faster location lookup in mobile environments, in: Proceedings of the 1st ACM International Conference on Mobile Computing and Networking (MOBICOM'95), October, 1995, pp. 161-169.
- P. Sistla, O. Wolfson, Temporal conditions and integrity constraints in active database systems, in: Proceedings of the ACM SIGMOD International Conference on Management of Data, May, 1995, pp. 269-280.
- M.T. Stanley, Y. Hong Va Leong, D. McLeod, A. Si, On multi-resolution document transmission in mobile web, SIGMOD Record 28 (3) (1999) 37-42.
- D.B. Terry, D. Goldberg, D.A. Nichols, B.M. Oki, Continuous queries over append-only databases, in: Proceedings of the ACM-SIGMOD International Conference on Management of Data, June, 1992.
- G.M. Voelker, B.N.B. Mobisaic, An information management system for mobile wireless computing environment, in: T. Imienlinski, H. Korth (Eds.), Mobile Computing, Kluwer Academic Publishers, 1996, pp. 375-395.
- G.D. Walborn, P.K. Chrysanthis, Supporting semantics-based transaction processing in mobile database applications, in: Proceedings of 14th IEEE Symposium on Reliable Distributed Systems, September, 1995, pp. 31-40.
- Wu Shiow-yang, Y. Change, An active replication scheme for mobile data management, in: IEEE Proceedings of 6th DASFAA, Taiwan, 1999.
- O. Wolfson, S. Jajodia, Distributed algorithms for dynamic replication of data, in: Proceedings of the Symposium on Principles of Database Systems, CA, 1992, pp. 149-163.
- O. Wolfson, A.P. Sistla, C. Sam, Y. Yelena, Updating and querying databases that track mobile units, Distributed and Parallel Databases 7 (3) (1999) 257-387.
- O. Wolfson, X. Bo, C. Sam, L. Jiang, Moving objects databases: issues and solutions, in: Proceedings of SSDBM, 1998, pp. 111-122.
- K. Wu, P.S. Yu, M. Chen, Energy Efficient caching for wireless

mobile computing, in: Proceedings of the 12th International Conference on Data Engineering, New Orleans, February, 1996.

- L.H. Yeo, A. Zaslavsky, Submission of transactions from mobile workstations in a cooperative multidatabase processing environment, in: Proceedings of the 14th IEEE International Conference on Distributed Computing Systems (ICDCS'94), June, 1994.

UNIT-IV

In mobile environment, users can retrieve information from wireless channels (with generally narrow bandwidth) anytime and anywhere. How to disseminate data efficiently to a large number of users in the mobile computing environment is challenging due to the necessity to consider time and energy efficiencies, given that mobile devices have limited energy capacities associated with their reliance on battery power.

The broadcast mechanism allows users to retrieve data with a lower power requirement (due to no user transmission being required) and with a cost that is independent of the number of users. However, the data broadcast has the drawback that data can only be accessed sequentially, and hence users must wait for desired data items to appear in the broadcast channel. Building an index of the broadcast data helps users to decide when and where their desired data items will be available, which allows the mobile device to be turned into a power-saving mode whilst waiting for desired data items.

A transaction in mobile environment is different than the transactions in the centralized or distributed databases. Due to the challenging characteristics of the mobile environments such as the mobility of mobile computers, the frequent disconnections of wireless networks and the limited processing power of mobile computers the traditional database transactions may not be able to efficiently support transactions in volatile mobile environments. Transaction processing in mobile environments is a very meaningful and challenging research area.

This unit contains:

- Data Management in Mobile Environment
- Wireless Data / Information Broadcast

- On-Disk vs On-Air Indexing
- Energy Efficient Indexing on Air
- Broadcast Disk and Transaction Processing
- Mobile Data Caching Schemes
- Database and Transaction Concepts
- Mobile Transaction Processing
- Mobile Database Research Directions
- Security and Fault Tolerance in Mobile Network
- Mobile Agents

UNIT 4

Transaction Management

4.1. DATA MANAGEMENT IN MOBILE ENVIRONMENT

4.1.1. Introduction

At present, many types of mobile computing devices such as laptops and Personal Digital Assistants (PDA) are available. The computing capacities of these mobile devices become more and more powerful in terms of processing speed, storage capacity and operating time. As a result, these mobile computing devices are becoming the essential work equipments. At the same time, many wireless network technologies are also developed and deployed, for example Bluetooth, wireless USB, wireless LAN or Universal Mobile Telecommunications System (UMTS).

The rapid expansion of both the wireless network technologies and the capacity of mobile computing devices has created a new work environment. With the support of wireless networks and mobile computing devices, people can carry out their work while being on the move. The environment for accessing and processing information is rapidly changing from stationary to mobile and location independent. This new work environment, called the mobile work environment, provides people a flexible and efficient work environment.

An Application Example

To illustrate the advantages of the mobile work environment, we will present and discuss a mobile IT (Information *T*echnology) support system. The mobile IT support system is a cooperative work system in which IT officers help users to deal with computer problems such as fixing a hardware problem or upgrading a software application as shown in

Fig. 4.1.The objective of the mobile IT support system is to solve as many computer problems as quickly as possible.

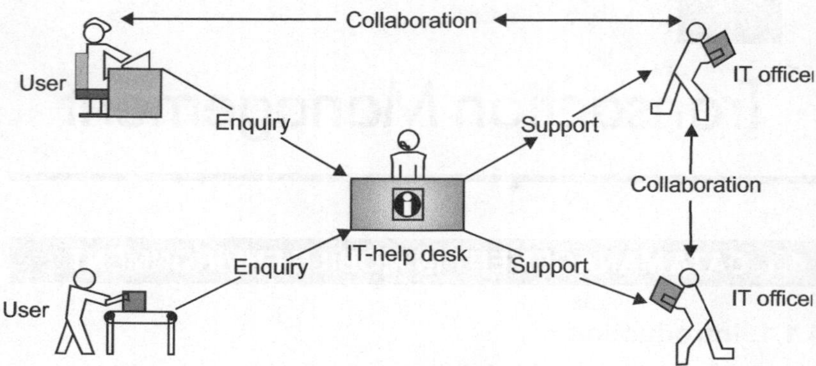

Fig. 4.1: The Mobile IT Support System

Users report computer problems by sending enquiries to the IT help desk. These computer problems will be handled by IT officers. An IT officer has to prepare in advance all the necessary data and tools to solve a computer problem. The IT officer also has to move around to specific locations like offices or computer labs where the computers and equipments are located. While handling a computer problem, an IT officer may need to contact the user, who submitted the inquiry, to clarify the problem. For example, to prepare necessary equipments for a multimedia lecture, the IT officer needs to know what types of computers and applications are used. Furthermore, when working on a difficult problem, an IT officer may also want to consult other colleagues for additional support. For each computer problem, a logbook is written to keep track of its progress. When a computer problem is solved, its logbook will be archived in the IT help desk system for future reference.

Traditionally, all the contact among IT officers and users must be carried out through the IT help desk system. The users must connect the IT help desk system to report computer problems. The IT officers must connect the IT help desk system from stationary and wire-connected computers to cooperate with users or other IT officers, and to update logbooks. There are several disadvantages of this work environment when the IT officer is unable to connect the IT help desk system. First, the IT officer is not able to update logbooks to keep the status of computer problems up-to-date. Therefore, the number of unsolved computer problems in the IT help desk system may incorrectly increase, and it is difficult to manage the progress of these enquiries. Second, if the description of a computer problem, which is handled by the IT officer, is modified, the IT officer will not be aware of it. Consequently, the IT officer is not well prepared to work efficiently on the computer problem.

With the support of mobile computing devices and wireless network technologies, the mobile IT support system can be extended to attack the above disadvantages and improve its performance. First, the logbook of a computer problem, which an IT officer is currently working on, can be first updated in the mobile computer of the IT officer. The logbook will also be saved in the IT help desk system via the wireless networks. This way, the mobile IT support system can effectively manage the user enquiries. Second, the IT officer can contact the IT help desk system to retrieve the up-to-date information of computer problems, and communicate with other colleagues while they are on the move.

Consequently, the IT officer is well prepared to solve the computer problems. Third, the IT help desk system can be informed about the current location of the IT officers. Computer problems, whose locations are nearby the location of an IT officer, can be assigned to this IT officer, i.e., saving the traveling time of the IT officer. As a result, more computer problems can be solved in shorter time. There are many challenges in mobile work environments. The wireless networks can be disconnected while an IT officer is working on a computer problem. Therefore, the status of this computer problem, which is currently stored in the mobile computer, can be different with the one stored in the IT help desk system. The mobile computers may not have the required capacity to support the IT officer to solve an enquiry. Consequently, some of the work may be delayed or suspended. Moreover, the collaborative activities among the IT officers and users can be carried out directly, i.e., without going through the IT help desk system. This leads to the demand for a new collaborative work model.

4.2. WIRELESS DATA / INFORMATION BROADCAST

Data broadcast has added another dimension in the area of mobile computing. Data access from wireless channels is a very useful facility because it allows users to get desired data through many computationally enabled devices. In an ideal scenario, assuming an abundance of wireless channels, servers can push all data users might ever need, and users can pull whatever they require. In reality, wireless channels are always fewer than the number required to satisfy user demands. Thus, the task of data dissemination technology is to develop ways for satisfying data demand with limited wireless resources.

Data broadcast is a 1-to-n process, enabling enhanced scalability. The capacity of data transfer from the server to the mobile client (downstream communication) is significantly larger than that of the mobile client to the server (upstream communication). The effectiveness of data dissemination systems is evaluated by its ability to provide users with required data ubiquitously. Data broadcast can be managed with three different modes:

- On-Demand,
- Push-Based, and
- Hybrid

Before describing the different operation modes, we present the basics of broadcast structures.

4.2.1. Broadcast Structure

In broadcast systems, there is no traditional network stack. Data is transmitted in the form of buckets. Buckets are also called data blocks or frames. Practically, buckets reside on top of the wireless Medium Access Control (MAC) protocol. In broadcast systems, mobile clients must wait until the server broadcasts the required information. Therefore, client waiting time is determined by the overall length of broadcast data, which is usually referred to as broadcast cycle. Clients must keep listening to the broadcast channel until the arrival of required information. The concept of selective tuning is introduced for reducing power consumption. By using selective tuning, mobile clients stay in doze mode most of the time and turn into active mode only when the requested information is expected to arrive. Indexing techniques are used to implement selective tuning in wireless environments. Indices are broadcast together with data to help mobile clients locate the required information, as shown in Fig. 4.2. In most systems, buckets are classified into index and data buckets.

Air indexing is fundamentally different than disk indexing. While disk indices represent a path or an offset in the disk (where accessibility is direct), air indices provide solely a time offset indicating when the pointed item is going to appear in the wireless channel. Therefore, established disk air indexing techniques were accordingly adapted. Most of these indexing schemes are based on three techniques:

- Index Tree
- Signature Indexing and
- Hashing

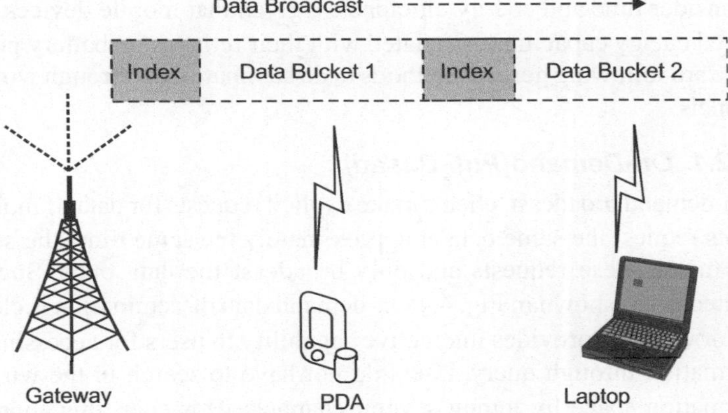

Fig. 4.2: Indexed Broadcast Composition

Hybrid indexing schemes have been proposed as well. Fig. 4.3 depicts an example of distributed indexing. The broadcast data is partitioned into several data segments. The index tree precedes each data segment in the broadcast. Users first traverse the index tree to obtain the time offset of the requested data item. After that, they switch to doze mode until the data item arrives.

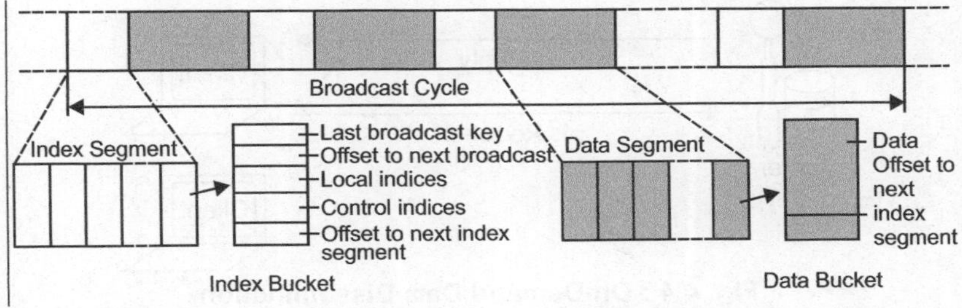

Fig. 4.3: Index and Data Organization of Distributed Indexing

4.2.2. Data Dissemination

The rapid advances in computer software, computer hardware, and wireless network technologies have led to the widespread implementation of mobile computing. In this environment, users can retrieve information from wireless channels (with generally narrow bandwidth) anytime and anywhere. How to disseminate data efficiently to a large number of users in the mobile computing environment is challenging due to the necessity to consider time and energy efficiencies, given that mobile devices have limited energy capacities associated with their reliance on battery power. There are following general methods to disseminate data through wireless channels:

4.2.2.1. On-Demand(Pull-Based)

In on-demand broadcast, clients make explicit requests for data. If multiple clients request the same data at approximately the same time, the server may match these requests and only broadcast the data once. Such an architecture is shown in Fig. 4.4 On-demand data dissemination is clearly user-oriented. It provides interactive capability to users for accessing the information through query. Users do not have to search in the wireless information space by tuning several channels. However, this approach has many disadvantages. First of all, it is resource intensive. Users require a separate channel to send requests to the server. The server, after receiving the request, composes the result and sends it to the user on a back channel (downstream) known to the user. Thus, every pull needs two channels for completing the process.

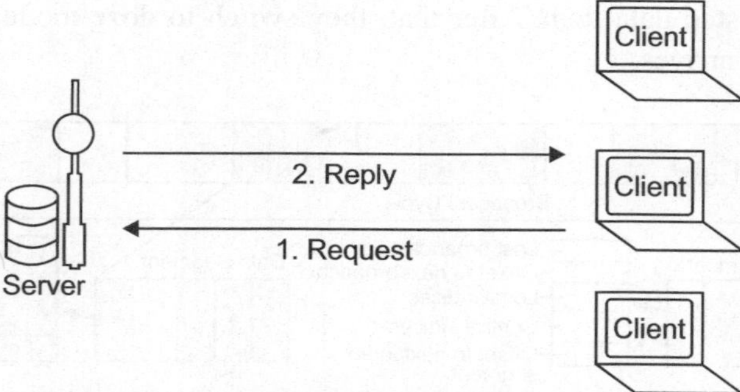

Fig. 4.4 : On-Demand Data Dissemination

Moreover, since incoming requests are usually not identical, the server cannot always efficiently group requests in order to exploit the advantages of broadcast. Obviously, this depends on the volume and the context of the incoming workload. To make things worse, client-server architectures are notoriously not scalable. When the number of incoming requests becomes too high, the server fails to keep up.

4.2.2.2. Broadcast (Push-Based)

In push-based systems, the server employs point-to-multipoint communication and sends data items in the absence of explicit client requests. In order to achieve that, the server maintains a broadcast schedule, which determines the order and the frequency in which data items are broadcast. Such an architecture is shown in Fig. 4.5 In this trivial example, the scheduler handles three data items (A, B and C), out of which B and C are broadcast with the same frequency and A twice more frequently, resulting in the transmission schedule: (A,B, A,C, A,B, A,C ...). The major feature of such systems is scalability. Client population does not influence the dissemination process because clients do not issue requests. The addition of new clients does not influence the server's incoming load or the client perceived access time.

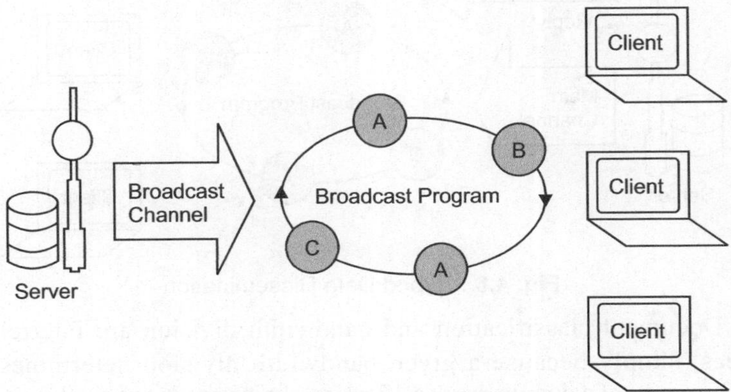

Fig. 4.5: Push-based data dissemination.

In addition to that, clients need few resources. Mechanisms such as wireless indexing, enable clients to efficiently locate data in the broadcast channel. Moreover, data can be kept actual, since the server can simply broadcast any updates. The major problem of push-based systems is their lack of self organization and adaptiveness. Since the server does not receive explicit client requests, it remains unaware of possible changes in client population or querying characteristics. This incurs several problems. Bandwidth for instance, can be unnecessarily utilized for a relatively low number of end clients. Apart from that, the push service requires more powerful hardware.

4.2.2.3. Hybrid Data Dissemination

As the name suggests, hybrid data dissemination is a combination of on-demand and push-based approaches. Data items are classified into popular and unpopular (respectively, hot and cold). Popular data items are delivered via push-based channels, while unpopular data items are disseminated via on-demand channels. Such an architecture is shown in Fig. 4.6. Typical design issues in hybrid systems are channel allocation (number of push and on-demand channels), data classification (cold or hot) and item scheduling (both on on-demand and push channel).

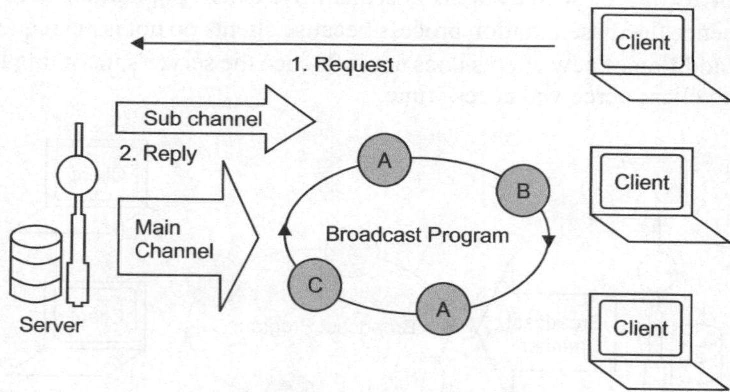

Fig. 4.6 : Hybrid Data Dissemination

Document classification and bandwidth division are interrelated issues, simply because a given bandwidth division determines the performance of a document classification choice and, conversely, a given document classification determines a bandwidth split that optimizes performance. In turn, both document classification and bandwidth division depend on the popularity of data items because download latency is smaller when hot items are assigned to multicast push, cold items to unicast pull, and the bandwidth is divided appropriately between the two channels.

4.2.3. Performance Measures

The mobile computing environment has a few characteristics that distinguish itself from the traditional wired network. In addition to the traditional access latency, mobile clients have limited energy power. As a result, access techniques must take energy consumption into consideration.

In on-demand access, power consumption is dominated by the number of request transmissions since all the client needs to do is to transmit the query and wait for the result, leaving all of the processing work to the server. In this regard, effective caching methods are vital in the reduction of the number of queries needed. For broadcast, since the client has to scan the channel for the interested data item, its power consumption can be considered as directly proportional to the time it is listening actively to the channel, which is referred to as *tuning time.*

4.3. ON-DISK VS ON-AIR INDEXING

Portable devices have limited power resources due to their small size. It is inefficient in terms of power consumption for the client to retrieve data by continuously listening to the channels until the desired data arrives. Imagine a client wanting to monitor the price of a stock. The device has to actively listen to thousands of stock symbols on the broadcast just to pick up one of them to display. Indexing can be used to guide the client in the listening process so that it will activate only when the data arrives and thus reducing power consumption. To contrast, while a traditional database index maps a key to where the key value is stored in memory, an index for broadcast data maps a key to the time when the key value is broadcast.

In traditional database indexes, data is stored on disks or in main memories. The data is always available and can be accessed randomly. However, in wireless broadcast, data is available "on air" in the sense that the data is available on the wireless channel only transiently and has to be accessed sequentially as dictated by the broadcast program. Search algorithms and index methods for wireless broadcast channels should avoid back-tracking. Existing database indexes obviously were not designed to meet this requirement and hence perform poorly on broadcast data.

When indexing is used, the broadcast cycle contains the index together with the actual data. When the client is looking for information, it tunes to the channel to locate the index for the broadcast cycle, from which it can obtain the broadcast time of the information and sleeps until it arrives.

Compared to the total size of the data records, the index only contains the key names and thus is relatively small. It achieves the objective of reducing power consumption without significantly increasing the access latency.

4.4. ENERGY EFFICIENT INDEXING ON AIR

The periodic broadcast of data over wireless communication channels can be considered in a sense a supplement to a mobile user's secondary storage. While accessing local hard drives consumes significant power, the reception of wireless broadcast data is a relatively low-power operation. When appropriate, periodic data broadcasts can be used to disseminate large volumes of data, e.g. a large common database, to an easily scalable population of listeners. However, even though wireless reception is a low-power operation when compared to hard drive access, it is not "free". In addition, because the data arrives at the mobile computer in a unique fashion, the schemes to organize and access the data must be unique.

Due to the dynamic nature of mobile computing in terms of wireless communication cell migration, changing information content, and the multiplexing of many different files over the same communication channels, researchers proposed broadcasting the directory of a broadcasted data file along with the data file in the form of an index. Without an index, the client would have to filter (listen to) the entire broadcast in the worst case, or half the broadcast on average. This is undesirable because such filtering requires the mobile unit to be in its active mode, consuming power unnecessarily. Therefore every broadcast (channel) contains all of the information needed—the file and the index. Again, the question is how to organize the data to be broadcast for optimal access by a mobile receiver.

For use in evaluating potential methods of organization and access, two parameters ***access time and tuning time*** are introduced. The access time is the average time between identification of desired data in the index portion of the broadcast, and download of the data in the data file portion of the broadcast. The tuning time is the amount of time spent by a mobile client actually listening to a broadcast channel. The goal is to find algorithms for allocating the index together with the data on a broadcast channel, and to do so in a means that struck a balance between the optimal *access time* algorithm and the optimal *tuning time* algorithm. The first organization method, called "(1, *m*) Indexing", broadcasts the entire index

m times (equally spaced) during the broadcast of one version of the data file. In other words, the entire index is broadcast every $1/m$ fraction of the data file. In the second method, "Distributed Indexing", the $(1, m)$ method is improved upon by eliminating much of the redundancy in the m broadcasts of the data file index. Their key observation is that only certain portions of the index tree are necessary between broadcasts of particular segments of the data file. Specifically, the periodically broadcasted index segments need only index the data file segment that follows it. By using fixed-sized "buckets" of data (both index and file data).

Both schemes achieve tuning times that are almost as good as that of an algorithm that had optimal tuning time. In terms of access time, both algorithms exhibit a savings that is a respectable compromise between the two extremes of an algorithm with optimal access time and an algorithm with optimal tuning time. The Distributed Indexing scheme is always better than the $(1, m)$ scheme.

In examples of practical implementations, their algorithms are compared to the extreme cases of an optimal tuning time algorithm, and an optimal access time algorithm. In one example for the $(1, m)$ algorithm, they show a per query reduction of power by a factor of 120 over the optimal access algorithm, but a 45% increase in access time. For the same $(1, m)$ example, they found that the power consumption was very similar to that of the optimal tuning algorithm, but that the access time had improved to 70% of that in the optimal tuning algorithm.

In looking at an example of the distributed indexing scheme, it was found that, a per query power reduction of 100 times smaller than that of an optimal access algorithm, while the access time increased by only 10%. Again when compared to an optimal tuning algorithm, they found similar power consumption, but again improved access time of 53% of that for an optimal tuning algorithm. The conclusion is that by using their distributed indexing scheme in periodic broadcasts, a savings of 100 times less energy can be realized. The fruits of this savings can of course be used for other purposes.

4.5 BROADCAST DISK AND TRANSACTION PROCESSING

In traditional client-server systems, data are delivered from servers to clients on demand. This form of data is called ***pull-based***. Another interesting trend is ***push-based*** delivery in a wireless environment. In wireless computing the stationary server machines are provided with a relative high bandwidth channel which supports broadcast delivery to all mobile clients located inside the cell.

In a push-based delivery, server repetitively broadcast data to clients without specific request. Clients monitor the broadcast and retrieve data items they need as they arrive on the broadcast channel. This is very important for a wide range of applications that involve dissemination of information to a large number of clients. Such applications include stock quotes, mailing lists, electronic newsletters, etc. Broadcast in a mobile computing has number of difficulties.

How to predict and decide about the relevance of the data to be broadcasted to clients. One way is that the clients may subscribe their interests to services. The server also needs to decide about either sending the data periodically or a periodically. Mobile clients are also resource poor and the communication environment is asymmetric. The problem also is to maintain the consistency of broadcast data. The commercial system, which supports the concept of broadcast data delivery, has been proposed. Recently, broadcast has received considerable attention in the area of transaction processing in mobile computing environment.

Some researchers addressed the problem of ensuring consistency and currency of client read-only transactions, when the values are being broadcast in the presence of updates at the server. They broadcast additional control information in the form of invalidation reports, multiple versions per item and serializability information. They propose different methods that vary in complexity and volume of control information transmitted and subsequently differs in response times, degree of concurrency, and space and processing overheads.

4.6. MOBILE DATA CACHING SCHEMES

In the information age, information itself has become an import commodity to cache and hoard. When we go on a trip, we fill our carry-on bags with books we may want to read while on the flight and laptop computer with files which we may want to work while waiting for the connecting flight. For people frequently on move, remembering to download all the files on to the laptop computer, which they may need while on the next trip, may easily become a cumbersome task. Further, on returning from the trip, the files have to be uploaded back to the permanent memory storage, say, on the home or office PC or server that is regularly backed up.

In general, caching is a very important technique in the computing world. A typical computer system consists of a several cache memories. A **cache** is a small fast memory for holding frequently used data. In fact, the different types of memories in a computer system, such as disk, main memory, and cache, can be viewed as a part of a *memory hierarchy* in which the closer a memory unit is to the processor the smaller is its capacity and *access time*. *How to reduce memory read/write latency in the presence of memory hierarchy*? – is the main problem for cache management in such systems. To achieve this, the system needs to (transparently) decide what data to cache (to copy from a farther memory unit to a closer memory unit) so that the cache (memory unit closer to the processor) can satisfy as many memory requests as possible - effectively achieving average access time close to that of the fast memory unit at the effective price of the large memory unit. Cache management techniques try to predict what data items would be most probably used in future and either copy them to a memory unit closer to the processor when they are accessed for the first time (i.e. on a *cache miss*) or to *pre-fetch* them well in advance so that they are available in the cache memory when they are needed. Many cache replacement algorithms such as Least-Recently Used (LRU) and pre-fetching algorithms have been developed to solve this problem.

4.6.1. Caching to Improve Data Availability in Distributed Systems

Data caching has been traditionally used in distributed (as well as non-distributed systems) system to improve performance (data access latency) by exploiting temporal and spatial locality in reference pattern. For such distributed systems, it is assumed that a high-bandwidth low-latency network connects the clients and servers and that network failures are infrequent. In cases where access latency is high and/or bandwidth is not sufficient data pre-fetching in conjunction with data caching can be used to hide communication latency and to cope with limited bandwidth. Both data caching and pre-fetching are performed transparently so that the applications do not have to do anything different when caching or pre-fetching is being employed than when it is not being employed. The only difference from the user's (application's) perspective is that the results are obtained faster (or in case of application such as video streaming, the quality of the output is better). Hence, caching/pre-fetching in such cases can only improve the situation and cause no harm.

Further, in distributed systems and network computing environments cache management schemes need to handle two different scenarios. In the first scenario, the data in the *shared memory* or the *server* can be *read/written* by different processors or *clients* concurrently. In the second scenario, the data is *read only* for the clients. Further, many a times the data may be replicated onto multiple servers for improving fault-tolerance and availability. An example of the former scenario is a distributed file system, while the latter scenario is often seen in the World Wide Web (WWW) system. In these environments, when a client accesses a cached data item, the server or another client could have just modified that data item. Hence, in distributed and network computing environments, the most crucial problem for caching is *how to maintain data consistency among the clients and the servers?* This problem is more difficult to solve than the problem of ensuring that the copy of the data in the higher-level memory is updated (through write-through or write-back schemes when the cached copy of the data in the lower-level memory has been updated. The complexity arises from the various failures that may occur – server failure, network failure, and client failure. To maintain cache consistency in distributed or network computing environment, different approaches have been developed. These approaches include polling-every-time, adaptive Time-to-Live (TTL), server-invalidation, and leases-based invalidation.

4.6.1.1. Cache Consistency

Caching of frequently accessed data plays an important role in mobile computing because of its ability to alleviate the performance and availability limitations during weak-connections and disconnections. Caching is useful during frequent relocation and connection to different DBS. In a wireless computing, caching of frequently accessed data items is an important technique that will reduce contention on the small bandwidth wireless network. This will improve query response time, and to support disconnected or weakly connected operations. If a mobile user has cached a portion of the shared data, he may request different levels of cache consistency. In a strongly connected mode, the user may want the current values of the database items belonging to his cache. During weak connections, the user may require weak consistency when the cached copy is a quasi-copy of the database items. Each type of connection may have a different degree of cache consistency associated with it. That is, weak connection corresponds to "weaker" level of consistency.

Cache consistency is severely hampered by both the disconnection and mobility of clients since a server may be unaware of the current locations and connection status of clients. The server can solve this problem by periodically broadcasting the actual data, invalidation report (reports the data items which have been changed), or even control information such as lock tables or logs. This approach is attractive in mobile environments since the server need not know the location and connection status of its clients and clients need not establish an up link connection to a server to invalidate their caches. There are two advantages of broadcasting. First, mobile host saves energy since they need not transmit data requests and second, broadcast data can be received by many mobile hosts at once with no extra cost.

Depending upon what is broadcasted, the appropriate schemes can be developed for maintaining consistency of data of a distributed system with mobile client. Given the rate of updates, the trade-off is between the periodicity of broadcast and divergence of the cached copies that can be tolerated. The more the inconsistency tolerated the less often the updates need to be broadcasted. Given a query, the mobile host may optimize energy costs by determining whether it can process the query using cached data or transmit a request for data. Another choice could be to wait for the relevant broadcast.

Cache coherence preservation under weak-connections is expensive. Large communication delay increases the cost of validation of cached objects. Unexpected failures increase the frequency of validation since it must be performed each time communication is restored. An approach that only validates on demand could reduce validation frequency but this approach would worsen consistency since it increases the possibility of some old objects being accesses while disconnected.

4.6.2. Issues in Designing Mobile Data Caching Schemes

It is challenging to design caching strategies for mobile environment since an efficient strategy should take into consideration various issues such as:

- Data access pattern
- Data update rate
- Communication/Access cost

- Mobility pattern of the client
- Connectivity characteristics (disconnection frequency, available bandwidth)
- Data currency requirements of the user (user expectations)
- Context-dependence of the information

In mobile computing environment, the cache management schemes needs to address the following problems:

- How to reduce client side latency?
- How to maintain cache consistency between various caches and the servers?
- How to ensure high data availability in presence of frequent disconnections?
- How to achieve high energy/bandwidth efficiency?
- How to determine the cost of cache miss and how to incorporate this cost in cache management scheme?
- How to manage location dependent data in the cache?
- How to enable cooperation between multiple peer caches?

The first two problems are not new to mobile computing environments. They have been extensively studied in distributed system and wired network-computing environments. The next four problems stem from the two features of mobile computing environments. And the last problem is to take advantage of the P2P paradigm of ad hoc networks. In the next section, we present several cache management schemes that have been developed to address these problems specific to mobile computing environments. Before looking at these management schemes let us look at some of the cache organization issues. These include:

- Where to cache?
- How many levels of caching to use (in the case of hierarchical caching architectures)?
- What to cache (when to cache a data item and how long)?
- How to invalidate cached items?
- Who is responsible for invalidations? What is the granularity at which the invalidation is done?
- What data currency guarantees the system can provide to the user?
- What are the costs involved? How to charge the users?

- What is the effect on query delay (response time) and system throughput (number of query completion rate)?

For example, in a mobile environment data can be cached at the server, at a proxy, or at a client. Furthermore, the data cached at each cache is dependent on the frequency/pattern of access and cost of access. In the case of server, data cached is dependent on aggregate access pattern and the cost of retrieving requested data from the data store (i.e. I/O cost). In the case of the proxy and at the client the caching strategy has to take into account the access pattern, communication cost, and also the update rate of the data being cached. In reality, data can be cached at several places. In order to maintain the consistency of the cached data, different strategies are employed based on the communication cost and design goals. If the goal is to minimize uplink queries by a mobile client (saving battery power of the mobile) and minimize contention on the narrow bandwidth wireless links (saving both bandwidth and energy) then the server can periodically broadcast invalidation reports . The invalidation report can be organized in different ways and at various data granularity levels.

4.6.2.1. Mobile Cache Maintenance

Data caching is especially important for mobile computing environment for improving data availability and access latencies – since, these computing environments are characterized by narrow bandwidth wireless links and frequent voluntary/involuntary disconnections from the static network. However, these very features of mobile environments, coupled with need to support seamless mobility, make maintaining consistent cache at the mobile client a challenging task. There are several reasons for this. First being that the underlying cache maintenance protocol should not overburden the wireless resources and mobile device. Secondly, these protocols should be energy-efficient, tolerant of disconnections, and adaptive to varying QoS provided by the wireless network.

4.6.2.2. Cache Consistency Maintenance

Cache consistency maintenance is required to ensure that whenever a value of data item is fetched from the cache it satisfies certain currency requirement. There are several cache consistency models supported in distributed systems. Under strong cache consistency model, the cache consistency maintenance protocol guarantees that the value of data item, say x, provided to the application at any time is the most recent value of x.

That is to say, if the data item *x* was accesses at time *t*, then the value of *x* is the value of the last write to x that occurred before time *t*. **Strong cache consistency** requirement implies that whenever data item *x* is accessed, checks are performed in consultation with the remote servers to determine whether the cached value of *x* is the most current. In implementations of strong cache consistency protocols such as that employed by Network File System (NFS), if the remote server is inaccessible because of either the network connecting the client and the server is down or the server itself is down, then the cache access to x just waits till the server becomes accessible. In some implementation the client machine even blocks any further cache accesses, practically freezing the client machines. Maintaining such strict consistency requirements can make mobile computing environments unusable when the disconnections become frequent.

Several cache consistency maintenance schemes have been designed for different distributed applications such as the world wide web, distributed file systems, and client-server databases. These techniques can be classified based on whether they detect or avoid access to stale data. These techniques provide different degree of consistency guarantees with varying cost and availability in presence of disconnections.

The classic techniques of maintaining cache coherency such as **callbacks** and **validity checks** were designed for computing environments consisting of workstations connected via reliable wired links. These techniques are not suitable for mobile computing environment consisting of battery-powered laptops connected via wireless links. For example, "callback breaks" (invalidation messages) lost while the mobile client is disconnected from the network may result in stale cached items in a client's cache. Hence, in the absence of any other mechanisms, a client may have to invalidate the entire cache upon each disconnection. Re-fetching of valid data items from server is wasteful in both wireless bandwidth and battery power. Same is true when validation checks are used for every data item before using it. To address these drawbacks of traditional techniques, new techniques have been developed for maintaining cache consistency in mobile environments that take into account the constraints and features of such environments.

In general, there are two different cache consistency requirements:

- *Strong Cache Consistency*

- *Weak Cache Consistency*.

Strong cache consistency enforces that the cached data is always up-to-date. Polling-every-time and invalidating data upon modification are two approaches to achieve strong cache consistency. On the other hand, weak cache consistency allows some degree of data inconsistency. TTL-based consistency strategies are used when it is sufficient to guarantee weak consistency for a data item. In mobile computing environments, the main challenge for consistency strategies is caused by weak connectivity, and resource constraints of mobile computing environments.

4.6.3. Cache Maintenance for Push-Based Information Dissemination

Traditional client-server information systems use pull-based communication schemes for information access where clients initiate data transfers by requesting a server. Such pull-based techniques are not suitable for architecture-based wireless network because it requires substantial upstream communications. To make use of the downstream communication capacity, *push-based* information system architectures have been developed, where data is pushed from the servers to clients. The idea is that the server periodically broadcasts frequently accessed data (hot data items) on the broadcast channel. The mobile can tune in to the broadcast channel at the start of the broadcast, determine when the data items it is interested in will be available on the channel by reading the index information and then go to sleep until the time when the data item is on the channel. Such push-based architecture brings up a new problem for cache management. Traditionally, caches are used to store the most frequently used data, but in the push-based environment the cost of obtaining the data should also be considered. Considered one the example:

Assume that data item x is accessed 1% of the time at a client C and is also broadcasted 1% of the time and another data item y is accessed 0.5% of the time at C but is broadcast only 0.1% of the time (which implies that time period between two occurrence of data item y on the broadcast channel, ty, is 10 times the broadcast period of data item x, tx). If we choose to cache x instead of y, then the client will experience longer delay when cache miss happens for y. This will adversely affect the average data access delay. Intuitively, the penalty for not caching a data item on the average data access latency is proportional to the product of frequency and broadcast period. For the example above, the product of frequency and broadcast period for data item y is higher than that for data item x.

Therefore, new cache management algorithms have been developed for pushed-based information systems that take into account the cost of cache miss. Note that in traditional cache systems all cache misses are assumed to have same cost. This is not so in push-based information access architecture. In general, an important metric to evaluate these cache management algorithms is the achievable *hit ratio*- the fraction of total data requests satisfied from the cache. This metric not only depends on cache management algorithms, but also depends on the cache size and particular request pattern. In mobile computing environments, hit ratio should not be the only metric to evaluate cache management algorithms, since its underlying assumption is that all cache misses have equal cost. This assumption does not necessarily hold in weakly connected environments, where cache miss cost also depends on data size and the timing. New metrics representing different cache cost in mobile computing environments are therefore needed.

4.7. DATABASE AND TRANSACTION CONCEPTS

A database is a collection of data items that is gathered over a period of time, and safety stored for further examination or analysis. A database is usually accompanied by a data structure and a set of constraint rules that specify what information a data item represents. For example, in an employee database, the employee age is an integer number and must be greater than eighteen and less than sixty five. A database state is a collection of all the stored data values of all the data items in the database at a specific time. A consistent state of a database is a database state in which all the data values fulfill all the constraint rules of the database. A set of operations is usually provided to support users in retrieving or modifying data items in the database. These provided operations can be simple, for example read and write operations, or more complex operations, for example deletion or modification operations. To assist users to perform much more complex operations rather than reading from and writing to the database, a piece of specialized software called a DataBase Management System (DBMS) is accommodated to the database. In general, a DBMS not only provides an easy-to-use and friendly interface to users for accessing and manipulating the database, but also manages all the database operations. In addition, the DBMS also protects the database from unauthorized users.

4.7.1. Database Transactions

Users can interact with the database by one or many database operations. The database operations can be gathered together to form a unit of execution program that is called a *transaction.* In other words, a transaction is a logical execution unit of database operations. A transaction transforms the database from one consistent state to another consistent state. Fig. 4.7 presents a programming model of a transaction.

```
        Begin_transaction (initial_consistent_state)
            One or more database operations

        if (reach new_consistent_state) then
        Commit_transaction (new_consistent_state)
    else
        Abort_transaction (initial_consistent_state)
```

Fig. 4.7: Transactional Programming Model

A transaction program starts from an initial consistent state of the database by invoking a *Begin_transaction* method call. After that, one or a set of database operations of the transaction program are executed. When these database operations are completed, i.e., a new consistent database state is established as designed, the transaction program saves this new consistent state into the database by calling the *Commit_transaction* method. The *Commit_transaction* call ensures that all the database operations of the transaction program are successfully executed and the results of the transaction are safely saved in the database. If there is any error during the execution of the transaction program, the initial consistent state of the database is re-established by the *Abort_transaction* call. The *Abort_transaction* call indicates that the execution of the transaction program has failed and this execution does not have any effect on the initial consistent state of the database. The transaction is said to be *committed* if it has successfully executed the *Commit_transaction* call, otherwise it is *aborted.* A transaction is called a *read-only transaction* if all of its database operations do not alter any database state.

4.7.2. The ACID Properties

In a database system, there may be a large number of transactions that are executed concurrently, i.e., the shared data items in the database are read and possible written by many transactions at the same time. Each transaction must ensure that it always preserves the consistency of the database system. In order to retain and to protect the consistency of the database system, transactions will have the following ACID (Atomicity, Consistency, Isolation, and Durability) properties:

• ***Atomicity***

Either all database operations of a transaction program are successfully and completely executed, or none of the database operation of this transaction program is executed.

• ***Consistency***

A transaction must always preserve and protect the consistency of the database, i.e., it transforms the database from one consistent state to another. In other words, the result of a transaction that has committed fulfills the constraints of the database system.

• ***Isolation***

An on-going transaction must not interfere with other concurrent transactions, or be able to view intermediate results of other concurrent transactions. In other words, a transaction is executed as if it is the only existing execution program on the database system at any given time.

• ***Durability***

The result of a transaction that has successfully committed is permanent in the database. The consistent state of the database is always survived despite any type of failures.

The ACID properties of a transaction ensure that:

- A transaction always keep the database in a consistent state,
- A transaction does not disturb other transactions during their concurrent execution processes,
- The consistent state of the database system that is established by a committed transaction withstands software or hardware failures.

In order to achieve the ACID properties, normally, two different sets of protocols named *Concurrency Control Protocols* and *Recovery Protocols* are needed.

4.8. MOBILE TRANSACTION PROCESSING

In this section, we have discussed the basic and essential components of a transaction processing system that manages the execution of transactions on a transaction-oriented database system.

4.8.1. Essential Components of a Transaction Processing System

A transaction processing system plays a role as a mediator that accepts transaction requests from users, dispatches these requests to the database system, coordinates the execution of the involved transactions, and forwards transaction results to the original acquirers. Fig. 4.8 illustrates an interaction model for a transaction-oriented database system. The common programming model for a transaction-oriented database system is the client-server model. Users or clients interact with the database system by submitting their transaction processes that consist of one or many database operations to the transaction processing system. The transaction processing system will coordinate and manage the execution of these transaction processes by subsequently sending these database operations to the database system. The database system will carry out the actual execution of the submitted database operations. Finally, the transaction results that reflect the consistent states of the database system are returned to the clients.

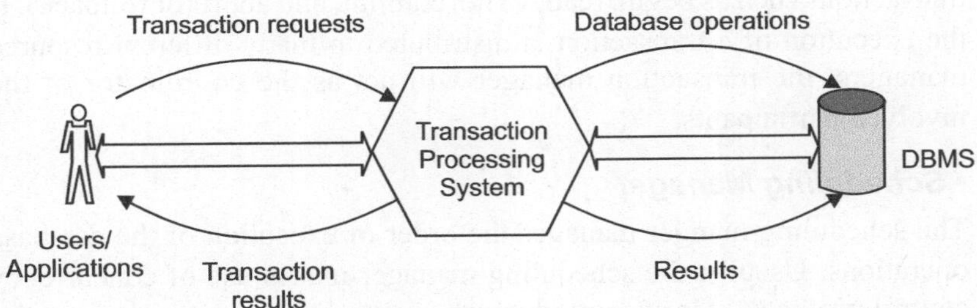

Fig. 4.8: Dataflow of Transaction-Oriented Database Systems

To protect the integrity constraint of the database system, the transaction processing system must ensure that the ACID properties of transactions are fulfilled. In order to achieve this, a set of essential components that includes a transaction manager, a scheduling manger and a log manger are deployed. Additional components such as communication manger or other resource managers can also be employed by the transaction processing system. However, in this section, we will focus our discussion on the three essential components. Fig. 4.9 presents the roles of the transaction processing system components.

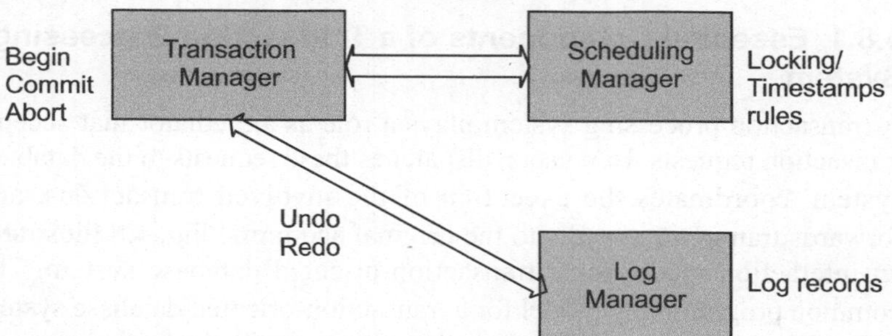

Fig. 4.9: Transaction Processing System Components

The role of each transaction processing component is described as follows:

- ***Transaction Manager***

The role of the transaction manager is to orchestrate the execution of transactions . Via the help of the scheduling and log managers (explained below), the transaction manager takes care of all important operations of transactions such as begin, read, write, commit, and abort (or rollback). If the execution of a transaction is distributed to many different resource managers, the transaction manager will act as the coordinator of the involved participants.

- ***Scheduling Manager***

The scheduling manger manages the order of execution of the database operations. Usually, the scheduling manager makes use of concurrency control protocols, for example locking or timestamp protocols, in order to control the execution of transactions. Thus, the scheduling manager supports the isolation and consistency properties of transactions. Based on the applied concurrency control protocol, the scheduling manager will determine an execution order in which the submitted database operations will be carried out. For example, if a locking protocol is used, the scheduling manager will decide whether a lock request will be granted to the acquired transaction, or if a timestamp protocol is applied, the scheduling manager will assess if a submitted operation will be allowed to be carried out.

• ***Log Manager***

The role of the log manager is to support the database system to recover from failures. The log manager keeps track of the changes of the database states by recording the history of transaction execution. Depending on the deployed recovery strategies, for example *undo* and/or *redo*, the log manger will record necessary information in a non-volatile logbook. The log manager ensures the atomicity and the durability properties of transactions. The cooperation among the transaction manager, the scheduling manger and the log manager will assure that the ACID properties of transactions in a transaction-oriented database system will be fulfilled.

4.8.2. Mobile Transaction Vs Centralized / Distributed Transaction

A transaction in mobile environment is different than the transactions in the centralized or distributed databases in the following ways:

- The mobile transactions might have to split their computations into sets of operations, some of which execute on mobile host while others on stationary host. A mobile transaction shares their states and partial results with other transactions due to disconnection and mobility.
- The mobile transactions require computations and communications to be supported by stationary hosts.
- When the mobile user moves during the execution of a transaction, it continues its execution in the new cell. The partially executed transaction may be continued at the fixed local host according to the instruction given by the mobile user. Different mechanisms are required if the user wants to continue its transaction at a new destination.
- As the mobile hosts move from one cell to another, the states of

transaction, states of accessed data objects, and the location information also move.

- The mobile transactions are long-lived transactions due to the mobility of both the data and users, and due to the frequent disconnections.

The mobile transactions should support and handle concurrency, recovery, disconnection and mutual consistency of the replicated data objects. To support mobile transactions, the transaction processing models should accommodate the limitations of mobile computing, such as unreliable communication, limited battery life, low bandwidth communication, and reduced storage capacity. Mobile computations should minimize aborts due to disconnection. Operations on shared data must ensure correctness of transactions executed on both stationary and mobile hosts. The blocking of a transaction's executions on either the stationary or mobile hosts must be minimized to reduce communication cost and to increase concurrency. Proper support for mobile transactions must provide for local autonomy to allow transactions to be processed and committed on the mobile host despite temporary disconnection.

4.8.3. Transaction Processing in Mobile Environments

In mobile environments, transaction processing systems consist of both mobile and non-mobile hosts, and can be divided into two different layers (see Fig. 4.10). The distributed transaction processing layer corresponds

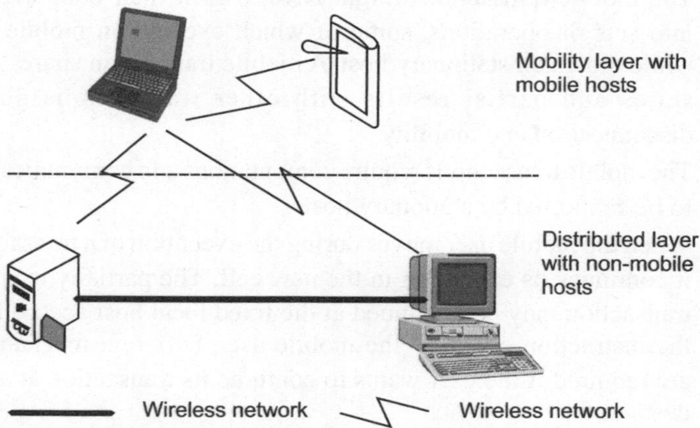

Fig. 4.10: Transaction Processing in Mobile Environments

to the execution of mobile transactions that are carried out on non-mobile hosts. The mobile transaction processing layer corresponds to the execution of mobile transactions that are carried out on a mobile host or distributed among mobile hosts. Due to the above distinguishing and challenging characteristics of mobile environments, transaction processing in mobile environments is more difficult than in distributed environments, especially in terms of concurrency control, data availability, and recovery mechanisms.

4.8.4. Architecture of Mobile Transaction Environments

In this section, we discussed the architecture of the mobile transaction environments. In general, the mobile transaction environments include three different components: Mobile Hosts (MH), Mobile Support Stations (MSS) and fixed hosts where Database Servers (DB) reside. Fig. 4.11 illustrates the mobile transaction environments.

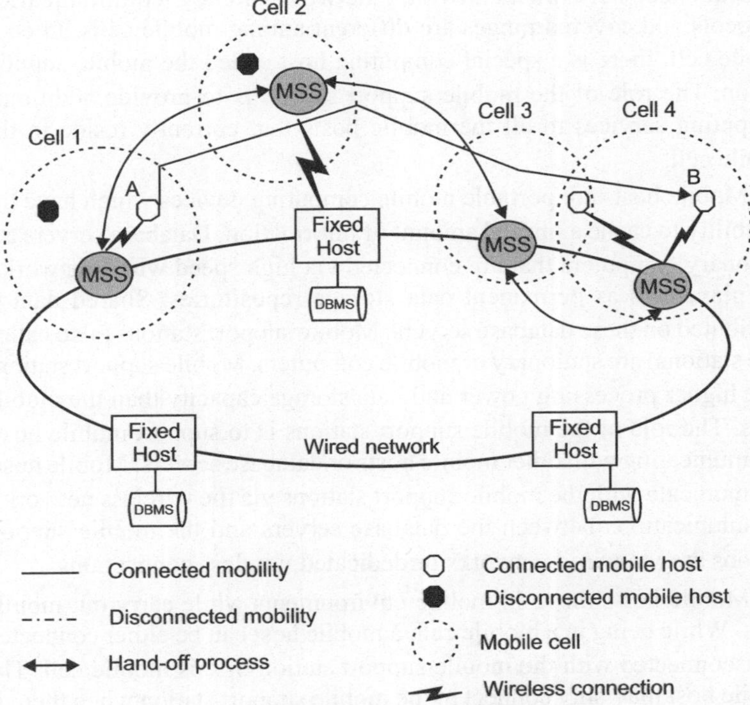

Fig. 4.11: Mobile Transaction Environments

A mobile environment is a geographical territory. The geographical territory is divided into a collection of areas called mobile cells. Wireless communications in each mobile cell is provided by a single low-power transmitter-receiver. There might be some areas in the mobile environments in which the wireless communication is not available. This could be caused by the limited service of the wireless communication providers or the structural of physical objects in the areas, for example concrete tunnels or remote islands. The geographical mobile environment, therefore, can be considered as a collection of mobile cells that are separated or overlapped with others. The size of mobile cells is not necessarily equal, due to the differences of operational power of the transmitter-receiver devices.

The wireless technologies that are provided in each mobile cell can be different, for example wireless LAN or wireless USB. As a consequence, network bandwidth, network latency, communication protocols and covered ranges are different among mobile cells. In each mobile cell, there is a special computing host called the mobile support station. The role of the mobile support station is to provide additional computing services to all the mobile hosts that currently reside in the mobile cell.

Mobile hosts are portable mobile computing devices which have the capability to cache a limited amount of information. Database servers are stationary computers that are connected via high speed wired-networks, and play roles as permanent data storage repositories. Shared data is distributed on these database servers. Mobile support stations (also called base stations) are stationary or mobile computers. Mobile support stations have higher processing power and data storage capacity than the mobile hosts. The role of the mobile support stations is to support mobile hosts communicating with other mobile hosts or database servers. Mobile hosts communicate with the mobile support stations via the wireless networks. Communications between the database servers and the mobile support stations are via wired networks or dedicated wireless connections.

Mobile hosts move in mobile environments while carry out mobile tasks. While being in a mobile cell, a mobile host can be either connected or disconnected with the mobile support station of this mobile cell. The mobile host may only connect to the mobile support station when there is a need for sharing of data. This will help to save the limited energy of the mobile host and to reduce the communication cost. On the other hand, because of the limitations of wireless networks, a mobile host may not always be able to establish a communication channel with the mobile support station. If a mobile host is in the area that is an intersection of two or more mobile cells, it can connect to any mobile support station.

The mobile hosts can move within one mobile cell or across a large area covered by several mobile cells. When a mobile host is leaving a mobile cell and entering a new mobile cell, the communication channel and other related information between the mobile host and the previous mobile support station will be transferred to the next mobile support station. This process is called *hand-over* or *hand-off* process. The new mobile support station at the new mobile cell will continue carrying out the support to the mobile host. However, it is not necessary that hand-over processes must happen every time the mobile host enters a new mobile cell. For example, the mobile host can operate in an autonomous mode when the wireless network is not supported in the new mobile cell. Furthermore, a mobile host does not have to disconnect from the old mobile support station before it can connect to the new mobile support station. A mobile host can connect to a new mobile support station while connecting to the old mobile support station. The hand-off process can be planned beforehand if the travel route of the mobile host is known in advanced and strictly followed. Otherwise, the hand-off process can only be carried out after the mobile host has established a connection with the new mobile support station, i.e., after the new destination of the mobile host is known.

In Fig. 4.11, there are four mobile cells in the mobile environments. Mobile cells one and two are separated, while mobile cells three and four are overlapped. A mobile host moves from position *A* in mobile cell one to position *B* in mobile cell four. The travel route of the mobile host passes through mobile cells two and three. When the mobile host is leaving cell one, it will enter a disconnected interval in the area between the mobile cells one and two. While in the mobile cell two, the mobile host will be supported by the mobile support station that is a dedicated mobile host. When the mobile host is in the mobile cell three, it may not connect to the mobile support station all the time. In the intersection region of the mobile cells three and four, the mobile host can connect to the mobile support station of either mobile cell three or mobile cell four. The hand-over processes occur when the mobile host moves from one mobile cell to another along the travel route.

4.8.5. Characteristics of Mobile Transactions

Transactions in mobile environments possess many challenging characteristics due to the characteristics of the mobile environments. In this section, we will discuss the characteristics of mobile transactions. The characteristics of mobile transactions are described as follows:

4.8.5.1. Mobility of Transactions

The execution of transactions in mobile environments is tightly coupled with the behavior of the mobile hosts. A mobile host can initiate mobile transactions or participate in the transaction execution processes. When a mobile host moves from one location to another, all the transactions that are being carried out at that mobile host will also move. Consequently, many computing activities associated with these transactions are moved or changed, for example handling hand-over processes, establishing new communication channels, or updating the routing tables.

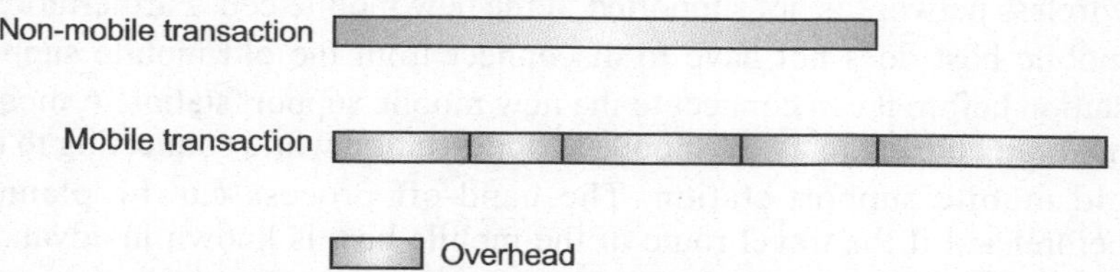

Fig. 4.12: Transaction Life-Time in Non-Mobile and Mobile Environments

In other words, the mobility of transactions causes the movement of related transaction resources, controls, and services.

4.8.5.2. Long-lived Transactions

Transactions in mobile environments have longer life (i.e., long-lived) than traditional ACID transactions. This is due to the overheads that are caused by two aspects: the data availability and the execution interruptions (see Fig 4.12)

4.8.5.3. Data Availability

In mobile environments, the data availability at a mobile host can be affected by many factors. First, the movement of the mobile host causes the movement of related information. This will cause additional overhead to the transaction execution time. Second, the bandwidth of wireless networks is limited; therefore it will take longer time to obtain the necessary data. Third, the mobile computing devices have limitations in storage capacity; therefore, the mobile host may not able to cache the required information to support disconnected transaction processing. In addition, due to the unexpected disconnections of the wireless networks, a transaction will not be able to release the controls on shared data to transactions at other hosts as scheduled; this means that this transaction blocks the execution of other transactions.

4.8.5.4. Execution Interruptions

The execution of transactions can be interrupted while being carried out at the mobile host. The interruptions can be caused by either the surrounding environment conditions or the limitation of computing capacity of the mobile host. For example, a wireless network disconnection suddenly occurs during the execution of transactions, or the performance of the mobile host is slowing down due to heavy computing load. The interruptions can happen frequently and cause transactions to be suspended or aborted.

4.8.5.5. Adaptive Transaction Processing

Due to the real-time movement of the mobile hosts, the limitations of the wireless networks, and the variation of the mobile resources, the execution plan of a transaction in mobile environments may not be as scheduled. Therefore, the mobile transaction processing system must have the ability to support adaptive transaction processing that includes: distributed and disconnected transaction processing.

4.8.5.6. Distributed Transaction Processing

Due to the limitations of processing capacity and resources, mobile hosts require additional support from other hosts to carry out transactions. For example, a transaction, which is initiated by a mobile host and accesses a large data set that is not cached at the mobile host, could be moved to stationary hosts for executing. This could reduce transaction processing time and avoid transferring a large amount of data through a slow wireless network, i.e., achieving higher throughput for the transaction processing system. Furthermore, the portable computing devices are easily damaged; therefore, the results of committed transactions must be saved at stationary database servers.

4.8.5.7. Disconnected Transaction Processing

A mobile host can be disconnected from the database servers for long periods; therefore, transactions that are executed at the mobile host may suffer from long blocking if the necessary data is not available at the mobile host. To deal with this problem, the mobile transaction processing system should have the capacity to cache enough data so that it can carry out the transactions while being disconnected from the database servers.

4.8.5.8. Temporary Data Inconsistency

Due to long disconnection periods, shared data among different mobile hosts may not be fully consistent all the time. For example, a transaction at a disconnected mobile host can modify a shared data item that is currently being read-only cached in a local storage of another disconnected mobile host. Data synchronization processes will be carried out when the disconnected mobile hosts reconnect to the database systems so that the data consistency of the database systems will be achieved.

4.8.5.9. Heterogeneous Processing

Many types of mobile devices can be involved in transaction execution processes. Interactions or communications among participating parties are carried out via the support of different types of wireless network technologies and protocols. Furthermore, different database systems are accessed during the execution of mobile transactions. All these factors contribute to the heterogeneous processing characteristic of mobile transactions.

4.8.6. Requirements of Transactions in Mobile Environments

In this section, we address in detail the requirements of a mobile transaction processing system. Because of the challenging characteristics of mobile transactions, the ACID properties of transaction are too strict to be applied in the mobile environments. More relaxing transaction properties have been introduced to support transaction processing in the mobile environments. A common approach is that the atomicity and isolation properties could be relaxed, while the consistency and durability properties must be preserved.

In order to achieve the objectives, we identify nine requirements that a mobile transaction processing system must have. The requirements are based on four categories: *mobility of transactions* (R1 and R2), *wireless networks* and *limited mobile resources* (R3 and R4), *customization of transaction properties* (R5, R6, and R7), and *recovery of transactions* (R8 and R9). The requirements are summarized in the following Table.

The above requirements are elaborated as follows:

R1. *The mobile transaction processing system must be able to effectively handle the hand-over control of mobile transactions.*

Mobility of hosts is one of the main challenging characteristics of mobile environments that cause the mobility of transactions. The mobility of a mobile transaction can be described in terms of hand-over processes that occur during the execution of the mobile transaction. Therefore, the mobile transaction processing system must be able to capture and control these hand-over processes. This can be achieved if the mobile transaction processing system is able to identify:

- when a hand-over process occurs, and
- which information is needed to move or to modify in accordance with the mobility pattern of mobile transactions.

R2. *The mobile transaction processing system must support interactions among transactions at different mobile hosts.*

While being on the move and disconnected from the database servers, mobile hosts can directly communicate with others by using short range and peer-to-peer communication technologies, for example infra-red, Bluetooth or wireless LAN. The mobile transaction processing system must be able to support direct interactions among transactions at different mobile hosts, i.e., without any support from the mobile support stations or the database servers.

R3. *The mobile transaction processing system must support disconnected transaction processing.*

In mobile environments, the mobile hosts are frequently disconnected from the database servers. Therefore, the mobile transaction processing system must support disconnected transaction processing, i.e., to deal with the disconnections of the wireless networks, especially long disconnection periods. This will allow the mobile hosts to continue processing transactions in isolation mode and, hence, reducing the delay of local transactions.

R4. *The mobile transaction processing system must support distributed transaction execution among mobile hosts and stationary hosts.*

Due to the limited computing resources of mobile devices, the mobile transaction processing system must be able to distribute the execution of transactions among available computing hosts. For example,

Categories	Requirements
Mobility of transactions	**R1.** The mobile transaction processing system must be able to effectively handle the hand-over control of mobile transactions. **R2.** The mobile transaction processing system must support interactions among transactions at different mobile hosts.
Wireless networks and limited mobile resources	**R3.** The mobile transaction processing system must support disconnected transaction processing. **R4.** The mobile transaction processing system must support distributed transaction execution among mobile hosts and stationary hosts.
Customization of transaction properties	**R5.** The mobile transaction processing system must have the ability to customize the atomicity property of transactions. **R6.** The mobile transaction processing system must support sharing partial states and status among transactions. **R7.** The mobile transaction processing system must assure the durability property of transactions.
Recovery of transactions	**R8.** The mobile transaction processing system must provide efficient recovery strategies **R9.** The mobile transaction processing system must support temporary data and transaction management.

if a mobile transaction requires a lot of processing capacity or the amount of requested data of the mobile transaction is large, the mobile transaction should be transferred to fixed hosts to be processed there. This approach, in addition, will avoid the problem of transferring a large amount of data from the database servers to the mobile host on the low bandwidth and frequently disconnecting wireless networks.

R5. *The mobile transaction processing system must have the ability to customize the atomicity property of transactions.*

The standard atomicity property of transactions is too strict in mobile environments, especially for long-lived transactions. Therefore, the mobile transaction processing system must provide mechanisms to customize the atomicity level of transactions. In other words, the mobile transaction processing system must support transactions to partially roll back when failures occur. For example, a transaction will be partially rolled back (i.e., not totally aborted) due to a failure caused by the exhausting power supply at the mobile host or the disconnection of wireless networks. The mobile transaction can be continued when these mobile resources become available. Customizing the atomicity property of transaction also avoids losing of useful work done due to the failures of the mobile hosts.

R6. *The mobile transaction processing system must support sharing partial states and status among transactions.*

Sharing partial results is essential in mobile environments. For example, if a shared data object is only accessible after the transaction that is being executed at a mobile host has finally committed at the database servers; other transactions can suffer long blocking periods. Furthermore, mobile transactions are long-lived transactions, therefore, the mobile transaction processing system must allow partial results of on-going transactions to be shared.

R7. *The mobile transaction processing system must assure the durability property of transactions.*

In mobile environments, mobile transactions are executed and locally committed at the mobile hosts, and globally committed at the database servers. Mobile computing devices are easily damaged; therefore, the results of committed transactions saved at mobile hosts can be lost if failures happen. Thus, the mobile transaction processing system must provide different methods to safely archive information in accordance with the commitment (i.e., locally or globally) of mobile transactions.

R8. *The mobile transaction processing system must provide efficient recovery strategies.* When a transaction fails, the recovery techniques support the database systems to restore consistent states. In mobile environments, failures are common due to many factors, for example the disconnections of wireless communications or the exhausting of the battery energy. Furthermore, cascading abort can happen if a transaction aborts after sharing their partial results to other transactions. Therefore, the transaction processing system must support different recovery methods to deal with different transaction failure situations.

For example, if a transaction that shares consistent data to other transactions aborts, those transactions that have read the shared consistent data should not be aborted.

R9. *The mobile transaction processing system must support temporary data and transaction management.*

The execution processes of mobile transactions can happen at different computing (mobile or non-mobile) hosts that can be asynchronously connected or disconnected. For example, a transaction at a disconnected mobile host reads a shared data object that is being modified at another mobile host. Therefore, the non-permanency of data and transactions behavior must be managed. The temporary management must also handle conflicts among transactions at different mobile hosts.

4.8.7. Issues Related to Mobile Transaction Processing Systems

In this section, we discuss issues that are related to mobile transaction processing systems. The three issues are:

- Mobile Database Replication,
- Advanced Transaction Commitment Protocols, and
- Mobile Data Sharing Mechanisms.

These three issues contribute in a vital way to the performance of transaction processes in mobile environments.

4.8.7.1. Mobile Database Replication

In mobile environments, to cope with the disconnections of the wireless networks, the mobile hosts must be able to cache necessary data to support disconnected transaction processing. A database portion that is cached at a mobile host is called the mobile database. Mobile databases offer higher level of data availability at disconnected mobile hosts; thus, enhance the performance of mobile transaction processing systems. Fig. 4.13 illustrates an example of the life cycle of mobile databases. Before the mobile hosts are disconnected from the database servers, shared data is cached at the mobile host. When the mobile host is disconnected from the database servers, cached data is modified. When the mobile hosts reconnect to the database server, shared data that has been modified at the local cache will be reconciled with the original versions.

Keeping data consistency among these copies all the time is difficult. Therefore, the main issue is how to avoid or be aware of data inconsistency among such copies. This can be achieved by several ways, for example an advanced locking protocol or signoff/ check-in/check-out operations. The pre-write lock is an additional lock layer that is deployed at the mobile support station to support mobile transactions to access shared data, i.e., without connecting to the database server. Transactions can connect to either the database server or the mobile support station to access shared data. If a shared data is modified, it will first be stored at the mobile

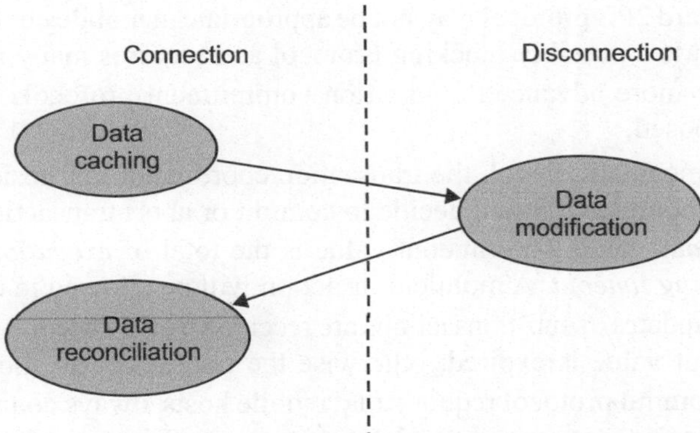

Fig. 4.13: Life Cycle of Mobile Databases.

support station before being updated in the database server. For sign-off/ check-in/check-out operations, consistent shared data is downloaded from the database server to mobile hosts via the support of a proxy-transaction (called a pseudo-transaction) to support disconnected transaction processing. When the mobile hosts reconnect to the database server, mobile transactions will be checked to ensure that they are serializable with other transactions at the database server. The mobile databases must be able to support mobile hosts to cope with different types of disconnections.

There are two forms of disconnection:

- Planned, and
- Unplanned

For planned disconnections, the mobile hosts inform the database servers about the disconnections so that the mobile databases can be well prepared. The strict mobile database replication model uses the standard shared and exclusive lock modes for controlling conflicting database operations among replicated copies. Relaxed mobile database replication model allows transactions to concurrently access replicated database portions at different mobile hosts as long as there is an acceptable execution schedule among involved transactions. For example, check-out with mobile read, checkout with system read, or relaxed check-out modes. To our knowledge, there is no mobile database model that supports mobile databases to deal with unplanned disconnections.

4.8.7.2. Advanced Transaction Commitment Protocols

The standard 2PC protocol may not be appropriate in mobile environments because it is a possibly blocking protocol and requires many messages. There are more advanced transaction commitment protocols that have been proposed.

In Timeouts Protocol, the transaction coordinator that resides at the mobile support station will decide to commit or abort transactions based on a *timeout* value. The timeout value is the total of *execution timeout* and *shipping timeout.* A mobile transaction will be allowed to commit if all of the updates of sub-transactions are received by the coordinator before the timeout value is expired; otherwise the transaction is aborted. The timeout commit protocol requires that mobile hosts always connect to the mobile support station and the database servers. The main drawback of this protocol is that it is hard to define or estimate the *execution* and *shipping* timeout values in mobile environments.

The Unilateral Commit Protocol is proposed to support transaction commitment in disconnected mode. This protocol reduces the number of exchanged messages by removing the second voting phase of the standard 2PC protocol (thus, this protocol is also called a one-phase commit protocol). If a mobile transaction reaches the prepare-to commit phase, it will commit.

There are other commit protocols that are developed by taking into account the special characteristics of mobile transactions. Some examples are the commitment of read-only transactions that are carried out separately from updating transactions (by exploring the special consistency requirements of read-only transactions), and the pre-commit protocol (by tolerating the difference between pre-committed and committed results which is specified by applications).

4.8.7.3. Mobile Data Sharing Mechanisms

In this section, we address the mechanisms that support sharing of data in mobile environments. In general, shared data is stored at dedicated non-mobile database servers. Mobile hosts need to connect to these database servers to access shared data. However, due to the disconnections in communication, the mobile hosts may not always be able to connect to the database servers. This leads to the demand of a temporary sharing workspace that is stored at dedicated hosts. Existing models that have been designed to support sharing data in distributed environments.

Recently, there are many research proposals that focus on supporting data sharing among mobile hosts in mobile environments. The two essential components that contribute to the mobile data sharing are:

- the dynamic mobile workgroup management, and
- the data access mechanisms.

The dynamic mobile workgroup management focuses on the organization and management of temporary mobile workgroups that are the collection of mobile hosts. The data access mechanisms are based on either the client-server or the peer-to-peer architecture. The Accessing Mobile Database (AMDB) architecture is based on the concepts of mobile agents and the client-server model. The main idea is to form a Mobile Database Community (MDBC) in which mobile clients access mobile databases that are stored at dedicated mobile hosts.

4.8.8. Mobile Transaction Processing Schemes: An Overview

Semantic based transaction processing models have been extended for mobile computing into increase concurrency by exploiting commutative operations. These techniques require caching large portion of the database or maintain multiple copies of many data items. In the scheme fragments data objects, fragment ability of data objects have been used to facilitate semantic based transaction processing in mobile databases. Each fragmented data object has to be cached independently and manipulated synchronously. That is, on request, a fragment of data object is dispatched to the MU. On completion of the transaction, the mobile hosts return the fragments to the BS. Fragments are then integrated in the object in any order and such objects are termed as reorderable objects. This scheme works only in the situations where the data objects can be fragmented like sets, stacks and queues.

In optimistic concurrency control based schemes, cached objects on mobile hosts can be updated without any co-ordination but the updates need to be propagated and validated for the commitment of transactions. This scheme leads to aborts of mobile transactions unless the conflicts are rare. Since mobile transactions are expected to be long-lived due to disconnection and long network delays, the conflicts will be more in mobile computing environment.

In pessimistic schemes in which cached objects can be locked exclusively, mobile transactions can be committed locally. The pessimistic schemes lead to unnecessary transaction blocking since mobile hosts can not release any cached objects while it is disconnected. Existing caching methods attempt to cache the entire data objects or in some case the complete file. Caching of these potentially large objects over low bandwidth communication channels can result in wireless network congestion and high communication cost. The limited memory size of the MU allows only a small number of objects can be cached at any given time.

The concept of transaction proxies is introduced to support recovery, in which for each transaction submitted at an MU, a dual transaction called proxy is submitted to the base station. The proxy transaction includes the updates of the original transaction. Proxy transaction takes the periodic backup of the computation performed at mobile host.

Similar to above, the notion of twin-transaction was introduced, which essentially replicate the process of executing transactions. In twin transaction model, each write's request will be mirrored and two equivalent transactions will be created. In this way, if a mobile host is disconnected, the transaction execution can still be proceed.

Dynamic object clustering has been proposed in mobile computing, which assumes a fully distributed system, and the transaction model is designed to maintain the consistency of the database. The model uses weak-read, weak-write, strict-read and strict-write. The decomposition of operations is done based on the consistency requirement. Strict-read and strict-write have the same semantics as normal read and write operations invoked by transactions satisfying ACID properties. A weak-read returns the value of a locally cached object written by a strict-write or a weak-write. A weak-write operation only updates a locally cached object, which might become permanent on cluster merging if the weak-write does not conflict with any strict-read or strict-write operation. The weak transactions use local and global commits. However, a weak transaction after local commit can abort and is compensated. A pre-committed transaction does not abort, hence require no undo or compensation. A weak transaction's updates are visible to other weak transactions whereas pre-writes are visible to all transactions.

4.9. MOBILE DATABASE RESEARCH DIRECTIONS

We see the following as upcoming mobile database research directions:

4.9.1. Location-Dependent Query Processing

Location can be a subject of more complex aggregate queries. For example, finding the number of hotels in the area you are passing or looking for a mobile doctor closest to your present location. Hence, the location information is a frequently changing piece of data. The objective is get the right data at different locations for processing a given query. The results returned in response to such queries should satisfy the location constraints with respect to the point of query origin, where the results are received, etc.

Data may represent SSN of a person, or maiden name, or sales tax of a city. In one representation the mapping of the data value and the object it represents is not subjected to any location constraints. For example, the value of SSN of a person remains the same no matter from which location it is accessed. This is not true in the case of sales tax data. The value of the sales tax depends on the place where sales query is executed. For example, sales tax value of West Lafayette is governed by a different set of criteria than the sales tax of Boston. We can therefore, identify the type of data whose value depends on the set of criteria established by the location and another type of data, which is not subject to the constraints of a location. There is a third type of data that is sensitive to the point of query.

We illustrate this data with the following example. Consider a commuter who is traveling in a taxi initiates a query on his laptop to find the nearby hotels in the area of its current location. The answer to this query depends on the location of the origin of the query. Since the commuter is moving he may receive the result at a different location. Thus, the query results should correspond to the location where the result is received or to the point of the origin of the query. The difference in the two correct answers to the query depends on the location and not on the hotel. The movement does not affect the answer to the query "find the cheapest hotel". The former depends on the location where as later on the object characteristics.

In most of the research projects it is considered, a database that represents information about moving objects and their location. Existing DBMS's are not well equipped to handle continuously changing data, such location of moving objects. One of the issue is location modelling by introducing the concept of dynamic attribute (whose value keeps changing), spatial and temporal query languages and indexing dynamic attributes.

4.9.2. View Maintenance in Mobile Computing

Accessing on-line database from the mobile computer may be expensive due to limited uplink bandwidth, and also due to the fact that sending messages consume lot of energy which is limited in the portable battery. These two problems can be solved by maintaining a materialized view i.e., storing the tuples of the view in the database at the mobile computer. This view will be updated as on-line database changes using wireless data messages. This will also localize access, thus improving access time. Therefore, to better deal with the problem of disconnection, reliability, and to improve response time, the view should be materialized at the mobile computer. The view maintenance will involve location-dependent data, time-dependent data, and dynamic allocation of a materialized view in the fixed and mobile network. The another problem is dynamic allocation of a materialized view in the mobile network. Another issue concerns the divergence of the materialized view at the mobile computer from the on-line database. In other words, how closely should the materialized view reflect the on-line database. An approach to divergence involves parameterizing each read at the mobile computer with the amount of divergence from the latest version it can accept. Another approach allows the user to specify triggers on the on-line database, the view is updated when the trigger is satisfied. Recently, this problem has also been discussed to emphasis the importance of data warehousing view maintenance in mobile computing environment.

There is a need to develop view maintenance algorithms in case of data warehousing environment where relational data is broadcasted.

Similarly, there is a need to do change management in the web data where changes are broadcast periodically and mobile host should capture the data and make the cached web data consistent.

4.9.3. Workflows in Mobile Environment

Workflow management systems are growing due to their ability to improve the efficiency of an organization by streamlining and automating business processes. Workflow systems have to be integrated with mobile computing environment in order to co-ordinate disconnected computing to enhance the system's resilience to failures. Specific issues that arise here include how the workflow models can co-ordinate tasks that are performed when mobile users work in disconnected mode and when they cross wireless boundaries. Also location sensitive activities might have to schedule to use an organization's resources effectively. Current workflow systems do not seem to have any provision to handle these requirements. During disconnected workflow clients can be supported while preserving the correctness of the overall execution and allowing co-ordinated interactions between the different users. The required activities (i.e., applications and data) are downloaded onto the mobile computer before performing a planned disconnection. The activities are performed in a disconnected mode and the results are then uploaded after reconnection at which time exceptions that occurred during the disconnected mode of operations are also handled. When mobile users cross the borders of wireless cells, hand-off (i.e., a mobile user's session is to migrate to a new information server) may need to be performed from the old workflow server to a new server. Consistency issues that arise when workflow instances migrate are to be handled carefully. For location sensitive routing of a mobile user's request, the modeling primitives should have provision to specify geographic information in the workflow definition.

4.9.4. Digital Library Services in Mobile Computing

Digital libraries bring about the integration, management, and communication of gigabytes of multimedia data in distributed environment. Digital library data includes texts, Figs, photographs, sound, video, films, slides, etc. Digital library system currently envisions users as being static when they access information. It is expected in the near future that users will have access to a digital library through wireless access. Provision to access digital library services through wireless networks is required by a wide range of applications from personal to research to customize business computing. Providing digital library services to users whose location is constantly changing, whose network connections are through a wireless medium, and whose computational power is low necessitates modifications to existing digital library systems. The queries in digital library are complex and involve processing, navigation, searching, and presenting of distributed heterogeneous repositories of multimedia data.

4.9.5. Mobile Web and E-commerce

There is a need to bring web on the mobile platform. Imagine a taxi that is equipped with mobile computer and the passenger there would like to browse web pages while waiting for its destination. The limited bandwidth will be a bottleneck in such a scenario. Another interesting application may be e-commerce on the mobile web. All these applications are ready to go on the *disconnected, highly unreliable, limited bandwidth and* unsecured platform where application demands reliability and security. Some efforts in this direction, where a WWW system designed to handle mobile users. It allows the documents to refer and react to current location of clients. One of the issue of mobile web is browsing through a multi-resolution transmission paradigm. The multi-resolution scheme allows various organizational units of a web document to be transferred and browsed according to the information contents. This will allow better utilization of limited bandwidth.

4.9.6. Mobile Data Security

Security is a prime concern in mobile databases due to nature of communication medium. New risks caused by mobility of users, portability of computers can compromise on confidentiality, integrity and availability including accountability. In a mobile database environment, it may be a good idea if data can be summarized or only metadata can be stored on mobile platform and more detailed data can be kept on Mobile Service Station (MSS) only. The higher frequency of disconnection also requires a more powerful recovery model. Such situations offer attackers the possibility of masquerade as either mobile host or MSS. This needs more robust authentication service.

Another issue is to maintain the privacy of location data of mobile hosts. Ideally only mobile user and home agent should have knowledge about mobile hosts current position and location data. All user identification information including message origin and destination has to be protected. In order to achieve anonymous communication, aliases can be used or communication can be channeled through a third trusted party. Further more, the identity of users may also need to be kept secret from other MSSs if required. Access based control policies can be adapted to provide data security on mobile platform.

4.10. SECURITY AND FAULT TOLERANCE IN MOBILE NETWORK

The security in mobile computing would be a major issue as individual, groups, and organizations are unlikely to put personal, important, and mission-critical information over an infrastructure that is either not secure or is not perceived to be secure. The security weaknesses of wireless and mobile infrastructure stems from both the use of multiple "incompatible" security schemes and due to "inherent" weaknesses in certain wireless security algorithm (such as wireless LANs). It should be noted that security issues are quite different in wireless networks and for variety of reasons strong security has not been implemented in wireless infrastructure.

There are many security issues in such environment, including confidentiality, authentication, integrity, authorization, non-repudiation, and accessibility. Other issues would include convenience, speed, ease-of-use, and standardization. Depending on the type of data and the cost of possible loss, modification, and stolen data, a security strategy must be devised and implemented. In addition to security and privacy risks, new vulnerabilities arise due to the use of wireless devices. Use of wireless infrastructure may involve multiple wireless networks with different levels of security. These could lead to possible change/deletion of information, and denial of service. In addition to these, many more security issues arise due to poor implementation, feature interactions, unplanned growth and new flaws that are created due to prior attacks (Fig. 4.14).

The end-to-end security issues are important in mobile environment as multiple networks, devices, applications and software will exist and inter-operate. The security issues can be addressed by mobile middleware.

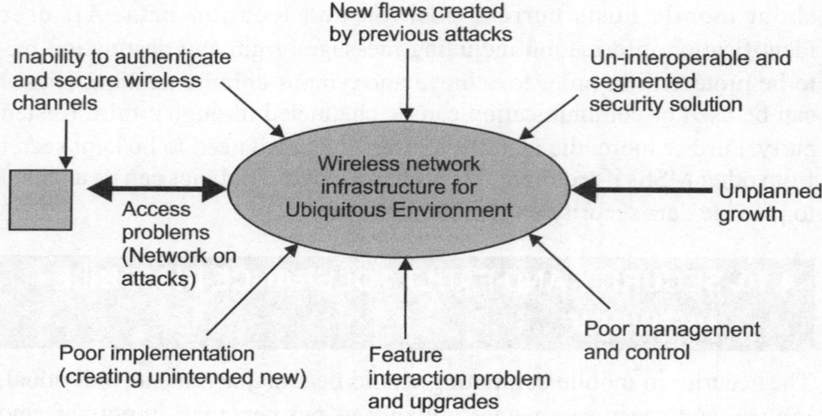

Fig. 4.14: Security Issues in the Mobile Environment

For example, WAP provides security using Wireless Transport Security Layer (WTLS), but it does not always result in the end-to-end security (only between device and WAP gateway). It is possible to add some security feature for financial services as GSM supports both user (PIN) and device authentication (SSL).

It has been shown that wireless security used in IEEE 802.11 has been compromised and several weaknesses have been exposed including breaking of key in few minutes by eavesdropping and analyzing the wireless network traffic. WEP is based on the use of single shared key (common to all users and kept in a software-accessible location) and no key management protocol defined so it is hard to re-key if a device is stolen or key becomes public.

We believe that secure and dependable wireless solutions must be designed and implemented before mission-critical data can be put on wireless infrastructure. The dependability problems arise due to component failures or caused by attacks. Both of these require very careful attention as far as enterprise environment is concerned. We also believe that techniques used for wireless dependability could also lead to increased security. To support dependable, secure, and integrated wireless access in the ubiquitous and pervasive environment, we propose a design solution as shown in Fig. 4.15.

The increased dependability is achieved by ***fault-tolerance*** or "added" redundancy in the wireless infrastructure. This fault-tolerance allows business transactions to be executed even when there are one or more failures in the infrastructure. This redundancy would also allow overcoming or at least alleviating denial of service attacks. If an attack occurs at device, access, network, or server levels, the redundancy would allow switching to another network, server, or device interface. The proposed solution is also scalable in terms of number of users, transactions, and the network size.

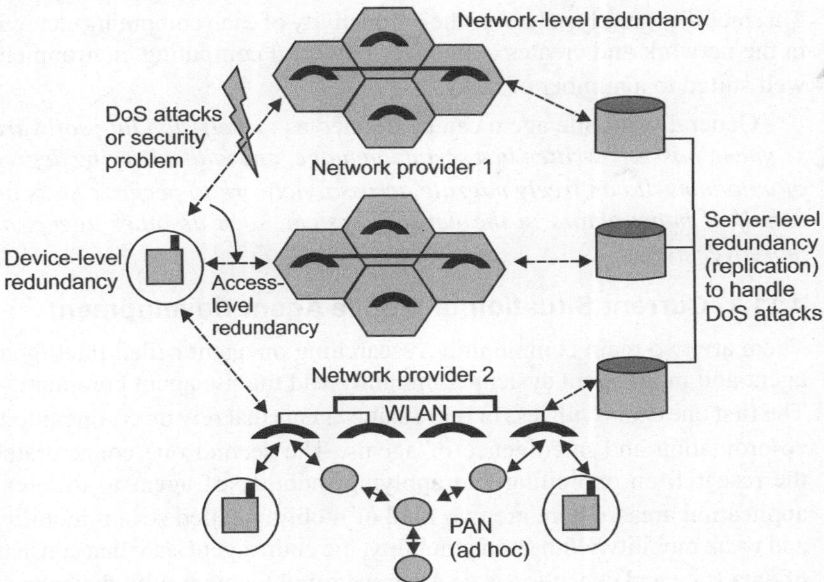

Fig. 4.15: A Dependable, Secure and Scalable Solution for Wireless Enterprise

4.11. MOBILE AGENTS

The term ***"agent"*** is heard frequently today. While it means a variety of things to a variety of people, commonly it is defined as an independent software program which runs on behalf of a network user. An agent may run when the user is disconnected from the network, even involuntarily. Some agents run on specialized servers, others run on standard platforms.

Mobile agent technology has recently emerged as one of the most promising paradigms, which has a wide potential for use in programming languages design and implementation, decision support and expert systems, management, in fact almost anywhere where there is a need for adaptive entities, with high degree of flexibility and dynamism.

A Mobile Agent is specialized in that in addition to being an independent program executing on behalf of a network user, it can travel to multiple locations in the network. As it travels, it performs work on behalf of the user, such as collecting information or delivering requests. This mobility greatly enhances the productivity of each computing element in the network and creates a uniquely powerful computing environment well suited to a number of tasks.

Generally, mobile agent can be defined as : *a self-standing software segment, possibly written in a script language, and with a varying degree of autonomy. It can freely migrate across a network to perform tasks on behalf of many actors in the network system, such as other agents or moreover users.*

4.11.1. Current Situation of Mobile Agent Development

There are two main communities researching on agent called intelligent agent and multi agent system community and mobile agent community. The first one deals with less or more static agents that rely on co-operation, co-ordination and intelligence of agents. The second one concentrates the research on exploiting and applying mobility of agent to different application areas. There are two kind of mobility called strong mobility and weak mobility. With strong mobility, the entire agent state that consists of data state and execution state are transferred together with the code to the new location. When agent arrives to its new location, its state is automatically restored. While weak mobility migrate only data state. There are many common features between mobile agent migration and process migration. They are reduction of network traffic, load balancing, fault resilience, asynchronous interaction and data access locality.

However, mobile agent does not have similar transparency requirements. It leads to the implementation of mobile agent systems and their applications are much simpler. Further, applications can be more easily modeled with mobile agent than with client-server model. Recent years, mobile agents have been developed very fast and they attract many attentions of researchers in academia and industry. As natural consequence, a large number of mobile agent systems, both in academia and industry, were developed. Some of the best known are: Telescript, Aglet, Voyager, Concordia, Agent Tcl, TACOMA and MOA.

Generally, each mobile agent system has private characters. For example, they can be either strong mobility or weak mobility. However common requirements of these systems on infrastructure are they need to provide the functions for the agents to migrate from one location to another, to communicate with each other and to interact with the hosts in network. Infrastructure must guarantee privacy and integrity for agents and the underlying computer system.

Infrastructure also needs to have ability to prevent malicious agents attacking other agents or the computer systems, and vice versa agents need to be protected against a potential malicious system when visiting them. Despite existing many mobile agent systems have been developed in academic environment well as industry but none of them has been successful in productizing agent system or widely deploying agent applications. There are potential capacities in mobile agent applications but only few have merged in practice. Basically, while mobile agent systems can substantially improve occasionally the system performance, most of the applications can be implemented efficiently by using traditional techniques also. In addition, environment where mobile agent can be accepted and executed still is not ready in order to mobile agent applications can be exploited widely in the real world.

There are many applications developed based on different mobile agent systems using programming language Java or script language such as Tcl. Problem is how applications that are developed on this mobile agent system can run and interact transparently with other systems. Different mobile agent systems have different characteristics but almost mobile agent systems allow an agent to freely migrate in heterogeneous networks. However, to use widely mobile agents, agent's code must be contingent upon the portability of the code across different mobile agent mechanisms that require a huge standardization effort. OMG MASIF is considered as the first standard mobile agent system. Now, there are various standardization efforts for mobile agent systems from the organizations such as the Agent Society, FIPA, the Object Management Group and GMD FOKUS and IBM Corp.

One other important major issue need the concern is security due to the existence of many open and unresolved problems. For example, the infrastructure of mobile agent systems, in principle, lacks the ability to protect an agent from potentially malicious system when visited by agents. However, security is very hard to achieve for mobile agent system due to security technique is insufficient to support mobile agent. In protection of mobile agent systems, to protect agents from malicious hosts is a problem that is not yet solved. There are four proposed directions to solve this problem. Currently, all of them are not applied yet to applications in real world due to only ongoing works. The organizational approach eliminates problems by allowing only trustworthy institutions to run mobile agent systems. The trust/reputation approach allows agents to move only to trusted hosts or good reputation. The manipulation approach offers mechanisms to detect manipulation of agent data or the execution of code but without protection from read attacks. The black box protection approach generates black box code out of agent code based on code obfuscating techniques. Agents are protected for certain time interval. After expiration of this interval, agent and data become invalid.

4.11.2. Mobile Agent Applications

Applications of mobile agents mainly focus on exploring two goals: reduction of network traffic and asynchronous interaction. There exist applications using mobile agent paradigm on different areas. In this part we will describe some application of mobile agent in communication networks, particular in network management, e-commerce, resource management, routing and fault tolerant.

Mobile agent is convenient and effective paradigm for distributed applications, particularly for partially connected computing where devices are often disconnected from network, have low bandwidth and unreliable connections and frequently change their address for each reconnection.

One mobile agent system developed by researchers is Agent Tcl. In this system, mobile agents can transparently migrate among mobile computers or between mobile computers and permanently connected computers. Hence, any mobile agent can carry out its pre-assigned duties on network hosts regardless of when mobile computer connect to the network.

One of applications based on Agent Tcl is to gather and retrieve information for its user. Retrieval information can be distributed collections of technical reports, medical records or mechanical drawings. This application is very useful, especially for networks with low bandwidth connection or networks where hosts are often disconnected to the network. In these networks, mobile agent can move to necessary information sources in Internet, access and filter them to obtain result data rather than transferring multiple requests and responses over the network. Since mobile agent is not affected by loss of connection, it can continue its tasks when computer is disconnected from network. When this computer is reconnected again, mobile agent can return with its result. It leads to applications can continue running even computer on the network is disconnected for long time. Other application of Agent Tcl is workflow. In this application, mobile agent carries the description of multi-step task from host to host, interacting with each user in order to complete a part of task at this site.

In network management, mobile agents are used to implement duties of network management by delegation and to deliver tasks. Mobile agents gather the information from the network elements, execute the required computations, and transfer only the result information to the network manager. Mobile agents with different functions are created and can communicate each other to execute tasks of network management. For example, mobile agent can be used to decentralize network management activities. They can autonomously carry out some daily duties of network administrator such as install and upgrade software and periodically monitor the networks, e.g. mobile agent can bring the software to perform the installation onto different computers in the network. In addition, due to using mobile agent, the network management policies can change and adapt quickly to the changes of today dynamic network environment. Hence, mobile agents can support for the provision better the services and performance in network management.

Mobile agent can be used to distribute code to SNMP agent. At each managed device, mobile agent interact with SNMP agent and gather necessary information instead of management station frequently sends requests to SNMP agents and waits to receive responses from SNMP agents.

Mobile agents with the code and data will migrate to managed entities and perform predefined management tasks along with pre-assigned travel. Using mobile agent can avoid the transportation of a large amount of data over the network, reduce bottleneck and network traffic across the network.

Therefore, mobile agent approach helps network management to over come technical limitations of centralized management using Simple Network Management Protocol (SNMP) such as scalability, reliability, performance degradation, and difficulties in delegation since networks are expanding and become more distributed.

Other application of mobile agent in network management is network monitoring. In this application, mobile agents will visit network nodes, interacts with network monitor at each network node to obtain local recent status information. In the same time, network monitor also will update its database with new status information that mobile agent bring from the rest of network. By this way, no extra messages are generated due to the cooperation of network monitors. Mobile agents can optimal locally the distribution of network status information in the situations where bandwidth is limited or network is congested. By using mobile agent, the limitations caused by centralized network monitoring when monitored network is large or low bandwidth can be eliminated.

In electronic commerce, mobile agents can roam on the Internet, search electronic catalogs to find the products with best prices that meet the customer's need, chose products and vendors, interact with billing, inventory, and shipping agents, arrange and negotiate the purchase on behalf of owner. Mobile agent can carry out these duties even while owner's computer is disconnected from network. When owner's computer is reconnected, all agents will return home with results so connectivity need only few seconds.

In resource management, mobile agents are used to provide flexible resource management. Service policies are implemented based on current requirements rather than policies that are embedded in the network elements. Mobile agents also are used to re-act to events behaviors in the network, modify dynamically route and redistribute resources.

In routing, mobile agent are used to discover and maintain routes in networks. Most of routing models proposed are based on the biological imitation of ants when they find the routes. In these models, mobile agents work as ants roaming the network to discover routes and update the routing tables in the various network components. Mobile agent seems to be very suitable in routing and has performed this duty effectively. In fault tolerant and secure networks, mobile agent are used to check the state of the network due to their mobility. When mobile agent detects fault it can restart back from previous state due to the capacity of mobile agent in storing its execution state. Therefore mobile agents have been considered as means to promote fault tolerant and secure networks.

4.11.3. Advantages of Mobile Agent

The following are the primary advantages of Mobile Agents:

- ***They facilitate high quality, high performance, economical mobile applications.*** Applications employing Mobile Agents transparently use the network to accomplish their tasks, while taking full advantage of resources local to the many machines in the network. They process data at the data source, rather than fetching it remotely, allowing higher performance operation. They use the full spectrum of services available at each point in the network, such as GUI's at the user and database interface on servers. They make best use of the network as they travel.
- ***They enable use of portable, low-cost, personal communications devices.*** Network support, including security, is contained in a lightweight server which manages the movement of agents in the network. Coupled with the sophisticated, self-contained programming model afforded by agents, this permits a small footprint to be achieved on user devices, without sacrificing functionality for the application.
- ***They permit secure Intranet-style communications on Public networks.*** Security is an integral part of the Mobile Agent framework, and it provides for secure communications even over public networks. Agents carry user credentials with them as they travel, and these credentials are authenticated during execution at every point in the network. Agents and their data are fully encrypted as they traverse the network. All this occurs with no programmer intervention.
- ***They efficiently and economically use low bandwidth, high latency, error prone communications-channels.*** The agent network employs a store and forward mechanism to transfer agents between nodes. This is well suited to the problematic nature of many communications channels, especially in the mobile arena. Queuing and persistent checkpoints enhance this further, to the point that agents can use such channels with no degradation in

reliability or response. Because the agent data processing takes place locally to the source, the network has no effect on the agent as it executes.

4.11.4. Breaking the Client/Server Barrier

4.11.4.1. The Limitations of Client/Server

Historically, distributed applications such as these are created with "client/server" programming. In this model, an operation is split into two parts across a network, with the client making requests from a user machine to a server which services the requests on a large, centralized system. A protocol is agreed upon and both the client and server are programmed to implement it. A network connection is established between them and the protocol is carried out.

The client/server model has the advantage of enabling the removal of the client to smaller, remote machines, and it works well for certain applications. However it breaks down under other situations, including highly distributed systems, slow and/or poor quality network connections, and especially in the face of changing applications.

In a system with a single central server and numerous clients, there is only a problem of simple scaling. When multiple servers become involved, the scaling problems multiply rapidly, as each client must manage and maintain connections with the multiple servers. The use of two-tier systems or proxies only moves this problem to the network: it does not eliminate the basic problem.

With client/server comes a need for good quality network connections. First, the client needs to connect reliably to its server, because only by setting up and maintaining the connection may it be authenticated and secure. Second, the client needs to be assured of a predictable response, since its many requests of the server require full round trips to be completed. Third, it needs good bandwidth, since due to its very nature; client/server must copy data across the network.

Finally, the protocol which a client and server agree upon is by its very nature specialized and static. Often, specific procedures on the server are codified in the protocol and become a part of the interface. Certain classes of data types are bound to these procedures and the end result is a special network version of an application programming interface. This interface is extensible, but only at the high cost of recoding the application, providing for protocol version compatibility, software upgrade, etc. As the applications grow and the needs increase, client/server programming rapidly becomes an impediment to change.

4.11.4.2. Mobile Agents to the Rescue

Mobile agents overcome all these inherent limitations in client/server.

First and foremost, the Mobile Agent shatters the very notion of client and server. With Mobile Agents, the flow of control actually moves across the network, instead of using the request/response architecture of client/server. In effect, every node is a server in the agent network, and the agent (program) moves to the location where it may find the services it needs to run at each point in its execution. For example, the same agent interacts with the user via a GUI to obtain request keys, then travels to a database server to make its request.

The scaling of servers and connections then becomes a straightforward capacity issue, without the complicated exponential scaling required between multiple servers. The relationship between users and servers is coded into each agent instead of being pieced out across clients and servers. It is the agent itself that creates the system, rather than the network or the system administrators. Server administration becomes a matter simply of managing systems and monitoring local load.

The problem of robust networks is greatly diminished, for several reasons. The hold time for connections is reduced to only the time required to move the agent in or out of the machine. Because the agent carries its own credentials, the connection is simply a conduit, not tied to user authentication or spoofing. No requests flow across the connection, the agent itself moves only once, in effect carrying a greater "payload" for each traversal. This allows for efficiency and optimization at several levels.

Last and most important, no application-level protocol is created by the use of agents. Therefore, compatibility is provided for *any* agent-based application. Complete upward compatibility becomes the norm rather than a problem to be tackled, and upgrading or reconfiguring an application may be done without regard to client deployment. Servers can be upgraded, services moved, load balancing interposed, security policy enforced, without interruptions or revisions to the network and clients.

4.11.5. Security Threats

Threats to security generally fall into three main classes: disclosure of information, denial of service, and corruption of information. There are a variety of ways to examine these classes of threats in greater detail as they apply to agent systems. Here, we use the components of an agent system to categorize the threats as a way to identify the possible source and target of an attack. It is important to note that many of the threats that are discussed have counterparts in conventional client-server systems and have always existed in some form in the past (e.g., executing any code from an unknown source either downloaded from a network or supplied on floppy disk). Mobile agents simply offer a greater opportunity for abuse and misuse, broadening the scale of threats significantly.

A number of models exist for describing agent systems; however, for discussing security issues it is sufficient to use a very simple one, consisting of only two main components: the agent and the agent platform. Here, an agent is comprised of the code and state information needed to carry out some computation. Mobility allows an agent to move, or hop, among agent platforms. The agent platform provides the computational environment in which an agent operates. The platform from which an agent originates is referred to as the home platform, and normally is the most trusted environment for an agent. One or more hosts may comprise an agent platform, and an agent platform may support multiple computational environments, or meeting places, where agents can interact. Since some of these detailed aspects do not affect the discussion of security issues, they are omitted from the agent system model depicted in Fig. 4.16.

Four threat categories are identified:

- Threats stemming from an agent attacking an agent platform,
- An agent platform attacking an agent,
- An agent attacking another agent on the agent platform, and
- Other entities attacking the agent system

The last category covers the cases of an agent attacking an agent on another agent platform, and of an agent platform attacking another platform, since these attacks are primarily focused on the communications capability of the platform to exploit potential vulnerabilities. The last category also includes more conventional attacks against the underlying operating system of the agent platform.

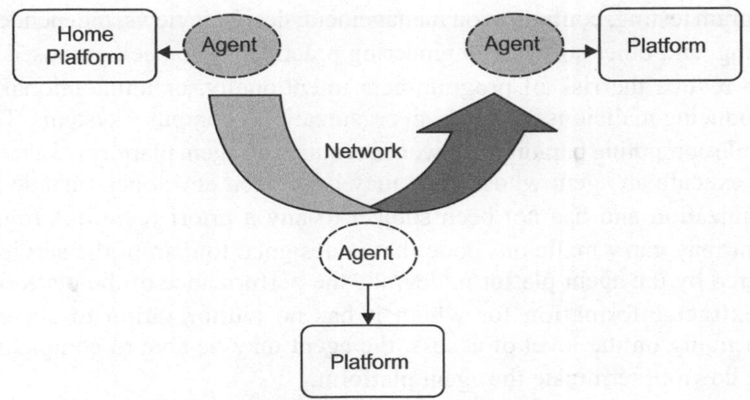

Fig. 4.16: Agent System Model.

4.11.5. 1. Agent-to-Platform

The agent-to-platform category represents the set of threats in which agents exploit security weaknesses of an agent platform or launch attacks against an agent platform. This set of threats includes masquerading, denial of service and unauthorized access.

4.11.5.1.1. Masquerading

When an unauthorized agent claims the identity of another agent it is said to be masquerading. The masquerading agent may pose as an authorized agent in an effort to gain access to services and resources to which it is not entitled. The masquerading agent may also pose as another unauthorized agent in an effort to shift the blame for any actions for which it does not want to be held accountable. A masquerading agent may damage the trust the legitimate agent has established in an agent community and its associated reputation.

4.11.5.1.2. Denial of Service

Mobile agents can launch denial of service attacks by consuming an excessive amount of the agent platform's computing resources. These denial of service attacks can be launched intentionally by running attack scripts to exploit system vulnerabilities, or unintentionally through programming errors. Security threats resulting from programming errors and intentional flaws have been written about since the early 1970's.

Program testing, configuration management, design reviews, independent testing, and other software engineering practices have been proposed to help reduce the risk of programmers intentionally, or unintentionally, introducing malicious code into an organization's computer systems. The mobile computing paradigm, however, requires an agent platform to accept and execute an agent whose code may have been developed outside its organization and has not been subject to any a priori review. A rogue agent may carry malicious code that is designed to disrupt the services offered by the agent platform, degrade the performance of the platform, or extract information for which it has no authorization to access. Depending on the level of access, the agent may be able to completely shut down or terminate the agent platform.

4.11.5.1.3. Unauthorized Access

Access control mechanisms are used to prevent unauthorized users or processes from accessing services and resources for which they have not been granted permission and privileges as specified by a security policy. Each agent visiting a platform must be subject to the platform's security policy. Applying the proper access control mechanisms requires the platform or agent to first authenticate a mobile agent's identity before it is instantiated on the platform. An agent that has access to a platform and its services without having the proper authorization can harm other agents and the platform itself. A platform that hosts agents representing various users and organizations must ensure that agents do not have read or write access to data for which they have no authorization, including access to residual data that may be stored in a cache or other temporary storage.

4.11.5.2. Agent-to-Agent

The agent-to-agent category represents the set of threats in which agents exploit security weaknesses of other agents or launch attacks against other agents. This set of threats includes masquerading, unauthorized access, denial of service and repudiation. Many agent platform components are also agents themselves. These platform agents provide system-level services such as directory services and inter-platform communication services. Some agent platforms allow direct inter-platform agent-to-agent communication, while others require all incoming and outgoing messages to go through a platform communication agent. These architecture decisions intertwine agent-to-agent and agent-to-platform security.

4.11.5.2.1. Masquerade

Agent-to-agent communication can take place directly between two agents or may require the participation of the underlying platform and the agent services it provides. In either case, an agent may attempt to disguise its identity in an effort to deceive the agent with which it is communicating. An agent may pose as a well-known vendor of goods and services, for example, and try to convince another unsuspecting agent to provide it with credit card numbers, bank account information, some form of digital cash, or other private information. Masquerading as another agent harms both the agent that is being deceived and the agent who's identity has been assumed, especially in agent societies where reputation is valued and used as a means to establish trust.

4.11.5.2.2. Denial of Service

In addition to launching denial of service attacks on an agent platform, agents can also launch denial of service attacks against other agents. For example, repeatedly sending messages to another agent, or spamming agents with messages, may place undue burden on the message handling routines of the recipient. Agents that are being spammed may choose to block messages from unauthorized agents, but even this task requires some processing by the agent or its communication proxy. If an agent is charged by the number of CPU cycles it consumes on a platform, spamming an agent may cause the spammed agent to have to pay a monetary cost in addition to a performance cost. Agent communication languages and conversation policies must ensure that a malicious agent doesn't engage another agent in an infinite conversation loop or engage the agent in elaborate conversations with the sole purpose of tying up the agent's resources. Malicious agents can also intentionally distribute false or useless information to prevent other agents from completing their tasks correctly or in a timely manner.

4.11.5.2.3. Repudiation

Repudiation occurs when an agent, participating in a transaction or communication, later claims that the transaction or communication never took place. Whether the cause for repudiation is deliberate or accidental, repudiation can lead to serious disputes that may not be easily resolved unless the proper countermeasures are in place. An agent platform cannot prevent an agent from repudiating a transaction, but platforms can ensure the availability of sufficiently strong evidence to support the resolution of disagreements. This evidence may deter an agent that values its reputation and the level of trust others place in it, from falsely repudiating future transactions. Disagreements may arise not only when an agent falsely repudiates a transaction, but also because imperfect business processes may lead to different views of events. Repudiation often occurs within non-agent systems and real-life business transactions within an organization. Documents are occasionally forged, documents are often lost, created by someone without authorization, or modified without being properly reviewed. Since an agent may repudiate a transaction as the result of a misunderstanding, it is important that the agents and agent platforms involved in the transaction maintain records to help resolve any dispute.

4.11.5.2.4. Unauthorized Access

If the agent platform has weak or no control mechanisms in place, an agent can directly interfere with another agent by invoking its public methods (e.g., attempt buffer overflow, reset to initial state, etc.), or by accessing and modifying the agent's data or code. Modification of an agent's code is a particularly insidious form of attack, since it can radically change the agent's behavior (e.g., turning a trusted agent into malicious one). An agent may also gain information about other agents' activities by using platform services to eavesdrop on their communications.

4.11.5.3. Platform-to-Agent

The platform-to-agent category represents the set of threats in which platforms compromise the security of agents. This set of threats includes masquerading, denial of service, eavesdropping, and alteration.

4.11.5. 3.1. Masquerade

One agent platform can masquerade as another platform in an effort to deceive a mobile agent as to its true destination and corresponding security domain. An agent platform masquerading as a trusted third party may be able to lure unsuspecting agents to the platform and extract sensitive information from these agents. The masquerading platform can harm both the visiting agent and the platform whose identity it has assumed. An agent that masquerades as another agent can harm other agents only through the messages they exchange and the actions they take as a result of these messages, but a malicious platform that masquerades as an authorized platform can do more harm to the duped agent than a single agent can do on its own.

4.11.5. 3.2. Denial of Service

When an agent arrives at an agent platform, it expects the platform to execute the agent's requests faithfully, provide fair allocation of resources, and abide by quality of service agreements. A malicious agent platform, however, may ignore agent service requests, introduce unacceptable delays for critical tasks such as placing market orders in a stock market, simply not execute the agent's code, or even terminate the agent without notification. Agents on other platforms waiting for the results of a non-responsive agent on a malicious platform must be careful to avoid becoming deadlocked. An agent can also become live locked if a malicious platform, or programming error, creates a situation in which some critical stage of the agent's task is unable to finish because more work is continuously created for it to do. Agent live lock differs from agent deadlock in that the live locked agent is not blocked or waiting for anything, but is continuously given tasks to perform and can never catch up or achieve its goal.

4.11.5.3.3. Eavesdropping

The classical eavesdropping threat involves the interception and monitoring of secret communications. The threat of eavesdropping, however, is further exacerbated in mobile agent systems because the agent platform can not only monitor communications, but also can monitor every instruction executed by the agent, all the unencrypted or public data it brings to the platform, and all the subsequent data generated on the platform. Since the platform has access to the agent's code, state, and data, the visiting agent must be wary of the fact that it may be exposing proprietary algorithms, trade secrets, negotiation strategies, or other sensitive information. Even though the agent may not be directly exposing secret information, the platform may be able to infer meaning from the types of services requested and from the identity of the agents with which it communicates. For example, someone's agent may be communicating with a travel agent, although the content of the message may not be exposed, this communication may indicate that the person on whose behalf the agent is acting is planning a trip and will be away from their home in the near future. The platform may share this information it has inferred with a suitcase manufacturer that may begin sending unsolicited advertisements, or even worse, the platform administrators may share this information with thieves who may target the home of the traveler.

4.11.5.3.4. Alteration

When an agent arrives at an agent platform it is exposing its code, state, and data to the platform. Since an agent may visit several platforms under various security domains throughout its lifetime, mechanisms must be in place to ensure the integrity of the agent's code, state, and data. A compromised or malicious platform must be prevented from modifying an agent's code, state, or data without being detected. Modification of an agent's code, and thus the subsequent behavior of the agent on other platforms, can be detected by having the original author digitally sign the agent's code. Detecting malicious changes to an agent's state during its execution or the data an agent has produced while visiting the compromised platform does not yet have a general solution. The agent platform may be running a modified virtual machine, for example, without the agent's knowledge, and the modified virtual machine may produce erroneous results. A mobile agent that visits several platforms on its itinerary is exposed to a new risk each time it is in transit and each time it is instantiated on a new platform. The party responsible for the malicious alteration of an agent's code, state, or data if not immediately detected may be impossible to track down after the agent has visited other platforms and undergone countless changes of state and data. Although check pointing and rollback of mathematical computations may be possible in non-agent environments, mobile agent frameworks make this task extremely difficult since an agent's final state and data on a platform may be the result of a series of non-deterministic events that depend on the behavior of autonomous agents whose previous behavior cannot be recreated.

The security risks resulting from an agent moving from its home platform to another is referred to as the "single-hop" problem, while the security risks resulting from an agent visiting several platforms is referred to as the "multi-hop" problem. The risks associated with the single-hop problem are easier to mitigate than the risks associated with a multihop scenario, since the protection mechanisms within the trust environment of the home platform are more difficult to use in the latter situation.

Agent platforms can also tamper with agent communications. Tampering with agent communications, for example, could include deliberately changing data fields in financial transactions or even changing a "sell" message to a "buy" message. This type of goal oriented alteration of the data is more difficult than simply corrupting a message, but the attacker clearly has a greater incentive and reward, if successful, in a goal-oriented alteration attack.

4.11.5.4. Other-to-Agent Platform

The other-to-agent platform category represents the set of threats in which external entities, including agents and agent platforms, threaten the security of an agent platform. This set of threats includes masquerading, denial of service, unauthorized access, and copy and replay.

4.11.5.4.1. Masquerade

Agents can request platform services both remotely and locally. An agent on a remote platform can masquerade as another agent and request services and resources for which it is not authorized. Agents masquerading as other agents may act in conjunction with a malicious platform to help deceive another remote platform or they may act alone. A remote platform can also masquerade as another platform and mislead unsuspecting platforms or agents about its true identity.

4.11.5.4.2. Unauthorized Access

Remote users, processes, and agents may request resources for which they are not authorized. Remote access to the platform and the host machine itself must be carefully protected, since conventional attack scripts freely available on the Internet can be used to subvert the operating system and directly gain control of all resources. Remote administration of the platform's attributes or security policy may be desirable for an administrator that is responsible for several distributed platforms, but allowing remote administration may make the system administrator's account or session the target of an attack.

4.11.5.4.3. Denial of Service

Agent platform services can be accessed both remotely and locally. The agent services offered by the platform and inter-platform communications can be disrupted by common denial of service attacks. Agent platforms are also susceptible to all the conventional denial of service attacks aimed at the underlying operating system or communication protocols.

4.11.5.4.4. Copy and Replay

Every time a mobile agent moves from one platform to another it increases its exposure to security threats. A party that intercepts an agent, or agent message, in transit can attempt to copy the agent, or agent message, and clone or retransmit it. For example, the interceptor can capture an agent's "buy order" and replay it several times, having the agent buy more than the original agent had intended. The interceptor may copy and replay an agent message or a complete agent.

4.11.6. Security Requirements

The users of networked computer systems have following main security requirements:

- Confidentiality,
- Integrity,
- Availability, and
- Accountability
- Anonymity

The users of agent and mobile agent frameworks also have these same security requirements. This section provides a brief overview of these security requirements and how they apply to agent frameworks.

4.11.6. 1. Confidentiality

Any private data stored on a platform or carried by an agent must remain confidential. Agent frameworks must be able to ensure that their intra- and inter-platform communications remain confidential. Eavesdroppers can gather information about an agent's activities not only from the content of the messages exchanged, but also from the message flow from one agent to another agent or agents. Monitoring the message flow may allow other agents to infer useful information without having access to the actual message content. A burst of messages from one agent to another, for example, may be an indication that an agent is in the market for a particular set of services offered by the other agent. The eavesdropping agent or external entity may use this information to gain an unfair advantage. Agents may be able to detect an Agent Communication Language (ACL) conversation signature pattern to infer further meaning from an agent conversation.

A procurement agent may, for example, send three messages to a vendor agent, followed by one message to its home platform, and conclude the transaction with two messages to the vendor agent. The vendor agent may send two messages to a credit-checking agency and conclude with a message to its banking agent. Although the contents of the messages have never been disclosed, an eavesdropper may be able to infer that the procurement and vendor agents have successfully completed a sale of some commodity or service.

Mobile agents may also want to keep their location confidential. Mobile agents may communicate through a proxy whose location is publicly known if the agents want to conceal their presence on a particular platform. Agents must be allowed to decide if their presence will be publicly available through platform directories, and platforms may enforce different security policies on agents that chose to be anonymous. An agent shopping for goods and services may wish to do so in privacy, but when a financial transaction is to be carried out the platform may require some form of authentication. Agents can assume a pseudonym to conceal their identity from other agents, but this pseudonym is reversible and cannot be used to conceal its identity from the platform itself. In addition, an agent may not want to disclose which platforms it has visited on its itinerary, but the platform security policy of its host may not be willing to accept agents that have been on certain platforms outside the authority of certain approved security domains.

Since audit logs maintain a detailed record of an agent's activities on the platform, the contents of the audit log must also be carefully protected and remain confidential. Access to the audit logs must be restricted to authorized administrators. A mobile agents' audit log may be distributed across several security domains, each having a different audit policy, so some agents may want to carry certain parts of their audit log with them for future reference. In some cases the mobile agent may require the host platform to sign portions of the audit log for which it was responsible.

4.11.6.2. Integrity

The agent platform must protect agents from unauthorized modification of their code, state, and data and ensure that only authorized agents or processes carry out any modification of shared data. The agent itself cannot prevent a malicious agent platform from tampering with its code, state, or data, but the agent can take measures to detect this tampering.

The secure operation of mobile agent systems also depends on the integrity of the local and remote agent platforms themselves. A malicious host can easily compromise the integrity of a mobile agent that is visiting a remote agent platform. The trend towards releasing open source platforms and operating systems makes it easier for unscrupulous administrators or organizations to make unauthorized modifications to the agent platform and the underlying framework. The agent's user and developer may have no knowledge of the behavior of this modified framework and the effects it will have on the agent's code, state and data that are under the platform's complete control. A malicious platform may make subtle changes in the execution flow of the agent's code and make changes to computed results that are difficult to detect. A malicious platform could interfere in transactions between agents representing different organizations and tamper with the audit trails. This could result in each organization involved in the transaction blaming the other for not delivering promised goods or services.

System access controls must be in place to protect the integrity of the agent platform from unauthorized users. Changes to the platform by unauthorized users are more likely to be detected over time than changes to the platform by authorized users. Intentional modification or tampering with the agent platform by authorized or unauthorized users places additional burden on mobile agents to be able to detect and recover from intentional corruption or alteration. Many security mechanisms available to the agent to protect itself may come at a serious performance and development cost and must be carefully weighed against the advantages offered by code mobility. If the agent is carrying out a critical or sensitive task for which it must assume an unreasonable risk or for which it cannot provide suitable protection, the agent developer or user may choose to restrict the agent's mobility. Thus, given the current security mechanisms available to mobile agents, agents may choose to forego mobility during certain security-sensitive transactions, and limit the types of security-sensitive transactions a mobile agent is authorized to conduct.

Goal-oriented attacks against agent communications aim to compromise the integrity of an intra- or inter-platform message by changing the content of the message, replacing the entire message, reusing an old message, deleting the message, or changing the source or destination of the message. Goal-oriented malicious attacks on the integrity of agent communications can do far greater harm to the agent than transmission errors resulting from poor or intermittent communication channels. Agent platforms rely on lower-level protocols to ensure the integrity of the agent communications. For example, TCP/IP ensures the detection of most transmission errors, and processes in the communications stack detect errors and arrange for retransmission. This error detection and correction is transparent to higher-level applications that rely on these protocols to ensure the integrity of their communications.

4.11.6.3. Accountability

Each process, human user, or agent on a given platform must be held accountable for their actions. In order to be held accountable each process, human user, or agent must be uniquely identified, authenticated, and audited. Example actions for which they must be held accountable include: access to an object, such as a file, or making administrative changes to a platform security mechanism. Accountability requires maintaining an audit log of security-relevant events that have occurred, and listing each event and the agent or process responsible for that event. Security-relevant events are defined in the platform security policy and should include, at a minimum, the following: user/agent name, time of event, type of event, and success or failure of the event. Audit logs must be protected from unauthorized access and modification. Measures need to be in place to prevent auditable events from being lost when the storage media reaches its capacity. These measures can include alerting the system administrator when the audit logs reach a certain capacity and depend on the system administrator to perform routine maintenance as part of their normal administrator duties.

Audit logs keep users and processes accountable for their actions. Mobile agents create audit trails across several platforms, with each platform logging separate events and possibly auditing different views of the same event (e.g., registration within a remote directory). In the case where an agent may require access to information distributed across different platforms it may be difficult to reconstruct a sequence of events. Platforms that keep distributed audit logs must be able to maintain a concept of global time or ordering of events. Auditing agent actions is very important considering the liability issues that may arise from the failure of a platform administrator to exercise due diligence in preventing known denial of service attacks. Legal issues may also come into play as rules governing the actions of agents may differ in states, countries, and regional trading blocks.

Audit logs are also necessary and valuable when the platform must recover from a security breach, or a software or hardware failure. Full recovery from a faulty or compromised system requires not only restoring the system to a safe state and performing some sort of fault diagnosis, but also sorting out which agents belonging to which organizations were affected. Audit logs are also necessary in cases of agents falsely repudiating their actions and for potential liability issues that are unique to agent societies.

Authentication mechanisms provide accountability for user actions. Agents must be able to authenticate their identity to platforms and other agents, while platforms must be able to authenticate their identity to agents and other platforms. The level of sensitivity of the transaction or data for which agents request access may require the agent to offer different degrees of authentication. In agent societies where reputation is valued and used as a means to establish trust, an agent platform must exercise due diligence to protect an agent's reputation from being harmed by other agents through masquerade.

An agent accessing publicly advertised product prices may not be required to authenticate itself at all and may only have "read access" to certain public data, but if this agent decides to purchase any of these products the agent must be able to authenticate itself before the transaction is completed. Similarly, the purchasing agent will require some proof of the selling agent's claimed identity. Both the purchasing and selling agent may require the agent platform to authenticate itself before they visit this platform. Humans must be able to authenticate themselves to agents through whatever means the agent platform makes available to the human user, for example, voice recognition, biometrics, passwords, or smart cards.

Accountability is also essential for building trust among agents and agent platforms. An authenticated agent may comply with the security policies of the agent platform, but still exhibit malicious behavior by lying or deliberately spreading false information. Additional auditing may be helpful in proving the malicious agent's attempts at deception. For example, the communication acts of an ACL conversation could be logged, but this results in costly overhead. If it is assumed that the malicious agent does not value its reputation within an agent community, then it would be difficult to prevent malicious agents from lying.

4.11.6.4. Availability

The agent platform must be able to ensure the availability of both data and services to local and remote agents. The agent platform must be able to provide controlled concurrency, support for simultaneous access, deadlock management, and exclusive access as required. Shared data must be available in a usable form, capacity must be available to meet service needs, and provisions for the fair allocation of resources and timeliness of service must be made. The agent platform must be able to detect and recover from system software and hardware failures. While the platform can provide some level of fault-tolerance and fault-recovery, agents may be required to assume responsibility for their own fault-recovery.

The agent platform must be able to handle the requests of hundreds or thousands of visiting and remote agents or risk creating an unintentional denial of service. In the event that a platform cannot handle its computational and communication load, the platform must provide graceful degradation of services and notify agents that it can no longer provide the level and quality of service expected by the agents requesting its services.

The threat of a denial of service attack being launched by rogue or flawed agents underscores the need for the control and monitoring of platform resources. A denial of service attack against the platform is an indirect attack on all the agents that rely on this platform for agent services and platform resources. Since the platform may be hosting agents from several other organizations, a denial of service attack on a single platform may adversely impact more than one agent, platform, or organization.

Ensuring confidentiality and integrity places restraints on availability and also has performance costs. Encrypting agents and messages in transit may impose unacceptable delays in environments where near real-time response is required. Ensuring accountability may also place restraints on the availability of platform services. For example, when the audit log storage media exhausts its capacity, many security policies disable all services that create records in the audit log. In an effort to maintain accountability, this policy may inadvertently create an opportunity for a denial of service attack by simply producing an inordinate amount of auditable events, such as repeated failed login attempts, and consume the remaining capacity of the audit log storage media.

4.11.6.5. Anonymity

The agent platform may need to balance an agent's need for privacy with the platform's need to hold the agent accountable for its actions. The platform may be able to keep the agent's identity secret from other agents and still maintain a form of reversible anonymity where it can determine the agent's identity if necessary and legal. Anonymity in human communities may help foster certain types of commerce or promote the freedom of expression by eliminating the fear of retribution for voicing unpopular viewpoints. There are many situations, however, in which the participants are reluctant or unwilling to engage in a transaction with an anonymous counterpart. Purchasers of goods and services may want to protect their privacy by remaining anonymous, but credit agencies would not extend credit to anonymous consumers without being able to verify their credit history and credit worthiness. The anonymity issues affecting human communities also apply to agent communities. The security policies of agent platforms and their auditing requirements must be carefully balanced with agent privacy expectations. The collection and use of audit information for uses other than security must also be understood by the agents visiting the agent platform. Moreover, what information belongs in public agent directories and under what conditions can the information be accessed from these directories must also be carefully controlled.

4.11.7. Robust and Fault -Tolerant Behavior

The ability of mobile agents to react dynamically to unfavorable situations and events makes it easier to build robust and fault-tolerant distributed systems. For example, if a host is being shut down, all agents executing on that machine are warned, whenever possible, and given time to dispatch and continue their operation on another host in the network.

The ability of the mobile agents to move from one platform to another in a heterogeneous environment has been made possible by the use of virtual machines and interpreters. Virtual machines and interpreters, however, can offer only limited support for preservation and resumption of the execution state in heterogeneous environments, because of differing representations in the underlying hardware.

Conventional fault-recovery and check-pointing techniques are challenged even further in the mobile agent computing paradigm. Even though an arsenal of techniques exist to provide security and fault-tolerance, the designer must be careful in selecting which mechanisms to use and how they impact the overall system performance and functionality. For example, check-pointing before and after an agent's arrival, and upon completion of certain transactions or events may be necessary to ensure for acceptable fault-recovery. With each check-pointing procedure and non-repudiation mechanism invoked, however, more overhead is introduced.

The fault-recovery techniques may also involve more than one machine, further complicating the recovery. Although mobile agents possess a great deal of autonomy and perform well in disconnected operations, the failure of the home platform or other platforms that the agents rely on to provide security services can seriously reduce their intended functionality. Even though a mobile agent can become more fault-tolerant by moving to another machine, the mobile agent's reliance on the safe operation of a safe home or trusted platform places restrictions on its functionality. Designers of mobile agent platforms are also faced with tradeoffs between security and fault-tolerance. For example, in order to address the security risks involved in "multi-hop" agent mobility, some agent architectures have been built on centralized client-server models requiring agents to return to a central server before moving on to another host machine. Clearly, addressing the security risks in this manner renders all the mobile agents vulnerable to a failure of the central server and raises scalability issues.

REFERENCES

- D. Barbara and T. Imielinski, "Sleepers and Workholics: Caching Strategies in Mobile Environments".
- J. Jing, A. Elmagramid, A. Helal, and R. Alonso, "Bit-Sequences: An adaptive cache invalidation method in mobile client/server environments", Mobile Networks and Applications 2, pp 115-127, 1997.
- L. Mummert and M. Satyanarayanan, "Large Granularity Cache Coherence for Intermittent Connectivity".
- G. Y. Liu and G. Q. Maguire Jr., "A Mobility-Aware Dynamic Database Caching Scheme for Wireless Mobile Computing and

Communications", Distributed and Parallel Databases 4, pp. 271-288, 1996.

- Q. Hu and D. K. Lee, "Cache algorithms based on adaptive invalidation reports for mobile environments", Cluster Computing 1, pp 39-50, 1998.
- A. P. Sistla, O. Wolfson, and Y. Huang, "Minimization of Communication Cost Through Caching in Mobile Environments", IEEE Transactions on Parallel and Distributed Systems, 9(4), pp 378-389, 1998.
- O. Wolfson and Y. Huang, "Competitive Analysis of Caching in Distributed Databases", IEEE Transactions on Parallel and Distributed Systems, 9(4), pp 391-409, 1998.
- S. Acharya, R. Alonso, M. Franklin, and S. Zdonik. Broadcast disks: data management for asymmetric communication environments. Proceedings of the ACM SIGMOD International Conference on the Management of Data, pp. 199-210, 1995.
- S. Acharya, M. Franklin, and S. Zdonik. Balancing push and pull for data broadcast. Proceedings of the ACM SIGMOD, pp. 183-194, May 1997.
- D. Barbara, T. Imielinski. Sleepers and workaholics: Caching strategies for mobile environments. Proceedings of the ACM SIGMOD Conference on Management of Data, pp. 1-12, 1994.
- D. Barbara, T. Imielinski. Sleepers and workaholics: Caching strategies for mobile environments (extended version). The VLDB Journal - The International Journal on Very Large Data Bases, Vol. 4, Issue 4, pp. 567-602, 1995.
- P. Cao, C. Liu. Maintaining Strong Cache Consistency in the World Wide Web., IEEE Transactions On Computers, Vol. 47, No. 4, pp. 445-457, 1998.
- V. Cate. Alex – a global file system. Proceedings of 1992 USENIX File System Workshop, pp. 1-12, May 1992.
- A. Chankhunthod, P. Danzig, C. Needaels, M.F. Schwartz, and K.J. Worrell. A hierarchical Internet object cache. In proceedings of the 1996 Usenix Technical Conference, San Diego, CA, Jan. 1996.
- R. Chandra, V. Ramasubramanian, K.P. Birman. Anonymous

Gossip: Improving Multicast Reliability in Mobile Ad-Hoc Networks. Proceedings of the 21st International Conference on Distributed Computing Systems, 2001.

- S. Dar, M.J. Franklin, B.T. Jonsson, D. Srivastava, and M. Tan. Semantic data caching and replacement. Proceedings of VLDB, pp 330-341, Bombay, India, September 1996.
- V. Garshnek, F. Burkle. Applications of telemedicine and telecommunications to disaster medicine: historical and future perspective. J Am Med Inf Assoc., Vol. 6, pp. 26-37, 1999.
- S. Gitzenis, N. Bambos. Power-controlled data prefetching/caching in wireless packet networks. Proceedings of IEEE INFOCOM, pp. 1405-1414, 2002.
- V. Grassi, Prefetching policies for energy saving and latency reduction in a wireless broadcast data delivery system. Proceedings of the 3rd ACM International Workshop on Modeling, Analysis and Simulation of Wireless and Mobile Systems, 2000.
- A. Kahol, S. Khurana, S. Gupta, P. Srimani. A strategy to manage cache consistency in a disconnected distributed environment. IEEE Transactions on Parallel and Distributed Systems, Vol. 12, No. 7, pp. 686-700, 2001.
- James Gwertzman and Margo Seltzer. World-wide web cache consistency. In Proceedings of the 1996 USENIX Technical Conference, San Diego, CA, January 1996.
- T. Hara, Effective Replica Allocation in Ad Hoc Networks for Improving Data Accessibility. Proceedings of IEEE INFOCOM, 2001.
- T. Hara. Cooperative Caching by Mobile Clients in Push-based Information Systems. Proceedings of the 11th International Conference on Information and Knowledge management, 2002.
- T. Hara. Replica Allocation in Ad Hoc Networks with Periodic Data Update. Proceedings of the Third International Conference on Mobile Data Management, 2002.
- Barron C. Housel, George Samaras and David B. Lindquist. Web Express: A client/intercept based system for optimizing Web browsing in a wireless environment. Mobile Networks and Applications 3 (1998) 419–431.
- T. Imielinski, S. Viswanathan, and B.R. Badrinath. Power efficient

filtering of data on air. Proceedings of EDBT Conference, pp 245-258, March 1994.

- T. Imielinski, S. Viswanathan, and B.R. Badrinath. Energy efficient indexing on air. Proceedings of 1994 ACM SIGMOD, pp 25-36, May 1994.
- Z. Jiang and L. Lkeinrock. Web prefetching in a mobile environment. IEEE Personal Communications, 5(5):25-34, 1998.
- Jin Jing, Ahmed Elmagarmid, Abdelsalam Sumi Helal, Rafael Alonso. Bit-Sequences: An Adaptive Cache Invalidation Method in Mobile Client/Server Environments. ACM Mobile Networks and Applications, Vol. 2, Issue 2, pp. 115-127, 1997.
- J. Kistler and M. Satyanarayanan. Disconnected operation in the coda file system. ACM Transactions on Computer Systems, Vol. 10, No. 1, February 1992, pp. 3-25.
- R. Krashinsky and H. Balakrishnan, Minimizing Energy for Wireless Web Access with Bounded Slowdown, Proc. Mobicom 2002, Atlanta, 2002.
- Mika Liljeberg, Heikki Helin, Markku Kojo, and Kimmo Raatikainen. Enhanced services for World-Wide Web in mobile WAN environment, University of Helsinki, Department of Computer Science, Series of Publications C, No. C-1996-28.
- S. Lyer, A. Rowstron, P. Druschel. Squirrel: a decentralized peer-to-peer web cache. The 21th ACM PODC 2002 (Symposium on Principles of Distributed Computing).
- P. Nuggehalli, V. Srinivasan etc. Energy-efficient caching strategies in ad hoc wireless networks. MobiHoc '03, Annapolis, Maryland, USA, June 2003.
- V. N. Padmanabhan and K. Sripanidkulchai. The Case for Cooperative Networking Proceedings of the First International Workshop on Peer-to-Peer Systems (IPTPS), Cambridge, MA, USA, March 2002
- Q. Ren, and M.H. Dunham. Using semantic caching to manage location dependent data in mobile computing. Proceedings of MOBICOM, 2000, Boston, MA, USA, 2000.
- F. Sailhan, V. Issarny. Energy-aware Web Caching for Mobile Terminals. Proceedings of the 22nd International Conference on Distributed Computing Systems Workshops, 2002.

- F. Sailhan, V. Issarny. Cooperative Caching in Ad Hoc Networks. Proceedings of the 4th International Conference on Mobile Data Management, 2003.
- M. Satyanarayanan. Fundamental challenges in mobile computing. Proceedings of the fifteenth annual ACM symposium on Principles of distributed computing, pp 1-7, 1996.
- A. Silberschatz and P. Galvin, Operating System Concepts, Addison Wesley, 1998.
- K. Tan, J. Cai, B. Ooi. An evaluation of cache invalidation strategies in wireless environments. IEEE Transactions on Parallel and Distributed Systems, Vol. 12, No. 8, pp. 789-807, 2001.
- J. Yin, L. Alvisi, and M. Dahlin etc. Using leases to support server-driven consistency in large-scale systems. In Proceedings of the 18th International Conference on Distributed Computing System, May 1998.
- J. Wang. A survey of web caching schemes for the internet. ACM Computer Communication Review, 29(5): 36-46, Oct. 1999.
- Z. Wang, S. Das, H. Che and M. Kumar. SACCS: Scalable Asynchronous Cache Consistency Scheme for Mobile Environments. International Workshop on Mobile and Wireless Networks, MWN2003, May, 2003.
- Varshney, U., Vetter, R. and Kalakota, R. “Mobile commerce: A New Frontier”, IEEE Computer: Special Issue on E-commerce, October 2000.
- Varshney, U. and R. Vetter, “Mobile Commerce: Framework, Applications, and Networking Support”, ACM/Kluwer Journal on Mobile Networks and Applications (MONET), vol. 7, no. 3, June 2002 (pp. 185-198
- Ghosh and Swaminatha, “M-commerce Security”, Communications of the ACM, Feb 2001
- Lange, D.B. and Oshima, M., Seven Good Reasons for Mobile Agents, Communications of ACM, March 1999. pp. 88-89
- Sunsted, Todd. Agents on The Move, Java World, July 1998
- Sundted, Todd. An Introduction to Agents . Java World, June 1998
- James E. White, Telescript Technology: The Foundation for The Electronic Marketplace, General Magic White Paper, 1994

- Vu Anh Pham, Ahmed Karmouch, Mobile Software Agent: An Overview, IEEE Communication Magazine, July 1998
- Crystaliz, Inc; General Magic , Inc; GMD Fokus and IBM Corp
- Gray, R.S., Agent TCL, 1997, pp. 58-95
- Ting Cai, Peter A. Gloor, Saurab Nog, Dartflow: A Workflow Management System on the Web Using Transportable Agents. Technical Report PCS-TR96-283, Dartmouth College, May 1996
- C.Sylvia, The Future With or Without SNMP, LAN Management 1996
- Wilmer Caripe, George Cybenko, Katsuhiro, and Robert Gray, Network Awareness and Mobile Agent System, Dartmouth College, IEEE Communication Magazine, july 1998, 44-49 pp

UNIT-V

With current advances in technology, wireless networks are increasing in popularity. Wireless networks allow users the freedom to travel from one location to another without interruption of their computing services. However, wireless networks require the existence of a wired Base Station (BS) in order for the wireless user to send/receive messages. Ad hoc networks, a subset of wireless networks, allow the formation of a wireless network without the need for a BS. All participating users in an ad hoc network agree to accept and forward messages, to and from each other. With this flexibility, wireless networks have the ability to form anywhere, at any time, as long as two or more wireless users are willing to communicate.

Ad hoc networks are dynamically created and maintained by the individual nodes comprising the network. They do not require a pre-existing architecture for communication purposes and do not rely on any type of wired infrastructure; in an ad hoc network all communication occurs through a wireless median. With current technology and the increasing popularity of notebook computers, interest in ad hoc networks has greatly peaked. Future advances in technology will allow us to form small ad hoc networks on campuses, during conferences, and even in our own homes. Further, the need for easily portable ad hoc networks in rescue missions and in situations located in rough terrain are becoming extremely common.

Readers would be able to explore the detailed knowledge about Mobile Ad hoc Networks under the following sections in this unit:

- Mobile Ad hoc Networks
- Characteristics of Mobile Ad-hoc Networks

- Network Architecture
- Basic Routing Schemes
- Classification of Ad hoc Routing Protocols
- Security in Ad Hoc Networks

UNIT

5

Ad hoc Networks

5.1. MOBILE AD HOC NETWORKS

5.1.1. Introduction

Wireless network is an emerging technology that will allow users to access information and services electronically, regardless of their geographic position. Recently, MOBILE AD HOC networks became a hot research topic among researchers due to their flexibility and independence of network infrastructures, such as base stations. Centralized networks, such as GSM, cannot be used in all situations. Significant examples of such scenarios include establishing survivable, efficient, dynamic communication for rescue operations, disaster relief efforts and military networks. Such network scenarios cannot rely on centralized and organized connectivity, they can be conceived as applications of Mobile Adhoc Networks (MANETs). The set of applications for MANETs is diverse, ranging from small, static networks that are constrained by power sources, to large-scale, mobile, highly dynamic networks. Due to unique characteristics, such as dynamic network topology, limited bandwidth, and limited battery power, routing in a MANET is a particularly challenging task compared to a conventional network.

Wireless networks can be classified in two ways:

- Infrastructured Network
- Infrastructureless Network

5.1.1.1. Infrastructured Networks

Infrastructured network consists of a network with fixed and wired gateways. A mobile host communicates with a bridge in the network (called base station) within its communication radius. The mobile unit can move geographically while it is communicating. When it goes out of range of one base station, it connects with new base station and starts communicating through it. This is called handoff. In this approach the base stations are fixed.

5.1.1.2. Infrastructureless Networks

Infrastructureless networks, in contrast to infrastructure based networks, in ad hoc networks all nodes are mobile and can be connected dynamically in an arbitrary manner. This may be done either because it may not be economically practical or physically possible to provide the necessary infrastructure or because the situation does not permit its installation.

Users may be so sparse or dense that the appropriate level of fixed infrastructure is not an economical investment. Sometimes fixed infrastructure exists but cannot be relied upon, such as during disaster recovery. Finally, existing services may not provide adequate service, or may be too expensive. Ad hoc mobile networks are attracting a lot of attention these days due to little efforts needed to deploy them. These networks prove to be economical in sparse areas. In emergency services such as disaster recovery these networks are the only possible options. There are no dedicated routers, servers, access points and cables. Because of its speedy and convenient deployment, robustness, and low cost, a MANET can find its applications in the following areas:

- Military use (e.g. a network in the battlefield)
- Search and rescue
- Temporary networks in meeting rooms, airports when friends or business associates would run into each other in an airport terminal and wish to exchange business cards, etc.
- Personal Area Networks connecting cell phones, laptops, smart watches, and other wearable computers

The cost and time associated in setting up the infrastructure required for networking does not justify its installation.

In ad hoc networks, nodes are wireless and mobile. They don't even have any base station. So ad hoc networks cannot have any centralized administration. Then the nodes themselves find their routes to other nodes in the network through distributed administration. Each node acts as a router with its own transmitter and receiver antennas and a battery source. A similar routing algorithm runs at each node in the network. If two nodes want to communicate with each other, they can do so only if they are in the transmission/reception range of each other, which is generally 10 to 20 Kms. To cover larger areas, we need to increase the power of transmitting /receiving antennas. Obviously, the size of power source i.e. battery will increase and the host will not be mobile.

Thus, in the case where only two hosts, within the transmission range, are involved in the ad hoc network, no real routing protocol or routing decisions are necessary. But in many practical ad hoc networks, two hosts that wish to correspond may not close enough to be within wireless transmission range of each other. These hosts could communicate if other hosts between them also participating in the ad hoc network are willing to forward packets for them.

As an example, consider the Fig. 5.1 shown below. Mobile host *C* is not within the range of host A's wireless transmitter (indicated by the circle around A) and host *A* is not within the range of host C's wireless transmitter. Now, if *A* and *C* wish to interact with each other, they may in this case procure the services of host *B* to forward packets for them, since host *B* lies within the transmission range of both *A* and C. A real ad hoc network may be more complicated than this example, due to the inherent non-uniform propagation characteristics of wireless transmissions and due to the possibility that any or all of the hosts involved may move at any time.

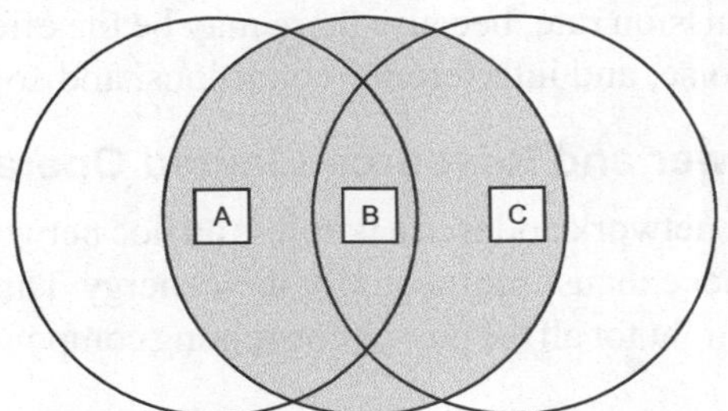

Fig. 5.1: Host A and C are 'connected' via host B

From a graph theory, we can view an ad hoc network as a graph, G (A, E (t)), which is formed by denoting each mobile host by a node and drawing an edge between the two nodes if they are with in the wireless communication range of each other. The set of edges (E (t)), is denoted as a function of time, as it keep changing as the node in the ad hoc networks move around. The topology can be very arbitrary since there are no restrictions on where the nodes are located and how they move with respect to each other. So, ***"An ad hoc network is a collection of wireless mobile hosts forming a temporary network without the aid of any centralized administration or standard support services regularly available on the wide-area network to which the hosts may normally be connected."***

5.2 CHARACTERISTICS OF MOBILE AD-HOC NETWORKS

Wireless mobile ad hoc networks have significant characteristics as follows:

5.2.1. Dynamic Network Topology

Each node in an ad hoc network is free to move randomly. This feature makes the network topology change unpredictably. Also, an ad hoc network may be comprised of both bi-directional and unidirectional links. Thus, using ad hoc networks could augment mobility and flexibility of nodes in the network.

5.2.2. Bandwidth-Limited and Fluctuating Capacity Links

Wireless links will remain to have substantially lower capacity compared to their hardwired counterparts. Besides, the throughput of wireless communications in real environments is often much less than a radios maximum transmission rate, because there may be the effects of multiple access, fading, noise, and interference conditions, and so on.

5.2.3. Low-Power and Resource-Limited Operation

In most cases, the network nodes in a wireless ad hoc network may depend on batteries or other exhaustible means for their energy. This feature makes the power budget tight for all the power-consuming components in a mobile device.

5.2.4. Constrained Physical Security

In general, mobile wireless networks are more likely to be vulnerable to physical security threats than are fixed-cable nets. For example, there is the increased possibility of eavesdropping, spoofing, and denial-of-service attack that should be carefully considered.

5.2.5. Decentralized Network Control

As an advantage, the decentralized nature of network control in mobile ad hoc networks supports extra robustness against the single points of failure of more centralized approaches.

5.3. NETWORK ARCHITECTURE

There are two approaches to provide network connectivity in an Ad hoc Mobile Networks:

5.3.1. Hierarchical Network Architecture

In hierarchical architectures, Fig. 5.2 aggregating nodes into clusters and clusters into super-clusters conceal the details of the network topology. Some nodes, such as cluster heads and gateway nodes have a higher computation communication load than other nodes. Hence, the mobility management becomes complex. The network reliability may also be affected due to single points of failure associated with the defined critical nodes. However, control messages may only have to be propagated within a cluster. Thus, the multilevel hierarchy reduces the storage requirement and the communication overhead of large wireless networks by providing a mechanism for localizing each node. In addition, hierarchical architectures are more suitable for low mobility case. Although flat architectures are more flexible and simpler than hierarchical one, hierarchical architectures provide more scalable approach.

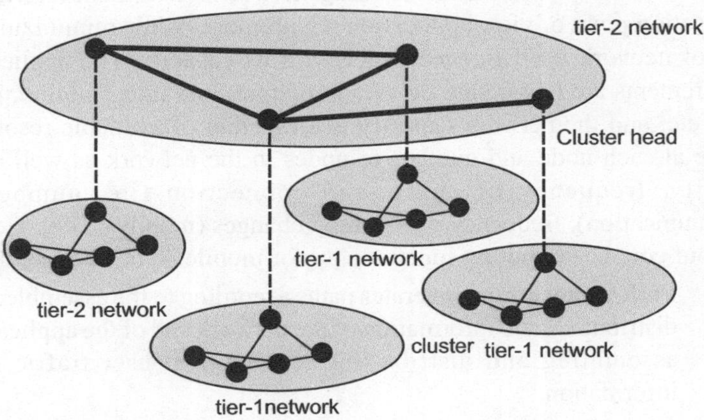

Fig. 5.2: Hierarchical Architecture

5.3.2 Flat-routed Architecture

In this approach all the nodes (Fig. 5.3) are identical in terms of responsibility, and there is no concept of special gateways. All nodes carry the same responsibility. Flat architectures do not optimize bandwidth resource utilization in large networks because control messages have to be transmitted globally throughout the network, but they are appropriate for highly dynamic network topology. The scalability decreases when the number of nodes increases significantly.

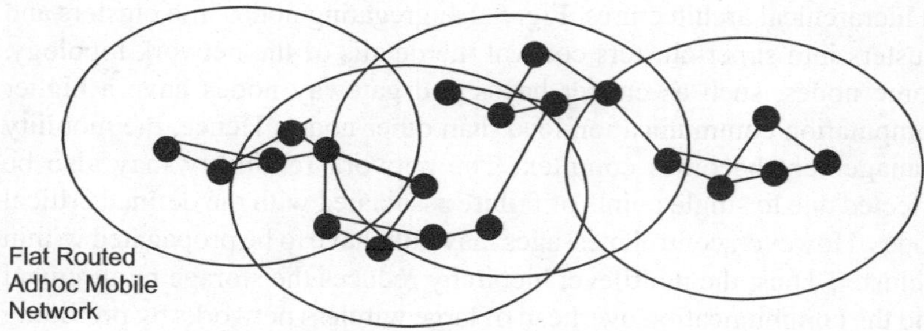

Fig. 5.3: Flat Bed Architecture

A routing protocol is the mechanism by which user traffic is directed and transported through the network from the source node to the destination node. Objectives include maximizing network performance form the application point of view application requirements while minimizing the cost of network itself in accordance with its capacity. The application requirements are hop count, delay, throughput, loss rate, stability, jitter, cost, etc; and the network capacity is a function of available resources reside at each node and number of nodes in the network as well as its density, frequency of end-to-end connection (i.e. number of communication), frequency of topology changes (mobility rate). Here is the four core basic routing functionality for mobile ad hoc networks:

- **Path Generation:** generates paths according to the assembled and distributed state information of the network and of the application, assembling and distributing network and user traffic state information.
- **Path Selection:** selects appropriate paths based on network and application state information

- **Data Forwarding:** forwards user traffic along the selected route, forwarding user traffic along the selected route.
- **Path Maintenance:** maintaining of the selected route.

Consequently routing is bounded by traffic requirements, network capacity. This is illustrated in Fig. 5.4.

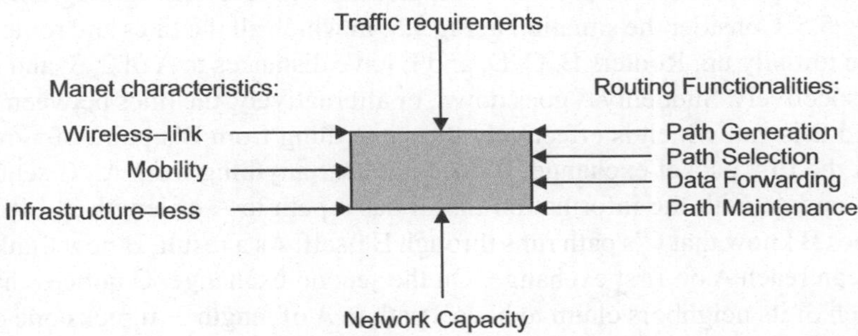

Fig. 5.4: Routing basics

5.4. BASIC ROUTING SCHEMES

In ad hoc networks, each node acts as a router. Routing algorithm must run at each node to allow it to discover path through the network to any other node. The dynamic routing algorithms like distance vector routing and link state routing, which were basically written for hardwired networks were adopted for routing in wireless ad hoc networks, essentially treating each mobile host as a router.

5.4.1. Distance Vector Routing

Distance vector routing is a routing protocol in which every node I maintains, for each destination x a set of distance { d_{ij}^{x} } where j ranges over the neighbors of i. Node I treats neighbor k as a next hop for a packet destination for x if   equals *min j* {   }.The succession of next hops chosen in this manner lead to x along the shortest path. In order to keep the distance estimates up-to-date, each node monitors the cost (if neighbor link is broken, cost will be infinity) of its outgoing links and periodically broadcasts, to each one of its neighbor, its current estimate of the shortest distance to every node in the network. In routing table we maintain the information <destination, next-hop, total_no_of _hops>.

The major drawback in this algorithm is that it can cause the formation of both short-lived and long-lived loops. The primary cause for formation of routing loops is that nodes choose their next-hops in a completely distributed fashion based on information which can possible be stale and, therefore, incorrect the loop formation is mainly due to the counting to infinity problem. This problem is explained with the help of diagram in Fig 5.5. Consider the situation in Fig 5.5, in which all the lines and routers are initially up. Routers B, C, D, and E have distances to A of 2, 3, and 4, respectively. Suddenly A goes down, or alternatively, the lines between A and B is cut, which is effectively the same thing from B's point of view. At the first packet exchange, B does not hear anything from A., C sends an update with the information that it has a path to A of length 2. Little does B know that C's path runs through B itself. As a result, B now thinks it can reach A on first exchange. On the second exchange, C notices that each of its neighbors claim to have a path to A of length 3. It picks one of them at random and makes its new distance to A as 4.

A	B	C	D	E	
1	2	3	4		Initially
3	2	3	4		After 1 exchange
3	4	3	4		After 2 exchanges
5	4	5	4		After 3 exchanges
5	6	5	6		After 4 exchanges
7	6	7	6		After 5 exchanges
7	8	7	8		After 6 exchanges
:	:	:	:		
:	:	:	:		

Till infinity

Fig. 5.5: Counting-to-infinity Problem

5.4.2. Link State Routing

Distance Vector Routing was replaced by an entirely new algorithm called Link State Routing. Link state routing eliminates the counting-to-infinity problem. In link state routing, each node maintains a view of the network topology with a cost (e.g. distance in terms of number of hops) for each link. To keep these views consistent, each node periodically broadcasts the link costs of its outgoing links to all other nodes using a protocol such as flooding. As a node views this information, it updates its view of the network topology and applies a shortest-path algorithm to choose its next hop for each destination. Some of the link costs in a node's view can be incorrect because of long propagation delays, partitioned network, etc. Such inconsistent views of network topologies might lead to formation of routing loops. These loops, however, are short-lived; because they disappear in the time it takes a message to traverse the diameter of the network.

5.5 CLASSIFICATION OF AD-HOC ROUTING PROTOCOLS

An **Ad hoc routing protocol** is a convention or standard that controls how nodes come to agree which way to route packets between computing devices in a mobile ad-hoc network (MANET).

In ad hoc networks, nodes do not have *a priori* knowledge of topology of network around them, they have to discover it. The basic idea is that a new node (optionally) announces its presence and listens to broadcast announcements from its neighbours. The node learns about new near nodes and ways to reach them, and may announce that it can also reach those nodes. As time goes on, each node knows about all other nodes and one or more ways how to reach them. Numerous protocols have been developed for ad hoc mobile networks to deal with the typical limitations of these networks, which include high power consumption, low bandwidth, and high error rates. Some of these routing protocols may generally be categorized as described in '***Annexure 5-A***' presented in the end of this chapter. Here author has tried to describe few of them as per the necessity, under the followings:

- Table–driven(Proactive) protocols
- Source-initiated (Reactive or On Demand) protocols
- Hybrid protocols

Despite being designed for the same type of underlying network, the characteristics of each of these protocols are quite distinct.

5.5.1. Table-Driven Routing Protocols

Table-driven routing protocols attempt to maintain consistent, up-to-date routing information from each node to every other node in the network. These protocols require each node to maintain one or more tables to store routing information, and they respond to changes in network topology by propagating updates throughout the network in order to maintain a consistent network view .The areas in which they differ are the number of necessary routing-related tables and the methods by which changes in network structure are broadcast.

5.5.1.1. Destination Sequenced Distance Vector (DSDV) Routing Algorithm

In DSDV, each node maintains a routing table containing the next hop information for each reachable destination. Each route is tagged with a sequence number originated by destination.

Update messages are periodically broadcasted through the network as in distance vector but with the only difference that in DSDV, while sending an update message, each node successively increases its even sequence number. Other nodes in the network when receive this update, modify their routing table only if this is the freshest information i.e. one with the greatest sequence number. If the two routes have equal sequence numbers, then one with the lower metric is used. In distance vector routing, looping was mainly due to "stale routes". In DSDV, looping problem is totally avoided because now only fresh routes are used for updates.

In addition to periodic updates, some event driven updates are also transmitted when there is any significant topology change e.g. a broken link. Mobile nodes cause broken links as they move from place to place. When a node finds that it has a broken link with its next hope, it sends an update with a metric to that next hop as "infinity" and an odd sequence number i.e. a sequence number one greater than the sequence number for the route that has broken.

Updates for broken links are immediately transmitted. While sending these updates, if there is still space in the packet, then routes whose sequence number has changed are sent. These routes are sent in turn so that for some routes the information may not get transmitted again and again unnecessarily.

Periodic updates can be sent both as "full dumps" or "incremental dumps". To conserve the network bandwidth, full dumps are sent relatively infrequently. Rather incremental dumps are sent. A full dump results in whole information broadcasted, an incremental dump causes only difference in the last update to be broadcasted.

As updated routes are broadcasted through the network, they may reach a node through different routes containing different metrics i.e. total number of hops to destination. Whenever a node receives an update with a lower metric (provided the sequence number is same); it will modify its table with the shortest path. This may cause fluctuations if routes with worse metric are received first. To avoid this problem, two routing tables are maintained, one for routing and one for broadcast. As any link cost change is detected by a node, it is not immediately transmitted rather it waits for some "settling time" .If the link cost remains same after the settling time, only then the entry is made in the routing table. Otherwise it is discarded. During the settling time, the route in the table can be used for forwarding any incoming packet. The most important parameter to be chosen is the time between rebroadcasts. However, whenever new info is received, it is broadcasted as soon as possible.

Limitations

DSDV is limited in that it provides only single path for routing between a source/destination pair. In a case a source node wants to send packet to destination but its corresponding entry has infinite metric, the source node will have to wait until it receives next update message originated by the destination in order to update its distance table entry for that destination. This implicit destination center synchronization leads to latency and security problem.

Since, in this case the source node can communicate with its destination if the corresponding metric entry has been updated. So, metric entry may be fakely updated by intruders because no security is provided. As a result of this the source can send packets in the illusion that there exists path to the desired destination and ultimately leading to loss of information.

Further more this protocol is table driven i.e. each node maintains a record of routes to all known destinations and periodically broadcast a part of this information for it to propagate through the network. This leads to network security threats as the information can be easily altered because routes are not secure.

5.5.1.2. Global State Routing (GSR)

Global State Routing (GSR) is similar to DSDV. It takes the idea of link state routing but improves it by avoiding finding of routing messages. In this algorithm, each node maintains a neighbour list, a topology table, a next hop table and a distance table. Neighbour list of a node contains the list of its neighbours (have all nodes that can be heard by a node are assured to be its neighbours). For each destination node, the topology table contains the link state information as reported by the destination and the time stamp of the information. For each destination, the next hop table contains the next hop to which the packets for this destination must be forwarded. The distance table contains the shortest distance to each destination node. The routing messages are generated on a link change as in link state protocols. On receiving a routing message the node updates its topology table of the sequence number of the msssage is newer than the sequence number stored in the table. After this the node reconstructs its routing table and broadcasts the information to its neighbors.

5.5.1.3. Fisheye State Routing (FSR)

Fisheye State Routing (FSR) is an improvement of GSR (both are based on the link state protocol). The large size of update messages in GSR uses a considerable amount of bandwidth.

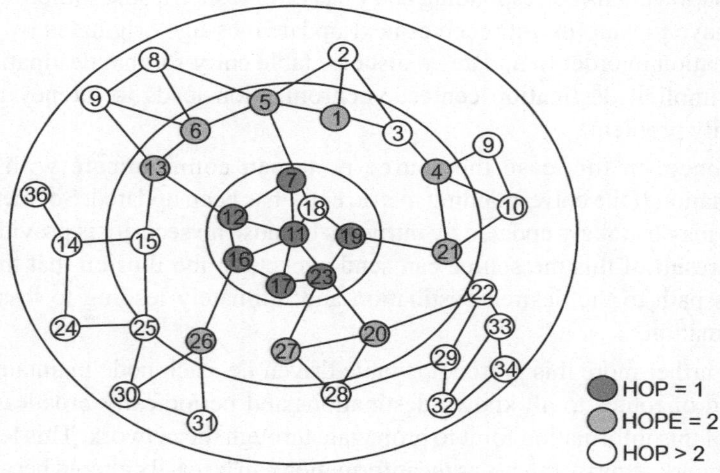

Fig. 5.6: Scope of Fisheye

General

- An example of a Fisheye's scope is shown above in Fig. 5.6 for the (node-II) center node.

- The scope is defined in terms of the number of hops needed to reach a certain node.
- In FSR, every update message doesn't contain information about all nodes in the network. Instead information about closer y

is exchanged more frequently than it is done about farther nodes, thus reducing the updates message size.
- The center node has most upto date information about all nodes in the inner circle and the accuracy of information decreases as the distance from node increases.
- This procedure of dividing the network into different scope levels is done at each node, meaning that it is independent on a central entity.
- Even if a node doesn't have accurate information about far away nodes, the packets will be routed correctly because the route information becomes more and more accurate as the packet gets closer to the destination.
- This means that FSR scales well to large networks as the overhead is controlled.

Protocol Operation

Fisheye state routing is a table-driven or proactive routing protocol.

FSR is based on link state routing and it is able of immediately providing route information when needed.

FSR is functionally similar to LS as it maintains a full topology map at each node.

The link state packets are exchanged periodically instead of event driven.

The topology tables are send to local neighbours only (instead of flooding the entire network) sequence numbers are used for entry replacement as well as for providing loop-free routing.

The Fisheye scope message updating scheme is highly accurate for inner scope nodes as entries in the routing table corresponding to nodes within the smallest scope are send to the neighbours with the highest frequency. For outer scope nodes, information may blue due to longer exchange interval but there is no need to find the destination firstly (as in on-demand routing).

The Fisheye scope technique allows exchanging link state messages at different intervals for nodes within different Fisheye scope distance, leading to a reduction of the link state message size.

The bold entries in Fig. 5.7 are propagated to the neighbours at the highest frequency, as they have low hop counts. The GST entry shows the neighbours corresponding to each node in the network.

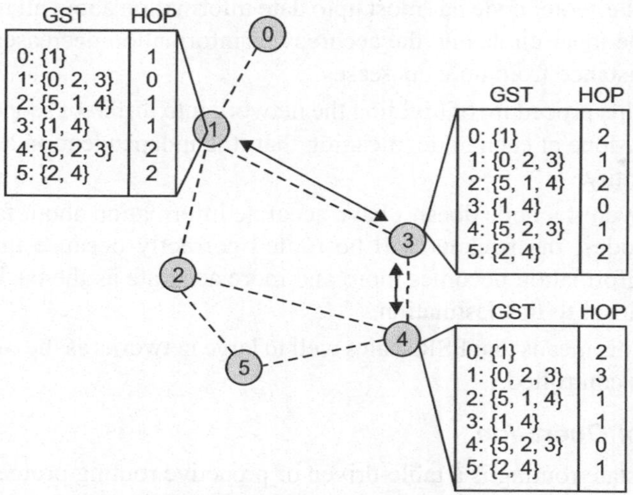

Fig. 5.7: Message reduction using Fisheye

Topology Table

The topology table is created by using the topology information obtained from the link state messages.

- Each destination has an entry in the table (full topology map).
- An entry consists of two parts : the link state information and a destination sequence number.
- Based on this table, the routing table will be calculated, the distance information will then be obtained from the routing table calculation. It is used to classify the node to a fisheye scope.

The topology table has following entries for every link state entry:

(a) Destination address

(b) Destination sequence number

(c) Link state list.

Neighbour Link State List

- On receiving a link state message, a node records/updates the sender in its neighbour list.
- If nothing is received for a time out interval, the corresponding station will be removed from the neighbour list.
- The following information is maintained for each neighbour node:

  (a) Neighbour node link state

  (b) Latest time stamp.

Routing Table

- The routing table provides next hop information to forward a packet to a destinations in the network. The entries are updated on a topology table change. The routing table consists of the following fields:

  (a) Destination address

  (b) Distance
- The inaccuracy for away nodes will increase in a mobile environment but a packet approaching its destination finds more and more accurate routing instructions as its enters sectors with higher refresh rates.

Advantages

- FSR is suitable for large and highly mobile network environments as it triggers no control messages on link failures broken link won't be included in the next link state message exchange. This means that a change on a link far away does not necessarily cause a change in the routing table.
- FSR is mainly based on simplicity, as it uses upto date shortest routes, it is robust to host mobility as it exchanges partial routing update information with neighbours only, thus reducing routing update traffic.
- FSR is quality of service ready, which means that it is possible to extend the definition of link state by adding bandwidth and channel quality information to the link entry.

Disadvantages

- It is easy to locate destinations due to the flat addressing scheme and topology map, but this also limits scalability.
- Other negative points are the routing table storage complexity and the processing overhead.
- FSR doesn't provide any form of security, as most other protocols.

5.5.1.4. The Wireless Routing Protocol (WRP)

- The Wireless Routing Protocol (WRP) is a table based distance-vector routing protocol. Each node in the network maintains a distance table, a routing table, a link cost table and a message retransmission list.
- The distance table of a node X contains the distance of each destination node Y via each neighbour Z of X. It also contains the downstream neighbour of Z through which this path is realized. The routing table of node X contains the distance of each destination node Y from node X, the predecessor and the successor of node X on this path. It also contains a tag to identify if the entry is a simple path, a loop or invalid. The storing predecessor and successor in the table is beneficial in detecting loops and avoiding, counting-to-infinity problem. The link cost table contains cost of link to each neighbour of the node and the number of time outs style an error-free message was received from that neighbour. The Message Retransmission List (MRL) contains information to let a node know which of its neighbour has not acknowledged. Its update message and to retransmit update message to that neighbour.
- Mode exchange routing table with their neighbours using update messages periodically as well as on link changes the nodes present on the response list of update message (formed using MRL) are required to acknowledge the receipt of update message. If there is no change in routing table since last update, the node is required to send an idle Hello message to ensure connectivity. On relieving an update message, the node modifies its distance table and looks for better paths using new information. Any new path so found is relayed bulk to the original nodes so that they can update their table. The node also updates its routing table of the new path better than the existing path. On receiving Acknowledgement, the node

updates its MRL. A unique failure of this algorithm is that it checks the consistency of all its neighbours every time. It detects a change in link of any of its neighbours. Consistency check in this manner helps eliminate looping situations in a better way and also has fast convergence.

5.5.1.5. Optimized Link State Routing (OLSR) Protocol:

OLSR is a proactive routing protocol, so the routes are always immediately available when needed. OLSR is a optimization version of a pure link state protocol. So the topological changes cause the flooding of topological information to all available hosts in the network. To reduce the possible overhead in the network, protocol uses Multipoint Relays (MPR). The idea of MPR is to reduce flooding of broadcasts in same regions in the network. Another reduce is to provide the shortest path. The reducing the time interval for the control messages transmission can bring more reactivity to the topological changes.

OLSR uses two kinds of the control messages: Hello and Topology Control (TC). Hello messages are used for finding the information about the link status and the host's neighbors. With the Hello message the Multipoint Relay (MPR) Selector set is constructed which describes which neighbors has chosen this host to act as MPR and from this information the host can calculate its own set of the MPRs. the Hello messages are sent only one hop away but the TC messages are broadcasted throughout the entire network. TC messages are used for broadcasting information about own advertised neighbors which includes at least the MPR Selector list. The TC messages are broadcasted periodically and only the MPR hosts can forward the TC messages. There is also Multiple Interface Declaration (MID) messages which are used for informing other host that the announcing host can have multiple OLSR interface addresses. The MID message is broadcasted throughout the entire network only by MPRs. There is also a "Host and Network Association" (HNA) message which provides the external routing information by giving the possibility for routing to the external addresses. The HNA message provides information about the network- and the netmask addresses, so that OLSR host can consider that the announcing host can act as a gateway to the announcing set of addresses. The HNA is considered as a generalized version of the TC message with only difference that the TC message can inform about route canceling while HNA message information is removed only after expiration time.

Limitations

We now discuss various security risks in OLSR. It did not include security measures in its design, like several other routing protocols. An attacker performing identity spoofing or message replay needs to change the Message Sequence Number field of the spoofed or replayed message. Otherwise, nodes that already have received a message with the same originator and MSN (according to their Duplicate Set) will drop the malicious message. Furthermore, accepting the malicious message causes message loss when a legitimate message having the same originator and MSN is received by the victim nodes, and dropped according to the protocol. Various attacks on OLSR protocol are as follows:

(a) **Incorrect traffic generation:** One way in which a node can misbehave is by generating control messages in a way that is not according to the protocol. Incorrect message generation can be due to:

- Incorrect HELLO message generation
- Incorrect TC message generation
- Incorrect MID/HNA message generation
- ANSN attack

(b) **Incorrect traffic relaying:** If control messages are not properly relayed, network malfunctions are possible. Incorrect traffic relaying may be due to:

- Black hole attack
- Replay attack
- Wormhole attack
- MPR attack

5.5.1.6. Zone-based Hierarchical Link State Routing Protocol

In Zone-based Hierarchical Link State Routing Protocol (ZHLS)[Joa-Ng99]*, the network is divided into non-overlapping zones. Unlike other hierarchical protocols, there is no zone-head. ZHLS defines two levels of topologies - node level and zone level. A node level topology tells how nodes of a zone are connected to each other physically. A virtual link between two zones exists if at least one node of a zone is physically connected to some node of the other zone. Zone level topology tells how zones are connected together. There are two types of Link State Packets

(LSP) as well - node LSP and zone LSP. A node LSP of a node contains its neighbor node information and is propagated with the zone where as a zone LSP contains the zone information and is propagated globally. So each node has full node connectivity knowledge about the nodes in its zone and only zone connectivity information about other zones in the network. So given the zone id and the node id of a destination, the packet is routed based on the zone id till it reaches the correct zone. Then in that zone, it is routed based on node id. A <zone id, node id> of the destination is sufficient for routing so it is adaptable to changing topologies.

*[Joa-Ng99] M Joa-Ng and I.-T. Lu, "A Peer-to-Peer zone-based two-level link state routing for mobile Ad Hoc Networks" IEEE Journal on Selected Areas in Communications, Special Issue on Ad-Hoc Networks, Aug. 1999, pp.1415-25.

5.5.1.7. Clusterhead Gateway Switch Routing Protocol

Clusterhead Gateway Switch Routing (CGSR) [Chiang97]* uses as basis the DSDV Routing algorithm described in the previous section.The mobile nodes are aggregated into clusters and a cluster-head is elected. All nodes that are in the communication range of the cluster-head belong to its cluster. A gateway node is a node that is in the communication range of two or more cluster-heads. In a dynamic network cluster head scheme can cause performance degradation due to frequent cluster-head elections, so CGSR uses a Least Cluster Change (LCC) algorithm. In LCC, cluster-head change occurs only if a change in network causes two cluster-heads to come into one cluster or one of the nodes moves out of the range of all the cluster-heads. The general algorithm works in the following manner. The source of the packet transmits the packet to its cluster-head. From this cluster-head, the packet is sent to the gateway node that connects this cluster-head and the next cluster-head along the route to the destination. The gateway sends it to that cluster-head and so on till the destination cluster-head is reached in this way. The destination cluster-head then transmits the packet to the destination.

In such type of protocol, each node maintains a cluster member table that has mapping from each node to its respective cluster-head. Each node broadcasts its cluster member table periodically and updates its table after receiving other nodeÆs broadcasts using the DSDV algorithm. In addition, each node also maintains a routing table that determines the next hop to reach the destination cluster. On receiving a packet, a node finds the nearest cluster-head along the route to the destination according to the cluster member table and the routing table. Then it consults its routing table to find the next hop in order to reach the cluster-head selected in step one and transmits the packet to that node.

[Chiang97]* C.-C. Chiang, "Routing in Clustered Multihop, Mobile Wireless Networks with Fading Channel" Proc. IEEE SICON'97, Apr.1997, pp.197-211.

5.5.2. Source Initiated (Reactive / On-Demand) Routing Protocol

A different approach from table-driven routing is source-initiated on demand routing. This type of routing creates routes only when desired by the source node. When a node requires a route to a destination, it initiates a route discovery process within the network. This process is completed once a route is found or all possible route permutations have been examined. Once a route has been established, it is maintained by a route maintenance procedure until either the destination becomes inaccessible along every path from the source or until the route is no longer desired.

5.5.2.1. Ad Hoc On Demand Distance Vector (AODV) Routing Protocol

The Ad Hoc On-Demand Distance-Vector (AODV) routing protocol is particularly designed for ad hoc wireless network. It provides very quick and efficient route establishment between communicating nodes because AODV nodes that do not lie on active paths neither maintain any routing information nor participate in any periodic routing table exchanges .Further a node does not have to discover and maintain a route to another node until the two need to communicate unless the former node is offering its services as an intermediate forwarding station to maintain connectivity between two other nodes. In most of the protocols the overhead is incurred by the fact that each packet transmitted contains the source route to the destination. AODV protocol eliminates this problem by maintaining only the next hop information to reach a particular destination. A monotonically increasing sequence number is used to prevent replay attacks and to ensure loop-free routing. The algorithm's primary objectives are:

- To broadcast discovery packets only when necessary.
- To disseminate information about changes in local connectivity to

those neighboring mobile nodes that are likely to need the information

5.5.2.1.1. Path Discovery

When a node needs to communicate wit another node but does not have the routing information the source node then initiates the path discovery process. Every node maintains two counters:

1. A node sequence number
2. A broadcast ID

The source node then broadcasts a Route Request (RREQ) packet to its neighbors. Each RREQ is uniquely identified by <IP address, Broadcast ID>. The value of broadcast ID is incremented every time a node issues a RREQ request.

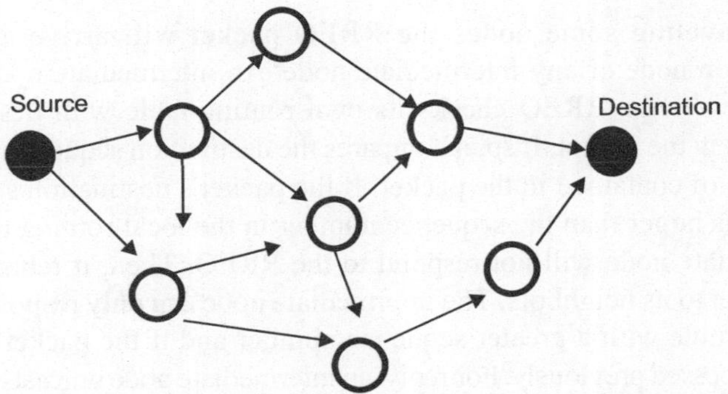

Fig 5.8: Propagation of RREQ Request

A node when receives a RREQ request have two options:

(a) Sends a reply RREP back to the source

(b) Increments the value of hop count filed and rebroadcasts the RREQ to its neighbors

Action i occur under either of the two conditions: the node is the destination or the intermediate node knows the route to the destination of the RREQ (with equal or higher sequence number). It is possible for a node to get multiple copies of same RREQ packet. Duplicate packets are simply discarded. Otherwise, it records the following information that is used for reverse and forward path set up procedures discussed in the next sections.

- Destination IP address
- Source IP address
- Broadcast ID address
- Expiration Time for the reverse path route entry
- Sequence number of the source

5.5.2.1.2. Reverse Path Setup

The RREQ packet travels from the source to several intermediate nodes and finally reaches the destination. In the mean time a reverse path from all nodes to the requesting node (source) is established as shown in the Fig. 5.8. To establish reverse path entry each intermediate node records the address of the neighbor node from which it got the first copy of the RREQ packet.

5.5.2.1.3. Forward Path Setup

After traveling some nodes the RREQ packet will arrive at either destination node or any intermediate node. An intermediate node when first receives the RREQ checks its own routing table with destination specified in the packet. If so, it compares the destination sequence number with that of contained in the packet. If the packet's destination sequence number is larger than the sequence number in the local routing table the intermediate node will not respond to the RREQ. Then, it rebroadcasts the packet to its neighbors. The intermediate node can only respond when it has a route with a greater sequence number and if the packet has not been processed previously. For reply, an intermediate node unicasts a Route Reply Packet (RREP) back to its neighbor from which it got the packet. The information of RREP packet is explained in the Fig. 5.9.

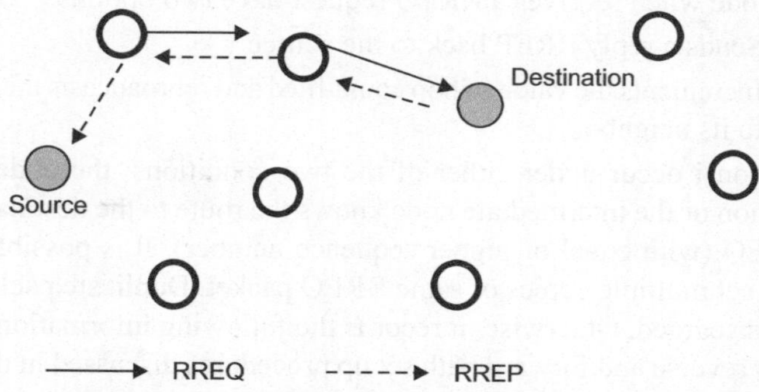

Fig 5.9: Propagation of route information

When an intermediate node receives a RREP, it establishes a forward path entry to the destination in its routing table. The forward path entry contains the following information:

- IP address of the destination
- The IP address of the neighbor from which the RREP came
- The hop count or distance to the destination

After processing the RREP the node forwards the reply towards the source. It is possible for a node to get multiple copies of the same reply from different neighbors. It forwards the first copy of the request. It will process the next copy if that copy contains a greater sequence number or less hop count. Otherwise the packet is discarded.

5.5.2.1.5. Route Maintenance

After the successful route discovery process the route is maintained as long as the source node requires it. Node movement is very common in ad hoc network environment. If the node movement does not affect the discovered path no action is taken by the protocol. If the source node moves during an active session, it reinitiates the route discovery process. When the destination or any intermediate node moves a Route Error message (RERR) is sent back to the corresponding nodes. The error message is initiated by the node that is closest to the source.

5.5.2.1.6.Local Connectivity Management

Neighboring information is maintained by periodically broadcast message. Each time a node receives a broadcast from its neighbor it updates the lifetime for that node in the local routing table. If a node does not broadcast anything within the last hello_interval, it then broadcasts a Hello packet to inform its neighbors to inform that it is still within its radio signal.

5.5.2.1.7. Limitations

In fact we consider AODV as the default routing protocol as it is presently going to be the acceptable standard for ad hoc network. So, we will highlight the major attacks on AODV or major flaws of this protocol. It is to be noted that it is not hard to transform similar type of attacks on other protocols, DSR for example. Known attacks on AODV are as follows:

- Traffic redirection by modification
- Replay attacks

- Loop formation by spoofing
- False Route Error

5.5.2.2. Dynamic Source Routing (DSR) Protocol

The Dynamic Source Routing protocol (DSR) is a simple and efficient routing protocol designed specifically for use in multi-hop wireless ad hoc networks of mobile nodes. Using DSR, the network is completely self-organizing and self configuring, requiring no existing network infrastructure or administration. Network nodes cooperate to forward packets for each other to allow communication over multiple "hops" between nodes not directly within wireless transmission range of one another. As nodes in the network move about or join or leave the network, and as wireless transmission conditions such as sources of interference change, all routing is automatically determined and maintained by the DSR routing protocol. Since the number or sequence of intermediate hops needed to reach any destination may change at any time, the resulting network topology may be quite rich and rapidly changing. The basic version of DSR uses explicit "source routing", in which each data packet sent carries in its header the complete, ordered list of nodes through which the packet will pass. This use of explicit source routing allows the sender to select and control the routes used for its own packets, supports the use of multiple routes to any destination (for example, for load balancing), and allows a simple guarantee that the routes used are loop-free; by including this source route in the header of each data packet, other nodes forwarding or overhearing any of these packets can also easily cache this routing information for future use.

The DSR protocol is composed of two main mechanisms that work together to allow the discovery and maintenance of source routes in the ad hoc network:

5.5.2.2.1. Route Discovery

It is the mechanism by which a node S wishing to send a packet to a destination node D obtains a source route D. Route Discovery is used only when S attempts to send a packet to D and does not already know a route to D.

When some source node originates a new packet addressed to some destination node, the source node places in the header of the packet a "source route" giving the sequence of hops that the packet is to follow on its way to the destination. Normally, the sender will obtain a suitable source route by searching its "Route Cache" of routes previously learned; if no route is found in its cache, it will initiate the Route Discovery protocol to dynamically find a new route to this destination node. In this case, we call the source node the "initiator" and the destination node the "target" of the Route Discovery. To initiate the Route Discovery, node A transmits a "Route Request" as a single local broadcast packet, which is received by (approximately) all nodes currently within wireless transmission range of A. When another node receives this Route Request (such as node B in this example), if it is the target of the Route Discovery, it returns a "Route Reply" to the initiator of the Route Discovery, giving a copy of the accumulated route record from the Route Request; when the initiator receives this Route Reply, it caches this route in its Route Cache for use in sending subsequent packets to this destination.

5.5.2.2.2. Route Maintenance

It is the mechanism by which node S is able to detect, while using a source route to D, if the network topology has changed such that it can no longer use its route to D because a link along the route no longer works. DSR uses two types of packets for route maintenance: Route Error (RERR) packets and ACKs. Whenever a node encounters fatal transmission error so that the route becomes invalid, a source receives a RERR message. Source then removes the erroneous hop from all of its route cache entries, and selects a new route, or if there are no more available routes, it initiates a new route discovery. ACK packets are used to verify the correct operation of the route links. Route maintenance for this route is used only when S is actually sending packets to D.

In DSR, Route Discovery and Route Maintenance each operate entirely "on demand". In particular, unlike other protocols, DSR requires no periodic packets of any kind at any layer within the network.

The DSR protocol is designed mainly for mobile ad hoc networks of up to about two hundred nodes, and is designed to work well with even very high rates of mobility.

5.5.2.2.3. Limitations

We expect large packet header, resulting in high protocol overhead, as the topology grows bigger. Securing the large packets is even more difficult.

5.5.2.3. Cluster Based Routing Protocols

In Cluster Based Routing Protocol (CBRP) [Jiang99]*, the nodes are divided into clusters. To form the cluster the following algorithm is used. When a node comes up, it enters the "undecided" state, starts a timer and broadcasts a Hello message. When a cluster-head gets this hello message it responds with a triggered hello message immediately. When the undecided node gets this message it sets its state to Routing Protocols for Ad Hoc Mobile Wireless Networks "member". If the undecided node times out, then it makes itself the cluster-head if it has bi-directional link to some neighbor otherwise it remains in undecided state and repeats the procedure again. Clusterheads are changed as infrequently as possible. Each node maintains a neighbor table. For each neighbor, the neighbor table of a node contains the status of the link (uni- or bi-directional) and the state of the neighbor (cluster-head or member). A cluster-head keeps information about the members of its cluster and also maintains a cluster adjacency table that contains information about the neighboring clusters. For each neighbor cluster, the table has entry that contains the gateway through which the cluster can be reached and the cluster-head of the cluster. When a source has to send data to destination, it floods route request packets (but only to the neighboring cluster-heads). On receiving the request a cluster-head checks to see if the destination is in its cluster. If yes, then it sends the request directly to the destination else it sends it to all its adjacent cluster-heads. The cluster-heads address is recorded in the packet so a cluster-head discards a request packet that it has already seen. When the destination receives the request packet, it replies back with the route that had been recorded in the request packet. If the source does not receive a reply within a time period, it backs off exponentially before trying to send route request again. In CBRP, routing is done using source routing. It also uses route shortening that is on receiving a source route packet, the node tries to find the farthest node in the route that is its neighbor (this could have happened due to a topology change) and sends the packet to that node thus reducing the route. While forwarding the packet if a node detects a broken link it sends back an error message to the source and then uses local repair mechanism. In local repair mechanism, when a node finds the next hop is unreachable, it checks to see if the next hop can be reached through any of its neighbor or if hop after next hop can be reached through any other neighbor. If any of the two works, the packet can be sent out over the repaired path.

***[Jiang99]** Mingliang Jiang, Jinyang Li, Y.C. Tay, "Cluster Based Routing Protocol" August 1999 IETF Draft, 27 pages. http://www.ietf.org/internet-drafts/draft-ietf-manet-cbrp-spec-01.txt

5.5.2.4. Associativity Based Routing

The Associativity Based Routing (ABR) protocol is a new approach for routing proposed in [Toh96,Toh99]*. ABR defines a new metric for routing known as the degree of association stability. It is free from loops, deadlock, and packet duplicates. In ABR, a route is selected based on associativity states of nodes. The routes thus selected are liked to be long-lived. All node generate periodic beacons to signify its existence. When a neighbor node receives a beacon, it updates its associativity tables. For every beacon received, a node increments its associativity tick with respect to the node from which it received the beacon. Association stability means connection stability of one node with respect to another node over time and space. A high value of associativity tick with respect to a node indicates a low state of node mobility, while a low value of associativity tick may indicate a high state of node mobility. Associativity ticks are reset when the neighbors of a node or the node itself move out of proximity. The fundamental objective of ABR is to find longer-lived routes for ad hoc mobile networks. The three phases of ABR are Route discovery, Route Reconstruction (RRC) and Route deletion. The route discovery phase is a broadcast query and await-reply (BQ-REPLY) cycle. The source node broadcasts a BQ message in search of nodes that have a route to the destination. A node does not forward Routing Protocols for Ad Hoc Mobile Wireless Networks a BQ request more than once. On receiving a BQ message, an intermediate node appends its address and its associativity ticks to the query packet. The next succeeding node erases its upstream node neighbors' associativity tick entries and retains only the entry concerned with itself and its upstream node. Each packet arriving at the destination will contain the associativity ticks of the nodes along the route from source to the destination. The destination can now select the best route by examining the associativity ticks along each of the paths. If multiple paths have the same overall degree of association stability, the route with the minimum number of hops is selected. Once a path has been chosen, the destination sends a REPLY packet back to the source along this path. The nodes on the path that the REPLY packet follows mark their routes as valid. All other routes remain inactive, thus avoiding the chance of duplicate packets arriving at the destination. RRC phase consists of partial route discovery, invalid route erasure, valid route updates, and new route discovery, depending on which node(s) along the route move. Source node movement results in a new BQ-REPLY process because the routing protocol is source-initiated. The Route Notification (RN) message is used to erase the route entries associated with downstream nodes. When the destination moves, the destination's immediate upstream node erases its route. A localized query (LQ [H]) process, where H refers to the hop count from the upstream node to the destination, is initiated to determine if the node is still reachable. If the destination receives the LQ packet, it selects the best partial route and REPLYs; otherwise, the initiating node times out and backtracks to the next upstream node. An RN message is sent to the next upstream node to erase the invalid route and inform this node that it should invoke the LQ [H] process. If this process results in backtracking more than halfway to the source, the LQ process is discontinued and the source initiates a new BQ process. When a discovered route is no longer needed, the source node initiates a route delete (RD) broadcast. All nodes along the route delete the route entry from their routing tables. The RD message is propagated by a full broadcast, as opposed to a directed broadcast, because the source node may not be aware of any route node changes that occurred during RRCs.

***[Toh96]** Chai-Keong Toh, "A novel distributed routing protocol to support Ad hoc mobile computing" Proc. 1996 IEEE 15th Annual Int'l. Phoenix Conf. Comp. and Commun., Mar. 1996, pp. 480-86.

***[Toh99]** C.-K. Toh, "Long-lived Ad-Hoc Routing based on the concept of Associativity" March 1999 IETF Draft, 8 pages.

5.5.2.5. Signal Stability Routing

Signal Stability-Based Adaptive Routing protocol (SSR) presented in *[Dube97]** is an on-demand routing protocol that selects routes based on the signal strength between nodes and a node's location stability.

This route selection criterion has the effect of choosing routes that have "stronger" connectivity. SSR comprises of two cooperative protocols: the Dynamic Routing Protocol (DRP) and the Static Routing Protocol (SRP).

The DRP maintains the Signal Stability Table (SST) and Routing Table (RT). The SST stores the signal strength of neighboring nodes obtained by periodic beacons from the link layer of each neighboring node. Signal strength is either recorded as a strong or weak channel. All transmissions are received by DRP and processed. After updating the appropriate table entries, the DRP passes the packet to the SRP. The SRP passes the packet up the stack if it is the intended receiver. If not, it looks up the destination in the RT and forwards the packet. If there is no entry for the destination in the RT, it initiates a route-search process to find a route. Route-request packets are forwarded to the next hop only if they are received over strong channels and have not been previously processed (to avoid looping). The destination chooses the first arriving route-search packet to send back as it is highly likely that the packet arrived over the shortest and/or least congested path. The DRP reverses the selected route and sends a route-reply message back to the initiator of route-request. The DRP of the nodes along the path update their RTs accordingly. Route-search packets arriving at the destination have necessarily arrived on the path of strongest signal stability because the packets arriving over a weak channel are dropped at intermediate nodes. If the source times out before receiving a reply then it changes the PREF field in the header to indicate that weak channels are acceptable, since these may be the only links over which the packet can be propagated. When a link failure is detected within the network, the intermediate nodes send an error message to the source indicating which channel has failed. The source then sends an erase message to notify all nodes of the broken link and initiates a new route-search process to find a new path to the destination.

***[Dube97]** R. Dube et al., "Signal Stability based adaptive routing for Ad Hoc Mobile networks", IEEE Pers. Comm., Feb. 1997, pp. 36-45.

5.5.2.6. Temporally-Ordered Routing Algorithm

Temporally Ordered Routing Algorithm (TORA) is a distributed routing protocol. The basic underlying algorithm is one in a family referred to as link reversal algorithms. TORA is designed to minimize reaction to topological changes. A key concept in its design is that control messages are typically localized to a very small set of nodes. It guarantees that all routes are loop-free (temporary loops may form), and typically provides multiple routes for any source/destination pair. It provides only the routing mechanism and depends on Internet MANET Encapsulation Protocol

(IMEP) for other underlying functions. TORA can be separated into three basic functions: creating routes, maintaining routes, and erasing routes. The creation of routes basically assigns directions to links in an undirected network or portion of the network, building a Directed Acyclic Graph (DAG) rooted at the destination as shown in the following Fig. 5.10.

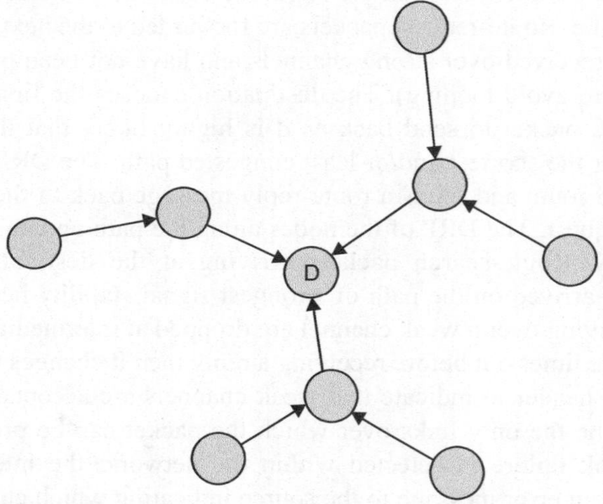

Fig. 5.10 : Directed acyclic graph rooted at destination.

TORA associates a height with each node in the network. All messages in the network flow downstream, from a node with higher height to a node with lower height. Routes are discovered using Query (QRY) and Update (UPD) packets. When a node with no downstream links needs a route to a destination, it will broadcast a QRY packet. This QRY packet will propagate through the network until it reaches a node that has a route or the destination itself. Such a node will then broadcast a UPD packet that contains the node height. Every node receiving this UPD packet will set its own height .to a larger height than specified in the UPD message. The node will then broadcast its own UPD packet. This will result in a number of directed links from the originator of the QRY packet to the destination. This process can result in multiple routes. Maintaining routes refers to reacting to topological changes in the network in a manner such that routes to the destination are re-established within a finite time, meaning that its directed portions return to a destination-oriented graph within a finite time. Upon detection of a network partition, all links in the portion of the network that has become partitioned from the destination are marked as undirected to erase invalid routes. The erasing of routes is done using clear (CLR) messages.

5.5.2.6.1. Properties

The protocols underlying link reversal algorithm will react to link changes through a simple localized single pass of the distributed algorithm. This prevents CLR packets to propagate too far in the network. A comparison made by the CMU Monarch project has however shown that the overhead in TORA is quite large because of the use of IMEP. The graph is rooted at the destination, which has the lowest height. However, the source originating the QRY does not necessarily have the highest height. This can lead to the situation, where multiple routes are possible from the source to the destination, but only one route will be discovered. The reason for this is that the height is initially based on the distance in number of hops from the destination.

5.5.2.7. Internet MANET Encapsulation Protocol

Internet MANET Encapsulation Protocol (IMEP) is a protocol designed to support the operation of many routing protocols in Ad-hoc networks. The idea is to have a common general protocol that all routing protocols can make use of (see Fig. 5.11). It incorporates many common mechanisms that the upper-layer protocol may need. These include:

- Link status sensing
- Control message aggregation and encapsulation
- Broadcast reliability
- Network-layer address resolution
- Hooks for inter router security authentication procedures

IMEP also provides an architecture for MANET router identification, interface identification and addressing. IMEPs purpose is to improve overall performance by reducing the number of control messages and to put common functionality into one unified, generic protocol useful to all upper-level routing.

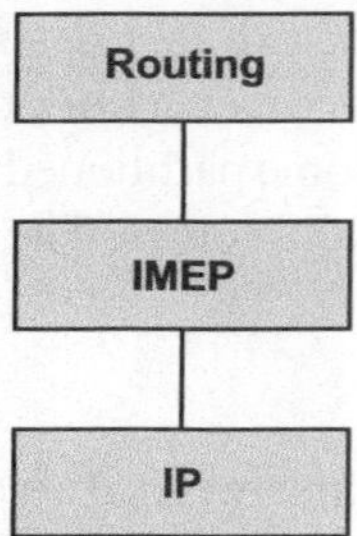

Fig. 5.11: IMEP in the protocol-stack.

Of the currently purposed protocols, only TORA and OLSR use IMEP.

5.5.2.7.1.Properties

The idea to have a general protocol for common basic features is good, but from a performance point of view this is not such a good idea. It adds another layer to the protocol stack. IMEP generates a lot of overhead, mainly because of IMEPs neighbor discovery mechanism that generates at least one hello message per second, but also because of the reliable in-order delivery of the packets that IMEP provides.

5.5.3. Hybrid Routing Protocols

Based on proactive and reactive routing protocols, some hybrid routing protocols are proposed to combine their advantages. The most typical hybrid one is Zone Routing Protocol.

5.5.3.1. Zone Routing Protocol

Zone Routing Protocol (ZRP) is a framework of hybrid routing protocol suites, which is made up following modules:

- Intrazone routing protocol
- Interzone routing protocol
- Bordercast resolution protocol

In ZRP, every node has a zone, which is defined to be the nodes within the distance of n hops (n configurable parameter). Within the zone, intra-zone routing protocol, which is a proactive protocol, is adopted maintain the local topology. When the route between different zones is needed, Intra-zone routing protocol, which a reactive protocol, is used to find the path between the source and destination. Bordercast is an efficient broadcast technique, which reduce the number of redundant forwarding in route discovery of inter-zone routing protocol. Fig. 5.12 illustrates the different components of ZRP.

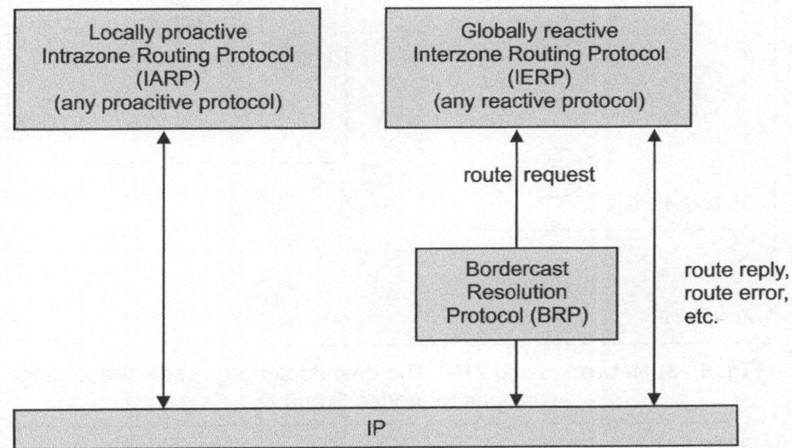

Fig. 5.12: Different Components of the Zone Routing Protocol

Routing Zone

A routing zone is defined as a set of nodes, within a specific minimum distance in number of hops from the node in question. The distance is referred to as the zone radius. In the example network (Fig. 5.13), node S, A, F, B, C, G and H, all lie within a radius of two from node F. Even though node B also has a distance on hops from node F, it is included in the zone since the shortest distance is only 2 hops. Border nodes or peripheral nodes are nodes whose minimum distance to the node in question is equal exactly to the zone radius. In Fig. 5.13, nodes B and F are border nodes to S.

Consider the network in Fig. 5.13. Node S wants to send a packet to node D. Since node D is not in the routing zone of S, a route request is sent to the border nodes B and F; Each border node checks to see if D is in their routing zone. Neither B nor F finds the requested node in their routing zone; thus the request is forwarded to the respectively border nodes. F sends the request to S, B, C and H while B sends the request to S, F, E and G. Now the requested node D is found within the routing zone of both C and E thus a reply is generated and sent back towards the source node S.

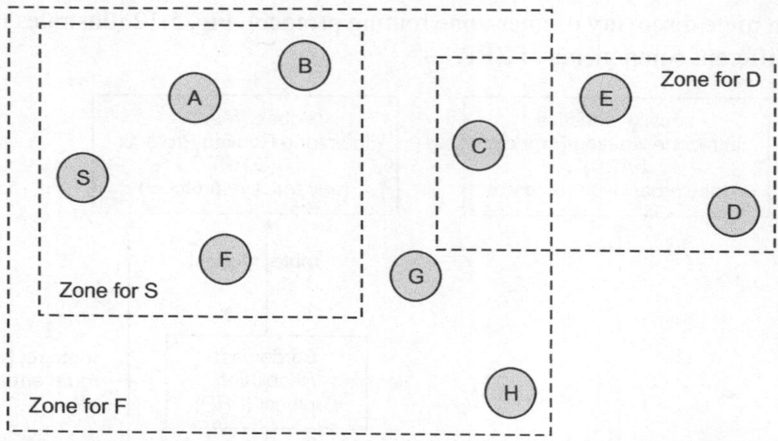

Fig. 5.13: Network-using ZRP. The dashed squares show the routing zones for nodes S and D.

ZRP is a very interesting protocol and can be adjusted of its operation to the current network operational conditions (e.g. change the routing *zone diameter*). *However this is not* done *dynamically*, but instead it is suggested that this zone radius should be set by the administration of the network or with a default value by the manufacturer. The performance of this protocol depends quite a lot on this decision. Since this is a hybrid between proactive and reactive schemes, this protocol use advantages from both. Routes can be found very fast within the routing zone, while routes outside the zone can be found by efficiently querying selected nodes in the network. One problem is however that the proactive intrazone routing protocol is not specified. The use of different intrazone routing protocols would mean that the nodes would have to support several different routing protocols. This is not a good idea when dealing with thin clients. It is better to use the same intrazone routing protocol in the entire network. ZRP also limits propagation of information about topological changes to the neighborhood of the change only (as opposed to a fully proactive scheme, which would basically flood the entire network when a change in topology occurred). However, a change in topology can affect several routing zones.

The advantages of ZRP are obvious:

- Because intra-zone routing protocol is proactive, the route towards the node within the zone is available before it's needed, thus the delay and overhead of route discovery is avoided.

- Because the periodic broadcast of topology information is confined within the zone, the change of status at one end of the network will not affect the other end of the network.
- The path between different zones is build on demand, which saves the overhead of periodic broadcast of topology information throughout the MANET, as what proactive routing protocols do;
- Proactive intrazone routing protocol helps the route maintenance of reactive interzone routing protocol. The broken link can be bypassed with the aid of local topology information, and route optimization can be achieved within the zone;
- Local topology information obtained from intrazone routing protocol helps efficient forwarding of broadcast packets, which transmits the packet from covered area of the network to uncovered part. The radius of the zone is a configurable parameter. Different zones may have different radii. With properly configured zone radius, ZRP will outperform both proactive routing protocols and reactive routing protocols.

5.6. SECURITY IN AD HOC NETWORKS

Mobile ad-hoc network is a relatively new innovation in the field of wireless technology. These types of networks operate in the absence of fixed infrastructure, which makes them easy to deploy at any place and at any time. The absence of any fixed infrastructure in mobile ad-hoc networks makes it difficult to utilize the existing techniques for network services, and poses number of various challenges in the area. Typical challenges include routing, bandwidth constraints, security and power.

Security is one of the important aspects of this technology and it needs some serious attention. Users within the network want their communication to be secure. As current mobile ad-hoc networks do not have any strict security policy, this could possibly lead active attackers to easily exploit or possibly disable the mobile ad-hoc network.

Mobile ad-hoc networks are highly dynamic; topology changes and link breakage happen quite frequently. Therefore, we need a security solution, which is dynamic, too. Any malicious or misbehaving nodes can generate hostile attacks. These types of attacks can seriously damage basic aspects of security, such as integrity, confidentiality and privacy of the node. Current ad-hoc routing protocols are completely insecure. Moreover, existing secure routing mechanisms are either too expensive or have unrealistic requirements.

Security requirements for ad-hoc routing protocols includes:

- Certain discovery, meaning the route should always be found if it exits between two nodes;
- Isolating misbehaving nodes, making sure misbehaving nodes should always be identified and isolated from routing; and
- Location privacy, protecting information about node location and network structure.

5.6.1. Attacks in Ad-hoc Routing Protocols

An ***active attack*** injects arbitrary packets and tries to disrupt the operation of the protocol in order to limit the availability, gain authentication, or attract packets destined or other nodes.

A **passive attack** does not disrupt the operation of the protocol, but tries to discover valuable information by listening to traffic.

Incorrect traffic generation includes attacks which consist in sending false control messages i.e. control messages sent on behalf of another node (identity spoofing),or control messages which contain incorrect or outdated routing information. The consequences of this attack are degradation in network communications, unreachable nodes and possible routing loops.

Incorrect traffic relaying disrupts network communications coming from legitimate, protocol compliant nodes that are polluted by misbehaving nodes.

In conclusion, most of the proposed routing solutions are, as yet, incomplete when it comes to security issues. We can trust a routing mechanism only when it guarantees that all transmission will be protected. Rather than treating these problems on individual basis, we'll need to work out routing along with security in mobile ad-hoc network designs going into the future.

5.6.2. Security Implementation Issues in MANETs

Securing wireless ad hoc networks is particularly difficult for many reasons including the following:

5.6.2.1. Vulnerability of Channels

As in any wireless network, messages can be eavesdropped and fake messages can be injected into the network without the difficulty of having physical access to network components.

5.6.2.2. Vulnerability of Nodes

Since the network nodes usually do not reside in physically protected places, such as locked rooms, they can more easily be captured and fall under the control of an attacker.

5.6.2.3. Absence of Infrastructure

Ad hoc networks are supposed to operate independently of any fixed infrastructure. This makes the classical security solutions based on certification authorities and on-line servers inapplicable.

5.6.2.4. Dynamically Changing Topology

In mobile ad hoc networks, the permanent changes of topology require sophisticated routing protocols, the security of which is an additional challenge. A particular difficulty is that incorrect routing information can be generated by compromised nodes or as a result of some topology changes and it is hard to distinguish between the two cases.

ANNEXURE-5A

List of Some Ad-hoc Routing Protocols

An **Ad hoc routing protocol** is a convention or standard that controls how nodes come to agree which way to route packets between computing devices in a mobile ad-hoc network (MANET).

In *ad hoc networks*, nodes do not have *a priori* knowledge of topology of network around them, they have to discover it. The basic idea is that a new node (optionally) announces its presence and listens to broadcast announcements from its neighbours. The node learns about new near nodes and ways to reach them, and may announce that it can also reach those nodes. As time goes on, each node knows about all other nodes and one or more ways how to reach them.

The following is a list of some ad-hoc network routing protocols:

1. Pro-active Routing (Table-driven)

2. Reactive Routing (On-demand)
3. Flow Oriented Routing
4. Adaptive Routing (Situation-Aware)
5. Hybrid (Pro-Active/Reactive)
6. Hierarchical Routing Protocols
7. Geographical Routing Protocols
8. Power Aware Routing Protocols
9. Multicast Routing
10. Geographical Multicast Protocols (Geocasting)

Pro-active Routing (Table-driven)

This type of protocols maintains fresh lists of destinations and their routes by periodically distributing routing tables throughout the network. The main disadvantages of such algorithms are -

1. Respective amount of data for maintenance.
2. Slow reaction on restructuring and failures.

Examples of proactive algorithms are -

- AWDS (Ad-hoc Wireless Distribution Service) - *Layer 2 wireless mesh routing protocol*,
- Babel, a protocol inspired by DSDV with faster convergence and ETX link quality estimation.
- CGSR (Clusterhead Gateway Switch Routing protocol) - *CHING-CHUAN CHIANG, HSIAO-KUANG WU, WINSTON LIU, MARIO GERLA Routing in Clustered Multihop, Mobile Wireless Networks with Fading Channel, IEEE Singapore International Conference on Networks, SICON'97, pp. 197-211, Singapore, 16.-17. April 1997, IEEE*
- DFR ("Direction" Forward Routing) - YENG-ZHONG LEE, MARIO GERLA, JASON CHEN, JIWEI CHEN, BIAO ZHOU AND ANTONIO CARUSO, Ad Hoc & Sensor Wireless Networks, Volume 2, Number 2, 2006.
- DBF (Distributed Bellman-Ford Routing Protocol) - *DIMITRI P. BERTSEKAS, ROBERT G. GALLAGER, Distributed Asynchronous Bellman-Ford Algorithm, Data Networks, pp. 325-333, Prentice Hall, Enlgewood Cliffs, 1987, ISBN 0-13-196825-4*

- DSDV (Highly Dynamic Destination-Sequenced Distance Vector routing protocol) - *C. E. PERKINS, P. BHAGWAT Highly Dynamic Destination-Sequenced Distance Vector (DSDV) for Mobile Computers Proc. of the SIGCOMM 1994 Conference on Communications Architectures, Protocols and Applications, Aug 1994, pp 234-244.*
- Guesswork - *TOM PARKER AND KOEN LANGENDOEN, Guesswork: Robust Routing in an Uncertain World, 2nd IEEE International Conference on Mobile Ad-hoc and Sensor Systems (MASS 2005), November 2005*
- HSR (Hierarchical State Routing protocol) - *ALAN O'NEILL HONGYI LI HIERARCHICAL STATE ROUTING PROTOCOL Internet Draft,*
- IARP (Intrazone Routing Protocol/pro-active part of the ZRP) - *ZYGMUNT J. HAAS, MARC R. PEARLMAN, PRINCE SAMAR The Intrazone Routing Protocol (IARP) for Ad Hoc Networks, Internet Draft,*
- LCA (Linked Cluster Architecture) - *M. GERLA, J. T. TSAI Multicluster, Mobile, Multimedia Radio Network ACM Wireless Networks, VOl 1, No.3, 1995, pp. 255-265*
- MMRP (Mobile Mesh Routing Protocol) - *K. GRACE Mobile Mesh Routing Protocol (MMRP*
- OLSR (Optimized Link State Routing Protocol) - *PHILIPPE JACQUET, PAUL MUHLETHALER, AMIR QAYYUM, ANIS LAOUITI, LAURENT VIENNOT, THOMAS CLAUSEN Optimized Link State Routing Protocol (OLSR), RFC 3626*
- TBRPF (Topology Dissemination based on Reverse-Path Forwarding routing protocol) - *BHARGAV BELLUR, RICHARD G. OGIER, FRED L. TEMPLIN Topology Dissemination Based on Reverse-Path Forwarding (TBRPF), RFC 3684, February 2004.*
- WAR (Witness Aided Routing) - Aron, I.D. and Gupta, S., 1999, "A Witness-Aided Routing Protocol for Mobile Ad-Hoc Networks with Unidirectional Links", Proc. of the First International Conference on Mobile Data Access, p.24-33.
- WRP (Wireless Routing Protocol) - *SHREE MURTHY, J.J. GARCIA-LUNA-AVECES A Routing Protocol for Packet Radio Networks, Proc. ACM International Conference on Mobile*

Computing and Networking, pp. 86-95, November, 1995. Citeseer: murthy95routing;

- SHREE MURTHY, J.J. GARCIA-LUNA-AVECES, An Efficient Routing Protocol for Wireless Networks, AACM/Baltzer Journal on Mobile Networks and Applications, Special Issue on Routing in Mobile Communication Networks, Vol. 1, No. 2, pp 183-197, ACM, October 1996

Reactive Routing (On-demand)

This type of protocols finds a route on demand by flooding the network with Route Request packets. The main disadvantages of such algorithms are-

1. High latency time in route finding.
2. Excessive flooding can lead to network clogging.

Example of reactive algorithms are -

- Multirate Ad-hoc On-demand Distance Vector Routing Protocol - *R. Guimaraes and Ll. Cerda*, Improving reactive routing on wireless multirate ad-hoc networks, In: Proceedings of 13th European Wireless 2007, https://upcommons.upc.edu/e-prints/bitstream/2117/1173/1/mr-aodv.pdf
- Reliable Ad-hoc On-demand Distance Vector Routing Protocol - *Sandhya Khurana, Neelima Gupta, Nagender Aneja,*
- Minimum Exposed Path to the Attack (MEPA) in Mobile Adhoc Network (MANET) - *Sandhya Khurana, Neelima Gupta, Nagender Aneja*
- Ant-based Routing Algorithm for Mobile Ad-Hoc Networks - *Mesuț Günes et al.*, ARA - the ant-colony based routing algorithm for manets, In Stephan Olariu, editor, Proceedings of the 2002 ICPP Workshop on Ad Hoc Networks (IWAHN 2002), pages 79-85, IEEE Computer Society Press,
- Admission Control enabled On demand Routing (ACOR) - *N. Kettaf, A. Abouaissa, T. Vuduong and P. Lorenz, (draft-kettaf-manet-acor-00.txt), July 2006,*
- Ariadne - *Y. Chu, A. Perrig, D. Johnson, Ariadne: A Secure On-Demand Routing Protocol for Ad Hoc Networks, Proc. ACM Conf. Mobile Computing and Networking (MobiCom), 2002.*
- Associativity-Based Routing - *CHAI-KEONG TOH: A Novel*

Distributed Routing Protocol To Support Ad hoc Mobile Computing, Proc. IEEE 15th Annual International Phoenix Conference on Computers and Communications, IEEE IPCCC 1996, 27 March-29, Phoenix, AZ, USA, pp. 480-486 / CHAI-KEONG TOH: Long-lived Ad Hoc Routing based on the Concept of Associativity, Internet Draft, March 1999

- Ad-hoc On-demand Distance Vector - *C. PERKINS, E.ROYER AND S. DAS Ad hoc On-demand Distance Vector (AODV) Routing, RFC 3561*
- Ad-hoc On-demand Multipath Distance Vector - *M. Marina, S. Das: On-demand Multipath Distance Vector Routing in Ad Hoc Networks, Proceedings of the 2001 IEEE International Conference on Network Protocols (ICNP), pages 14—23, IEEE Computer Society Press, 2001.*
- Backup Source Routing - *SONG GUO, OLIVER W. YANG Performance of Backup Source Routing (BSR) in mobile ad hoc networks p 440-444, Proc. 2002 IEEE Wireless Networking Conference*
- CHAMP - CacHing And MultiPath routing - ALVIN C. VALERA, WINSTON K.G. SEAH AND S.V. RAO, *Cooperative Packet Caching and Shortest Multipath Routing in Mobile Ad hoc Networks*, Proceedings of 22nd Annual Joint Conference of the IEEE Computer and Communications Societies (INFOCOM 2003), Mar 30-Apr 3, 2003
- Dynamic Source Routing - *DAVID JOHNSON, DAVID MALTZ, YIH-CHUN HU: The Dynamic Source Routing Protocol for Mobile Ad Hoc Networks for IPv4, RFC 4728 / DAVID B. JOHNSON, DAVID A. MALTZ: Dynamic Source Routing in Ad Hoc Wireless Networks, Mobile Computing, Thomasz Imielinski and Hank Korth (Editors), Vol. 353, Chapter 5, pp. 153-181, Kluwer Academic Publishers, 1996*
- Flow State in the Dynamic Source Routing - *YIH-CHUN HU, DAVID B. JOHNSON, DAVID A. MALTZ Flow State in the Dynamic Source Routing Protocol Internet Draft, draft-ietf- manet-dsrflow-00.txt,*
- Dynamic NIx-Vector Routing - *Young J. Lee and George F. Riley, Dynamic NIx-Vector Routing for Mobile Ad Hoc Networks.*

Proceedings of the IEEE Wireless Communications and Networking Conference (WCNC 2005), New Orleans, Mar. 13 - 17, 2005.

- Dynamic Manet On-demand Routing - *I. Chakeres AND C. Perkins: Dynamic MANET On-demand Routing Protocol (DYMO), Internet Draft, draft-ietf-manet-dymo-04.txt,*
- Mobile Ad-hoc On-Demand Data Delivery Protocol - *Humayun Bakht and Others: Mobile Ad-hoc On-Demand Data Delivery Protocol (MAODDP),*

Flow Oriented Routing

This type of protocols finds a route on demand by following present flows. One option is to unicast consecutively when forwarding data while promoting a new link The main disadvantages of such algorithms are -

1. Takes long time when exploring new routes without a priori knowledge.
2. May refer to entitative existing traffic to compensate for missing knowledge on routes.

Examples of flow oriented algorithms are -

- GB (Gafni-Bertsekas), *E. Gafni, D. Bertsekas: Distributed Algorithms for Generating Loop-free Routes in Networks with Frequently Changing Topology, IEEE Transactions on Communication, Vol. 29, No. 1, Jan, 1981, pp.11-15. The first Link Reversal Routing (LRR) algorithm.*
- IERP (Interzone Routing Protocol/reactive part of the ZRP) - *ZYGMUNT J. HAAS, MARC R. PEARLMAN, PRINCE SAMAR The Interzone Routing Protocol (IERP) for Ad Hoc Networks, Internet Draft,*
- LBR (Link life Based routing), *B. S. Manoj, R. Ananthapadmanabha, and C. Siva Ram Murthy, "Link life Based Routing Protocol for Ad hoc Wireless Networks", Proc. of The 10th IEEE International Conference on Computer Communications 2001 (IC3N 2001), October 2001.*
- LMR (Lightweight Mobile Routing protocol) - *M.S. CORSON AND A. EPHREMIDES Lightweight Mobile Routing protocol (LMR), A distributed routing algorithm for mobile wireless networks, Wireless Networks 1 (1995).A Link Reversal Routing*

(LRR) algorithm.

- LQSR (Link Quality Source Routing) - Microsoft Version of DSR with Link Quality Metrics,
- LUNAR (Lightweight Underlay Network Ad hoc Routing) - *CHRISTIAN TSCHUDIN AND RICHARD GOLD Lightweight Underlay Network Ad hoc Routing (LUNAR)*
- MOR - Multipath On-demand Routing Protocol, *Biagioni and Chen, A reliability layer for ad-hoc wireless sensor network routing,*
- MPRDV (Multipoint Relay Distance Vector protocol) - *Géraud Allard, Philippe Jacquet and Laurent Viennot. "Ad hoc routing with multipoint relaying",*
- QuaSAR (QoS aware source initiated ad-hoc routing) - QuaSAR has both reactive and proactive mechanisms that aim to diminish the communication disruption time experienced in highly mobile ad-hoc networks. *Knut-Helge Vik and Sirisha Medidi, "Quality of Service aware source initiated ad-hoc routing", 1st IEEE International Conference on Sensor and Ad hoc Communications and Networks; Santa Clara, CA, USA; October 2004.*
- RDMAR (Relative-Distance Micro-discovery Ad hoc Routing protocol) - *G. AGGELOU, R. TAFAZOLLI Relative Distance Micro-discovery Ad Hoc Routing (RDMAR) protocol Internet Draft, draft-ietf-manet- rdmar-00.txt, work in progress, September 1999.*
- SrcRR DSR and ETX based, optimized for performance *D. AGUAYO, J. BICKET, R. MORRIS, "SrcRR: A High-Throughput Routing Protocol for 802.11 Mesh Networks (DRAFT)",*
- SSR (Signal Stability Routing protocol) - *R. DUBE, C. D. RAIS, K. WANG, AND S. K. TRIPATHI Signal Stability based adaptive routing (SSR alt SSA) for ad hoc mobile networks, IEEE Personal Communication, Feb. 1997.*
- PLBR (Preferred link based routing) — *R. S. Sisodia, B. S. Manoj, and C. Siva Ram Murthy, "A Preferred Link Based Routing Protocol for Ad Hoc Wireless Networks", Journal of Communications and Networks, Vol. 4, No. 1, pp. 14-21, March 2002*

Adaptive Routing (Situation-Aware)

This type of protocols combines the advantages of proactive and of reactive routing. The routing is initially established with some proactively prospected routes and then serves the demand from additionally activated nodes through reactive flooding. Some metrics must support the choice of reaction. The main disadvantages of such algorithms are

1. Advantage depends on amount of nodes activated.
2. Reaction to traffic demand depends on gradient of traffic volume.

Example of adaptive algorithms is:

TORA (Temporally-Ordered Routing Algorithm routing protocol) *V. Park, S. Corson: Temporally-Ordered Routing Algorithm (TORA) Version 1, Functional Specification, Internet Draft, IETF MANET Working Group, June 2001, A Link Reversal Routing (LRR) algorithm.*

Hybrid (Pro-Active/Reactive)

This type of protocols combines the advantages of proactive and of reactive routing. The routing is initially established with some proactively prospected routes and then serves the demand from additionally activated nodes through reactive flooding. The choice for one or the other method requires predetermination for typical cases. The main disadvantages of such algorithms are:

1. Advantage depends on amount of nodes activated.
2. Reaction to traffic demand depends on gradient of traffic volume.

Examples of hybrid algorithms are:

- ARPAM, specialized for aeronautical MANETs.
- HRPLS (Hybrid Routing Protocol for Large Scale Mobile Ad Hoc Networks with Mobile Backbones) - *Ashish Pandey, Md. Nasir Ahmed, Nilesh Kumar, P. Gupta: A Hybrid Routing Scheme for Mobile Ad Hoc Networks with Mobile Backbones, IEEE International Conference on High Performance Computing, HIPC 2006, pp. 411-423, Dec 2006.*
- HSLS (Hazy Sighted Link State routing protocol) - Uses a mathematical optimization to mix link state and reactive routing to optimize network data updates in space and time, *CESAR SANTIVANEZ AND RAM RAMANATHAN Hazy Sighted Link State routing protocol (HSLS), BBN Technical Memorandum No. 1301, 31 August 2001. There's an open-source version.*

- OORP (OrderOne Routing Protocol) - proactive/reactive distance vector combined with a hierarchy that is not used to route data.
- ZRP (Zone Routing Protocol) - ZYGMUNT J. HAAS, MARC R. PEARLMAN, PRINCE SAMAR The Zone Routing Protocol (ZRP) for Ad Hoc Networks, Internet Draft, Hierarchical Routing Protocols

With this type of protocols the choice of proactive and of reactive routing depends on the hierarchic level where a node resides. The routing is initially established with some proactively prospected routes and then serves the demand from additionally activated nodes through reactive flooding on the lower levels. The choice for one or the other method requires proper attributation for respective levels. The main disadvantages of such algorithms are:

1. Advantage depends on depth of nesting and addressing scheme.
2. Reaction to traffic demand depends on meshing parameters.

Examples of hierarchical routing algorithms are:

- CBRP (Cluster Based Routing Protocol) - *M. JIANG, J. LI, Y. C. TAY Cluster Based Routing Protocol (CBRP) Functional Specification Internet Draft,*
- CEDAR (Core Extraction Distributed Ad hoc Routing) - *RAGHUPATHY SIVAKUMAR, PRASUN SINHA, VADUVUR BHARGHAVAN Core Extraction Distributed Ad hoc Routing (CEDAR) Specification, Internet Draft, draft-ietf-manet-cedar-spec-00.txt;*
- *PRASUN SINHA, RAGHUPATHY SIVAKUMAR, VADUVUR BHARGHAVAN CEDAR: A Core-Extraction Distributed Ad Hoc Routing Algorithm, The 18th Annual Joint Conference of the IEEE Computer and Communications Societies, INFOCOM '99 New York, NY, USA, pp. 202-209 IEEE, March 1999*
- DART (Dynamic Address Routing) - *JAKOB ERIKSSON, MICHALIS FALOUTSOS, SRIKANTH KRISHNAMURTHY Scalable Ad Hoc Routing: The Case for Dynamic Addressing, in proceedings of INFOCOM 2004.*
- DDR (Distributed Dynamic Routing Algorithm) - *NAVID NIKAEIN, HOUDA LABIOD, CHRISTIAN BONNET Distributed Dynamic Routing Algorithm (DDR) for Mobile Ad Hoc Networks, in proceedings of the MobiHOC 2000 : First Annual Workshop on Mobile Ad Hoc Networking & Computing*

- FSR (Fisheye State Routing protocol) - *MARIO GERLA, GUANGYU PEI, XIAOYAN HONG, TSU-WEI CHEN Fisheye State Routing Protocol (FSR) for Ad Hoc Networks Internet Draft, draft-ietf-manet-fsr-00.txt,*
- GSR (Global State Routing protocol) - *Global State Routing protocol (GSR) [Chen98] Tsu-Wei Chen and Mario Gerla, "Global State Routing: A New Routing Scheme for Ad-hoc Wireless Networks" Proc. IEEE ICC'98, Atlanta, GA, USA, June 1998, pp. 171-175.*
- HARP (Hybrid Ad Hoc Routing Protocol) - *NAVID NIKAEIN, CHRISTIAN BONNET, NEDA NIKAEIN Hybrid Ad Hoc Routing Protocol - HARP, in proceeding of IST 2001: International Symposium on Telecommunications*
- HSR (Host Specific Routing protocols)

This type of protocols requires thorough administration to tailor the routing to a certain network layout and a distinct flow strategy. The main disadvantages of such algorithms are -

1. Advantage depends on quality of administration addressing scheme.
2. Proper reaction to changes in topology demands reconsidering all parametrizing.

- HSR (Hierarchical State Routing) - *Scalable Routing Strategies for Ad Hoc Wireless Networks*
- LANMAR (Landmark Routing Protocol for Large Scale Networks) - *MARIO GERLA, XIAOYAN HONG, LI MA, GUANGYU PEI Landmark Routing Protocol (LANMAR) Internet Draft, draft-ietf-manet- lanmar-01.txt, June 2001.*
- ATR (Augmented Tree-based Routing) - *MARCELLO CALEFFI, GIANCARLO FERRAIUOLO, LUIGI PAURA Augmented Tree-based Routing Protocol for Scalable Ad Hoc Networks, in proceedings of MHWMN 2007: The Third IEEE International Workshop on Heterogeneous Multi-Hop Wireless and Mobile*

Geographical Routing Protocols

This type of protocols acknowledges the influence of physical distances and distribution of nodes to areas as significant to network performance. The main disadvantages of such algorithms are:

1. Efficiency depends on balancing the geographic distribution versus occurrence of traffic.
2. Any dependence of performance with traffic load thwarting the negligence of distance may occur in overload.
   - ALARM (Adaptive Location Aided Routing Protocol - Mines) - *J. Boleng and T. Camp, Adaptive Location Aided Mobile Ad Hoc Network Routing, Proceedings of the 23rd IEEE International Performance, Computing, and Communications Conference (IPCCC '04), pp. 423-432, 2004.*
   - BGR (Blind Geographic Routing) - *MATTHIAS WITT, VOLKER TURAU BGR: Blind Geographic Routing for Sensor Networks. In Proceedings of the Third Workshop on Intelligent Solutions in Embedded Systems (WISES'05). Hamburg, Germany, May 20, 2005.*
   - DREAM (Distance Routing Effect Algorithm for Mobility) - *S. BASAGNI, I. CHLAMTAC, V. R. SYROTIUK, B. A. WOODWARD A Distance Routing Effect Algorithm for Mobility (DREAM) In Proc. ACM/IEEE Mobicom, pages 76-84, October 1998.*
   - GLS(Grid) (Geographic Location Service) - *JINYANG LI, JOHN JANOTTI, DOUGLAS S. J. DE COUTU, DAVID R. KARGER, ROBERT MORRIS A Scalable Location Service for Geographic Ad Hoc Routing M.I.T. Laboratory for Computer Science*
   - LAR (Location-Aided Routing protocol) - *Y.-B. KO, V. N. H. Location-Aided Routing in mobile Ad hoc networks In Proc. ACM/IEEE Mobicom, pages 66-75, October 1998.*
   - GPSAL (GPS Ant-Like Routing Algorithm) - *Daniel Câmara, Antonio Alfredo F. Loureiro, A Novel Routing Algorithm for Hoc Networks, Baltzer Journal of Telecommunications Systems, 18:1-3, 85-100, Kluwer Academic Publishers, 2001.*
   - ZHLS (Zone-Based Hierarchical Link State Routing) - *JOA NG, I-TAI LU Zone-Based Hierchical Link State Routing (ZHLS). An abstract routing protocol and medium access protocol for mobile ad hoc networks Submitted for partial fulfillment of the requirements for the degree of doctor of philosophy (Electrical engineering) in January 1999.*

- *MARIO JOA-NG, I-TAI-LU A Peer-to-Peer Zone-Based Two-Level Link State Routing for Mobile Ad Hoc Networks, IEEE Journal on Selected Areas In Communication, Vol. 17, No. 8, pp. 1415-1425, August 1999*. A improving approach can be find in ZHLS-GF (Zone-Based Hierarchical Link State Routing Protocol with Gateway Flooding).
- GPSR (Greedy Perimeter Stateless Routing) - *BRAD N. KARP, H. T. KUNG GPSR: Greedy Perimeter Stateless Routing for Wireless Networks, Proceedings of the sixth annual ACM/IEEE International Conference on Mobile computing and networking (MobiCom '00), pages 243-254, August 2000.*
- Greedy Face Greedy (GFG) - *Prosenjit Bose and Pat Morin and Ivan Stojmenovic and Jorge Urrutia*: Routing with guaranteed delivery in ad hoc wireless networks, DIALM '99: Proceedings of the 3rd international workshop on Discrete algorithms and methods for mobile computing and communications, Seattle, Washington, United States, pages 48-55, 1999,
- SiFT (Simple Forwarding over Trajectory) - *A. Capone, I. Filippini, M.A. Garcia de la Fuente, L. Pizziniaco, SiFT: An efficient method for Trajectory Based Forwarding, International Symposium on Wireless Communication Systems 2005 (ISWCS2005), Siena, Sept. 2005.*

Power Aware Routing Protocols

Energy required to transmit a signal is approximately proportional to d˜ , where d is the distance and $\alpha > 2$ is the attenuation factor or path loss exponent, which depends on the transmission medium. When = 2 (which is the optimal case), transmitting a signal half the distance requires one fourth of the energy and if there is a node in the middle willing spend another fourth of its energy for the second half, data would be transmitted for half of the energy than through a direct transmission - a fact that follows directly from the inverse square law of physics. The main disadvantages of such algorithms are:

1. This method induces a delay for each transmission.
2. No relevance for energy network powered transmission operated via sufficient repeater infrastructure.

- ISAIAH (Infra-Structure Aodv for Infrastructured Ad Hoc networks) - *ANDERS LINDGREN AND OLOV SCHELÉN Infrastructured ad hoc networks In Proceedings of the 2002 International Conference on Parallel Processing Workshops (International Workshop on Ad Hoc Networking (IWAHN 2002)). pages 64-70. August 2002.*
- PARO (Power-Aware Routing Optimization Protocol) - *J. GOMEZ, A. T. CAMPBELL, M. NAGHSHINEH, C. BISDIKIAN, T.J. WATSON POWER-AWARE ROUTING OPTIMIZATION PROTOCOL (PARO)*
- EADSR (Energy Aware Dynamic Source Routing Protocol) - *T.X. Brown, S. Doshi, S. Bhandare, University of Colorado-Boulder, draft-brown-eadsr-00.txt, June 2003,*
- PAMAS (PAMAS-Power Aware Multi Access Protocol with Signaling Ad Hoc Networks) - *S. SINGH, C.S. RAGHAVENDRA PAMAS & PAMAS-Power Aware Multi Access Protocol with Signaling Ad Hoc Networks*
- DSRPA (Dynamic Source Routing Power-Aware) D. Djenouri N. Badache, The International Journal of Ad Hoc and Ubiquitous Computing (IJAHUC), volume 1, number 3, pp 126-136, May 2006, Inderscience publisher.

Multicast Routing

- ABAM (On-Demand Associativity-Based Multicast) - Chai-Keong Toh, Guillermo Guichal, and Santithorn Bunchua: "On-demand associativity-based multicast routing for ad hoc mobile networks (ABAM)", In *Proc. of the 52nd IEEE VTS Vehicular Technology Conference (VTC) 2000 Fall*, vol. 3, pages 987 - 993, Boston, MA, September 2000.
- ADMR (Adaptive Demand-Driven Multicast Routing) - Jorjeta G. Jetcheva and David B. Johnson: "Adaptive Demand-Driven Multicast Routing in Multi-Hop Wireless Ad Hoc Networks", In *Proc. of the 2nd ACM International Symposium on Mobile and Ad-hoc Networking & Computing (MobiHOC)*, pages 33 - 44, Long Beach, CA, October 2001.
- AMRIS (Ad hoc Multicast Routing protocol utilizing Increasing id-numberS) - Chun Wei Wu and Yong Chiang Tay: "AMRIS: A

Multicast Protocol for Ad Hoc Wireless Networks", In *Proc. of the IEEE Military Communications Conference (MILCOM)*, pages 25 - 29, Atlantic City, NJ, November 1999.

- AMRoute (Adhoc Multicast Routing Protocol) - Mingyan Liu, Rajesh R. Talpade, Anthony McAuley, and Ethendranath Bommaiah: "AMRoute: Adhoc Multicast Routing Protocol", *University of Maryland CSHCN Technical Report 1999-1*, College Park, MD, 1999.
- AQM (Ad Hoc QoS Multicast) - Kaan Bür and Cem Ersoy: "Ad Hoc Quality of Service Multicast Routing", *Elsevier Science Computer Communications*, vol. 29, no. 1, pages 136 - 148, December 2005.
- BEMRP (Bandwidth-Efficient Multicast Routing Protocol) - T. Ozaki, Jaime Bae Kim and T. Suda: "Bandwidth-efficient multicast routing protocol for ad-hoc networks", In *Computer Communications and Networks, 1999. Proceedings. Eight International Conference*, pages 10-17, Boston, MA, September 1999.
- CAMP (Core-Assisted Mesh Protocol) - J. J. Garcia-Luna-Aceves and Ewerton L. Madruga: "The Core Assisted Mesh Protocol", *IEEE Journal on Selected Areas in Communications, Special Issue on Ad-Hoc Networks*, vol. 17, no. 8, pages 1380 - 1394, August 1999.
- CBM (Content Based Multicast) - Hu Zhou and Suresh Singh: "Content based multicast (CBM) in ad hoc networks", In *Proc. of the 1st ACM International Symposium on Mobile and Ad-hoc Networking & Computing (MobiHOC)*, pages 51 - 60, Boston, MA, August 2000.
- DCMP (Dynamic Core Based Multicast Routing Protocol) - Subir Kumar Das, B. S. Manoj, and C. Siva Ram Murthy: "A Dynamic Core Based Multicast Routing Protocol for Ad hoc Wireless Networks", In *Proc. of the 3rd ACM International Symposium on Mobile and Ad-hoc Networking & Computing (MobiHOC)*, pages 24 - 35, Lausanne, Switzerland, June 2002.
- DDM (Differential Destination Multicast) - Lusheng Ji and M. Scott Corson: "Differential Destination Multicast-A MANET Multicast Routing Protocol for Small Groups", In *Proc. of the 20th Annual Joint Conference of the IEEE Computer and*

Communications Societies (INFOCOM), pages 1192 - 1202, Anchorage, AK, April 2001.

- DSR-MB (Simple Protocol for Multicast and Broadcast using DSR) - Jorjeta G. Jetcheva, Yih-Chun Hu, David A. Maltz, and David B. Johnson: "A Simple Protocol for Multicast and Broadcast in Mobile Ad Hoc Networks", *Internet Draft draft-ietf-manet-simple-mbcast-01.txt*, July 2001.
- ExOR (wireless network protocol) - Opportunistic Multi-Hop Routing for Wireless Networks; Sanjit Biswas, Robert Morris, 2005; Uses standard 802.11 radios
- FGMP (Forwarding Group Multicast Protocol) - Ching-Chuan Chiang, Mario Gerla, and Lixia Zhang: "Forwarding Group Multicast Protocol (FGMP) for Multihop, Mobile Wireless Networks", *ACM-Baltzer Journal of Cluster Computing: Special Issue on Mobile Computing*, vol. 1, no. 2, pages 187 - 196, December 1998
- LAM (Lightweight Adaptive Multicast) - Lusheng Ji and M. Scott Corson: "A Lightweight Adaptive Multicast Algorithm", In *Proc. of the IEEE Global Telecommunications Conference (Globecom)*, pages 1036 - 1042, Sydney, Australia, November 1998.
- MAODV (Multicast Ad-hoc On-Demand Distance Vector routing) - Elizabeth M. Royer and Charles E. Perkins: "Multicast Operation of the Ad-hoc On-Demand Distance Vector Routing Protocol", In *Proc. of the 5th annual ACM/IEEE International Conference on Mobile Computing and Networking (MobiCom)*, pages 207 - 218, Seattle, WA, August 1999.
- MOLSR (Multicast Optimized Link State Routing) - Anis Laouiti, Philippe Jacquet, Pascale Minet, Laurent Viennot, Thomas Clausen, Cedric Adjih: "Multicast Optimized Link State Routing", INRIA research report,RR-4721, Feb 2003
- MCEDAR (Multicast Core-Extraction Distributed Ad hoc Routing) - Prasun Sinha, Raghupathy Sivakumar, and Vaduvur Bharghavan: "MCEDAR: Multicast Core-Extraction Distributed Ad hoc Routing", In *Proc. of the Wireless Communications and Networking Conference (WCNC)*, pages 1313 - 1317, New Orleans, LA, September 1999.

- MZR (Multicast Zone Routing) - Vijay Devarapalli, Ali A. Selcuk, and Deepinder Sidhu: "MZR: A Multicast Protocol for Mobile Ad Hoc Networks", In *Proc. of the IEEE International Conference on Communications (ICC)*, pages 886 - 891, Helsinki, Finland, June 2001.
- ODMRP (On-Demand Multicast Routing Protocol) - Sung-Ju Lee, Mario Gerla, and Ching-Chuan Chiang: "On-Demand Multicast Routing Protocol", In *Proc. of the Wireless Communications and Networking Conference (WCNC)*, pages 1298 - 1302, New Orleans, LA, September 1999.
- PUMA (Protocol for Unified Multicasting Through Announcements) - Vaishampayan, Ravindra. and Garcia-Luna-Aceves, J.J.: " Efficient and Robust Multicast Routing in Mobile Ad Hoc Networks", In *2004 IEEE International Conference on Mobile Ad-hoc and Sensor Systems*, pages 304- 313, Fort Lauderdale, FL, October 2004.
- SMF (Simplified Multicast Forwarding) - Joseph Macker, editor, SMF Design Team: "Simplified Multicast Forwarding for MANET",
- SPBM (Scalable Position-Based Multicast) - Matthias Transier, Holger Füßler, Jörg Widmer, Martin Mauve, and Wolfgang Effelsberg: "Scalable Position-Based Multicast for Mobile Ad-hoc Networks", In *Proc. of the 1st International Workshop on Broadband Wireless Multimedia: Algorithms, Architectures and Applications (BroadWim)*, San José, CA, October 2004.
- SRMP (Source Routing-based Multicast Protocol) - Hasnaa Moustafa and Houda Labiod: "SRMP: A Mesh-based Protocol for Multicast Communication in ad hoc networks", In *Proc. of the 2002 International Conference on Third Generation Wireless and Beyond*, pages 43 - 48, San Francisco, CA, May 2002.
- EraMobile (Epidemic-based Reliable and Adaptive Multicast) - Zulkuf Genc and Oznur Ozkasap: "EraMobile: Epidemic-based Reliable and Adaptive Multicast for MANETs", In *Proc. of the Wireless Communications and Networking Conference (WCNC)*, Hong Kong, China, March 2007.
- OBAMP (Overlay, Boruvka-based, Ad-hoc multicast Protocol) - Andrea Detti, Nicola Blefari-Melazzi: "Overlay, Boruvka-based,

Ad-hoc multicast Protocol: description and performance analysis", Wireless Communications and Mobile Computing, Wiley, 2008

Geographical Multicast Protocols (Geocasting)

- LBM (Location Based Multicast) - *Y.KO AND VAIDYA 1998 Location Based Multicast (LBM)*
- GeoGRID (Geographical GRID (see GLS)) - *WEN-HWA LIAO AND JANG-PING SHEU AND YU-CHEE TSENG GeoGRID & Geographical GRID: A Fully Location-Aware Routing Protocol for Mobile Ad Hoc Networks, Telecommunication Systems 2001,volume 18, number 1-3, pages 37-60*
- GeoTORA (Geographical TORA (see TORA)) - *Y. KO AND N. VAIDYA A protocol for geocasting in mobile ad hoc networks (GeoTORA) Tech. Rep. 00-010, Dept. of Computer Science, Texas A&M University, March 2000. 23*
- MRGR (Mesh-Based Geocast Routing) - *BOLENG, CAMP AND TOLETY 2001 Mesh-Based Geocast Routing (MRGR)*
- MOBICAST (Mobile Just-in-time Multicasting) - *Q. Huang, C. Lu and G-C. Roman, Mobicast: Just-in-time multicast for sensor networks under spatiotemporal constraints, Lecture Notes in Computer Science, Vol 2634, pages 442-457*
- Abiding Geocast / Stored Geocast (Time Stable Geocasting) - C. Maihöfer, T. Leinmüller, E. Schoch: Abiding Geocast: Time-Stable Geocast for Ad Hoc Networks, Second ACM International Workshop on Vehicular Ad Hoc Networks (VANET 2005), Cologne, Germany, September 2, 2005

REFERENCES

- A. Perrig, R. Canetti, J. D. Tygar, and D. X. Song, "Efficient authentication and signing of multicast streams over lossy channels", IEEE Symposium on Security and Privacy, 2000, pp 56–73.
- A.S. Dalghan, Mohamad M. Gamloush, R.M. Zeitouny, and Y.M. Shaer "Securing Mobile Ad Hoc Networks", Electrical and Computer Engineering Department American University of Beirut, Beirut – Lebanon.
- Charles E. Perkins and Elizabeth M. Belding-Royer, "Ad hoc On-

Demand Distance Vector (AODV) Routing", IETF, Internet draft, draft-ietf-manet-aodv-13.txt, 2003

- Charles E. Perkins & Pravin Bhagwat, "Highly Dynamic Destination-Sequenced Distance-Vector Routing (DSDV) for Mobile Computers", ACM SIGCOMM Symposium on Communication, Architecture and Protocols.1994. pp 234-244.
- David B. Johnson, David A. Maltz and Yih-Chun Hu, "Dynamic source Routing protocol for Mobile Ad hoc networks", IETF internet draft, draft-ietf -manet-dsr10.txt, July 2004.
- Elizabeth Royer and C-K Toh, "A Review of Current Routing Protocols for Ad-Hoc Mobile Wireless Networks", IEEE Personal Communications Magazine, April 1999, pp. 46-55.
- E. M. Royer, and C-K. Toh, "A Review of Current Routing Protocols for Ad-Hoc Mobile Wireless Networks", IEEE Personal Communications, April 1999, pp. 46-55.
- George Coulouris, Jean Dollimore and Tim Kindberg "Distributed Systems concepts and Design", 3rd Edition, Pearson Education, 2004, pp 251-289.
- Jihye Kim and Gene Tsudik, "SRDP: Securing Route Discovery in DSR", Computer Science Department University of California, Irvine.
- Josh Broch, David A. Maltz, David B. Johnson, et al. "A Performance Comparison of Multi-Hop Wireless Ad Hoc Network Routing Protocols", MOBICOM'98, October 1998.
- J. Zhen and Sampalli Srinivas, "Preventing Replay Attacks for Secure Routing in Ad Hoc Network", ADHOC-NOW 2003, LNCS 2865, pp. 140-150.
- L. Zhou and Z.J. Haas, "Securing ad hoc networks," IEEE Network, 0890-8044, November/December 1999, pp. 24-30.
- M. Guerrero Zapata and N. Asokan, "Securing Ad Hoc Routing Protocols", Proc. ACM Workshop on Wireless Security (WiSe), ACM Press, 2002, pp. 1–10.
- Mike Burmester, Tri Van Le and Matt Weir, "Tracing Byzantine Faults In Ad Hoc Networks" ,Department of Computer Science, Florida State University, Tallahassee, Florida 32306, USA.

- N.Asokan and P. Ginzboorg, "Key agreement in adhoc networks", Elsevier Science, Computer Communications 23, 0140-3664/00, PII:S0140- 3664(00)00249-8, 2000, pp.1627-1637.
- S. Marti et al. Mitigating Routing Misbehaviour in Mobile Ad Hoc Networks. Proc. 6th Ann. Int'l Conf. Mobile Computing and Networking (MobiCom 2000), ACM Press, 2000, pp. 255–265.
- T. Clausen and P. Jacquet "Optimized Link State Routing Protocol (OLSR)." RFC 3626, IETF Network Working Group, October 2003.
- Thomas Clausen and Emmanuel Baccelli, "Securing OLSR problem statement", Internet-Draft, draft-clausen-manet-solsr-ps-00.txt. IETF MANET Working Group, February 14, 2005.
- William Stallings, Cryptography and Network Security, 2nd Edition, 1999, Chapter 13, 403.
- Y.-C. Hu, A.Perrig, and D.B. Johnson.Ariadne, "A secure on-demand routing protocol for ad hoc networks", MOBICOM, 2002.
- Y.C. Hu, D.B. Hohnson, and A. Perrig. SEAD: "Secure Efficient Distance Vector Routing in Mobile Wireless Ad Hoc Networks." Proceedings of 4th IEEE Workshop on Mobile Computing Systems and Applications (WMCSA 02), IEEE Press, 2002, pp.3-13
- Zygmunt J. Haas, Marc R. Pearlman, and Prince Samar, "The Zone Routing Protocol (ZRP) for Ad Hoc Networks", draft-ietf-manet-zone-zrp-04.txt, July, 2002.
- Elizabeth M. Royer, Chai-Keong Toh, "A Review of Current Routing Protocols for Ad Hoc Mobile Wireless Networks", IEEE Personal Communications, Vol. 6, No. 2, pp. 46-55, April 1999.
- C.E. Perkins and P. Bhagwat, "Highly Dynamic Destination-Sequenced Distance-Vector Routing (DSDV) for Mobile Computers", Comp. Comm. Rev., Oct. 1994, pp.234-244.
- C.-C. Chiang, "Routing in Clustered Multihop, Mobile Wireless Networks with Fading Channel" Proc. IEEE SICON'97, Apr.1997, pp.197-211.
- S. Murthy and J.J. Garcia-Luna-Aceves, "An Efficient Routing Protocol for Wireless Networks", ACM Mobile Networks and App. J., Special Issue on Routing in Mobile Communication Networks, Oct. 1996, pp. 183-97.

- Tsu-Wei Chen and Mario Gerla, "Global State Routing: A New Routing Scheme for Ad-hoc Wireless Networks" Proc. IEEE ICC'98, 5 pages.
- Iwata, C.-C. Chiang, G. Pei, M. Gerla, and T.-W. Chen, "Scalable Routing Strategies for Ad Hoc Wireless Networks" IEEE Journal on Selected Areas in Communications, Special Issue on Ad-Hoc Networks, Aug. 1999, pp.1369-79.
- M Joa-Ng and I.-T. Lu, "A Peer-to-Peer zone-based two-level link state routing for mobile Ad Hoc Networks" IEEE Journal on Selected Areas in Communications, Special Issue on Ad-Hoc Networks, Aug. 1999, pp.1415-25.
- Mingliang Jiang, Jinyang Li, Y.C. Tay, "Cluster Based Routing Protocol" August 1999 IETF Draft, 27 pages.
- Charles E. Perkins, Elizabeth M. Royer, Samir R. Das, "Ad Hoc On-demand Distance Vector Routing", October 99 IETF Draft, 33 pages.
- David B. Johnson, Davis A. Maltz, "Dynamic Source Routing in Ad Hoc Networks", Mobile Computing, T. Imielinski and H. Korth, Eds., Kulwer, 1996, pp. 152-81.
- David B. Johnson, Davis A. Maltz, "The Dynamic Source Routing Protocol for Mobile Ad Hoc Networks" October 1999 IETF Draft, 49 pages.
- VD Park and MS Corson "A highly adaptive distributed routing algorithm for mobile wireless networks", Proc. INFOCOM'97, Apr. 1997, 9 pages.
- Chai-Keong Toh, "A novel distributed routing protocol to support Ad hoc mobile computing" Proc. 1996 IEEE 15th Annual Int'l. Phoenix Conf. Comp. and Commun., Mar. 1996, pp. 480-86.
- C.-K. Toh, "Long-lived Ad-Hoc Routing based on the concept of Associativity" March 1999 IETF Draft, 8 pages.
- R. Dube et al., "Signal Stability based adaptive routing for Ad Hoc Mobile networks", IEEE Pers. Comm., Feb. 1997, pp. 36-45.
- Z. J. Haas and M.R. Pearlman, "The Performance of Query Control Schemes for the Zone Routing Protocol," ACM SIGCOMM'98.

- Gupta B.K., Sharma V., and Sharma S.C.: "Dynamic Source Routing (DSR) Protocol for Multi-Hop Wireless Ad Hoc Networks : A Review",, In Proceedings National Conference on IT Research and Application, pp. 323 – 327, 16 –18 Nov., 2007, Haryana, India
- Chugh. T., Gupta B.K.,: "Security in Ad Hoc On Demand Distance Vector Routing Protocol Networks" In Proceedings National Conference on "Issues and Challenges in Internet & Mobile Computing" 28th March, 2008, Ghaziabad. India.
- Gupta Brijesh Kr . Chugh. T.: "Simulation Study for Ad Hoc on Demand Distance Vector Routing Protocol Networks" National Conference on "Technologies & Trends in Advance Computing" 2-3 May, 2008, Ghaziabad. India.
- Bhandari P., Verma A.K., : " A Comparative Study of Mobile Ad-hoc Network Routing Protocols, Proc. International Conference on Intelligent Systems and Networks (IISN) pp. 92-99, 23rd –25th May, 2007, Haryana, India.
- David F. Bantz and Fr´ed´eric J. Bauchot. Wireless LAN Design Alternatives. IEEE Network, 8(2):43–53, March/April 1994.
- Vaduvur Bharghavan, Alan Demers, Scott Shenker, and Lixia Zhang. MACAW: A Media Access Protocol for Wireless LAN's. In Proceedings of the ACMSIGCOMM'94 Conference, pages 212–225. ACM, August 1994.
- Robert T. Braden, editor. Requirements for Internet Hosts—Communication Layers. RFC 1122, October 1989.
- Josh Broch, David A. Maltz, David B. Johnson, Yih-Chun Hu, and Jorjeta Jetcheva. A Performance Comparison of Multi-Hop Wireless Ad Hoc Network Routing Protocols. In Proceedings of the Fourth Annual ACM/IEEE International Conference on Mobile Computing and Networking (MobiCom'98), pages 85–97, Dallas, TX, October 1998.
- Josh Broch, David B. Johnson, and David A. Maltz. The Dynamic Source Routing Protocol for Mobile Ad Hoc Networks. Internet-Draft, draft-ietf-manet-dsr-03.txt, October 1999.
- Josh Broch, David A. Maltz, and David B. Johnson. Supporting Hierarchy and Heterogeneous Interfaces in Multi-Hop Wireless Ad Hoc Networks. In Proceedings of The International Symposium

on Parallel Architectures, Algorithms and Networks Workshop on Mobile Computing, Perth, Western Australia, June 1999. IEEE Computer Society.

- Robert Casta˜neda and Samir R. Das. Query Localization Techniques for On-demand Routing Protocols in Ad Hoc Networks. In Proceedings of the Fifth International Conference on Mobile Computing and Networking (MobiCom'99). ACM, August 1999.
- Stuart Cheshire and Mary Baker. Internet Mobility 4x4. In Proceedings of the SIGCOMM '96, pages 318–329. ACM, August 1996.
- Stephen E. Deering and Robert M. Hinden. Internet Protocol, Version 6 (IPv6) Specification. RFC 2460, December 1998.
- Ralph Droms. Dynamic Host Configuration Protocol. RFC 2131, March 1997.
- Rohit Dube, Cynthia D. Rais, Kuang-Yeh Wang, and Satish K. Tripathi. Signal Stability-Based Adaptive Routing (SSA) for Ad HocMobile Networks. IEEE Personal Communications, 4(1):36–45, February 1997.
- Deborah Estrin, Daniel Zappala, Tony Li, Yakov Rekhter, and Kannan Varadhan. Source Demand Routing: Packet Format and Forwarding Specification (Version 1). Internet-Draft, January 1995.
- Daniel M. Frank. Transmission of IP Datagrams over NET/ROM Networks. In ARRL Amateur Radio 7th Computer Networking Conference, pages 65–70. American Radio Relay League, October 1988.

Question Bank

UNIT-I

Part A

1. Define a cell.
   The smallest geographical area covered by wireless communication is said to be a cell.
2. What are the shapes related to a cell?
   In early days three shapes namely.
   a. Circle
   b. Square
   c. Hexagon
   Were suggested for a cell. But coverage of signal was very accurate with hexagonal shaped cells and in later stage it was taken as standard.
3. What is a periodic signal?
   In a signal if a particular signal pattern repeats over a time period systematically it is a periodic signal.
4. What is a "Aperiodic" signal?
   In a signal if the same signal pattern does not repeat itself over a time period it is known as 'Aperiodic' signal.
5. Give an example for a periodic and aperiodic signals.
   a. periodic signal $\rightarrow x(t+T) = x(t)$.
      where $-\infty < t < +\infty$
   b. Aperiodic signal $\rightarrow x(t+T) \neq x(t)$.

6. Differentiate analog and digital signals.
   If there is no discontinuity in a signal such a smooth signal is an analog signal. All the input signals are usually of analog in nature. On the other hand if there are discontinuities or break in the signal it is a digital signal. The signal strength varies in this signal. It is always better to have signals in digital format for processing.
7. What is the importance of digital signals?
   The signal processing is better with digital signal formats (0's and 1's) where noise is minimized. Hence analog to digital converters are used to convert input analog signal to its equivalent digital signal and after processing the signal is again converted to original analog signal with digital to analog signal a the end entity for proper reception of the signal.
8. Define wavelength.
   The wavelength of a signal represents its distance or range it takes for one cycle. It is denoted as 'λ'. Wavelength $\lambda = c/f$.
9. What is a bandwidth?
   Bandwidth is the range of frequencies and represented as BW = $f_2 - f_1$, where $f_1 - f_2$ are the first and last frequencies of the signal graph.
10. Differentiate between signal and data.
    The term 'data' represents message or information where the signal is the representation of the data, and it is also termed as information bearing signal.
11. Define attenuation.
    It is nothing but reduction in signal strength mainly at higher frequency ranges, and at receiving end this attenuated signal has reduced voltage levels.
12. Tabulate two differences between analog and digital signals.

	Analog signal	Digital signal
1	It is a continuously varying signal	It is a regular sequence of voltage pulses.
2	Media used for signal propagation is like a. Space propagation b. Copper wire media.	Media used for propagation is like a. Copper wire medium

13. Give the equation for signal to noise ratio.

    Signal to noise ration (SNR) = $10 \log_{10} \frac{\text{Signalpower}}{\text{Noisepower}}$

    It is expressed in decibel units.

14. What is the normal operating range of frequency for cell phones?
    The operating frequency range for cell phones are 825 MHz to 845 MHz (approx).

15. What is the frequency range of microwave transmission?
    The frequency of microwave transmissions are 2 GHz to 40 GHz.

16. Draw the diagram of multiplexing.

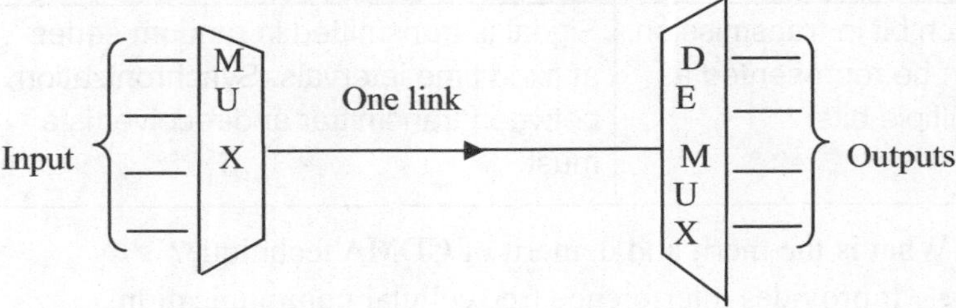

17. What is the principle used in multiplexers?
    The principle used in multiplexer is 'many to one' concept. Many inputs are combined as one link or one output from a MUX unit where a DEMUX unit at the receiver reproduces the same many units at the end entity.

18. What are the important multiplexing schemes?

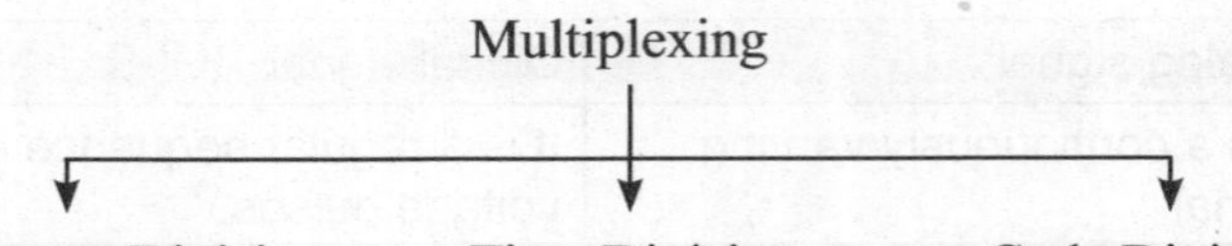

19. What are the multiple access schemes?
    a. FDMA
    b. TDMA
    c. CDMA
20. Define guard band.
    It is unused (dummy) frequency inserted with actual spectrum to reduce adjacent channel interference to enhance accuracy.
21. What are the types of spread spectrum?
    a. FHSS - Frequency Hopping Spread Spectrum
    b. DSSS – Direct Sequence Spread Spectrum.
22. Differentiate DSSS and FHSS.

DSSS	FHSS
Each bit in transmission can be represented as multiple bits.	Signal is transmitted in random series at fixed time intervals. Synchronization between transmitter and receiver is a must.

23. What is the merit and demerit of CDMA technique?
    - It provides interference free cellular communication.
    - It is not economical to use this scheme.
24. At what frequencies ground waves and sky wave propagation takes place?
    a. Ground wave propagation → below 2 MHz.
    b. Sky wave propagation → 2 to 30 MHz.
25. What are the basic shift keying methods?
    (i) Amplitude shift keying.
    (ii) Frequency shift keying
    (iii) Phase shift keying.

26. What are the different kinds of mobility?
    (i) User Mobility: refers to a user who has access to the same or similar telecommunication services at different places. [eg. Call forwarding service]
    (ii) Device portability: the communication device moves. [eg. Mobile Phone System].
27. Give examples for mobile and wireless devices.
    Sensor, Embedded controllers, pager, mobile phones, personal digital assistant, pocket computer and laptop / Notebook computer.
28. State inverse square law.
    Even if no matter exists between the sender and the receiver (i.e, if there is a vacuum), the signal still experiences the free space loss. The received power Pr is proportional to 1/d2 with d being the distance between sender and receiver.
29. Classify the radio waves based on the frequency used.
    (i) Ground wave uses <2MHz
    (ii) Sky wave uses 2-30 MHz
    (iii) Line of sight uses > 30 MHz
30. State the different types of additional propagation effects of a signal.
    (i) Blocking (or) shadowing
    (ii) Reflection
    (iii) Refraction
    (iv) Scattering
    (v) Diffraction
31. Define Delay Spread.
    Radio waves emitted by the sender can either travel along a straight line, or they may be reflected at a large building, or scattered at smaller obstacles. In reality, many more paths are possible. Due to the finite speed of light, signals traveling along different paths with different lengths arrive at the receiver at different times. This effect (caused by multi-path propagation) is called delay spread: the original signal is spread due to different delays of parts of the signal.

32. Why is digital modulation not enough for radio transmission?
    (i) Antenna height is based on the signal's wavelength.
    (ii) FDM can't be applied
    (iii) Medium characteristics like path-loss, penetration of obstacles, reflection, scattering and diffraction depend on the wavelength of the signal.
33. What is a good code for CDMA?
    A code for a certain user should have a good auto correlation and should be orthogonal to other codes.

Part B

1. Explain the different applications of wireless networks and mobile communications.
2. Write notes on the following
   (i) Frequencies for radio transmission
   (ii) Signals and their representation
3. Discuss the types of antennas.
4. What are the additional propagation effects? Explain them?
5. What is multi path propagation? What are the effects of it? What are the ways of mitigating those effects?
6. Explain the different types of multiplexing in detail.
7. Explain the different types of digital modulation techniques.
8. What is spread spectrum technique? What are the types of it? Explain.
9. Why does CSMA/CD scheme fail in wireless networks?
10. Explain the different types of TDMA scheme.
11. Explain CDMA scheme with an example.
12. Compare SDMA, TDMA, FDMA and CDMA techniques.

UNIT-II

Part A

1. Define BTS.

   BTS is the base transceiver station available in each cellular region.

2. What is a MSC?

   It is mobile services switching center and it enables connectivity between BTS and PSTN.

3. What is known as 'handoff'?

   Handoff is a principle used to continue the call established in mobile communication. When the subscriber is towards the cell boundary the signal strength reduces by which the BTS of that cell hand over the call to the next BTS of another cell where the subscriber enters.

4. What are the types of handoff?

   a. Hard hand off.

   b. Soft handoff.

5. What are the three types of switching methods?

   a. Circuit switching

   b. Message switching

   c. Packet switching

6. What are FACCH and GGSN?

   FACCH – Fast associated control channel

   GGSN – Gateway GPRS support node

7. What is SMS and EMS?

   SMS → Short Message Service

   EMS → Enhanced Message Service

8. What are the technologies that opt for SMS facility?

   a. GSM

   b. GPRS

   c. EDGE

   d. UMTS

9. Write short note on QoS in GPRS.
   In GPRS the users can specify the QoS profile where the profile determines important things like reliability class, delay class and service precedence.
10. What is expansion of SGSN and GR?
    (i) SGSN - Serving GPRS Support Node.
    (ii) GR - GPRS Register.
11. What is a DECT?
    It is basically a digital cellular network termed as "Digital Enhanced Cordless Telecommunications" systems and it was specified by ETS1 in the year 1999.
12. What is the advantage of DECT system?
    a. DECT replaced analog cordless phone system of early days.
    b. DECT is more flexible and powerful than other digital system. DECT's access points can be easily established with PSTN.
13. Draw the DECT protocol architecture.
    a.

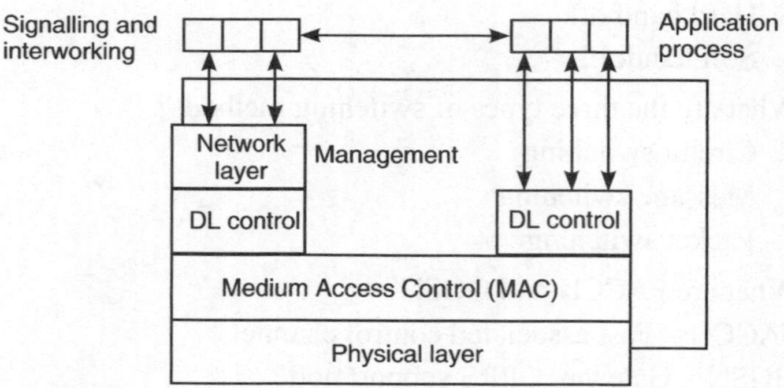

14. What are the tele-services related GSM?
    a. Message services
    b. Encrypted voice transmissions
    c. Data communication
15. What are the subsystems under GSM?
    a. Radio subsystem (RSS)
    b. Operation subsystem (OSS)
    c. Network and switching subsystem (NSS).

16. What are the parameters that the transmission characteristics depend on?

    It depends on the cable parameters like

    a. Conductor spacing
    b. Wire diameter
    c. Dielectric constant of the insulator

17. Define a phase jitter.

    It is one form of the incidental phase modulation, and it causes uncontrolled variations in zero crossing of the signal.

18. Define crosstalk.

    Crosstalk is an unwanted coupling that may interfere with the actual signal from the original signal path into another signal path. It is mainly a kind of disturbance created in a channel by other communication channels.

19. Write a short note on GSM.

    Global system for mobile (GSM) is developed as an ETS1 standard in the 1982. It was developed for second generation pan-European digital cellular with facility of international roaming. The main aim of this second generation standard was to avoid roaming complexities in European countries.

20. List all the services provided by GSM.

    a. Tele services
    b. Bearer services
    c. Supplementary services

21. What are the different managements under GSM protocol architecture?

    (i) Mobility management
    (ii) Connection management
    (iii) Radio resource management
    (iv) Message transfer

22. What is a TCH/H GSM channel?

    It is half rate traffic channel that supports traffic channels with half-rate speech coding. It can use up to 16 slots in one frame with a data rate of 11.4 kbps/sec.

23. What are the common control channels?

The common control channels (CCCH) are used for call establishment and they are basically one way channels.

24. What are types of CCCH?

a. Random access channel (RCH)
b. Paging channel (PCH)
c. Access grant channel (AGCH)

25. What is a RCH?

For establishing a call RCH (Random access channel) is used by mobile station to access the base station involved.

26. What is DCCH?

It is duplicated control channels known as two way channels and it is useful for signaling and control operations for individual subscribers.

27. What are the types of DCCH?

DCCH types

a. Stand alone dedicated control channel (SDCCH)
b. The slow associated control channel (SACCH)
c. The fast associated control channel (FACCH)

28. What are the applications of DECT?

a. Large and small business system.
b. Wireless data access systems.
c. Public cordless access systems.

29. List two functions supported by physical layer of DECT.

a. Modulation and demodulation of radio carriers with data rates of bit streams.
b. Monitoring radio environment

30. What are the functions of MSC in network and switching subsystem?

a. It is like a normal switching node for PSTN fixed telephone and for cellular subscribers of the same network.
b. It is possible to have functions like registration, location updating, and authentication, call routing etc.

31. What is the use of SS7?
    a. In network subsystem the SS7 (signaling system number 7) is used for signaling between different functional entities.
    b. SS7 is used for SMS, roaming prepaid network functions.
    c. SS7 is also used for trunk signaling.
32. What is the function of an AuC?
    The authentication center (AuC) maintains copy of secret key that is stored in each and every subscribers SIM card. It is used to protect user's database.
33. What are the parameters considered for defining QoS in GPRS technology?
    a. Service precedence
    b. Delay
    c. Throughput
    d. Reliability
34. Compare MEO and LEO satellite types.

Characteristics	MEO	LEO
Satellite lifetime	10 to 15 years	4 to 8 years
Altitude range	10,000 to 20.000 km	500 to 2000 km
Round - trip delay	40 to 80 msec	5 to 10 msec

35. What is a GEO?
    The communication satellite (GEO) orbits in geo stationary orbit which is at 36000 km above earth's surface. The satellite revolves with same speed as that of the earth (1 Rev/day) that revolves around sun.
36. What are examples of global mobile satellite system?
    a. Iridium
    b. Teledesic
    c. Global star
37. Give three specifications of Global star and Iridium systems.

Characteristic	Global star	Iridium
System type	LEO	LEO
Data speed	7.2 kbps	2.4 kbps
Launched year	1999	1998

38. What are the advantages of Iridium satellite system?
    a. Inter-satellite links are possible.
    b. Number of satellites possible is 66 and 6 numbers of satellites can be maintained as spares.
    c. The terminal types can be of dual mode, mobile or handheld.
39. Write short note on ICO.
    ICO is basically a MEO satellite system. The aim of ICO is to provide services related to handheld phones. The multiple access used here is TDMA technique.
40. What are the four versions used by global star satellite system with maximum transmission power capability?
    Single – mode – Global star.
    Dual – mode – Global star / GSM.
    Dual – mode - Global star / CDMA cellular.
    Triple – mode – Global star / CDMA cellular / AMPS cellular.
41. Draw the IMT-2000 family member system interface specified by ITU.

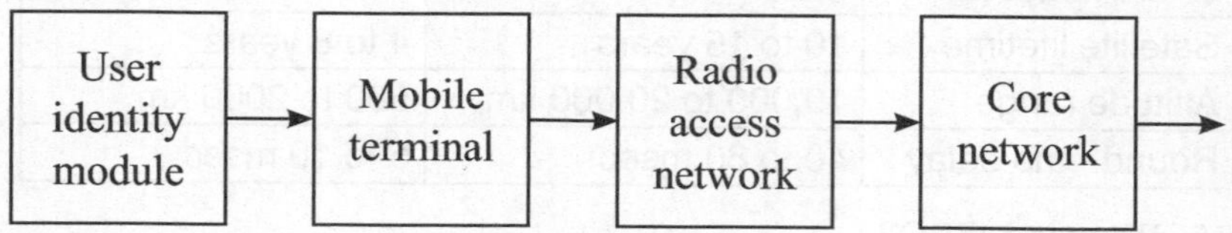

42. What are the benefits of IMT-2000 over 2G systems? (Give any three).
    a. Circuit and packet bearer capability up to 144 kbps.
    b. User authentication and ciphering.
    c. Multimedia services.
    d. Emergency and priority calls.
43. Give few advantages of GEO satellites.
    a. They have large footprints and provide large coverage.
    b. Used for communication related applications.
44. What is the demerit of GEO satellite?
    Their round trip time delay is long due to high altitudes, and it results in qua1ity degradation.

45. What is the goal of teledesic satellite system?
    It extends the terrestrial infrastructures to provide advanced information and communication services over earth mainly to support Internet access communication rather than mobility services.
46. List few specifications of teledesic.
    The plan of teledesic satellite systems includes the features likes usage of 840 LEO satellites at altitude of 700 km and (roughly) it deploys 288 active low earth orbit satellites at an altitude of 1350 km.
47. List two radio aspects of GSM.
    a. Up / down link frequencies are 890-915 MHz/935-960 MHz.
    b. GSM uses TDMA and FDMA schemes.
48. What are the physical elements of a BTS?
    BTS processor, radio transceivers, equalizers, channel coders, transcoders, encryption unit, combiners, pre-selectors, interleaving and deinterleaving units.
49. What are the new supplementary services in GSM? List any three.
    Call completion to the busy subscribers, private numbering plan, and malicious call identification.
50. What is a CAMEL?
    'CAMEL' is 'customized applications for mobile network enhanced logic' a feature that enables GSM to support flexible customer service creations particularly for roaming subscribers.
51. What are the advantages of LEO satellites?
    a. LEO satellites provide higher global coverage.
    b. High spectrum utilization.
    c. The propagation delay is lower (say $\approx$ 5 to 10 msec).
52. What are the demerits of LEO system?
    a. The network architecture is complex
    b. Satellite movement is rapid and analysis is tough.
    c. Routing mechanism is difficult.
    d. Long period of deployment.

53. What is the significance of GPRS?
This system mainly focuses on packet oriented data transmission. The time slots are allocated on demand basis so that channels are efficiently used. The data transfer possible is up to 150 kbits per second. GPRS is also capable of providing point to point packet transfer data services.
54. What is HSCSD?
It is a circuit switched protocol used for multimedia and large file transfer applications. TDMA scheme is applied to increase HSCSD data rate.
55. What are the components of GPRS.
    a. Home location register (HLR)
    b. Visitor location register (VLR)
    c. Mobile services switching center (MSC)
    d. Mobile station (MS)
    e. Base station subsystem (BSS)
    f. Terminal adoption functions (TAF)
    g. Serving GPRS support node (SGSN)
    h. Gateway GPRS support node (GGSN)
    i. Interworking functions (IWF)
    j. Terminal equipment (TE)
    k. Public switched telephone network (PSTN)
    l. Public switched data network (PSDN).
56. What is MSRN and MSISDN?
MSRN – Mobile Station Roaming Number.
MSISDN – Mobile Station ISDN Number.

Part B

1. Explain the system architecture of GSM.
2. Explain the radio interface of GSM.
3. Discuss the protocol architecture of GSM.
4. What is a handover? Explain the different types of it in GSM.
5. Explain the protocol architecture of DECT.

6. List the tasks of RNC in UMTS.
7. Explain the types of handover in UMTS.
8. Explain the characteristics of different orbits of satellites.
9. Draw and explain the components of a DAB sender.
10. Explain how DVB can be used for high-speed internet access.
11. Compare the security features of GSM, UMTS and DECT.

UNIT-III

1. State the modes possible when the slave is in connection state in Bluetooth.
   (i) Active
   (ii) Sniff
   (iii) Hold
   (iv) Park
2. What are elements available under link security of Bluetooth technology?
   a. Authentication
   b. Key management
   c. Encryption
3. What is a LMP?
   It is "link manager specification" that is responsible for radio link between the master and slave in Bluetooth. This protocol also involves message exchanges in the form of LMP-PDU's.
4. List three security services under LMP.
   a. Authentication
   b. Change link key
   c. Encryption
5. What are the synchronizing mechanisms possible under LMP?
   a. Slot offset information
   b. Clock offset request
   c. Timing accuracy information request.
6. What are the PDU's that is used to exchange messages about communicating devices in LMP?
   There are two PDU's used namely LMP version and Bluetooth radio with link controller as supported feature are related with communicating devices.
7. What are the PDU's under LMP that are used to manage Bluetooth device states and modes? List any five.
   a. Slave role/switch master
   b. Name request

c. Sniff mode
d. Park mode
e. Power control

8. List any four LMP supported features.
a. Encryption
b. CVSD
c. Paging scheme
d. Timing accuracy

9. List any three Bluetooth user scenarios.
a. Internet bridge
b. Cordless desktop
c. Instant digital postcard

10. List few functions of Bluetooth.
a. It can make call from a headset (wireless) to a mobile phone which is at a distant place.
b. It can trigger MP3 players on some other machines to download audio signals like music in wireless environment.
c. It mainly eliminates cables in many user applications.

11. What is Bluetooth?
It is a low power short range wireless standard and it can operate in situations where several users are involved. At the maximum eight different devices can communicate in a network using this standard.

12. Write short note on protocol architecture of Bluetooth.
Bluetooth is said to be layered protocol architecture and it comprises of 4 protocols namely,
a. Core protocols
b. Cable replacement protocol
c. Telephony control protocol
d. Adopted protocol

13. Differentiate piconet and scatternet in Bluetooth technology.
a. Piconet: It is a basic network supported by Bluetooth standard where one master and seven slaves (total eight devices) can interact.

b. Scatternet: A device in one piconet either a master or slave can interact with other device that is overlapping of one piconet on other piconet is possible and termed as a “Scatternet”.

14. What is known as ad hoc network topology?
Ad hoc network is also called as distributed network that is mainly a reconfigurable network and it is infrastructure independent.

15. Compare ad hoc and infrastructure network topologies.

Parameter	Ad hoc network topology	Infra network topology
Flexibility	More flexible	Less flexible
Control	It is complex	Centralized control
Routing complexity	It does not exist	It does not exist
Coverage	Less Greater coverage	

16. Which standard supports multihop ad hoc network topology?
The ETSI BRAN’s HIPERLAN standard supports multihop ad hoc network topology for several commercial applications.

17. Write is a TCH/H GSM channel?
It is half rate traffic channel that supports traffic channels with half-rate speech coding. It can use up to 16 slots in one frame with a data rate of 11.4 kb/sec.

18. List two applications of WLAN.
   a. Wireless financial services for layer stock exchanges.
   b. Wireless campus area networks called as WLAN’s for providing wireless classroom.

19. What are the three main management wings under IEEE 802.11 standard?
   a. MAC management
   b. PHY management
   c. Station management

20. What are the two services linked with handoff mechanism in IEEE 802.11?
   a. Re-association service
   b. Dissociation service

21. Give the packet frame for WATM.

Wireless header	ATM header	ATM payload	Wireless trailer
	→ 5 bytes	→ 48 bytes	

22. What are the two main challenges that a WATM design has to meet to develop the network?
    a. The wireless medium is unreliable in wideband frequency ranges and there might be complexities in transmission mechanisms.
    b. ATM switches were designed to support QoS. In a wireless environment there will be channel condition fluctuations and a negotiated QoS cannot be guaranteed, but it is the most expected feature of WATM.
23. Give two functional requirements of HIPERLAN-1.
    a. Coverage up to 100m
    b. Data rates (speed) should be of 23.529 Mb/sec.
24. What are the two features that are necessary in integration of WLAN with cellular systems?
    a. Vertical roaming support
    b. Support for QoS control.
25. What is a dynamic frequency selection (DFS)?
    The HIPERLAN-2 standard supports the basic mechanism for measuring power and to communicate with adjacent AP's and this is called as dynamic frequency selection.
26. Mention any two standards that supports multi-channel operation.
    a. 802.11
    b. HIPERLAN-2
27. List three functional requirement of IEEE802.15 WPAN.
    a. Distance – 0 to 10 m
    b. Power – Low current
    c. Size – Small in size → 0.5 cubic inches without an antenna

28. What is the of modulation scheme used in HIPERLAN standards?
HIPERLAN-1 → GMSK
HIPERLAN-2 → OFDM
29. What are the frequency bands used in IEEE 802.11b and 802.11a standards?
IEEE 802.11b → 2.4 GHz.
IEEE 802.11a → 5.2GHz.
30. Differentiate Bluetooth and Wi-Fi technologies with respect to number of devices connectivity.
In Bluetooth technology there can be up to seven devices connected whereas in Wi-Fi it can be increased up to 32 devices that can be connected.
31. What are the bandwidths allocated for IEEE 802.11a and IEEE 802.11b standards?

IEEE standard	Bandwidth
802.11a	5.2 GHz
802.11b	2.4 GHz

32. What are the industrial applications of Wi-Fi technology?
They are device oriented services, security services, wireless automation with controlling services, and instrumentation monitoring services etc.
33. Compare 802.11, 802.11b standards.

	802.11b	802.11a	802.11
Application	WLAN	WLAN	WLAN
Maximum possible data rate	11 Mbps	54 Mbps	2 Mbps
Frequency band	5 GHz	2.4 GHz	2.4 GHz

34. Compare HIPERLAN-1, HIPERLAN-2, HIPERLAN-3 and HIPERLAN-4 standards.

	HIPERLAN-1	HIPERLAN-2	HIPERLAN-3	HIPERLAN-4
Application	WLAN	WATM (Indoor access)	Fixed wireless access-WATM – (Remote access)	Wireless point to point links – WATM
Maximum possible data rate	23.5 Mbps	20 Mbps	20 Mbps	155 Mb/sec
Frequency band	5 GHz	5 GHz	5 GHz	17 GHz

35. What are the main requirements of WLAN?

WLAN should support and provide,

a. Number of nodes (say 100's)
b. Maximum throughput
c. Energy saving
d. Robustness and secured environment
e. Handoff-Roaming facilities
f. Reduced propagation delay
g. Dynamic topology
h. Multimedia applications etc.

36. What are the security procedures opted by IEEE 802.11 standard?

Two security procedures are mainly defined by this standard.

a. Encrypted frame transmission.
b. Authentication between the two communicating stations.

37. How power saving is achieved by IEEE 802.11 standard?

Power saving is achieved by the principle of buffering of traffic at transmitting station that is whenever a mobile unit is in sleep mode all the traffic related to it will be buffered till the node wakes up.

38. Write short note on IEEE 802.11g standard.

The goals of this 802.11g group under 802.11 is to make use of OFDM scheme where data rates will be up to 54 Mb/sec. Backward compatibility should be available to support other working groups.

39. List any three main requirements of MAC protocol in WATM.

    It should allow decreased complexity at mobile nodes with less energy consumption.

    - Should support required QoS under load variations.
    - Should provide low delay values under channel assignments.

40. What is an 'IrDA' standard?

    'IrDA' is a standard that is specified by Infrared Data Association formed in the year 1993. It was developed mainly to enhanced point-to-point or point-to-multipoint communication. It is dependant on line of sight (LOS) operation.

    The infrared rays can be used wherever LOS is preferred and useful for this indoor consumer applications.

41. What are the specifications of 'IrDA'?

    The IrDA standard 1.0 supports the data rate up to 115.2 kb/sec. for the range up to 1m and next version 'IrDA 1.1" developed later supports data transfers up to 35 times faster when compared to "IrDA 1.0".

42. What are the new specifications supported by current Bluetooth?

    The short range Bluetooth technology is improved for meeting the distance of 100m in open air and 30 m within building infrastructures for it's operation. It works with data rate of 1 Kbps.

43. What re the two kinds of profiles in Bluetooth 1.1 version?

    The two main profile classification is nine application profiles and four system profile and as a whole thirteen profiles are supported by Bluetooth 1.1 version.

44. What are the system profiles used in Bluetooth 1.1 version?

    The system profiles are generic object exchange, object push, file transfer and synchronization profiles.

UNIT-IV

Part A

1. State the requirements of mobile IP.
   (i) Compatibility
   (ii) Transparency
   (iii) Scalability and efficiency
   (iv) Security
2. What is COA? How is it assigned?
   Care-or address (COA): The COA defines the current location of the MN from an IP point of view.
   There are two different possibilities for the location of the COA:
   - Foreign agent COA
   - Co-located COA
3. How does a MN identify that it has moved?
   Mobile IP describes two methods: agent advertisement and agent solicitation, which are in fact router discovery methods plus extensions.
4. What are the contents of mobility binding?
   Mobility binding containing the mobile node's home IP address and the current COA. Additionally, the mobility binding contains the lifetime of the registration which is negotiated during the registration process.
5. Define encapsulation.
   Encapsulation is the mechanism of taking a packet consisting of packet header and data and putting it into the data part of new packet. The reverse operation, taking a packet out of the data part of another packet, is called decapsulation.
6. List the types of encapsulation.
   - IP-in-IP encapsulation
   - Minimal encapsulation
   - Generic routing encapsulation
7. What are the messages used for mobile IP optimization?
   - Binding request

- Biding update
- Binding acknowledgement
- Binding warning

8. State the reasons for reverse tunneling.
   - Firewalls
   - Multi-cast
   - TTL
9. State any 4 features of IPv6.

   No special mechanisms as add-ons are needed for securing mobile IP registration. Every IPv6 node masters address auto configuration – the mechanisms for acquiring a COA are already built in. Neighbor discovery as a mechanism mandatory for every node is also included in the specification; special foreign agents are no longer needed to advertise services. Combining the features of auto configuration and neighbor discovery means that every mobile node is able to crate or obtain a topologically correct address for the current point of attachment.

   Every IPv6 node can send binding updates to another node, so the MN can send its current COA directly to the CN and HA.
10. State the advantages of cellular IP.

    Advantage:

    Manageability: Cellular IP is mostly self-configuring, and integration of the CIPGW into a firewall would facilitate administration of mobility-related functionality.
11. State the disadvantages of cellular IP.

    Disadvantages:
    - Efficiency : Additional network load is induced by forwarding packets on multiple paths.
    - Transparency: Changes to MNs are required.
    - Security : Routing tables are changed based on messages sent by mobile nodes. Additionally, all systems in the network can easily obtain a copy of all packets destined fro an MN by sending packets with the MN's source address to the CIPGW.

12. State the advantages of Hawaii.

    Advantages:

    - Security: Challenge-response extensions are mandatory. In contrast to Cellular IP, routing changes are always initiated by the foreign domain's infrastructure.
    - Transparency: HAWAII is mostly transparent to mobile nodes.

13. State the disadvantages of Hawaii.

    Disadvantages:

    - Security: There are no provisions regarding the setup of IPSec tunnels.
    - Implementation: No private address support is possible because of co-located COAs.

14. State the advantages of HMIPv6.

    Advantages:

    - Security: MNs can have (limited) location privacy because LCOAs can be hidden.
    - Efficiency: Direct routing between CNs sharing the same link is possible.

15. State the disadvantages of HMIPv6.

    - Transparency: Additional infrastructure component (MAP).
    - Security: Routing tables are changed based on messages sent by mobile nodes. This requires strong authentication and protection against denial of service attacks. Additional security functions might be necessary in MAPs.

16. List out the messages used in DHCP for client initialization.

    DHCPDISCOVER, DHCPOFFER, DHCPREQUEST, DHCPACK and DHCPRELEASE.

17. State the uses of mobile ad hoc networks.

    - Instant infrastructure
    - Disaster relief
    - Remote areas
    - Effectiveness

18. State any 4 differences between wired networks and ad hoc wireless networks related to routing.
    a. Asymmetric links
    b. Redundant links
    c. Interference
    d. Dynamic topology
19. Why can't we apply traditional routing algorithms for ad hoc networks? State any 2 reasons.
    - Routing in wireless ad-hoc networks cannot rely on layer three knowledge alone. Information from lower layers concerning connectivity or interference can help routing algorithms to find a good path.
    - Centralized approaches will not really work, because it takes to long to collect the current status and disseminate it again. Within this time the topology has already changed.
    - Many nodes need routing capabilities. While there might be some without, at lease one router has to be within the range of each node. Algorithms have to consider the limited battery power of these nodes.
20. What are the features added by DSDV to distance vector algorithm?
    DSDV now adds two things to the distance vector algorithm:
    - Sequence numbers: Each routing advertisement comes with a sequence number. Within ad-hoc networks, advertisements may propagate along many paths. Sequence numbers help to apply the advertisements in correct order. This avoids the loops that are likely with the unchanged distance vector algorithm.
    - Damping: Transient changes in topology that are of short duration should not destabilize the routing mechanisms. Advertisements containing changes in the topology currently stored are therefore not disseminated further.
21. What are the parts of on-demand routing algorithm?
    Dynamic source routing (DSR), therefore, divides the task of routing into two separate problems:

- Route discovery: A node only tries to discover a route to a destination if it has to send something to this destination and there is currently no known route.
- Route maintenance: If a node is continuously sending packets via a route, it has to make sure that the route is held upright. As soon as a node detects problems with the current route, it has to find an alternative.

22. What are the other metrics considered for routing in ad hoc network?

    h-Hops, i-interference, r-reliability, e-error rate

    cost of a pat $\alpha h + \beta i + \theta r + \delta e + ...$ where α, β, θ, δ are weights.

Part B

1. Explain the role of different entities in mobile IP with an example.
2. What are the types of registration in mobile IP? Explain.
3. Explain the different types of encapsulation techniques in mobile IP.
4. Explain the different routing techniques available for mobile ad hoc network with an example.
5. Explain the agent discovery process in mobile IP.
6. Explain the different approaches available for IPv6 to support mobility.
7. Compare the features of wired network with ad hoc network related to routing.

UNIT-V

1. State any 4 improvements to the classical TCP.
   a. Indirect TCP
   b. Mobile TCP
   c. Snooping TCP
   d. Fast retransmit/Fast recovery.
2. State any 2 advantages of I-TCP.
   - I-TCP does not require any changes in the TCP protocol as used by the hosts in the fixed network or other hosts in a wireless network that do not use this optimization. All current optimizations for TCP still work between the foreign agent and the correspondent host.
   - Due to the strict partitioning into two connections, transmission errors on the wireless link, i.e., lost packets cannot propagate into the fixed network. Without partitioning, retransmission of lost packets would take place between mobile host and correspondent host across the whole network. Now only packets in sequence, without gaps leave the foreign agent.
3. State any 2 disadvantages of I-TCP.
   - The loss of the end-to-end semantics of TCP might cause problems if the foreign agent partitioning the TCP connection crashes. If a sender receives an acknowledgement, it assumes that the receiver got the packet. Receiving an acknowledgement now only means (for the mobile host and a correspondent host) that the foreign agent received the packet. The correspondent node does not know anything about the partitioning, so a crashing access node may also crash applications running on the correspondent node assuming reliable end-to-end delivery.
   - In practical use, increased handover latency may be much more problematic. All packets sent by the correspondent host are buffered by the foreign agent besides forwarding them to the mobile host (if the TCP connection is split at the foreign agent.) The foreign agent removes a packet from the buffer as soon as the appropriate acknowledgement arrives. If the

mobile before the old foreign agent can forward the buffered data to the new foreign agent. During this time more packets may arrive. All these packets have to be forwarded to the new foreign agent first, before it can start forwarding the new packets redirected to it.

4. State any 2 advantages of S-TCP.
   - The end-to-end TCP semantic is preserved. No matter at what time the foreign agent crashes (if this is the location of the buffering and snooping mechanisms), neither the correspondent host nor the mobile host have an inconsistent view of the TCP connection as is possible with I-TCP. The approach automatically falls back to standard TCP if the enhancements stop working.
   - The correspondent host does not need to be changed; most of the enhancements are in the foreign agent. Supporting only the packet stream from the correspondent host to the mobile host does not even require changes in the mobile host.
5. State any 2 disadvantages of S-TCP.
   - Snooping TCP does not isolate the behaviour of the wireless link as well as I-TCP. Assume, for example, that it takes some time until the foreign agent can successfully retransmit a packet from its buffer due to problems on the wireless link (congestion, interference). Although the time-out in the foreign agent may be much shorter than the one of the correspondent host, after a while the time-out I the correspondent host triggers a retransmission. The problems on the wireless link are now also visible for the correspondent host and not fully isolated. The quality of the isolation, which snooping TCP offers, strongly depends on the quality of the wireless link, time-out values, and further traffic characteristics. It is problematic that the wireless link exhibits very high delays compared to the wired link due to error correction on layer 2 (factor 10 and more higher). This is similar to i-TCP. If this is the case, the timers in the foreign agent and the correspondent host are almost equal and the approach is almost ineffective.

- Using negative acknowledgements between the foreign agent and the mobile host assumes additional mechanisms on the mobile host. This approach is no longer transparent for arbitrary mobile hosts.

6. State any 2 advantages of M-TCP.
   - It maintains the TCP end-to-end semantics. The SH does not send any ACK itself but forwards the ACKs form the MH.
   - If the MH is disconnected, it avoids useless retransmissions, slow starts or breaking connections by simply shrinking the sender's window to 0.
7. State any 2 disadvantages of M-TCP.
   - As the SH does not act as proxy as in I-TCP, packet loss on the wireless link due to bit errors is propagated to the sender. M-TCP assumes low bit error rates, which is not always a valid assumption.
8. State any 2 advantages of Transmission / time out freezing.
   The advantage of this approach is its simplicity. Only minor changes in the mobile host's software already result in a performance increase. No foreign agent or correspondent host has to be changed.
9. The main disadvantage of this scheme is the insufficient isolation of packet losses. Forcing fast retransmission increases the efficiency, but retransmitted packets still have to cross the whole network between correspondent host and mobile host. If the handover from one foreign agent to another takes a longer time, the correspondent host will have already started retransmission. The approach focuses on loss due to handover: packet loss due to problems on the wireless link is not considered. This approach requires more cooperation between the mobile IP and TCP layer making it harder to change one without influencing the other.
10. State any 2 advantages of Transmission / time out freezing.
    The advantage of this approach is that it offers a way to resume TCP connections even after longer interruptions of the connection. It is independent of any other TCP mechanism, such

as acknowledgements or sequence numbers, so it can be used together with encrypted data.

11. State any 2 disadvantages of Transmission / time out freezing.
    Not only does the software on the mobile host have to be changed, to be more effective the correspondent host cannot remain unchanged. All mechanisms rely of the capability of the MAC layer to detect future interruptions. Freezing the state of TCP does not help in case of some encryption schemes that use time-dependent random numbers. These schemes need resynchronization after interruption.
12. State any 2 advantages of selective retransmission.
    The advantage of this approach is obvious: a sender retransmits only the lost packets. This lowers bandwidth requirements and is extremely helpful in slow wireless links. The gain in efficiency is not restricted to wireless links and mobile environments. Using selective retransmission is also beneficial in all other networks.
13. State any 2 disadvantages of selective retransmission.
    More buffer is necessary to re-sequence data and to wait for gaps to be filled. But while memory sizes and CPU performance permanently increase, the bandwidth of the air interface remains almost the same. Therefore, the higher complexity is no real disadvantage any longer as it was in the early days of TCP.
14. State any 2 advantages of Transaction oriented TCP.
    The obvious advantage for certain applications is the reduction in the overhead which standard TCP has for connection setup and connection release.
15. State any 2 disadvantages of Transaction oriented TCP.
    This solution no longer hides mobility. Furthermore, T/TCP exhibits several security problems.
16. Who have formed the WAP forum?
    Ericsson, Motorola, Nokia, and Unwired Planet.
17. State the features of WAP Forum solutions.
    All solutions must be:
    - interoperable

- scaleable
- efficient
- reliable
- secure

18. State the layers in WAP architecture.
    a. Transport layer
    b. Security layer
    c. Transaction layer
    d. Session layer
    e. Application layer
19. State any 4 WAP working groups.
    a. WAP architecture working group
    b. WAP wireless protocol working group
    c. WAP wireless security working group
    d. WAP wireless application working group
20. What are the service primitives available in T-SAP?
    a. T_D Unit data.req(DA, DP, SA, SP, UD)
    b. T_D Unit data.ind(SA, SP, UD)
    c. T_DError.ind(EC)

    DA – destination address   SA – Source Address
    DP – destination port   SP – Source Port
    UD – user data   EC – Error code.
21. What are the different security levels offered by WTLS?
    a. privacy
    b. data integrity
    c. authentication
22. What are the different services offered by WTP?
    a. Class 0: unreliable message transfer without any result message.
    b. Class 1: reliable message transfer without any result message.
    c. Class 2: reliable message transfer with exactly one result message.
23. How is reliability achieved in WTP?
    a. duplicate removed

b. retransmission
c. acknowledgements
d. unique transtion identifier.

24. What are the types of PDU exchanged between WTP entities?
a. invoke PDU
b. ack PDU
c. result PDU

25. What are the functions of WSP?
a. session management
b. capability negotiation
c. content encoding

26. State the features of WSP/B.
a. HTTP1.1 functionality
b. Exchange of session headers
c. Push & Pull data transfer
d. Asynchronous requests.

27. List any 4 basic features of WML.
a. Text and images representation
b. User interaction
c. Navigation
d. Context management

28. List any 4 capabilities of WML script.
a. Validity check of user input
b. Access to device facilities
c. Local user interaction
d. Extension to the device software

29. What are the standard libraries available for WML script?
a. Lang
b. Float
c. String
d. URL
e. WML Browser
f. Dialogs

30. What are the libraries available for WTA?
    a. Common network services
    b. Network specific services
    c. Public services.

Part B

Very Short Answer Type Questions:

1. State the features of I-TCP.
2. Explain the features of S-TCP.
3. State the features of M-TCP.
4. Explain the architecture of WAP.
5. Explain the features of WML.
6. Explain the function of WDP.
7. Explain the services offered by WSP.
8. Explain the services offered by WTA with an example.

Short Answer Type Questions:

1. Define CDMA.
2. Define Signal.
3. What is digital modulation?
4. Define code division multiplexing.
5. List out the advantages of frequency division multiplexing.
6. What are the several versions in CSMA?
7. What is Quadrature Amplitude Modulation?
8. What are the 2 sub layers in DLC?
9. Define time division multiplexing.
10. List out the different types of frequencies used for data transmission.
11. Define Antenna.
12. List out the different types of antennas.
13. Define Modulation.
14. What is hidden and exposed terminal problem?

15. Define polling.
16. What is spread spectrum?
17. List out the different types of spread spectrum techniques.
18. Distinguish between ALOHA and slotted ALOHA.
19. Define fading.
20. Distinguish between DSSS and FHSS.
21. What are the 3 fundamental propagation behaviors depending on their frequency?
22. What is multipath propagation?
23. What is guard space?
24. What are the 3 different basic schemes analog modulation?
25. What is the use of Phase Lock Loop (PLL)?
26. What is hopping sequence?
27. What is dwell time?
28. What are the advantages of cellular systems?
29. What is browsing channel allocation and fixed channel allocation?
30. What are the disadvantages of cellular systems?
31. What is digital sense multiple access?
32. What is Network and Switching subsystem?
33. What is authentication centre?
34. What is called burst and normal burst?
35. What are the basic groups of logical channels?
36. Define traffic multiframe and control multiframe?

Long Answer Type Questions:

1. Explain different TDMA schemes in detail.
2. Explain multiplexing in detail.
3. Discuss Modulation techniques in detail.
4. Account on CDMA Scheme.
5. Explain FDMA in detail.

6. Discuss SDMA in detail.
7. Explain major types of networks.
8. Explain types of Antennas in detail.
9. Explain the various applications of mobile computing.
10. Explain about the signal propagation.
11. Discuss about the cellular system.
12. List the difference between S/T/F/CDMA.
13. What is spread spectrum with its types.
14. Why do MAC scheme in wired network fail in wireless networks and how dose the multiple access with collision avoidance (MACA) scheme work.
15. Define modulation and explain the method for analog modulation techniques in details.
16. Discuss briefly the advanced phase shift keying.

Short Answer Type Questions:

1. What is Handover?
2. What are the categories of Mobile services?
3. What is TETRA?
4. What is meant by GPRS?
5. What are subsystems in GSM system?
6. What is meant by GEO?
7. Define the inclination angle and perigee.
8. Define the elevation angle and footprint.
9. What is MSC?
10. What are the different types of disk?
11. What are the goals of DVB?
12. Name some of the formats supported by MOT?
13. What are the advantages of DAB?
14. What is object repetition?
15. What is EIT?

16. What are the service information sent by DVB?
17. What is Active scanning?
18. What is Passive Scanning?
19. What is FIC?
20. What are the registers maintained by the gateway of satellite?
21. Specify the security services offered by GSM.
22. What is the frequency range of uplink and downlink in GSM network?
23. What are the two basic groups of logical channels in GSM?
24. What are the control channel groups in GSM?
25. List out the numbers needed to locate an MS and to address the MS.
26. What are the four possible handover scenarios in GSM?
27. What are the security services offered by GSM?
28. What is meant by GGSN?
29. What is meant by SGSN?
30. What is meant by BSSGP?
31. Define the protocol architecture of DECT.
32. Specify the standards offered by TETRA.
33. How many ITU standardized groups of 3G radio access technologies are there in IMT-2000?
34. What are the steps perform during the search for a cell after power on?
35. What are the two basic classes of handover?
36. What are the two basic transport mechanisms used by DAB?
37. What are the two transport modes defined for MSC?
38. Define the terms: i. Earth Station. ii. Uplink.
39. Define Elevation Angle.
40. What are the factors limited the number of sub channels provided within the satellite channel?

Long Answer Type Questions:

1. Write notes on DECT and TETRA.
2. Write notes on UMTS and IMT – 2000.
3. Explain broadcast systems in detail.
4. Explain satellite systems in detail.
5. Explain GSM systems in detail.
6. Explain GPRS systems in detail.
7. Explain DAB in detail.
8. Explain DVB in detail.
9. Explain the following a)Routing b)Hand over c)Localization.
10. Explain the various satellite orbit and the parameters associated.
11. Compare GEO, MEO and LEO

Short Answer Type Questions:

1. What is the primary goal of IEE 802.11?
2. What is meant by SIFS?
3. What are Advantages of wireless LAN?
4. What are Design Goals of Wireless LAN?
5. What are the three Low Power States provided by Bluetooth?
6. What is SCO?
7. What are Advantages and Disadvantages of Infrared?
8. What are the system integration functions of MAC management?
9. What do you meant by roaming?.
10. What is mobile routing?
11. What are the functions which support service and connection control?
12. What are the examples for service scenarios identified in WATM?
13. What is BRAN?
14. What are the different network types of BRAN?
15. What is the main problem for WATM during handover?

16. What are the different segments in ATM end-to-end connection?
17. What is anchor point? .
18. What are different types of handover?
19. What is mobile terminal and wireless terminal?.
20. Mention some of the disadvantages of WLANS?
21. Mention the design goals of WLANS?
22. What is the difference between infrastructure and ad-hoc networks?
23. Mention the features of infrared transmission?
24. What are the disadvantages of infrared transmission?
25. Mention the features of radio transmission?
26. What are the disadvantages of radio transmission?
27. Define frequency hopping spread spectrum?
28. Define random back off time?
29. What is Traffic Indication Map?
30. What is Delivery Traffic Indication Map?
31. What is Ad-hoc TIM?
32. Mention the features of HIPERLAN1?
33. What are the three phases of medium access in EY-NPMA?
34. Mention the elements of Bluetooth core protocols?
35. What is the purpose of sniff state?
36. What is the use of hold state?
37. What is the purpose of park state?

Long Answer Type Questions:

1. Explain the architecture and features of IEEE 802.11 in details
2. Write notes on WATM services and Functions.
3. Write notes on WATM handover.
4. Write notes on location management, addressing and access point control protocol.
5. Give a detail note on HYPERLAN

6. Account on BLUETOOTH in detail.
7. Discuss in detail about the different services of IEEE802.11.
8. Explain in detail about Adhoc networks.
9. List out the Advantages and Disadvantages of Infrastructure network and adhoc network.
10. Explain the MAC layer in IEEE802.11
11. Explain how power management is done in IEEE 802.11 infrastructure based and ad hoc networks.
12. Discuss how to increase the quality of service in an ad hoc network.

Short Answer Type Questions:

1. What is generic routing encapsulation?
2. Define COA.
3. What is meant by Transparency?
4. What is Binding Request?
5. What are the possibilities for the location of care-of-address (COA)?
6. What are the requirements for the development of mobile IP standard?
7. Why is need of routing?
8. What is Dynamic source Routing?
9. Define Mobile node.
10. What is Encapsulation and Decapsulation?
11. Define Compatibility.
12. What is Home Agent (HA)?
13. Define Foreign Agent (FA).
14. Define Agent Advertisement.
15. Define Registration.
16. Define Key distribution.
17. Applications of Dynamic Host Configuration Protocol.
18. Define DSDV (Destination Sequenced Distance Vector).

19. List the examples for interference based routing.
20. Define tunneling.
21. What are the requirements of mobile IP?
22. Mention the different entities in a mobile IP.
23. What do you mean by mobility binding?
24. Define a tunnel.
25. Define an outer header
26. Define an inner header.
27. What is the use of network address translation?
28. Define triangular routing.
29. What is meant by a binding cache?
30. Define binding request.
31. *What is known as Binding update*?
32. Explain binding acknowledgement.
33. Define binding warning.
34. Explain cellular IP.
35. What are the advantages of cellular IP?
36. What is known as mobility anchor point?
37. Explain destination sequence distance vector routing.
38. What are the two things added to the distance vector algorithm?
39. How the dynamic source routing does divide the task of routing into two separate problems?

Long Answer Type Questions:

1. Explain mobile IP in detail.
2. Give a detailed account of mobile ad-hoc networks.
3. Explain about DHCP: Dynamic Host Configuration Protocol.
4. Discuss about Adhoc-networks.
5. Explain about Traditional routing algorithms in detail.
6. Explain about DSDV (Destination Sequenced Distance Vector) in detail.

7. State Dynamic source routing in detail.
8. Discuss about inference routing in detail.
9. Explain the following :
   (a) Agent Advertisement
   (b) Encapsulation
10. Explain the following:
    (a) Registration
    (b) Tunneling.
11. (a) What are the requirements of a mobile IP? (8)
    (b) Describe Dynamic host configuration protocol. (8)
12. (a) Discuss the routing algorithm in ad-hoc network (8)
    (b) What are the entities in mobile IP? (8)
13. (a) Discuss how optimization in achieved in mobile IP (8)
    (b) Explain tunneling and encapsulation in mobile IP. (8)
14. Explain how dynamic source routing protocols handles routing with an example (16)

Short Answer Type Questions:

1. What are the two functions of the transport layer in the internet?
2. What is called the exponential growth of the congestion window?
3. List out the advantages of I-TCP.
4. List out disadvantages of I-TCP.
5. Define Slow Start.
6. How does data transmission takes place?
7. What is mean by Slow Start?
8. What is mean by SCPS-TP?
9. What are Advantages and Disadvantages of MobileTCP?
10. What is Fast retransmit?
11. What is fast recovery?
12. What is HTTP?
13. What is WAP?

14. What is WML Browser?
15. List out advantages of Transmission Freezing.
16. Define WAE.
17. What is WML?
18. Write short notes on WAP forum.
19. Distinguish between Traditional TCP and wireless TCP?
20. What is WTP? What are its classes?
21. List out the network elements of WAP.
22. What is the purpose of congestion window in classical TCP?
23. What is slow start?
24. What is the use of congestion threshold?
25. What led to the development of Indirect TCP?
26. What is the goal of M-TCP?
27. What do you mean by persistent mode?
28. What are the characteristics of 2.5G/3.5G wireless networks?
29. What are the configuration parameters to adapt TCP to wireless environments?
30. State the requirements of WAP.
31. Name the layers of WAP.
32. Name some ICMP messages.
33. What is WTP? What are its classes?
34. What is WSP?
35. Name some features of WSP adapted to web browsing.
36. What is WML?
37. What are the features of WML?
38. What are the advantages of WML Script over WML?
39. Name the libraries specified by WML Script.
40. What are the classes of libraries?
41. Name the operations performed by PAP.
42. What are the components of WAP2.0?

Long Answer Type Questions:

1. Explain in detail about traditional TCP.
2. Explain about Classical TCP improvement techniques in detail.
3. Write notes on WDP and WTLS.
4. Write notes on wireless sessions protocol
5. Explain in detail about WAP.
6. Discuss about WAE and WTP.
7. Explain the following: Snooping TCP and Indirect TCP.
8. Explain the following: Selective repeat and Fast retransmit and recovery.
9. Explain the following: Freezing and transaction oriented TCP.
10. Explain about WML and WML script with the help of an example.
11. Explain classical TCP *improvements and snooping* TCP.
12. Explain the concept of wireless markup language.
13. Explain wireless application protocols with the it's version WAP 2.0in detail.
14. Describe the operation of the window flow control mechanism

Mobile Computing (MCA-E34) ODD Semester 2012-13

SECTION A

Question 1

a.

- Low Bandwidth
- Weak and Discontinuous Connectivity
- High Bandwidth
- Limited Geographical Coverage
- Risk to data (Mobile elements are easier to be accidently
- damaged, stolen, or lost)
- Mobile elements rely on battery of low power
- Small User Interface
- Small storage capacity

b.

- **Soft Handoff:** Soft handoff (or handover) is a mobile cellular network technology commonly used in CDMA (Code-division multiple access) systems that enables the overlapping of the repeater coverage zones, so that every cell phone set is always well within range of at least one of the base stations. Since, a Soft handoff mechanism works by first switching and establishing connection with another base station before disconnecting from the existing base station in the network, it is also sometimes referred to as "Make-before-Break" Handoff.

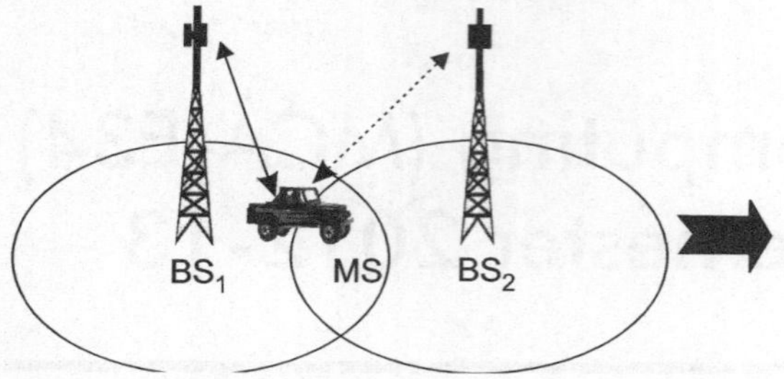

a. Before handoff

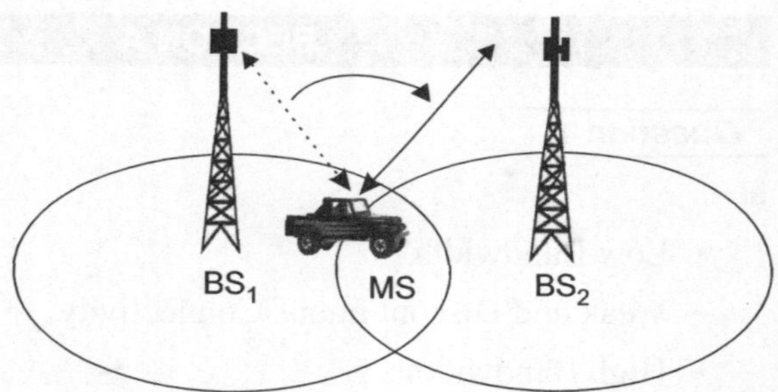

b. After handoff

- **Hard Handoff:** In a mobile cellular communication network, a Hard handoff (or Hard handover) is a typical Handoff mechanism in a communication network which is designed to work by first breaking off from the initial connection with a base station before switching to another base station. This is done in order to retain communications in a session for mobile users after incurring a non perceptible and insignificant brief interruption. A Hard handoff is also referred to as "Break-before-Make" handover.

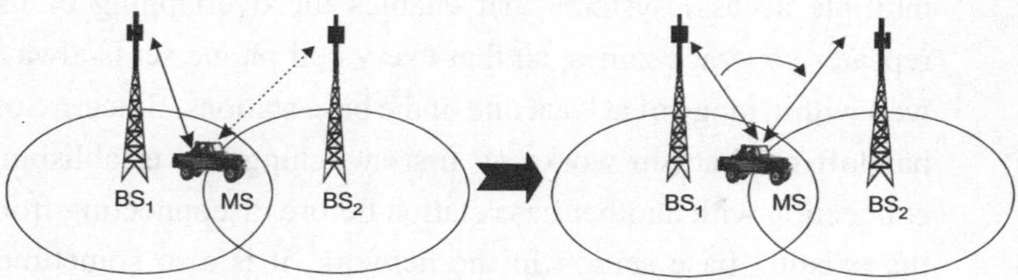

a. Before handoff　　b. After handoff

c. Various Control Channels in logical channels of GSM

- Broadcast Channels (BCH)
  - Frequency Correction Channel (FCCHJ
  - Synchronization Channel (SCH)
  - Broadcast Control Channel CBCCH)
- Common Control Channels (CCCH)
  - Paging Channel (PCH)
  - Random Access Channel (RACH)
  - Access Grant Channel (AGCH)
- Dedicated Control Channels (DCCH)
  - Stand alone Dedicated Control Channel (SDCCH)
  - Slow Associated Control Channel (SACCH)
  - Fast Associated Control Channel (FACCH)

d. I-TCP splits the connection into two parts: A wired/fixed and a wireless/mobile part. This isolates problems on the wireless link from the fixed network. However, this also requires that intermediate systems are able to look into IP packets to split the connection. This prevents the usage of IPsec- end-to-end security and I-TCP (or proxy solutions in general) does not go together.

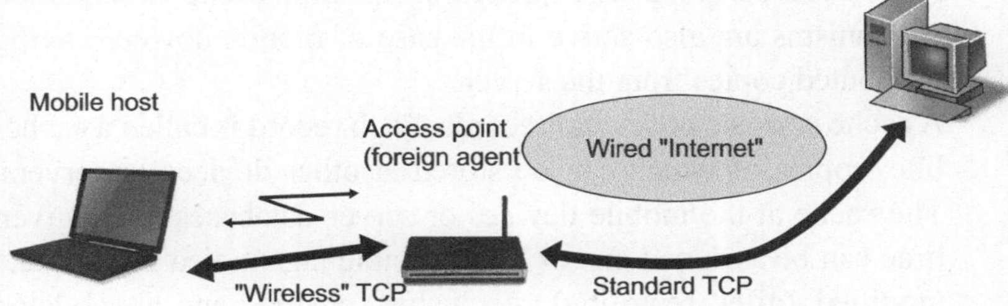

e. Power saving Mechanism in Blue tooth

- *Sniff state:* The sniff state has the highest power consumption. The device listens to thepiconet at a reduced rate.
- *Hold state:* The device does not release its AMA but stops ACL transmission. A slavemay still exchange SCO packets.

- *Park state:* In this state the device has the lowest duty cycle and the lowest powerconsumption. The device releases its AMA and receives a parked member address.The device is still a member of the piconet, but gives room for another device tobecome active.

f. **Agent Solicitation:** A method by which an MN visiting anetwork discovers the FA and the COA incase COA not found from advertisements. If an advertisement is not listened to,solicitation can be done three times at 1 sintervals. Later this interval can be increased.

   If the MN docs not receivc any address as response lo its solicitation messages then to avoid network flooding MN should reduce the rate of solicitation

g. A cached record at the client device may be invalidated. This may be due to expiry or modification of the record at the database server. Cache invalidation is a process by which a cached data item or record becomes invalid and thus unusable because of modification, expiry, or invalidation at another computing system or server. Cache invalidation mechanisms are used to synchronize the data at other processors whenever the cache-data is written (modified) by a processor in a multiprocessor system, cache invalidation mechanisms are also active in the case of mobile devices having distributed copies from the server.

   A cache consists of several records. Each record is called a cache-line, copies of which can be stored at other devices or servers. The cache at the mobile devices or server databases at anygiven time can be assigned one of four possible tags indicating its state modified (after rewriting), exclusive, shared, and invalidated (after expiry or when new data becomes available) at any given instance. These four states are indicated by the letters M, E, S, and I, respectively (MESI). The states indicated by the various tags are as follows:

   - The E tag indicates the exclusive state which means that the data record is for internal use and cannot be used by any other device or server.

- The S tag indicates the shared state which indicates that the data record can be used by others.
- The M tag indicates the modified state which means that the device cache
- The I tag indicates the invalidated state which means that the server database no longer has a copy of the record which was shared and used for computations earlier.

h. **Mobile subscriber ISDN number (MSISDN):** Mobile Station International Subscriber Directory Number (MSISDN) is a number used to identify a mobile phone number internationally. The number dialed to reach aGSM subscriber. The MSISDN will determine which gateway MSCto use. At the MSC, the MSISDN is mapped onto a HLR whichis queried to get the latest data related to the called mobile. The HLR provides*the mobile station roaming* number (MSRN). This is used by theGMSC to get to the MSC of the current location of the mobile. TheMSISDN consists of: country code (CC) used by PSTN, national destinationcode (NDC) and subscriber number (SN). The NDC can be either the networkof the suscriber or the geographical area of the subscriber's home system(in the US NDCs are the telephone area codes).

i. **Proactive Routing Protocol:** Proactive routing protocols maintain routes to all destinations,regardless of whether or not these routes are needed. In order to maintain correct routeinformation, a node must periodically send control messages. Therefore, proactiverouting protocols may waste bandwidth since control messages are sent out unnecessarilywhen there is no data traffic. The main advantage of this category of protocols is thathosts can quickly obtain route information and quickly establish a session.

- Table driven
- Continuously evaluate routes
- No latency in route discovery
- Large network capacity to keep info. current
- Most routing information may never be used

Advantage:

- Updated Information.
- Availability of alternate routes.

Disadvantages:

- Large database required to store all paths
- More overhead

Example areDestination-Sequenced Distance Vector (DSDV), Global State Routing (GSR), Fisheye State Routing (FSR).

j. **Care-of-address:** In Internet routing, a care-of address is a temporary IP address for a mobile node (mobile device) that enables message delivery when the device is connecting from somewhere other than its home network. The care-of address identifies a mobile node's current point of attachment to the Internet and makes it possible to connect from a different location without changing the device's home address (permanent IP address). This works similarly to the way the postal system might forward letters through a care-of address: messages sent to the known permanent address are rerouted to the care-of address while the recipient can be reached there. Thus, the recipient avoids having to change their official address to the temporary one when they change their location, and change it back again when they return home.

SECTION B

Question 2

a.

1.

- *Sender A*
  - sends $A_d = 1$, key $A_k = 010011$ {assign: "0"= –1, "1" = +1)
  - sending signal $A_s = A_d * A_k = (-1, +1, -1, -1. +1, +1)$
- *Sender B*
  - sends $B_d = 0$, key $B_k = 110101$ (assign: "0"= –1, "1" = +1}
  - sending signal $B_s = B_d * B_k = \{-1, -1, +1 , -1, +1, -1)$

- Both signals superimpose in space
  - interference neglected (noise etc.)
  - $A_s + B_s = (-2, 0, 0, -2, +2, 0)$
- Receiver wants to receive signal from sender A
  - apply key A_k bitwise (inner product)
    - $A_e = (-2, 0, 0, -2, +2, 0)$
    - $A_k = 2 + 0 + 0 + 2 + 2 + 0 = 6$
    - result greater than 0, therefore, original bit was "1"
  - receiving B
    - $B_e = (-2, 0, 0, -2, +2, 0)$
    - $B_k = -2 + 0 + 0 - 2 - 2 + 0 = -6$, i.e. "0"

2.

International Mobile Subscriber Identity (IMSI)

- Uniquely identifies the subscriber and is stored in the SIM, HLR, and AuC
- Hierarchical addressing (example: MCN=262 for Germany, MNC = 01.02,03,07 for T-Mobile, Vodafone, Eplus, 02)
- Used, e.g., for billing

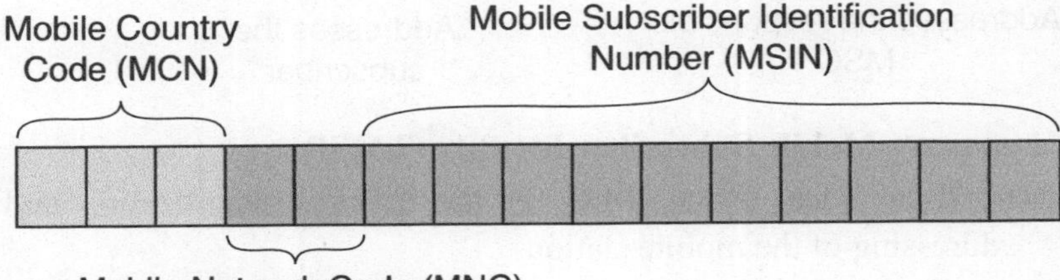

Mobile Subscriber ISDN Number (MSISDN)

- Real telephone number of a subscriber
- Subscriber can have several MSISDNs, e.g., to distinguish several services (voice, data, fax,...}
- Thus, automatic activation of service-specific resources is already possible during setup of connection

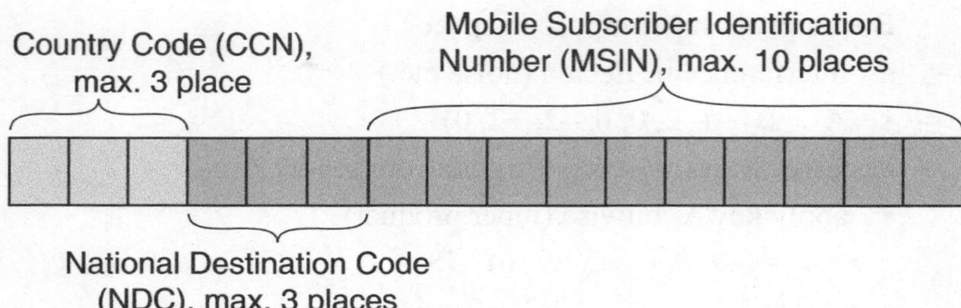

Mobile Station Roaming Number (MSRN)

- Temporary location-dependent ISDN number
- Required to make routing descisions and to identify the responsible MSC
- Assigned by the locally responsible VLR to each mobile station in its area and passed to the HLR
- Generated at each registration or when the HLR requests it for call setup (on a call-by-call basis)

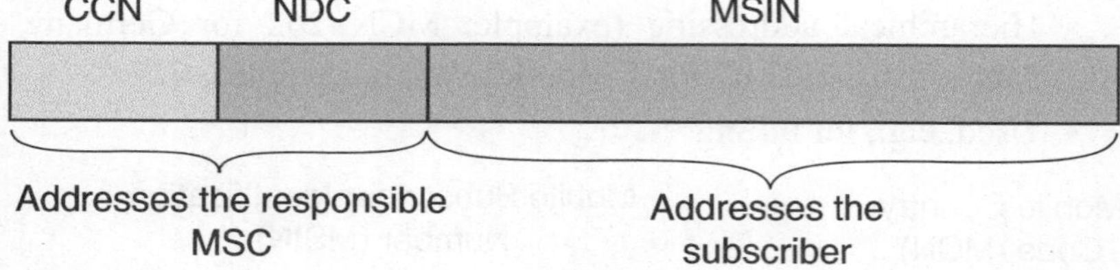

Temporary Mobile Subscriber Identity (TMSI)

- Used in place of the IMSI for the definite identification and addressing of the mobile station
- Avoids to determine the identity of the subscriber by listening to the radio channel
- Assigned during the mobile station's presence in the area of one VLR (by that VLR) and can be changed during this period (ID hopping)
- Is stored by the mobile station on the SIM card
- Is stored on the network side on|ly in the VLR, not in the HLR
- Is assigned in an operator specific way and consists of 4x8 Bits

- Subscriber can be uniquely identified; IMSI is replaced by (TMSI, LAI)

Type Approval Code (TAC), centrally assigned

Serial Number (SNR), assigned by the manufacturer.

Finally Assembly Code (FAC), assigned by the manufacturer.

Spare (SP), not used

International Mobile Station Equipment Identity (IIMEI)

- Uniquely identifies mobile stations internationally
- Allocated by the manufacturer, registered by the network operator and stored in the EIR
- Characterizes a mobile station and gives clues about the manufacturer and the date of manufacturing

Location Area Identifier (LAI)

- Internationally unique identification of a location area
- Regularly broadcasted by the base station
- "Heard" by the mobile station in order to decide whether or not a new LA has been entered

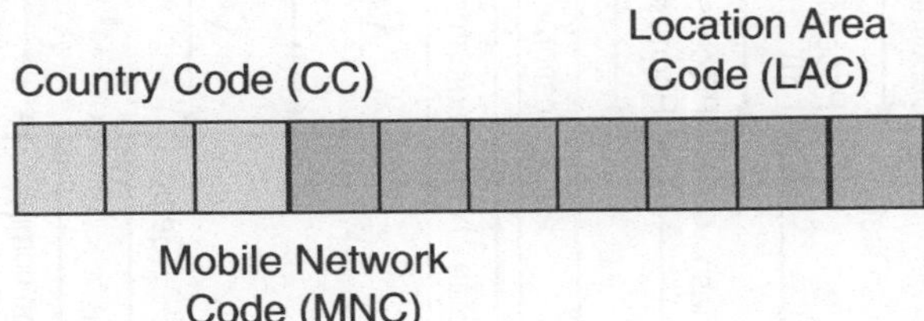

Cell Identifier (CI)

- Uniquely identification of cells within an LA
- Length of CI: 2x8 bits
- Internationally unique identification with the Global Cell Identity (LAI+CI)

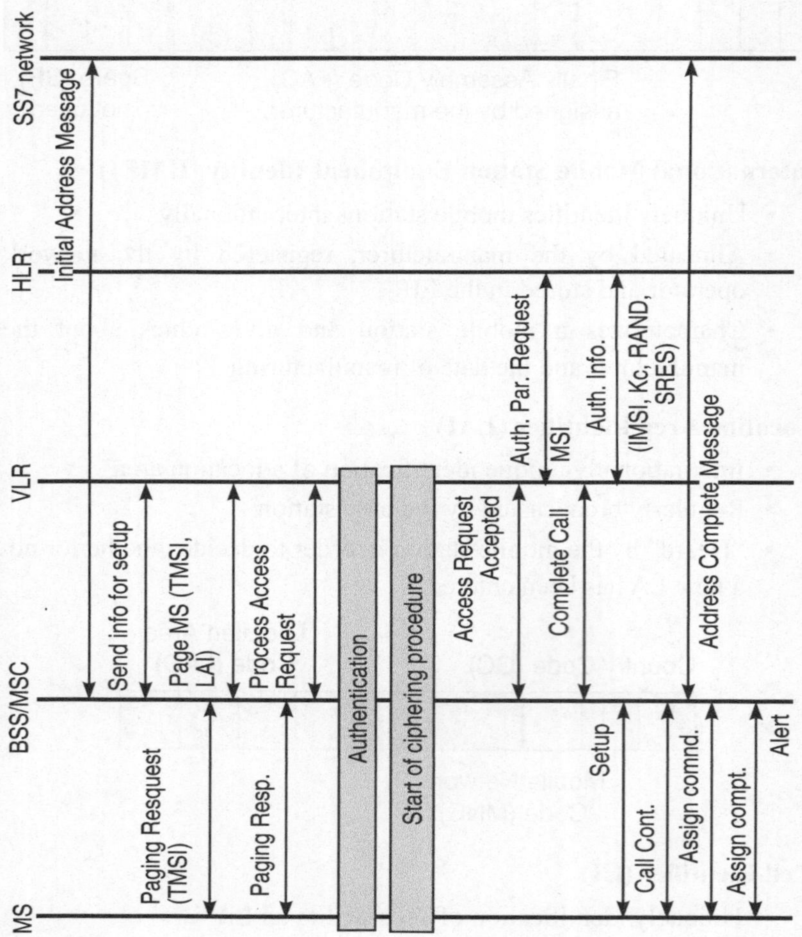
MS
BSS/MSC
VLR
HLR
SS7 network
Initial Address Message
Send info for setup
Page MS (TMSI, LAI)
Process Access Request
Paging Resquest (TMSI)
Paging Resp.
Authentication
Start of ciphering procedure
Access Request Accepted
Auth. Par. Request
MSI
Auth. Info.
(IMSI, Kc, RAND, SRES)
Complete Call
Address Complete Message
Setup
Call Cont.
Assign comnd.
Assign compt.
Alert

Location Registration

- Must be executed in order to get access to a GSM network, i.e., to receive or to initiate calls
- Registration with home network or a foreign network (roaming; provided there is a roaming agreement between home and foreign network)
  - *Steps:*
    - Sending IMSI and LAI to the network
    - Authentication
  - Start of ciphering
  - Generation of an TMSI (stored in the associated VLR) and an MSRN (stored in the central HLR)
  - MS receives TMSI and saves it in the SIM storage

Location Update

- Purpose: Tracking the mobile user in order to deliver calls or SMS

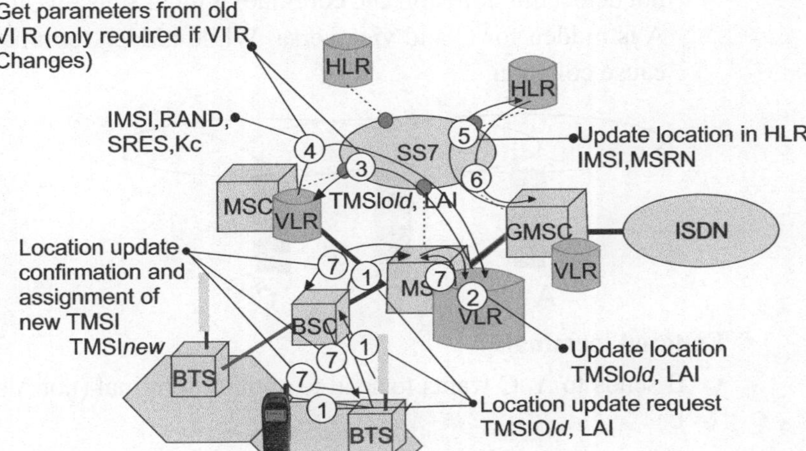

- Hybrid location updating
  - Execution on LA crossing: mobile station recognizes that it is in a new LA by regularly reading the LAI broadcasted in each cell

- Periodic execution: Periodic execution of location updates (independent of "Execution on LA crossing")

- Difference between location registration and location update: location update is based on TMSI (which is only unique in connection with an LAI) instead of the IMSI

b.

1.

- **Hidden terminals**
  - The transnsmission range of A reaches B, but not C.
  - C reaches B, but not A and finally, B reaches A & C.
  - A can not detect C and C can not detect A.
  - Collision at B, A cannot receive the collision (CD fails)
  - A is "hidden" for C
    - A starts sending to B, C does not receive this transmission. C also wants to send some data to B and sense the medium. Thus C starts sending causing a collision at B. But A can not detect this collision and continues with its transmission. A is hidden for C and vice versa. While hidden terminals cause collision.

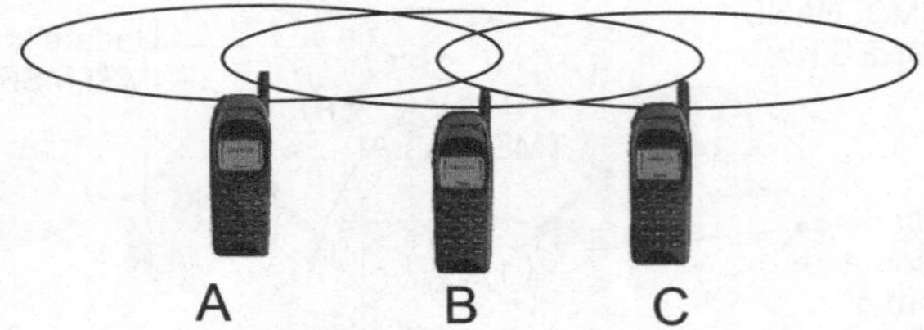

- **Exposed terminals**
  - B sends to A, C wants to send to another terminal (not A or B)
  - C has to wait, CS signals a medium in use
  - n but A is outside the radio range of C, therefore waiting is not necessary
  - C is "exposed" to B

- Now B sends something to A and C wants to send data to some other phone outside the range of A,B and C. C senses the carrier and detects that carrier is busy. Hence C post pones its transmission. But as A is outside the interference range of C, waiting is not necessary. So in this situation , C is exposed to B,

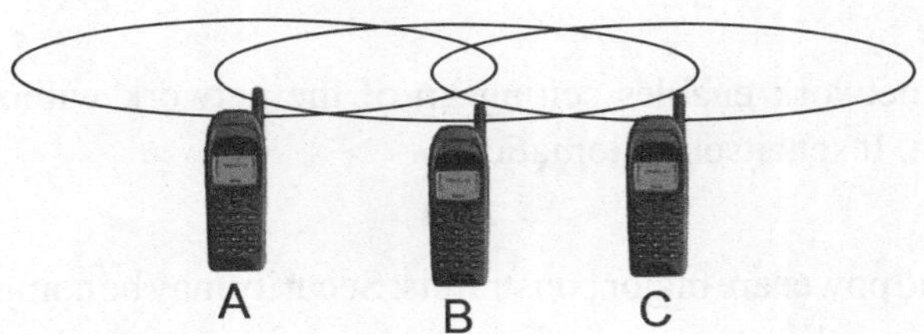

2. Packet Forwarding Mechanism in Bluetooth

Packet Forwarding

TUc Network. Aqocss Pt>Lnt or Group ad-huc Network acts as a bridge and. forwards packets between PAN users. It performs a subset of the operations specified by the IEEE

Each PAN user is itemed as if it whs a bridge port, so mtlfic is forwarded w and fiw each user. For Network Access Points the Ethernet connection is also treated as a bridge port. Broadcast traffic must be sent to ail ports, although devices are allowed to develop their own means of efficient!}' handling the problem of supporting brihadcasts to PAN users in low power models.

Which packet types ane fbrwajded and which are filtered ii decided by the packet filtering database. The 602. LD standard gives [he definitive set of mln for filtering and forwarding. It is not as simple at just looking at the type and deciding whether lo drop a packet or forward it: as packcts are sent, information is learned which affects decisions,

The Network Access Point or Group jtd-hoc Network mny add its own intelligent algorithms to the rules laid mil in 602.1 LD. For exmple. Ethernet carry AdJrehs Resolution Protocol (ARP) Frames. Address Resolution Protocol is use J to translate IP addresses into ethemet addresses. IP and cthcmel addresses arc allocated completely separately, so (0 find out which ethemet address corresponds to an IP address, a broadcast ARP request is sent out to every computer on the Ethernet. The ARP request contains an IP address which some device Ls trying to match up with an IP address. Every computer receives the packet, and the one with the matching IP address replies with a response giving its match-

Advantage

Bluetooth network enables setting up of the network without much preparation. It sets itself automatically.

Problems

Security and power are major constraints. Security may be compromised and power may be spent on traffic not meant for a particular device.

c.

1.

Initial goals of the WAP Forum

- Bring Internet based content & services to handheld wireless devices
- Work across global network technologies
- Allow creation of content that works across many types of link layers and device types
- To use existing standards wherever possible

Devices designed for WAP

- Includes mobile phones, pagers, PDAs
- Devices with limited CPU, memory & battery life
- Devices with a simple user interface
- Low bandwidth & high latency environments Unpredictable availability & stability

Bring Internet/Intranet information and advanced data services to digital cellular phones and other wireless terminals

Create global wireless protocol specifications that work across differing wireless network technologies

Enable the creation of content and applications that scale from very low-end bearer networks and devices

Embrace and extend existing standards and technology wherever they are appropriate

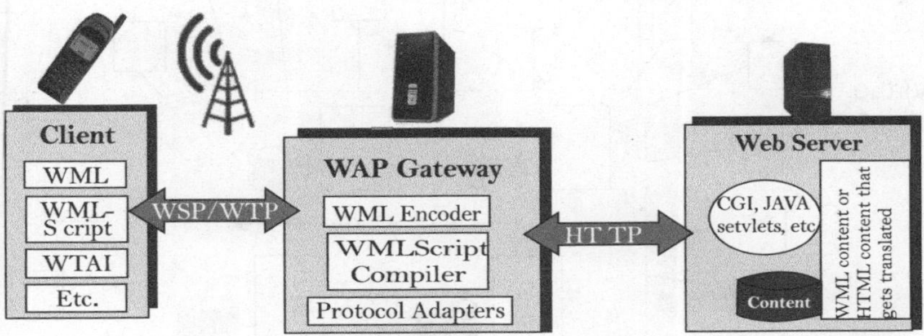

High level view of WAP Architecture

2. ODA FileSystem

Coda has beendeveloped at Carnegie Mellon University (CMU) in the 1990s, and is nowintegrated with a number of popular UNIX-based operating systems such as Linux.Coda is in many ways different from NFS, notably with respect to its goal for highavailability. This goal has led to advanced caching schemes that allow a client tocontinue operation despite being disconnected from a server.

Coda was designed to be a scalable, secure, and highly available distributedfile system. An important goal was to achieve a high degree of naming and locationtransparency so that the system would appear to its users very similar to apure local file system. By also taking high availability into account, the designersof Coda have also tried to reach a high degree of failure transparency.

Coda follows the same organization as AFS. Every Virtue workstation hosts auser-level process called Venus, whose role is similar to that of an NFS client. AVenus process is responsible for providing access to the files that are maintainedby the Vice file servers. In Coda, Venus is also responsible for allowing the clientto continue operation even if access to the file servers is (temporarily) impossible. This additional role is a major difference with the approach followed in NFS.

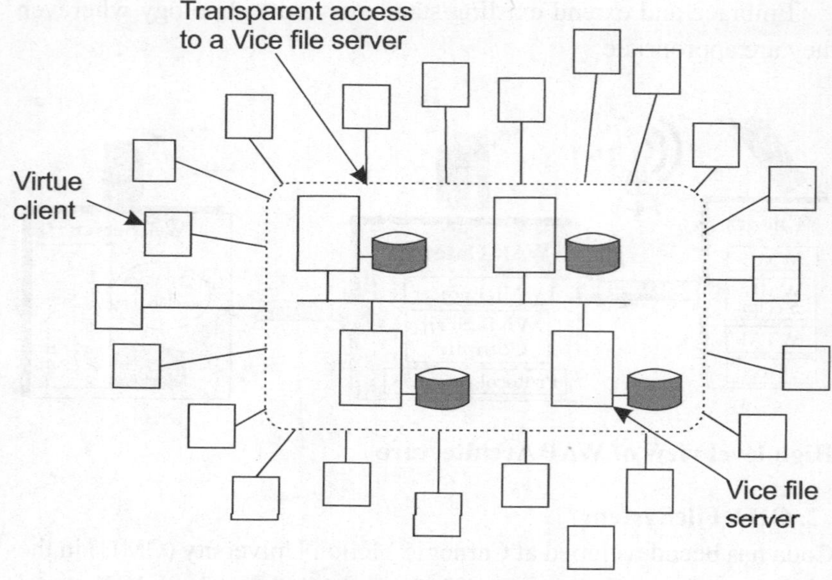

Figure The overall organization of AFS.

A client is said to be disconnected with respect to avolume, if its AVSG for that volume is empty. In other words, the client cannotcontact any of the servers holding a copy of the volume. In most file systems (e.g.,NFS), a client is not allowed to proceed unless it can contact at least one server. Adifferent approach is followed in Coda. There, a client will simply resort to usingits local copy of the file that it had when it opened the file at a server.Closing a file (or actually, the session in which the file is accessed) whendisconnected will always succeed. However, it may be possible that conflicts aredetected when modifications are transferred to a server when connection is establishedagain. In case automatic conflict resolution fails, manual intervention willbe necessary. Practicalexperience with Coda has shown that disconnected operationgenerally works, although there are occasions in which reintegration fails dueto unresolvable conflicts.

Types of sending an invalidation message by server.

The success of the approach followed in Coda is mainly attributed to the factthat, in practice, write-sharing a file hardly occurs. In other words, in practice it israre for two processes to open the same file for writing. Of course, sharing filesfor only reading happens a lot, but that does not impose any conflicts. Theseobservations have also been made for other file systems. Furthermore, thetransactional semantics underlying Coda's file-sharing model also makes it easyto handle the case in which there are multiple processes only reading a shared fileat the same time that exactly one process is concurrently modifying that file.

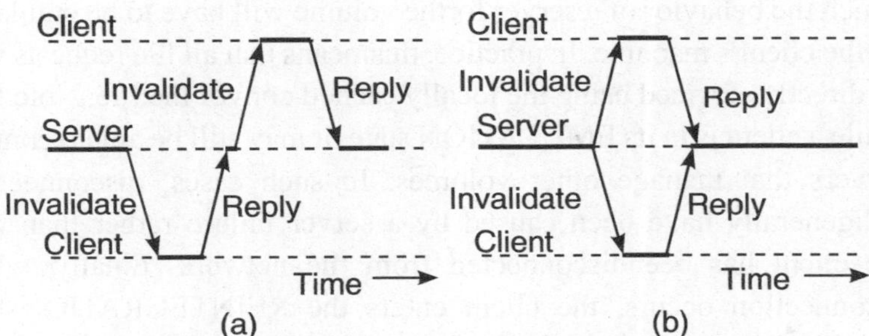

Figure (a) Sending an invalidation message one at a time. (b) Sending invalidation messages in parallel.

The main problem that needs to be solved to make disconnected operation asuccess is to ensure that a client's cache contains those files that will be accessedduring disconnection. If a simple caching strategy is followed, it may turn out thata client cannot continue as it lacks the necessary files. Filling the cache inadvance with the appropriate files is called hoarding. The overall behavior of aclient with respect to a volume (and thus the files in that volume) can now besummarized by the state-transition diagram shown in following Fig.

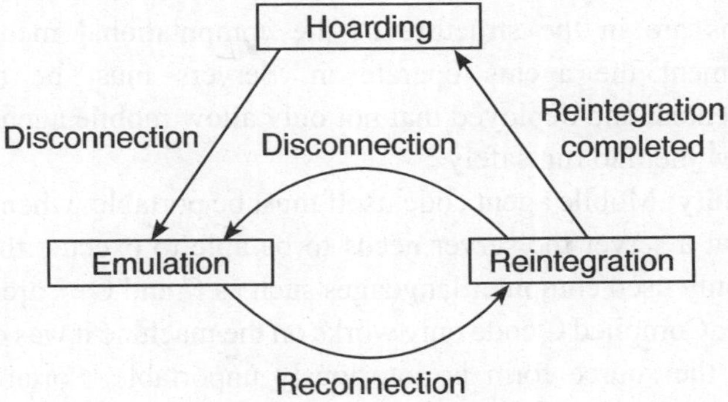

Normally, a client will be in the HOARDING state. In this state, the client isconnected to (at least) one server that contains a copy of the volume. While in thisstate, the client can contact the server and issue file requests to perform its work.Simultaneously, it will also attempt to keep its cache filled with useful data (e.g.,files, file attributes, and directories).At a certain point, the number of servers in the client's AVSG will drop tozero, bringing it into an EMULATION state in which the behavior of a server forthe volume will have to be emulated on the client's machine. In practice, thismeans that all file requests will be directly serviced using the locally cached copyof the file. Note that while a client is in its EMULATION state, it may still be ableto contact servers that manage other volumes. In such cases, disconnection willgenerally have been caused by a server failure rather than that the client has beendisconnected from the network. Finally, when reconnection occurs, the client enters the REINTEGRATIONstate in which it transfers updates to the server in order to make them permanent.It is during reintegration that conflicts are detected and, where possible, automaticallyresolved. As shown in Fig. above, it is possible that during reintegration theconnection with the server is lost again, bringing the client back into the EMULATIONstate.

d.

Requirements for Mobile Agent Systems

While mobile agents are a useful approach to distributed computation, in practice they have seldom been used. There are many technical challenges to implementing mobile agent systems. Most of these problems are in the structure of the computational medium, the environment the agents operate in. Servers must be designed, implemented, and deployed that not only allow mobile agents to run, but allow them to run safely.

Portability: Mobile agent code itself must be portable; when an agent arrives at a server the server needs to be able to execute that agent. Commonly used computer languages such as C and C++ are not very portable. Compiled C code only works on the machine it was compiled for and the source form is notoriously unportable. Portability can be achieved by running computer programs inside virtual machines interpreters, but overhead has limited the use of interpreted languages. Most mobile agent systems under development now rely at least in part on virtual machines to standardize the execution environment.

Ubiquity: In order for mobile agents to be successful they need access to many different computer resources. Servers for agents must be commonplace; there needs to be a widely accepted framework for executing mobile agents deployed on many machines across the Internet. In practice the requirement of ubiquity means that the execution environment needs to have market acceptability, be freely available, and be unencumbered by restrictive intellectual property requirements.

Network Communication: Mobile agents that live in the network need to be written in a language that makes network access simple. It must be easy to transfer objects across the network and to invoke methods of remote objects. Traditional computer languages treat networking structures as an afterthought, usually providing only a minimal socket library. Languages that better support network access have typically not been widely used. This situation is improving with the current development of language-neutral distributed object frameworks such as CORBA and OLE.

Server Security: A major concern specific to mobile agents is the protection of the servers running the agents. Running arbitrary programs on a machine is dangerous: a hostile program could destroy the hard drive, steal data, or do all sorts of other undesirable things. This risk must be thoroughly addressed if mobile agent environments are to succeed. Two types of security are possible to protect servers from malfunctioning and hostile agents: physical and social.

Physical security refers to building servers for agents in such a way that the agents cannot harm the server. The ''laws of physics'' of the server execution environment can be designed to make dangerous operations difficult or impossible. Common approaches involve creating a ''sandbox'' for visiting agents, restricting access to resources (preventing disk writes, for instance) and ensuring the agent cannot escape those restrictions. This approach to security is attractive; when it works, it is entirely effective. But the viability of physical security in the face of design complexity and server implementation bugs is unclear. In addition, physical security is typically focussed on protecting some underlying aspect of the server from the sandbox the agent is trapped in. But if multiple agents are put in the same sandbox how can the server guarantee that one agent cannot harm another? As we put more trust in the computations that take place inside sandboxes, the security of those sandboxes themselves becomes important. A second approach to server security is using social enforcement mechanisms to punish the creators of harmful agents. If a server administrator can find out who is responsible for a malicious agent, then that person can be held accountable via social mechanisms (such as lawsuits). Digital signature technology makes identifying the authors of agents possible. But there are limitations to a purely social approach to security. It may not be clear which agent is responsible for damage, nor will it be easy to determine ahead of time which agent authors are trustable. In practice some combination of social and physical enforcement of server security will be useful.

Agent Security: The complement of server security is agent security: whether the agent can trust the server on which it is executing. A mobile agent might contain secret information such as proprietary data and algorithms. Worse, servers might have an incentive to subvert the computation of a visiting agent. In the Internet-based DES cracking effort currently under design a major concern is protecting the computation from sites that pretend to do pieces of the problem but return false answers . Physical security answers to this problem are difficult. Secure, trusted hardware on the server could guarantee agent safety but is unlikely to be widely deployed. Agent programmers can protect their agents by obfuscating their code and verifying the results of the remotely- performed computation but the general applicability of these techniques are unknown. Social solutions may be possible in the form of reputation systems for servers. This area of security has largely been unexamined.

Resource Accounting: If economic control and incentive are going to be factors in net- wide resource use some mechanism to account for the resources that an agent uses and a way for receiving payment for those resources is necessary. In theory these requirements are not difficult to meet. Servers can keep track of the resource usage of agents, explicitly accounting CPU, memory, bandwidth and disk usage. Digital cash systems can be used to pay for services. In practice, these technologies are not widely deployed and the overhead they impose presents an engineering challenge.

1. Difference between Cellular and Ad-hoc Network

Differences between Cellular and Ad Hoc Wireless Networks

Cellular	Ad Hoc Wireless Networks
Infrastructure networks	Infrastructureless networks
Fixed, prelocated cell sites and base station	No base station, and rapid deployment
Static backbone network topology	Highly dynamic network topologies with multihop
Relatively caring environment and stable connectivity	Hostile environment (noise, losses) and irregular connectivity
Detailed planning before base station can be installed	Ad hoc network automatically forms and adopts to changes
High setup costs	Cost-effective
Large setup time	Less setup time

e.

1. Compare and Contrast DSR and AODV

i. *Genral:* While DSR and AODV share the on-demand behavior, many of their routing mechanisms are very different.

- DSR use.s source routing, whereas AODV uses a table-driven routing framework and desti-
- By virtue of source routing, DSR has access to a significantly greater amount of routing information than AODV. For example, in DSR, by using a single request-reply cycle,

the source can learn routes to each intermediate node on the route in addition to the intended destination

- DSR replies to all requests reaching a destination from a single request cycle. In AODV, on the other hand, the destination replies only once to the request arriving first and ignores the rest.
- The route deletion activity using KERR is also conservative in AODV. By way of active neighbour list, RERR packets reach all nodes using a failed link on its route to any destination. In DSR, however, an RERR simply backtracks the data packet that meets a failed link. Nodes thayire not on the upstream route of this data packet, but use the failed link, are

ii. Routing overhead: DSR always demonstrates a lower routing overhead than AODV. The major contribution to routing overhead in AODV is from RERRs, while RRERs constitute a large fraction of routing overhead in DSR. AODV has more RERRs than DSR, and the con-

iii. Effect of mobility: Link failures can happen very frequently in MANETs, They trigger new route discoveries in AODV, since it has at most one route per'destination in its routing table. However, route discovery is delayed in DSR until all cached routes fail. With high mobility,

2. The entities of Mobile IP are as follows:

Mobile node (MN): A mobile node is an end-system or router that can change its point of attachment to the internet using mobile IP. The MN keeps its IP address and can continuously communicate with any other system in the internet as long as link-layer connectivity is given. Mobile nodes are not necessarily small devices such as laptops with antennas or mobile phones; a router onboard an aircraft can be a powerful mobile node.

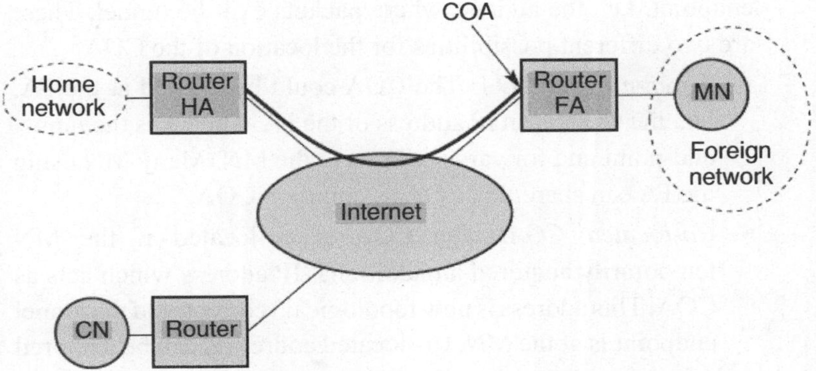

- **Correspondent node (CN):** At least one partner is needed for communication. In the following the CN represents this partner for the MN. The CN can be a fixed or mobile node.
- **Home network:** The home network is the subnet the MN belongs to with respect to Its IP address. No mobile IP support is needed within the home network.
- **Foreign network:** The foreign network is the current subnet the MN visits and which is not the home network.
- **Foreign agent (FA):** The FA can provide several services to the MN during its visit to the foreign network. The FA can have the CO A (defined below), acting as tunnel endpoint and forwarding packets to the MN. The FA can be the default router for the MN. FAs can also provide security services because they belong to the foreign network as opposed to the MN which is only visiting. For mobile IP functioning, FAs are not necessarily needed. Typically, an FA Is implemented on a router for the subnet the MN attaches to.
- **Care-of address (COA):** The COA defines the current location of the MN from an IP point of view. All IP packets sent to the MN are delivered to the COA, not directly to the IP address of the MN. Packet delivery toward the MN is done using a tunnel, as explained later. To be more precise, the COA marks the tunnel

endpoint, i.e., the address where packets exit the tunnel. There are two different possibilities for the location of the COA:

- *Foreign agent COA:* The COA could be located at the FA, i.e., the COA is an IP address of the FA. The FA is the tunnel end-point and forwards packets to the MN. Many MN using the FA can share this COA as common COA.
- *Co-located COA:* The COA is co-located if the MN temporarily acquired an additional IP address which acts as COA. This address is now topological^ correct, and the tunnel endpoint is at the MN. Co-located addresses can be acquired using services such as DHCP. One problem associated with this approach is the need for additional addresses if MNs request a COA. This is not always a good idea considering the scarcity of IPv4 addresses.

- **Home agent (HA):** The HA provides several services for the MN and is located in the home network. The tunnel for packets toward the MN starts at the HA. The HA maintains a location registry, i.e., it Is informed of the MN's location by the current COA. Three alternatives for the implementation of an HA exist.

Data Transfer from Landline to MN

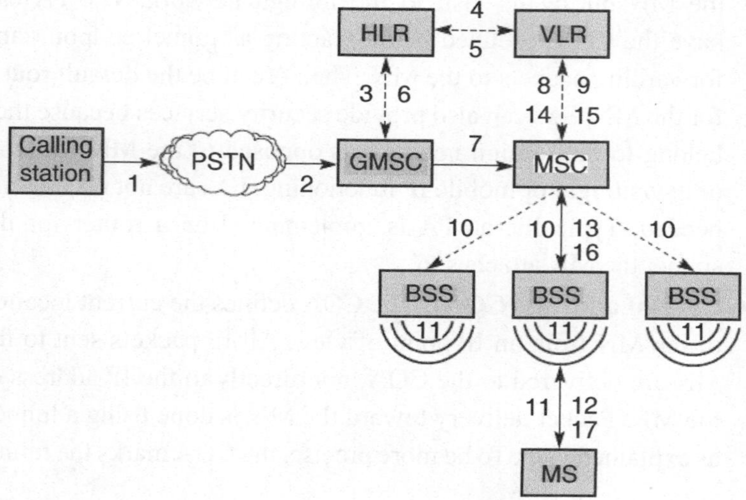

SECTION C

Question 3

System Architecture

A GSM Public Land Mobile Network (PLMN) consists of at least one Service Area controlled by a Mobile Switching Center (MSC) connected to the Public Switched Telephone Network (PSTN), see

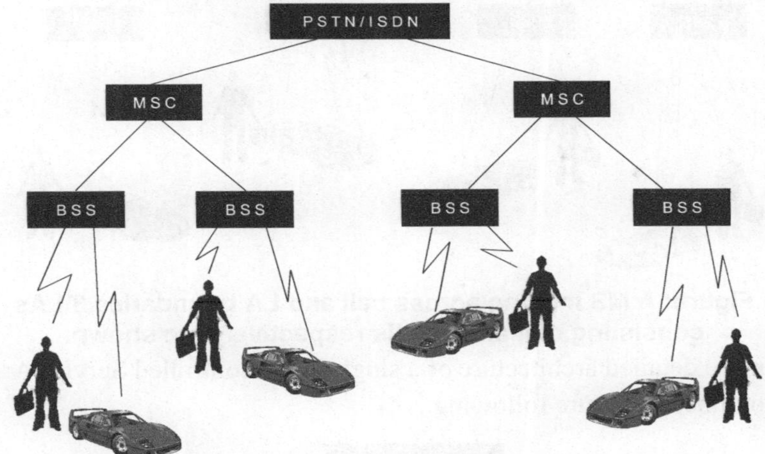

Figure: The architecture of a GSM Public Land Mobile Network (PLMN)

A Base Station Subsystem (BSS) consists of

- a Base Station Controller (BSC)
- at least one radio saccess point or Base Transceiver Station (BTS) for Mobile Stations (MS), which are mobile phones or other handheld devices (for example PDA computers) with phone interface.

A BTS, with its aerial and associated radio frequency components, is the actual transmission and reception component. A Network Cell is the area of radio coverage by one BTS. One or more BTSs are in turn managed by a BSC. A network cell cluster covered by one or several BSSs can be managed as a Location Area (LA). All these BSSs must however be controlled by a single MSC. In below Figure it is shown three LAs of 3, 4 and 4 cells respectively with a MS moving across cell and LA boundaries.

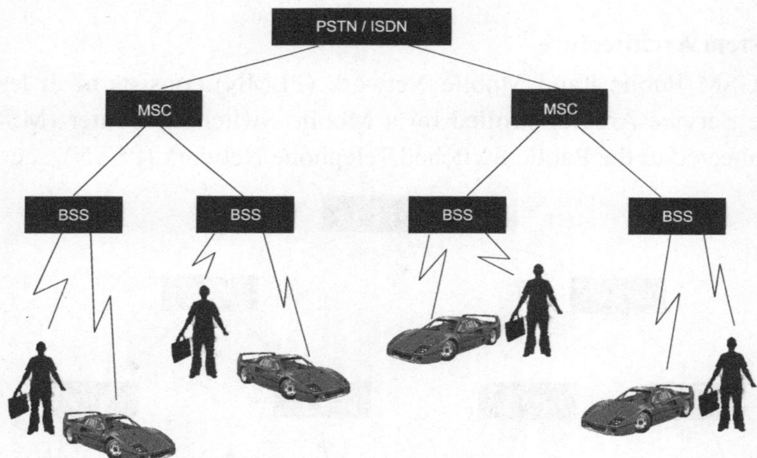

Figure: A MS moving across cell and LA boundaries.3 LAs consisting of 4 and 5 cells respectively are shown.

A more detailed architecture of a single MSC controlled Service Area is outlined in Figure following.

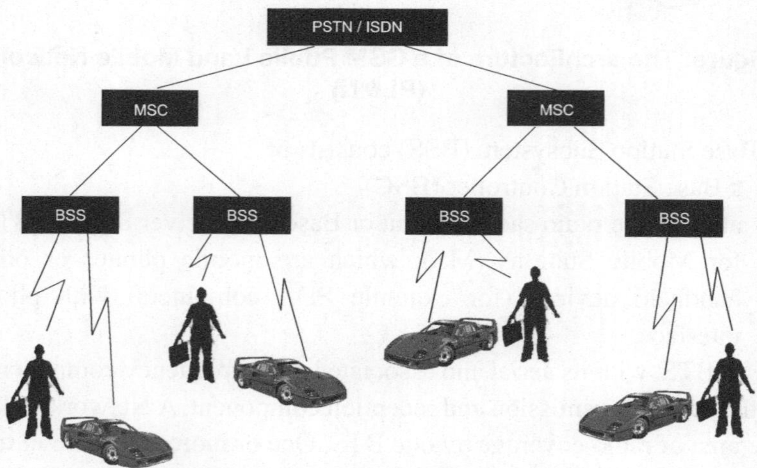

Figure: The GSM network architecture for a single MSC controlled Service Area

The components of the tree GSM network subsystems

- Radio Subsystem (RSS) consisting of the BSSs and all BSS connected MS devices.
- Network and Switching Subsystem (NSS)
- Operation Subsystem (OSS)

Specified in GSM 01.02 ('General description of a GSM Public Land Mobile Network (PLMN)') and the GSM components are shown in Figure gsm3.

ME = Mobile Equipment
BTS = Base Receiving Station
BSC = Base Station Controller
MSC = Mobile Switching Center
VLR = Visitor Location Register
OMC = Operation and Maintenance Center
AuC = Authentication Center
HLR = Home Location Register
EIR = Equipment Identity Register
SMSC = Short Message Service Centre

A MSC is also through a Gateway MSC (GMSC) connected to other MSCs and to the Public Switched Telephone Network (PSTN) with the Integrated Services Digital Network (ISDN) option. The Inter-Working Function (IWF) of GMSC connects the circuit switched data paths of a GSM network with the PSTN/ISDN. A GMSC is usually integrated in an MSC, see next Figure.

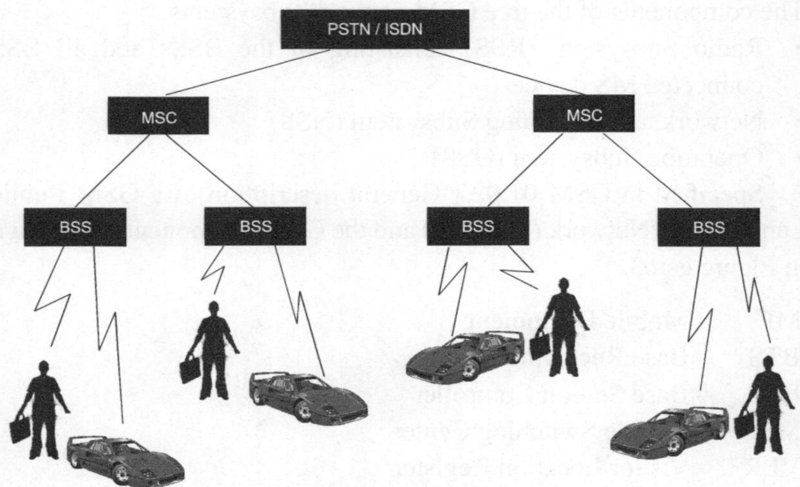

Figure: Basic GSM network components

3. Network and Switching Subsystem (Nss)

NSS consists of the Mobile Switching Center (MSC) and the Visitor Location Register (VLR). A MSC manages multiple BSSs and is responsible for

- setting up, managing and shutting down connections,
- handling call charges
- supervising supplementary services, such as call forwarding, call blocking and conference calling.

VLR contains information about all MSs currently within range of the associated MSC. This information is needed for routing a call to a particular MS (mobile telephone) via the proper BSS and radio cell. The VLR also maintains a list of MSs belonging to subscribers of other GSM networks. Such subscribers have logged or roamed into the network of the associated MSC. The area covered by a MSC is actually called a MSC/VLR Service Area, which can consist of several LAs as is shown in Figure next.

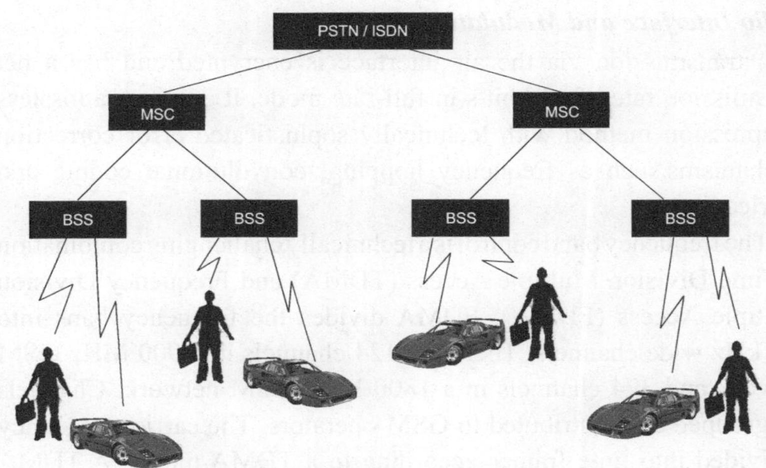

Figure: A MSC/VLR Service Area

4. Operation Subsystem (OSS)

The OSS consists of

- the Operation and Maintenance Center (OMC)
- the Authentication Center (AuC),
- the Home Location Register (HLR)
- the Equipment Identity Register (EIR).

OMC is responsible for

- regular network operation
- subscriber administration
- call billing.

AuC is the security component on the network side. AuC generates and manages all cryptographic keys and algorithms needed for network operation, especially for authentication of the MSs (i.e., the SIMs). HLR contains all of the subscriber data as well as the localization data for each of the MS. EIR contains essential data, such as the serial numbers of all MSs represented in the network. OSS alsocontrols the Short Message Service Centre (SMSC) for transmission of SMS messages. SMSC need information in HLR for the routing of SMS messages.

Radio Interface and Modulation

Data transmission via the air interface is encrypted and has a net transmission rate of 13 kbit/s in full-rate mode. It employs a lossless compression method with technically sophisticated error correction mechanisms,such as frequency hopping, convolutional coding and interleaving.

The frequency band control is a technically challenging combination of Time Division Multiple Access (TDMA) and Frequency Division Multiple Access (FDMA). FDMA divides the frequency bans into 200 kHz wide channels. There are 124 channels in a 900 MHz GSM network and 374 channels in a 1800 MHz GSM network. Channels are grouped and distributed to GSM operators. The carrier frequency is divided into time frames according to a TDMA model. A TDMA frame consists of 8 time intervals called slots. A message in one slut is called a burst. A logical channel uses one slot in a frame. A typical receiver module for a BTS has eight 200 kHz channels. In theory a receiver module can thus concurrently maintain eight active links to MSs. In practice, only seven active links are usually used, since one channel is usually reserved for administrative communications. One, three or six receiver modules are usually fitted in each BTS.

Characteristics of frequency hopping are:

- 216.7 hops/second
- the frequency is changed after each burst according to a predefined pattern
- disturbances are spread
- eavesdropping is made more difficult.

Modulation of radio signals means that the carrier frequency characteristics are changed while the signals are sent. GSM uses the Gaussian Modulation Shift Keying (GMSK), which is a compromise between a fairly high spectrum efficiency (of the order of 1 bit/Hz) and a reasonable demodulation complexity. The main features of GMSK are:

- The input bit stream is differentially encoded.
- The encoded signal is passed to a filter with a Gaussian impulse response function. The filtered bit waveform shows smooth

transitions and results in a narrow occupied frequency spectrum. Steep phase jumps would require more bandwidth.

- The Gaussian filtered waveform is applied to a phase modulator, which produces a phase shift of +90° or -90° for each differential bit value.

Advantages of 2G GSM

- GSM is mature; this maturity means a more stable network with robust features.
- Less signal deterioration inside buildings.
- Ability to use repeaters.
- Talktime is generally higher in GSM phones due to the pulse nature of transmission.
- The availability of Subscriber Identity Modules allows users to switch networks and handsets at will.
- GSM covers virtually all parts of the world so international roaming is not a problem.
- Disadvantages of 2G GSM
- Pulse nature of TDMA transmission used in 2G interferes with some electronics, especially certain audio amplifiers. 3G uses W-CDMA now.
- Intellectual property is concentrated among a few industry participants, creating barriers to entry for new entrants and limiting competition among phone manufacturers.
- GSM has a fixed maximum cell site range of 35 km, which is imposed by technical limitations.

Question 4

A limited amount of bandwidth is allocated for wireless services. A wireless system is required to accommodate as many users as possible by effectively sharing the limited bandwidth. Therefore, in the field of communications, the term multiple access could be defined as a means of allowing multiple users to simultaneously share the finite bandwidth with least possible degradation in the performance of the system. There are several techniques how multiple accessing can be achieved. The are four basic schemes:

i. Frequency Division Multiple Access (FDMA)
ii. Time Division Multiple Access (TDMA)
iii. Code Division Multiple Access (CDMA)
iv. Space Division Multiple Access (SDMA)

1. Frequency Division Multiple Access (FDMA)

FDMA is one of the earliest multiple-access techniques for cellular systems when continuous transmission is required for analog services. In this technique the bandwidth is divided into a number of channels and distributed among users with a finite portion of bandwidth for permanent use. The vertical axis that represents the code is shown here just to make a clear comparison with CDMA (discussed later in this chapter). The channels are assigned only when demanded by the users. Therefore when a channel is not in use it becomes a wasted resource.

FDMA channels have narrow bandwidth (30Khz) and therefore they are usually implemented in narrowband systems. Since the user has his portion of the bandwidth all the time, FDMA does not require synchronization or timing control, which makes it algorithmically simple. Even though no two users use the same frequency band at the same time, guard bands are introduced between frequency bands to minimize adjacent channel interference. Guard bands are unused frequency slots that separate neighboring channels. This leads to a waste of bandwidth. When continuous transmission is not required, bandwidth goes wasted since it is not being utilized for a portion of the time. In wireless communications, FDMA achieves simultaneous transmission and reception by using Frequency division duplexing (FDD). In order for both the transmitter and the receiver to operate at the same time, FDD requires duplexers. The requirement of duplexers in the FDMA system makes it expensive.

Time Division Multiple Access (TDMA)

In digital systems, continuous transmission is not required because users do not use the allotted bandwidth all the time. In such systems, TDMA is a complimentary access technique to FDMA. Global Systems for Mobile communications (GSM) uses the TDMA technique. In TDMA, the entire bandwidth is available to the user but only for a finite period of time. In most cases the available bandwidth is divided into fewer channels compared to FDMA and the users are allotted time slots during which they have the entire channel bandwidth at their disposal. TDMA requires careful time synchronization since users share the bandwidth in the frequency domain. Since the number of channels are less, inter channel interference is almost negligible, hence the guard time between the channels is considerably smaller. Guard time is a spacing in time between the TDMA bursts. In cellular communications, when a user moves from one cell to another there is a chance that user could experience a call loss if there are no free time slots available. TDMA uses different time slots for transmission and reception. This type of duplexing is referred to as Time division duplexing (TDD). TDD does not require duplexers.

Code Division Multiple Access

In CDMA, all the users occupy the same bandwidth, however they are all assigned separate codes, which differentiates them from each other typical Walsh codes used for this purpose. CDMA systems utilize a spread spectrum technique in which a spreading signal, which is uncorrelated to the signal and has a large bandwidth, is used to spread the narrow band message signal. Direct Sequence Spread Spectrum (DS-SS) is most commonly used for CDMA.

In DS-SS, the message signal is multiplied by a Pseudo Random Noise Code (PN code), which has noise-like properties. Each user has his owncodeword which is orthogonal to the codes of other users. In order to detect the user, the receiver is required to know the codeword used by the transmitter. Unlike TDMA, CDMA does not require time synchronization between the users. A CDMA system experiences a problem called self-jamming which arises when the spreading codes used for different users are not exactly orthogonal. While dispreading, this leads to a significant contribution from other users to the receiver decision statistic. If the power of the multiple users in a CDMA system is unequal, then the user with the strongest signal power will be demodulated at the receiver. The strength of the received signal raises the noise floor for the weaker signals at the demodulators. This reduces the probability that weaker signals will be received. This problem, known as the near-far problem can be taken care of by using power control. This ensures that all the signals within the coverage of the base station arrive with same power at the receiver

Space Division Multiple Access (SDMA)

SDMA utilizes the spatial separation of the users in order to optimize the use of the frequency spectrum. A primitive form of SDMA is when the same frequency is re-used in different cells in a cellular wireless network. However for limited co-channel interference it is required that the cells be sufficiently separated. This limits the number of cells a region can be divided into and hence limits the frequency re-use factor. A more advanced approach can further increase the capacity of the network. This technique would enable frequency re-use within the cell. It uses a Smart Antenna technique that employs antenna arrays backed by some intelligent signal processing to steer the antenna pattern in the direction of the desired user and places nulls in the direction of the interfering signals. Since these arrays can produce narrow spot beams, the frequency can be re-used within the cell as long as the spatial separation between the users is sufficient. There are three users served by SDMA using the same channel within the cell. In a practical cellular environment it is improbable to have just one transmitter fall within the receiver beam width. Therefore it becomes imperative to use other multiple access techniques in conjunction with SDMA. When different areas are covered by the antenna beam, frequency can be re-used, in which case TDMA or CDMA is employed, for different frequencies FDMA can be used.

Question 5

a. If a terminal has a packet ready to transmit, it will sense the medium first. If the medium is idle for DIFS, it will transmit RTS, then wait for the CIS from the receiver Therefore, the earliest time foir the receiver to send CPS massage is:

$$3\alpha + 5\alpha + \alpha + \alpha = 10\alpha$$

b. When the senjder receives the CTS from the receiver, it waits for SIFS, and then sends its data packet. Therefore, the shortest time for the receiver to send the ACK signal is:

$$3\alpha + 5\alpha + \alpha + \alpha + 5\alpha + \alpha + \alpha + 100\alpha + \alpha + \alpha = 119\alpha$$

Note that we should include the propagation delay also.

c. This is to give priority to some packets. For example after transmitting the DATA packets the receiver should be allowed to send ACK packets without any collisions. To accomplish this, we transmit the ACK packets immediately after SIFS time interval before any other node can transmit and interrupt the ACK packet,

d. No. SIFS is the turnaround time required to change from transmit (receive) mode to receive (transmit) mode. Thus it is compulsory to have finite SIFS time.

Question 6

The given Network:

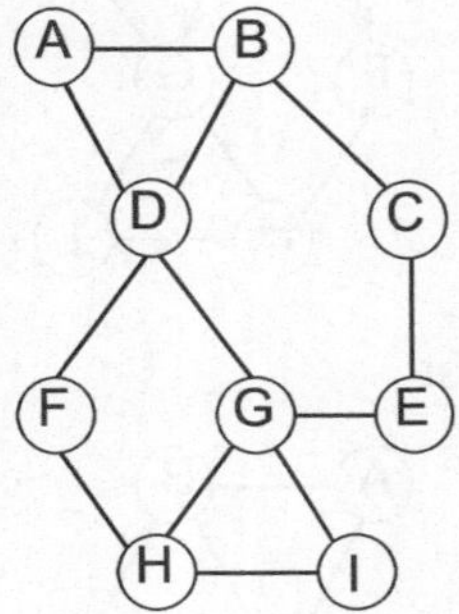

Step 1: The A will broadcast RREQ

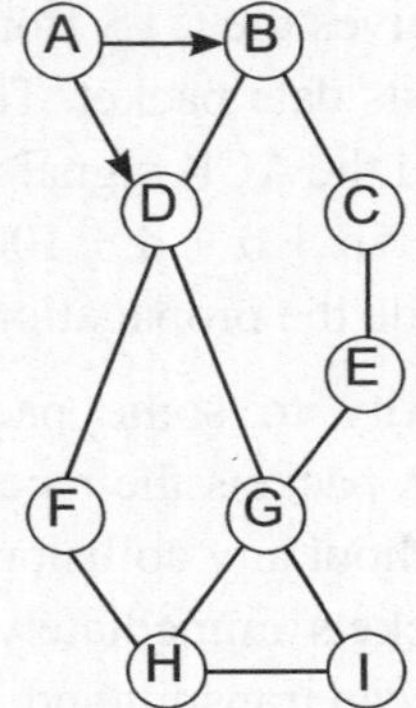

Step 2: Now B, D will broadcast.

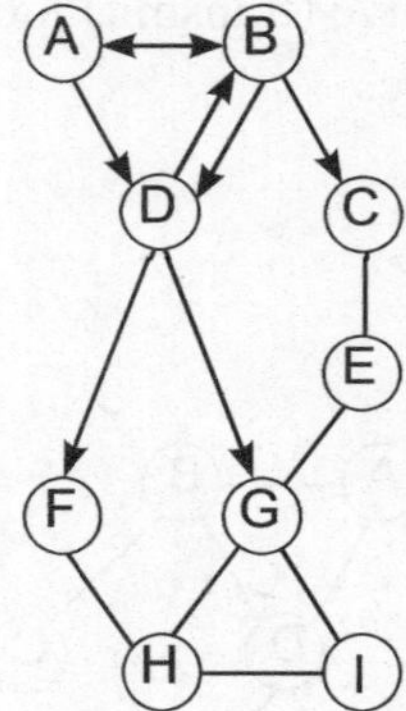

Step 3: The will broadcast

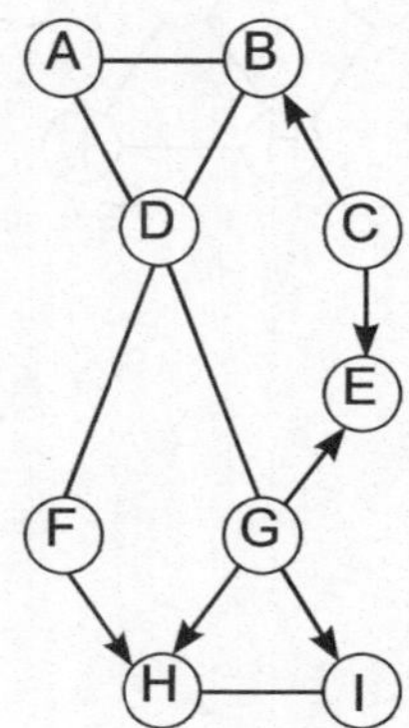

Step 4: Now H, G, E, I will broadcast

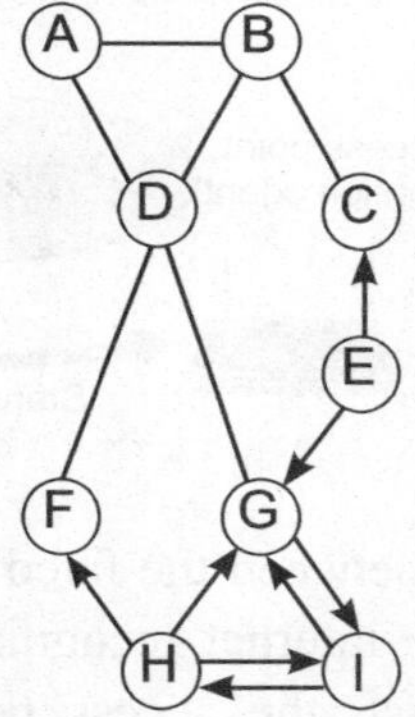

The path A, D, G, I will be stored in the A along with other path. If this path fails than A will select another path from its and each, if no path present then again discovery mechanism will take place.

Question 7

Together wtth the introduction of WLANs in the mid-nineties several research projects were started with the goal to Increase TCP's performance in wireless and mobile environments.|

Indirect TCP

Two competing insights led to the development of indirect TCP (l-TCP) (Bakre, 1995). One Is that TCP performs poorly together with wireless links; the other is that TCP within the fixed network cannot be changed, [-TCP segments a TCP connection into a fixed pa it and a wireless part. Figure 9.1 shows an example with a mobile host connected via a wireless link and an access point to the 'wired' internet where the correspondent host resides. The correspondent node could also use wireless access. The following would then also be applied to the access link of the correspondent host.

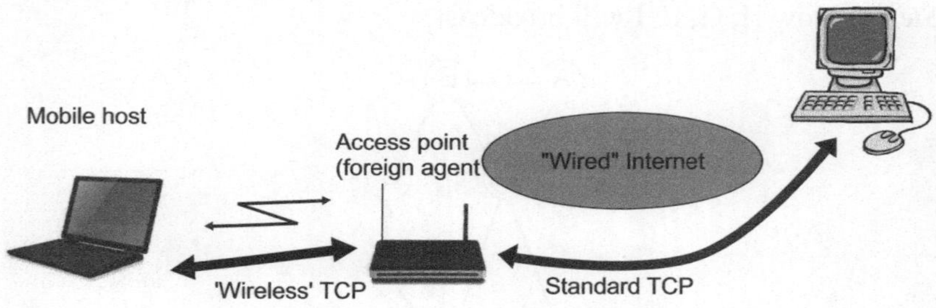

Standard TCP is used between the fixed computer and the access point. No computer in the internet recognizes any changes to TCP. Instead of the mobile host, the access point now terminates the standard TCP connection, acting as a proxy. This means that the access point is now seen as the mobile host for the fixed host and as the fixed host for the mobile host. Between the access point and the mobile host, a special TCP, adapted to wireless links, is used. However, changing TCP for the wireless link is not a requirement. Even an unchanged TCP can benefit from the much shorter round trip time, starting retransmission much faster. A good place for segmenting the connection between mobile host and correspondent host is at the foreign agent of mobile IP (see chapter 8). Hie foreign agent controls the mobility of the mobile host anyway and can also hand over the connection to the next foreign agent when the mobile host moves on. However, one can also imagine separating the TCP connections at a special server, e.g., at the entry point to a mobile phone network (e.g., 1WF in GSM, GGSN in GPRS).

The correspondent host in the fixed network does not notice the wireless link or the segmentation of the connection. The foreign agent acts as a proxy and relays all data in both directions. If the correspondent host sends a packet, the foreign agent acknowledges this packet and tries to forward the packet to the mobile host. If the mobile host receives the packet, it acknowledges the packet. However, this acknowledgement is only used by the foreign agent. If a packet is lost on the wireless link due to a transmission error, the correspondent host would not notice this. In this case, the foreign agent tries to retransmit this packet locally to maintain reliable data transport.

Similarly, if the mobile host sends a packet, the foreign agent acknowledges this packet and tries to forward it to the correspondent host. If the packet is lost on the wireless link, the mobile hosts notice this much faster due to the lower round trip time and can directly retransmit the packet. Packet loss in the wired network is now handled by the foreign agent.

I-TCP requires several actions as soon as a handover takes place. As Figure demonstrates, not only the packets have to be redirected using e.g., mobile IP. In the example shown, the access point acts as a proxy buffering packets for retransmission. After the handover, the old proxy must forward buffered data to the new proxy because it has already acknowledged the data. As explained in chapter 8, after registration with the new foreign agent, this new foreign agent can inform the old one about its location to enable packet forwarding. Besides buffer content, the sockets of the proxy, too, must migrate to the new foreign agent located in the access point. The socket reflects the current state of the TCP connection, i.e., sequence number, addresses, ports etc. No new connection may be established for the mobile host, and the correspondent host must not see any changes in connection state.

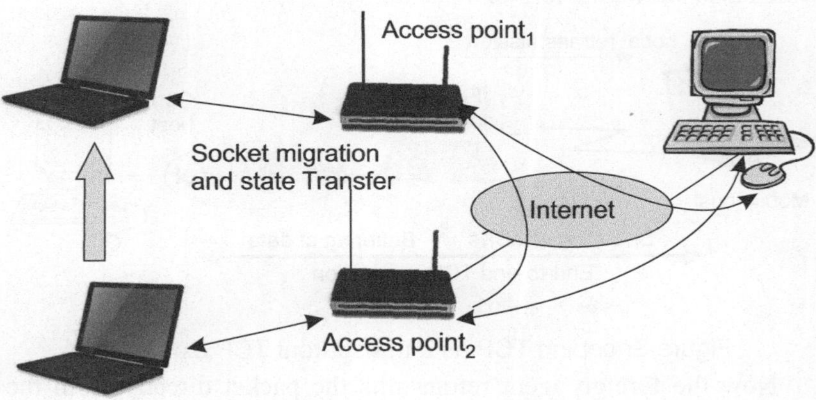

Figure Socket and state migration after handover of a mobile host

Snooping TCP

One of the drawbacks of I-TCP is the segmentation of the single TCP connection into two TCP connections. This loses the original end-to-end TCP semantic. The following TCP enhancement works completely transparently and leaves the TCP end-to-end connection intact. The main function of the enhancement is to buffer data close to the mobile host to perform fast local retransmission in case of packet loss. A good place for the enhancement of TCP could be the foreign agent in the Mobile IP context.

In this approach, the foreign agent buffers all packets with destination mobile host and additionally 'snoops' the packet flow in both directions to recognize acknowledgements. The reason for buffering packets toward the mobile node is to enable the foreign agent to perform a local retransmission in case of packet loss on the wireless link. The foreign agent buffers every packet until it receives an acknowledgement from the mobile host. If the foreign agent does not receive an acknowledgement from the mobile host within a certain amount of time, either the packet or the acknowledgement has been lost. Alternatively, the foreign agent could receive a duplicate ACK which also shows the loss of a packet.

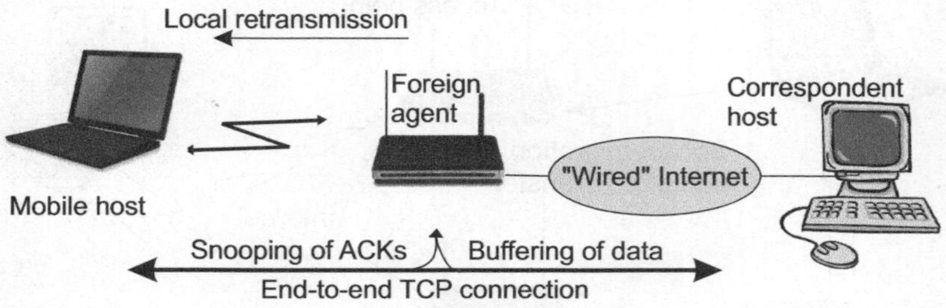

Figure Snooping TCP as a transparent TCP extension

Now the foreign agent retransmits the packet directly from the buffer, performing a much faster retransmission compared to the correspondent host. The time out for acknowledgements can be much shorter, because it reflects only the delay of one hop plus processing time.

To remain transparent, the foreign agent must not acknowledge data to the correspondent host. This would make the correspondent host believe that the mobile host had received the data and would violate the end-to-end semantic in case of a foreign agent failuie. However, the foreign agent tail filter the duplicate acknowledgements to avoid unnecessary retransmissions of data from the correspondent host. If the foreign agent now crashes, the time-out of the correspondent host still works and triggers a retransmission. The foreign agent may discard duplicates of packets already retransmitted locally and acknowledged by the mobile host. This avoids unnecessary traffic on the wireless link.

Data transfer from the mobile host with destination correspondent host works as follows. The foreign agent snoops into the packet stream to detect gaps in the sequence numbers of TCP. As soon as the foreign agent detects a missing packet, it returns a negative acknowledgement (NACK) to the mobile host. The mobile host can now retransmit the missing packet immediately. Reordering of packets is done automatically at the correspondent host by TCP.

Question 8

Data-delivery mechanisms can be classified into three categories, namely, push- based mechanisms (publish-subscribe mode), pull-based mechanisms (on-demand mode), and hybrid mechanisms (hybrid mode).

Push-based Mechanisms: The server pushes data records from a set of distributed computing systems.Examples are advertisers or generators of traffic congestion, weather reports, stock quotes, and news reports. The mobile user has to request to service provider activate the particular services. Once the service is activated the requested data broadcasted to the mobiles after regular intervals.

Figureabove shows a push-based data delivery mechanism in which a server or computing system pushes the data records from a set of distributed computing systems. The data records are pushed to mobile devices by broadcasting without any demand.

Advantages of Push Based Mechanism:

- Push-based mechanisms enable broadcast of data services to multiple devices.
- The server is not interrupted frequently by requests from mobile devices.

Disadvantages of Push Based Mechanism:

- Push-based mechanisms disseminate of unsolicited, irrelevant, or out-of-context data, which may cause inconvenience to the user.

Pull Based data Delivery Mechanism: Figure The user-device or computing system pulls the data records from the service provider's application database server or from a set of distributed computing systems. Examples are music album server, ring tones server, video clips server, or bank account activity server.

Records are pulled by the mobile devices on demand followed by the selective response from the server. Selective response means that server transmits data packets as response selectively, for example, after client-authentication, verification, or subscription account check.

Advantages of Pull based mechanisms:

- With pull-based mechanisms, no unsolicited or irrelevant data arrives at the device and the relevant data is disseminated only when the user asks for it.

Disadvantages of Pull based mechanisms:

- The server faces frequent interruptions and queues of requests at the server may cause congestion in cases of sudden rise in demand for certain data record.

Question 9

Wireless Application Protocol (WAP) is the de facto worldwide standard for providing Internet communications and advanced services on digital mobile devices, such as handheld phones, pagers, and other wireless devices. This protocol is an open, global specification that allows users of the referenceddigital devices to securely access and interact with Internet, intranet, andextranet applications and services. According to researchers, there will be more than 530 million wireless subscribers by the end of 2001. Some estimates report that the number of wireless subscribers will be more than one billion by the year 2004. Most of the phones sold in the near future will have multimedia capabilities that include:

- Retrieving e-mail
- Accessing data from company databases
- Executing stock trading
- Bill paying
- Making travel reservations
- Running other exciting applications

Based on these forecasts, wireless service providers, manufacturers of handheld devices, and software development companies see a huge new market of information-hungry users.

The WAP protocol family mirrors the layered OSI stack , and like the OSI stack some layers are not mandatory. At the lowest level, the WAP Datagram Protocol (WDP) moves information from receiver to sender and is modeled after UDP as a least effort method of delivery. On top of WDP sits the WAP Transaction Protocol (WTP) which ensures that the data fragments sent over the line are actually received, through typical ACK/NACK communication. Higher up, the WAP Session Protocol (WSP) handles the session between communicating systems. All sessions are granted unique IDs and are started/stopped/ terminated accordingly.

WAP Architecture and Reference Model

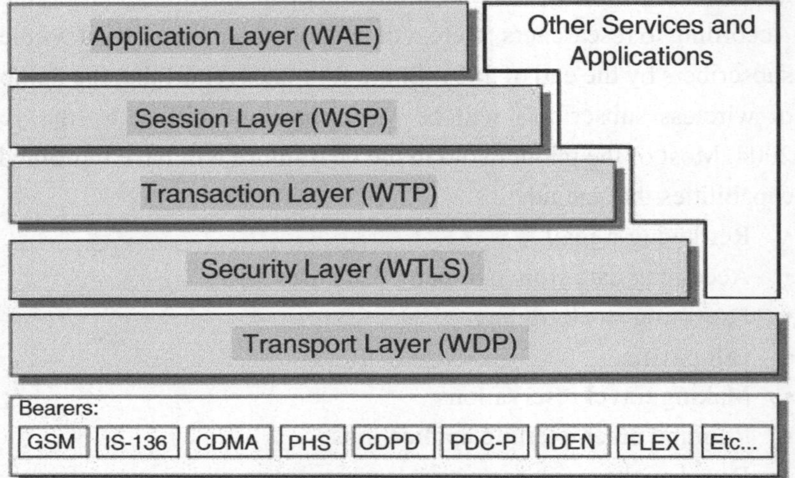

Wireless Transaction Protocol

WTP provides a mechanism especially designed for WAP terminals withlimited resources over networks, and with low to medium bandwidth. Thistechnology allows more subscribers on the same network, due to reducedbandwidth utilization.

WTP provides unreliable and reliable data transfer based on request/replyparadigm. Unlike TCP, there is no connection setup and tear down.Compared to TCP, where a SYN and ACK flow is started before the first dataare transmitted, WTP carries data already in the first packet of the protocolexchange.WTP works message oriented, not stream oriented, like TCP.

Index

B

C

D

E

F

G

I

J

O

P

S

W

NOTES

NOTES

NOTES

NOTES